Studies in Eighteenth-Century Culture

VOLUME 26

EDITORIAL BOARD
for
Studies in Eighteenth-Century Culture
Volume 26

Morris Brownell
University of Nevada—Reno

J. G. Barker-Benfield
State University of New York at Stony Brook at Albany

Carol Houlihan Flynn
Tufts University

Charles Hinnant
University of Missouri

John A. McCarthy
Vanderbilt University

Ruth Plaut Weinreb
State University of New York at Stony Brook

Studies in Eighteenth-Century Culture

VOLUME 26

Edited by

Syndy M. Conger
Western Illinois University

and

Julie C. Hayes
University of Richmond

Published by The Johns Hopkins University Press for the
American Society for Eighteenth-Century Studies

The Johns Hopkins University Press
Baltimore and London

©1998 American Society for Eighteenth-Century Studies
All rights reserved. Published 1998
Printed in the United States of America
02 01 00 99 98
5 4 3 2 1

This book is printed on recycled acid-free paper

The Johns Hopkins University Press
2715 North Charles Street
Baltimore, Maryland 21218-4363
The Johns Hopkins Press Ltd., London

ISBN 0-8018-5627-2
ISSN 0360-2370

Articles appearing in this annual series are abstracted
and indexed in *Historical Abstracts* and *America: History and Life*.

Editorial Readers for Volume Twenty-Six

JANET AIKINS / English / University of New Hampshire
PAUL ALKON / English / University of Southern California
BRENDA AMETER / English / Troy State University
PAULA BACKSCHEIDER / English / Auburn University
LINDA BAMBER / English / Tufts University
RICHARD BARNEY / English / University of Oklahoma
LISA BLANSETT / English / Florida International University
LIZ BOHLS / English / University of Illinois at Urbana
THOMAS F. BONNEL / English / Saint Mary's College
JANICE BRODER / English / Bloomsburg University
HELEN BURKE / English / Florida State University at Tallahassee
BONNIE BURNS / English / Tufts University
J. DOUGLAS CANFIELD / English / University of Arizona
RANITA CHATTERJEE / English / University of Utah
LISA CODY / History / Stanford University
PETER V. CONROY / French / University of Illinois at Chicago
EDWARD COPELAND / English / Pomona College
PATRICIA CRADDOCK / English / University of Florida
ROBERT CRITCHIE / Historian / Director of the Huntington Library
CATHERINE CUTTET / French / Yale University
JOANNA CUTTING-GRAY / Independent Scholar / Mobile, Alabama
RICHARD DAMMERS / Dean's Office / Illinois State University
JAMES DAVIS / Rare Books Library Special Collections / University of California at Los Angeles Research Library
THOMAS F. DILLINGHAM / English / Stephens College
THOMAS DIPIERO / French and Cultural Studies / University of Rochester
MARGARET ANNE DOODY / English / Vanderbilt University
JULIA DOUTHWAITE / French / University of Notre Dame
JOHN DUSSINGER / English / University of Illinois at Urbana
JULIA L. EPSTEIN / English / Haverford College
C. Y. FERDINAND / History / Magdalen College, Oxford
MOIRA FERGUSON / English / University of Nebraska
DIANE FOURNY / French / University of Kansas

CHRISTOPHER FOX / English / University of Notre Dame
CATHERINE GALLOUËT / French / Hobart and William Smith Colleges
LISA GASBARRONE / French / Franklin and Marshall College
JAY GASCO / Anthropology / Occidental College
ANNE BARBEAU GARDINER / English / John Jay College
JULIE GENSTER / English / Boston College
DUSTIN GRIFFIN / English / New York University
JEANNE GRIGGS / English / Kenyon College
GEORGE HAGGERTY / English / University of California at Riverside
ELIZABETH HARRIS / English / Smith College
PHILLIP HARTH / English / University of Wisconsin
ROBERT HAY / History / Marquette University
RAYMOND F. HILLIARD / English / University of Richmond
HOWARD HINKEL / English / Stephens College
SONIA HOFKOSH / English / Tufts University
GRANT HOLLY / English / Hobart and Smith Colleges
CATHERINE INGRASSIA / English / Virginia Commonwealth University
CHRISTOPHER M. S. JOHNS / Art History / University of Virginia
SARAH JORDAN / English / Albion College
MADELEINE KAHN / English / Mills College
TONY KAUFMAN / English / University of Illinois at Champaign
THOMAS M. KAVANAGH / French / University of California at Berkeley
LAURA KENNELLY / English / University of North Texas
BETH KOWALESKI-WALLACE / English / Boston College
ELIZABETH KRAFT / English / University of Georgia
MARIE-PAULA LADEN / French / University of California at Davis
MARCO LOVERSO / English / Concordia College
ELIZABETH J. MACARTHUR / French / University of California at Santa Barbara
ROBERT MACCUBBIN / English / College of William and Mary
W. DUNCAN MCARTHUR / English / Furman University
BRIAN MCCREA / English / University of Florida
ALAN MCKENZIE / English / Purdue University
DEBORAH MCLEOD / Independent Scholar / Paderborn, Germany
WARREN MONTAG / English / Occidental College
DAVID MORRIS / Independent Scholar / Alburquerque, New Mexico
JOHN C. O'NEAL / French / Hamilton College
CATHERINE PARKE / English / University of Missouri at Columbia

ANNIE PECAISTANG / Romance Languages / Tufts University
RUTH PERRY / English / Massachusetts Institute of Technology
RICHARD PETERSON / English / St. Olaf College
ALEXANDER PETTIT / English / University of North Texas
MARK PHILLIPS / History / Carleton University, Ottawa
JULIE-ANNE PLAX / Art History / University of Arizona
JEREMY D. POPKIN / History / University of Kentucky
ROY PORTER / History / Wellcome Institute for the History of Medicine, London
P. M. RICHARDS / English / Colgate University
DEBORAH ROGERS / English / University of Maine
SHIRLEY SAMUELS / English / Cornell University
NEAL SALISBURY / History / Smith College
VIRGINIA SAPIRO / Political Science / University of Wisconsin
GORDON SAYRE / English / University of Oregon
MONA SCHEUERMANN / English / Oakton Community College
SANDRA SHERMAN / English / Georgia State University
SEAN SHESGREEN / English / Northern Illinois University
ANNE B. SHTEIR / Humanities and Women's Studies / York University, Ontario
HARRY M. SOLOMON / English / Auburn University
KRISTINA STRAUB / English / Carnegie Mellon University
ERIC STIFFLER / Philosophy and Religious Studies / Western Illinois University
MICHAEL SUAREZ / History / Oxford University
CHARLOTTE SUSSMAN / English / University of Colorado at Boulder
VIRGINIA SWAIN / French / Dartmouth College
CLAUDIA THOMAS / English / Wake Forest University
DOWNING A. THOMAS / French / University of Iowa
JAMES TIERNEY / English / University of Missouri at St. Louis
JAY TRIBBY / History / University of Florida
CHARLES TROCANO / English / Tufts University
MARY TROUILLE / French / Illinois State University
ELEANOR TY / English / Wilfrid Laurier University
JAMES VAN DER LAAN / German / Illinois State University
JANIE VANPÉE / French / Smith College
ANN VAN SANT / English / Tufts University
WILLIAM WARNER / English / State University of New York at Buffalo
LELAND E. WARREN / English / Kansas State University

DONALD WEHRS / English / Auburn University
ARTHUR WEITZMAN / English / Northwestern University
STEPHEN WERNER / French / University of California at Los Angeles
HUGH A. WEST / History / University of Richmond
ANN WITHINGTON / History / University of Richmond
CALHOUN WINTON / English / University of Maryland
GORDON S. WOOD / History / Brown University
CAROLYN WOODWARD / English / University of New Mexico
ROSE ZIMBARDO / English / State University of New York at Stony Brook
EVERETT ZIMMERMAN / English / University of California at Santa Barbara

Contents

Editor's Note xi

The Presidential Forum
    RONALD C. ROSBOTTOM 1

Surveying the Frontier of Culture: Pastoralism in
Eighteenth-Century England
    MICHAEL MCKEON 7

Letters: Painted/Penned/Purloined
    MARY SHERIFF 29

"Opposition Augustanism" and Pope's *Epistle to Augustus*
    THOMAS KAMINISKI 57

Phillis Wheatley, the Aesthetic, and the Form of Life
    FRANK SHUFFELTON 73

"Struggling Manfully" through Henry Fielding's *Amelia:* Hysteria,
Medicine, and the Novel in Eighteenth-Century England
    GLEN COLBURN 87

Figures of Female Alienation: The Use of Periphrasis in
Lettres d'une Péruvienne
    BARBARA KNAUFF 125

Wieland and Wezel: Divergent Trends within the German
Enlightenment
    FRANZ A. BIRGEL 139

Wilkes and Libertinism
    JOHN SAINSBURY 151

Gender Bending and Corporeal Limitations: The Modern Body in
Tristram Shandy
    MIRIAM L. WALLACE 175

Ut Pictura Poesis Non Erit: Diderot's Quest for the
Limits of Expression in the *Salons*
    HUGUETTE COHEN 195

Isabelle de Charrière's *Sainte Anne*, or A Woman's
Wayward Quest for Knowledge
    JACQUELINE LETZTER 209

The Unaverted Eye: Dangerous Charity in Burney's
Evelina and *The Wanderer*
    SHARON LONG DAMOFF 231

Pre-Romantic Elements in the Aesthetic and Moral
Theories of François Hemsterhuis (1721–1790)
    A. P. DIERICK 247

The Road to Wisdom in Mozart's *Magic Flute*
    JULIE D. PRANDI 273

Gothic Gold: The Sadleir-Black Gothic Collection
    FREDERICK S. FRANK 287

Contributors 313

Executive Board 1995–96 317

Patron Members 319

Sponsoring Members 319

Institutional Members 321

Index 323

Editor's Note

The riches of the Miscellany (and what could be a more appropriate genre for eighteenth-century specialists to contrive together?) speak for themselves: a dozen disciplines dance in pairs or singly to offer new insights into the texts and contexts of eighteenth-century culture in America, Britain, and the European continent. Together they also shed light on some of the ideas that captured our society's collective imagination in 1995–96; in the order that they occur, pastoralism, letters in / and paintings, Augustanism, the aesthetic, hysteria, female alienation, German Enlightenment, libertinism, corporeal limitations, the limits of expression, knowledge, charity, the moral, wisdom, Gothicism. Since *SECC* readers selected these sixteen essays from nearly one hundred submissions to the annual volume, it is also fair to say that they also represent some of the best conference papers heard at regional and the national meetings during 1995–96 that time; among them are a Clifford lecture and a keynote address from the national meeting in Tucson. During the long selection and editing process, contributors—models of patience and gratitude—often thank readers and editors for their suggestions and work on essays; so in closing it seems appropriate to pass on those expressions of gratitude to *SECC* board members, manuscript reviewers, and society members and other scholars who consult this book. May you find it as stimulating as the conferences from which its contents were distilled.

Syndy M. Conger
Western Illinois University

Studies in Eighteenth-Century Culture

VOLUME 26

The Presidential Forum

RONALD C. ROSBOTTOM
ASECS President, 1994-95

In an effort to challenge the Society to think about itself, Barbara Stafford (President, 1995–96) and I devised the idea of a Presidential Forum to replace the traditional Presidential Address at our Annual Meeting. Concerned that ASECS, and other learned societies, did not provide adequate "space" for discussion of our cultural and intellectual organization, we offered an alternative in April 1995 at the Tucson meeting, and did so again at the Austin meeting (1996). Our purpose was to examine the interdisciplinary premises on which the Society was founded and by which it operates. My task was to organize a Forum around the relationships between curricular interdisciplinarity and academic administration; Professor Stafford's was to raise the issue of inter- and transdisciplinarity as viable intellectual concepts. The current debates over fiscal priorities within the academy and of our political influence outside will make investigation of our intellectual organization increasingly pertinent.

For my Forum, I invited three colleagues to present remarks which we hoped would elicit a lively discussion. I asked our Second Vice President, Paul Hunter (English, Chicago), to speak to concerns that have preoccupied him as an English professor and a former academic dean. I invited my Amherst College colleague, Margaret Hunt (History and Women's and Gender Studies), to give us an aperçu of how she has grown up in an interdisciplinary program at a small liberal arts college. And, I also looked to my colleague Barbara Stafford (Art History, Chicago) for help; her work on the role of the visual in modern humanistic and scientific disciplines has led her to ask questions about how knowledge is packaged by the academy.

The title of the Forum was "What Does It Mean to be Disciplined?" an arch way of bringing the ideas of control as well as order to the front of the discussion. This is a subject that is attracting more and more scholarly attention. In a recent collection of essays, *Knowledges: Historical and Critical Studies in Disciplinarity,* the editors write in their preface:

> For only two centuries, knowledge has assumed a disciplinary form; for less than one, it has been produced in academic institutions by professionally trained knowers. Yet we have come to see these circumstances as so natural that we tend to forget their historical novelty and fail to imagine how else we might produce and organize knowledge. . . .
>
> Socially and conceptually, we are disciplined by our disciplines. First, they help produce our world. They specify the objects we can study . . . and the relations that obtain among them. . . . They provide criteria for our knowledge . . . and methods . . . that regulate our access to it.
>
> Second, disciplines produce practitioners, orthodox and heterodox, specialist and generalist, theoretical and experimental. . . .
>
> Third, disciplines produce economies of value. They manufacture discourse in abundance . . . ; they provide jobs . . . ; they secure funding . . . ; they generate prestige. . . .
>
> Finally, disciplines produce the idea of progress. They proliferate objects to study and improve explanations. . . . They tell stories of progress.[1]

At our Forum, Margaret Hunt adroitly drew our attention to the advantages of "being disciplined": "[Disciplines have] clear intellectual regimens, as in the case of history (my favorite discipline), with centuries of precedent. There's a common sensibility, which one gets less often in interdisciplinary work, where [one gropes] for commonalities. Being within an already-established discipline is, in some ways, less exhausting [than being in a newer, interdisciplinary one]."

Another theme of the Forum was that we are members of a conservative intellectual profession. Once we establish a "discipline," no matter how it may have been in the avant garde at its inception, professionalism will soon attenuate the intellectual flexibility that occasioned the adventure. Said Professor Hunter: "Institutional structures of interdisciplinarity—when formed historically at a particular time in interdisciplinary relations—can be a highly conservative factor as new interdisciplinary ideas, relationships, and needs develop. One almost inviolable law in institutions involves inertia: once something is created it is almost impossible to uncreate it." This is our central conundrum, both as members of particular college and university faculties, and as members of our professional learned societies: how do we use disciplinary grounded-ness as an engine for change—or can we?

Disciplines—then their bureaucratic analogs, departments—evolved to structure the activities of the ungovernable intelligentsia. Academic departments, at least in this country, were originally formed to *control* an increasingly powerful professorate. As a counterweight to institutional bureaucracies, at about the same time, professional associations like ours served, as "invisible colleges," to give disciplinary identity and independence. Another use was to attenuate "amateurism," always threatening to the "expert." Being "disciplined" meant that wherever one was, one was the same. Not even an institution of employment could tell a professor that she was not doing what she should be doing: her professional organizations had already validated her work—and her worth. "Disciplining" is a reification of activity, not of ideas or things; it is a result of the idea of "progress," the movement to perfection that has been left us by our Enlightenment forebears.

As Paul Hunter repeated, though, disciplines do tend to make us more rigid rather than flexible. Arguing that there is nothing to prevent us from thinking and working, as individuals, in an interdisciplinary context, he concludes, "teaching is another matter, however. There is little direct support, and the departmental determination of courses and teaching loads often means it is hard to mount interdisciplinary—if we mean interdepartmental—courses and programs. It's easy to blame this on higher administration, but actually the difficulty just as often comes from inflexible or selfish departments and faculty individuals." It is important, in such a situation, to rely on the "benign neglect" of administrations rather than on their attention, which can often freeze a department into the most conservative of stances.

Professor Hunter touched on a subject that could well lead us out of these contradictions: through emphasizing *teaching* rather than "research," we might just be able to build a new ethos of intellectual activity that urges us to consider new conceptions of how we do our research. It is in the classroom where we are, for the most part, left alone; one of the frustrations of those who want to control the intelligentsia is indeed this freedom to teach how and what we want. This is an idea that especially interests—and concerns—Barbara Stafford who drew our attention to the fact that the classroom, as we know it, is being radically transformed. Our profession—as teachers and as critics and scholars—is changing before our eyes our LED consoles. Increasingly, the educational establishment will lose control of its "possessions" and of the means of its production. This is most obvious in the libraries that sustain us. They are becoming on many campuses the center for digitalized information and computing as well as depositories for books and manuscripts. Librarians are having to retrain themselves both technically and conceptually. No longer can they control what is held and what is allowed out; they must now educate—train—and explain to a public suddenly overwhelmed with what is available to it. Education is leaving the library and the archives the classroom and the campus, to occur on the Internet and in other telecommunicational modes. As Stafford argues: "In the coming electronic era, interactive 'home learning' will place a greater premium on the viewer's choice. This opens up the possibility of a truly weblike interdisciplinarity; conversely, it raises the specter of a new narrowness in the face of the almost limitless choice offered by five hundred cable channels and Mosaic or America On-Line. This dispersal into cyber-space adds an additional note of uncertainty since it is difficult to predict which disciplines will continue, emerge or fade in the virtual, digital university."

Not insignificantly, should we plan as we should, this transformation will lead us inexorably into a discussion about the costs of education and its delivery. The academy's success at making appropriate use of the radical changes in the creation and transmission of information will be greatly influenced by the real fiscal restraints under which we must operate. "Downsizing" is an attractive fiscal concept to many administrators who have yet to address the complexity of the intellectual enterprise and of the traditions and structures that now are embedded in American higher education. (This is a subject worthy of a preface all its own.)

It is somewhat unusual in a preface to a book containing some of our Society's best scholarly work to write about the real and mundane difficulties that confront out careers as scholars and teachers. But if a learned society is to have more than self-congratulatory value, it must use its meetings and publications to enable members to talk about *themselves*—who they are and how they work together—and how they *teach* as well as about the discoveries and products of their research. For, professionalization is powerful. An emotional and intellectual commitment to one's chosen field(s), it begins as early as our undergraduate major, and is firmly inculcated during graduate study where thinking about intellectual boundary-crossing is generally casual, if not counter-intuitive. How we organize ourselves professionally can either solidify that sense of disciplinary commitment or provide alternatives to it. We intellectuals still control our destinies, and we must not allow our nervousness of each other, our xenophobia, to keep us from maintaining an orderly house. We must work hard to avoid becoming, as Paul Hunter suggested, the "fossils of hubris or overreaching." We should not choose the interdisciplinary way in order to enhance our power or to satisfy selfish interests, but rather see that way as the most effective means by which we can remain "disciplined," yet still imaginative and tolerant. We must use the curiosity and faith in common sense that drew us to these professions to set limits of change while challenging the power of tradition. Otherwise, we will increasingly become insignificant to a world that is impatient with what we do.[2]

NOTES

1. Ellen Messer-Davidow, David R. Shumway, David J. Sylvan, eds., *Knowledges: Historical and Critical Studies in Disciplinarity* (Charlottesville: University Press of Virginia, 1993), vii–viii.

2. I would like to thank two of my Amherst College colleagues for their suggestions and patience as I worked my way through what I wanted this Forum to do: they are Professor Arthur Zajonc of the Physics Department and Professor Hugh Hawkins of the History and American Studies departments.

Surveying the Frontier of Culture: Pastoralism in Eighteenth-Century England

MICHAEL MCKEON

I first met James Clifford on the sixth floor of Philosophy Hall at Columbia University, in the fall of 1966. Burdened down by old volumes, he was making his way to the seminar room at the end of the hall, where he would pass around first editions for his Ph.D. students to inspect as they discussed modern paperback reprints of the same texts. Not yet arrived at this exalted stage of graduate study, I wondered if I'd ever attain the bibliographical mastery required to satisfy a scholar of Clifford's stature. It turned out I didn't need to. I think it would be right to describe graduate study under James Clifford as a kind of apprenticeship, but it was not a laborious and daunting discipline. Even before I left Columbia I'd come to see that in Clifford I'd had a mentor whose notion of his job included, but went beyond, intellectual and technical pedagogy. Like many graduate students, I lived my life as a mixture of overweening fantasy and cynical self-loathing. Through the kindness and unfeigned interest with which he treated me, Clifford tacitly refused to play his part in this wretched drama. He showed me that graduate study needn't be a degradation ceremonial, and he seemed to care less about putting us through the hoops than about helping us imagine ourselves as professional adults.

Once, when I was passing his office, he almost ran me down when he suddenly emerged into the hallway, one hand dragging John Richetti in his wake, the other jubilantly waving the letter from Oxford University Press that had just accepted John's revised dissertation for publication. In seminar he would hang expectantly on our reports on recent criticism, sometimes emitting little gasps, sharp intakes of breath, and low-pitched whistling noises to acknowledge the rigor and ferocity of our critiques. My orals were scheduled for the spring of 1968, when buildings were being occupied by protestors, and students were being offered the option of postponing their exams in deference to the occupation and its cause. Torn as I was between intractable political ambivalence and a paralytic dread of orals, my despair felt somehow paradigmatic of my entire graduate school existence. Wasn't it true—wasn't it obvious to everyone—that I was a charlatan and a hypocrite, canceling my exam on the pretence of political conviction but really out of abject personal cowardice and intellectual incompetence? Clifford patiently heard me out in my agony, and managed to convey respect for both the horns of what seemed my ignominious dilemma. In the end I postponed orals, took them later on, and, swallowing my panic, acquitted myself well enough on the canonical figures for Clifford to end by inquiring roguishly: "Well, what can you tell us about Eustace Budgell?" And I was surprised to find I could reply, "Nothing at all," with some equanimity and almost no abjection. In the end, James Clifford gave me the rarest gift, a simple model of humanity. For this reason it gives me the greatest pleasure to honor his memory by delivering the Clifford lecture today.

Our topic this year, "the frontiers of culture," may be said to have a special relevance to eighteenth-century studies. The acknowledgment of cultural difference—its power, its deep prevalence, its indefeasible legitimacy—is a central feature of modernity that gains a crucial momentum during the Enlightenment. This momentum is inseparable, however, from the celebrated and apparently contrary Enlightenment discovery of "general nature," of a uniformity and permanence in both nature and human nature, a deep ontological grounding whose existence had gone undetected in previous eras. The relationship could hardly be otherwise. The modern categories "nature" and "culture" entirely depend, for their antithetical authority, on each other's capacity to carve out a territory whose boundaries define the limits—but therefore also the scope—of the other's dominion.

Of course, surveying the frontiers of nature and culture is the work of all times and all cultures. In the West, the ancient genre of pastoral is the discourse most explicitly dedicated to this work. From one perspective, the history of pastoral in the eighteenth century is quite continuous with the history that precedes it. From another, eighteenth-century pastoral is an unprecedentedly innovative version of the form, a radical instrument of inquiry that provides a model for how the frontiers of culture may be experimentally negotiated. In the following talk I'll explore some highlights of this negotiation as it occurs in English literature of the period, but I'll begin with a few words about pastoral as such.

Whatever its more particular literary form, pastoral partakes of an oppositional structure that's based in a geographical antithesis between the country and the city, the rural and the urban, a structure that yields a familiar series of value-laden extensions: simplicity versus sophistication, innocence versus corruption, contemplation versus action, contentment versus ambition, private retirement versus public activity, *otium* versus *negotium,* female versus male, peace versus war, communal affiliation versus individual aggression, and the like. The spatial opposition finds its temporal equivalent in the antithesis between past and present, Golden Age and Iron Age; and at the most basic level, all these analogous articulations are mutually translatable as the abstract opposition between nature and artifice—or simply art.

From the beginning, however, pastoral has functioned both to sponsor and to question this oppositional structure. An artful impersonation of nature, pastoral deploys the sophisticated technology of poetic culture to represent its absence, and it's in the self-consciousness of this paradox that we recognize the characteristic complexity of the genre. We often distinguish Virgil's pastoral eclogues from his georgics, where the norm is not the natural tranquillity of animal herding but the industrious technology of land cultivation, the improvement of nature by techniques of art. But the eclogue and the georgic operate within the same basic scheme of opposition, and enforce different facets of the same system of values. Recollecting his own youthful exercise in pastoral song, Virgil in fact ends the *Georgics* with the opening line of the *Eclogues*. The antithesis, in other words, is also a circle. Pastoral works both to affirm and to suspend the opposition between nature and cultivation, to oppose them in such a way as to intimate simultaneously their complex interpenetration. It's felt to be inseparably "about" both nature, and the techniques by which nature is acculturated, enclosed, and represented. Pastoral is the supreme poetic form of conventionality: not only because it presents itself as a critique of social, political, and poetic convention; nor only because it (inevitably) elaborates this critique in conventional ways; but because, in seeking to be mindful of both these conditions at once, it takes as its subject the problem of conventionality itself.

By this way of thinking, the instability of pastoral is not an adventitious accident or a historical accretion, but congenital and constitutive of it as a genre. The eighteenth-century difference is therefore one not of kind but of degree. It entails a reconception of the frontier between nature and art whose very confidence is the precondition for its obscuring complication. If I were to try to explain this development, I would want to have recourse to a number of factors, among them the material and social transformations entailed in the capitalist revolution of the English countryside. My aim today is rather to describe this development, to suggest the dimensions of pastoral innovation by reference to some exemplary and well-known texts. I'll introduce these readings with a brief allusion to the famous debate about pastoral propriety that occupied the pages of the *Guardian* in 1713.

That this exchange was indeed a debate was not immediately evident to its readers—partly because of the parodic subtlety of Alexander Pope's contribution, and partly because his pastoral principles can seem rather close to those of his supposed antagonist, Thomas Tickell. Even on the issue of how far the procedures of the ancient pastoralists may be naturalized to a modern English setting, the two are by no means utterly at odds. Tickell, for his part, instances Sannazaro's piscatory eclogues as the negative limit-case of naturalization.[1] Having drawn this line, Tickell is pleased to assure his reader that "I shall now direct him where he may lawfully deviate from the ancients." A country scene, he says, is essential, but lawful deviations may be indulged with respect to climate, soil, vegetation, and such customs as rustic superstition.[2] Tickell's phrase is suggestive, and I'll use it to explore a broad range of pastoral experimentation. During the eighteenth century, the standard of "lawful deviation" operates, both explicitly and tacitly, as a sliding measure of how the frontiers of culture may be surveyed.

Sannazaro's impropriety consists, in Tickell's words, in having "changed the scene in this kind of poetry from woods and lawns, to the barren beach and boundless ocean. . . ."[3] How much more illicit must be a change of scene from the pastoral countryside to its antithesis, to the city itself? Jonathan Swift's famous "descriptions" of the city, which appeared in the *Tatler* in 1709 and 1710, clearly exemplify the problems in generic categorization that are created by the willingness to indulge certain kinds of pastoral "deviation." By Tickell's standards, Swift's poems must surely be seen as parodic and self-canceling "anti-pastorals." But Sir Richard Steele's introduction praises them, with some plausibility, for their innovative and highly particularized realism: the author "never forms Fields, or Nymphs, or Groves, where they are not, but makes the Incidents just as they really appear. For an Example of it," Steele continues, "I stole out of his Manuscript the following Lines: They are a Description of the Morning, but of the Morning in Town; nay, of the Morning at this End of the Town. . . ."[4] As Oliver Goldsmith later remarked of the six eclogues that compose John Gay's extreme exercise in the theocritean mode, *The Shepherd's Week* (1714), "they were originally intended, I suppose, as a burlesque . . . but, perhaps without designing it, he has hit the true spirit of pastoral poetry."[5] From this perspective, Swift's poems have often been seen as *lawful* deviations, *urban* or "town" pastorals (or perhaps, town *georgics*) that extend the ancient form by accommodating its celebration of rural nature to the domain of urban culture. To put it this way may appear to reduce to absurdity the founding, oppositional principle of pastoral. Yet Swift's strategy entails the microscopic rediscovery, within the supposedly discrete category of urban culture, of the same opposition that divides the city itself from the natural countryside. Thus "The Description of a City Shower" subjects the heterogeneous variety of city culture to the homogenizing effects of the rainstorm, a natural force that submerges all cultural difference within the uniformity of the flood (reinforced by the uniformity of the ending triplet):

Sweepings from Butchers Stalls, Dung, Guts, and Blood,
Drown'd Puppies, stinking Sprats, all drench'd in Mud,
Dead Cats, and Turnip-Tops come tumbling down the Flood.[6]

In this way, some eighteenth-century pastoralists deviate from standard practice by disclosing the country at the center of the city. Thus Tobias Smollett's Matthew Bramble, in thrall to a vision of bucolic purity, is distracted by the paradoxical presence of "public gardens" at the heart of London, and he later complains of "noisy rustics" hawking their produce under his window.[7] Thus James Boswell observes the odd capacity of the London crowd to confer anonymity and solitude, to reproduce the rural retreat in other terms: "London is undoubtedly a place where men and manners may be seen to the greatest advantage.... the satisfaction of pursuing whatever plan is most agreeable, without being known or looked at, is very great.... Indeed there is a great difference between solitude in the country, where you cannot help it, and in London, where you can in a moment be in the hurry and splendour of life."[8] This sort of deviation might be seen as a spatial displacement of rural values onto the city. The displacement phenomenon is even more striking in what might be called the eighteenth-century "macro-pastoral," in which the *intra*national opposition between city and country is projected outward as the *inter*national or imperial opposition between England and other nations. To find the implication of such macro-pastoral displacement one need look no further than the titles of some contemporary Virgilian experiments—like William Collins's *Persian Eclogues* (1742), Thomas Chatterton's *African Eclogues* (1770), Edward Rushton's *West-Indian Eclogues* (1787), or Robert Southey's *Botany-Bay Eclogues* (1797). But the macro-pastoral impulse also permeates a diverse range of English texts that are not strictly virgilian, and it complicates the pastoral opposition between English city and countryside by ignoring the frontier between these locales so as to conjoin them into a metropolitan unit that stands over against the underdeveloped rusticity of the colony.

One of the more compelling examples of this sort of spatial deviation is Collins's "Ode on the Popular Superstitions" (composed 1750). Addressed to John Home on his return to Scotland, Collins's ode urges his cultivated friend to emulate the native Highlander (or "untutored swain"), to recover in Scotland what can no longer be found farther south: "Nor thou, though learned, his homelier thoughts neglect; / Let thy sweet muse the rural faith sustain. . . ."[9] It is significant that Collins associates "the rural faith" not with religion, but with popular superstition. Scotland is to England as the country is to the city in the highly temporalized sense that it represents an archaic mode of belief whose authority resides in its very anachronism. Sheltered from modernity and its cultural overdevelopment, the highlands are still populated by notional beings—fairy people, old runic bards, wizard seers, pigmy folk— who bespeak not religious but poetic spirituality. Spatial distance facilitates the aura of historical distance, which in turn underscores the aesthetic distance required to conceive Highland culture as an imaginative construct, and therefore (paradoxically) more natural than our own. Insistently theatrical, Collins's exhortations also insist upon the aesthetic mechanism whereby the acknowledgment of artifice only promotes the feeling of the natural:

> Proceed, nor quit the tales which, simply told,
>   Could once so well my answering bosom pierce;
> Proceed, in forceful sounds and colours bold
>   The native legends of thy land rehearse;
> To such adapt thy lyre and suit thy powerful verse.
>
> In scenes like these, which, daring to depart
>   From sober Truth, are still to Nature true. . . .
>   (ll. 183–89)

By reconceiving the local, intranational opposition between nature and art as a single English unit within a structure of opposition that is international, macro-pastoral displacement obliges us to rethink the ethics of conflict that in "strict" pastoral terms appears normative. By the time Smollett's hero comes to ponder the supposedly absolute difference between the highlands and the lowlands, the contrast between Scotland itself and England— and indeed, between numerous paired locales *within* England—has already rendered pastoral opposition an exercise in relativity. Samuel Johnson's juvenalian satire *London* (1738) opposes the corruptions of the English metropolis to several alternative and increasingly far-flung realms of the rural: "the wilds of Kent," the shores of Wales, the rivers of Hereford and Staffordshire, the rocks of Scotland.[10] Despite their regional and even national disparateness, all these British locales are able in some fashion to figure a natural innocence that stands in contrast to the monolithic artifice and corruption of London. Once we leave Britain, however, the scheme of values becomes more complicated:

> London! the needy villain's gen'ral home,
> Ile common shore of Paris and of Rome;
> With eager thirst, by folly or by fate,
> Sucks in the dregs of each corrupted state.
> Forgive my transports on a theme like this,
> I cannot bear a French metropolis.
> (ll. 93–98)

It's not that London loses her artifice and corruption. It's rather that her vices are so relentlessly derived from a foreign source that London becomes a mere metonymy for Britain, and Britain a land of innocent bumpkins ripe for the cultural imperialism of metropolitan France:

> Obsequious, artful, voluble and gay,
> On Britain's fond credulity they prey.
> No gainful trade their industry can 'scape,
> They sing, they dance, clean shoes, or cure a clap;
> All sciences a fasting Monsieur knows,
> And bid him go to hell, to hell he goes.
> ....
> These arts in vain our rugged natives try,
> Strain out with fault'ring diffidence a lye,
> And get a kick for aukward flattery.
> ....
> For arts like these preferr'd, admir'd, caress'd,
> They first invade your table, then your breast;
> Explore your secrets with insidious art,
> Watch the weak hour, and ransack all the heart. . . .
> (ll. 111–16, 129–31, 152–55)

The effect of the macro-pastoral displacement is a reversal of values that throws the dominant perspective on London corruption into question. The rural and the urban bleed together—a relativizing effect that Johnson also achieves in the space of a single couplet: "Scarce can our fields, such crowds at Tyburn die, / With hemp the gallows and the fleet supply" (ll. 242–43).

The *beatus ille* of Horace's second Epode informs a broad spectrum of eighteenth-century thought with the paradigm of a pastoral retreat from the cares of public life to the contentment of private retirement. In his verse epistle "To my Honour'd Kinsman" (1700), John Dryden employs a range of classical and Christian pastoral topics to praise his cousin, "shunning Civil Rage," as a paragon of private virtue.[11] We see him as the pacific J.P. who resolves neighborly disputes; as the confirmed bachelor who wisely avoids the duplicity of marriage; as the paternalistic landlord who dispenses supplies and health to his people. But around the middle of the poem, as he concludes this medical topic, Dryden's private encomium explicitly modulates to a public register:

> He scapes the best, who Nature to repair,
> Draws Phisick from the Fields, in Draughts of Vital Air.
> You hoard not Health, for your own private Use;
> But on the Publick spend the rich Produce:
> When, often urg'd, unwilling to be Great,
> Your Country calls you from your lov'd Retreat,
> And sends to Senates, charg'd with Common Care,
> Which none more shuns; and none can better bear.
> (ll. 115–22)

The modulation turns on the fact that Dryden's cousin was not only a J.P. but also an M.P. In the latter half of the poem, Dryden recapitulates the very topics of his former praise, now finding in the public man the same virtues that formerly had defined private retirement *against* public ambition. The rural countryside is refigured as the "country" of England; the cousin's medical charity is refigured as his ministration to the English body politic; his pacific settlement of local suits at law is refigured as the successful advocacy of the Treaty of Ryswick in 1697; and his inveterate bachelorhood—indeed, his pastoral retreat itself—is refigured as an isolationist foreign policy.

Dryden's deviation, unlawful by Tickell's standards, supersedes the essential rurality of horatian retreat even as it preserves the crucial ethics of that form within the innovative territory of international politics. Also traditional to the retreat was a gentlemanly exclusivity that partook both of status and gender bias. In "The Petition for an Absolute Retreat" (1713), Anne Finch addresses this gender bias by imagining herself into the tradition:

> Give me O indulgent Fate!
> Give me yet before I Dye,
> A sweet, but absolute Retreat,
> 'Mongst Paths so lost, and Trees so high,
> That the World may ne'er invade,
> Through such Windings and such Shade,
> My unshaken Liberty.[12]

The virtues of friendship are by no means alien to the male tradition of pastoral retreat. But in Finch's deviation, the value of retreat is largely predicated on company. In Dryden's epistle, marriage is associated with the weakness of Eve and the duplicity of the Fall:

> Minds are so hardly match'd that ev'n the first,
> Though pair'd by Heav'n, in paradise, were curs'd.
> ....
> How could he stand, when put to double pain,
> He must a weaker than himself sustain!
> (ll. 21–22, 27–28)

But in Finch's version of retreat—indeed, of "absolute" retreat—prelapsarian bliss fully depends upon human companionship:

> Give me there (since Heaven has shown
> It was not Good to be alone)
> A *Partner* suited to my Mind,
> Solitary, pleas'd and kind;
> ....
> When but Two the Earth possest,
> 'Twas their happiest Days, and best;
> ....
> Give then, O indulgent Fate!
> Give a Friend in that Retreat
> ('Tho withdrawn from all the rest). . . .
> (ll. 104–7, 112–13, 196–98)

And yet the partner Finch names is not her husband, but rather the woman to whom she dedicates her poem. The revaluation of pastoral solitude as a peculiarly pristine mode of sociability is sharpened by the suggestion that sociability itself may be peculiarly female.

Something similar occurs in Mary Leapor's "Complaining *Daphne.* A *Pastoral*" (1751). On the face of it, Leapor's verse is not a retreat poem at all. As its title suggests, it's rather a pastoral complaint, modeled ultimately on Virgil's second eclogue. Wandering through a "blooming Grove" one spring afternoon, "lonely" Celia overhears Daphne complaining of the inconstancy of the swain Cynthio.[13] Leapor's first innovation therefore consists in making the nymph not the object but the subject of love complaint. But in the middle of her monologue, Daphne stops short and radically changes her tack:

> Ye gentle Winds! O, bear my darling Swain,
> My lovely *Cynthio,* to his native Plain.

> Ye Pow'rs!—but hold—Those happy Forms above,
> My sacred Guardians, heed no Tales of Love;
> And mystic Fate perhaps foresaw it wise,
> To ravish *Cynthio* from my aking Eyes.
> (ll. 58–63)

Recognizing Cynthio's fickleness for its duplicitous artifice, Daphne repudiates him as unworthy of pastoral desire, which yet persists through a generic transformation (and this is Leapor's second innovation) of her pastoral complaint into a pastoral retreat:

> Then stay, O stay, far from our peaceful Plain,
> Nor let me see that pleasing Face again.
> Go, fly, my *Cynthio,* where Ambition calls,
> And smiling Flatt'ry paints her gilded Walls:
> Let happier *Daphne* spend her equal Days
> With guiltless Pleasure, and substantial Ease.
> . . . .
> Come, sweet Content, and long-desired Rest!
> Two welcome Strangers! to my aking Breast:
> Purl on, ye Streams! ye Flow'rets, smile again!
> Your chearful *Daphne* shall no more complain. . . .
> (ll. 70–75, 102–5)

In the process of this transformation, Daphne narrates a memory that gives to her retreat a complex resonance. In her infancy, "when *Daphne* wander'd by her Mother's Side" in the fragrant summer meadows, she was told tales of "harmless" maids seduced and abandoned by false men. And whatever their beginnings, the tales would always end: *"Child, beware of Man"* (ll. 79, 93, 99). The memory carries two distinct but entwined associations. First, it associates nature with the mother, both temporalizing and internalizing the *locus amoenus* as the return of the Golden Age of maternal society before the Fall into adolescence. Second, it associates artifice with men, rendering Daphne's retreat a generic flight from male "ambition" and *negotium* as such, to female "ease" and *otium.* Bound by the logic that only he who has been active in the corrupting world can retreat from it, the horatian tradition presumes a male actor. But Leapor claims that logic for women, too, by figuring their worldly activity as nothing else than the corrupt company of men. Now reclaimed as a feminine strategy, pastoral retreat may even (as in Finch) entail female companionship. In the above passage, Daphne invokes Content and Rest as "Ye Sylvan Sisters! come; ye gentle Dames, / Whose tender Souls are spotless as your Names!" (ll. 108–9). And what's become of the lonely Celia? The very fact that the intimate frame with which the poem opens—Celia overhearing Daphne's lament—ostentatiously remains open (we never return to Celia) may suggest a closure that its absence ostensibly denies. Certainly the uncompleted frame has the effect of identifying us, Leapor's readers, with Daphne's unseen but deeply sympathetic female auditor.

At significant points in her poem, Leapor figures Daphne's pastoral drama as a specifically mental activity. In this way, the physical seclusion entailed in pastoral retreat is closely associated with that entailed in the *micro*-pastoral purification of, and withdrawal into, the mind. This pastoral "deviation" into the landscape of the mind, made famous by Andrew Marvell, became increasingly "lawful" in pastoral practice during the eighteenth century. James Thomson's *The Seasons* (1746), forward enough in its modernization of ancient pastoral settings, is quite bold in their internalization. Here is a passage from "Winter":

> Now, all amid the Rigours of the Year,
> In the wild Depth of Winter, while without
> The ceaseless Winds blow Ice, be my Retreat,
> Between the groaning Forest and the Shore,
> Beat by the boundless Multitude of Waves,
> A rural, shelter'd, solitary, Scene. . . .[14]

Thomson's wintry "scene" quickly modulates into a mental screen on which are projected a train of ancient heroes and poets, seen in the mind's eye. He then returns to the topics of an objective horatian retreat—friendly converse, pleasant prospects—only to watch the scene shift inexorably to a subjective register:

> Thus in some deep Retirement would I pass,
> The Winter-Glooms, with Friends of pliant Soul,
> Or blithe, or solemn, as the Theme inspir'd:
> . . . .
> Hence larger Prospects of the beauteous Whole
> Would, gradual, open on our opening Minds:
> And each diffusive Harmony unite,
> In full Perfection, to th' astonish'd Eye.
> Then would we try to scan the *moral World,*
> . . . .
> Then . . . we
> Would learn the private Virtues; how to glide
> Thro Shades and Plains, along the smoothest Stream
> Of rural Life: or snatch'd away by Hope,
> Thro the dim Spaces of Futurity,
> With earnest Eye anticipate those Scenes

> Of Happiness, and Wonder; where the Mind,
> In endless Growth and infinite Ascent,
> Rises from State to State, and World to World.
> (ll. 572–74, 579–83, 600–608)

Here the internalization of pastoral retreat as a micro-pastoral landscape of the mind is achieved through its mental allegorization. In *The Deserted Village* (1770), Oliver Goldsmith famously pursues Leapor's more temporalized mode of micro-pastoral internalization by conflating the recent history of the English countryside with the poet's own life history. Ostensibly, the problem the poem sets out to document is, in Goldsmith's words, the objective "depopulation" of the land, the "desertion" of the village under the pressures of large-scale social change.[15] It's because of this large-scale change, Goldsmith says, that he is now unable to experience the horatian *beatus ille*, the return to the "seats of my youth" (l. 6):

> In all my wanderings round this world of care,
> In all my griefs—and God has given my share—
> I still had hopes my latest hours to crown,
> Amidst these humble bowers to lay me down;
> ....
> O blest retirement, friend to life's decline,
> Retreats from care, that never must be mine,
> How happy he who crowns in shades like these
> A youth of labour with an age of ease;
> Who quits a world where strong temptations try
> And, since 'tis hard to combat, learns to fly.
> (ll. 83–86, 97–102)

Yet the crucial change, we slowly come to see, is not in the land and its inhabitants, but in the subjective history of the poet himself. And the crucial "depopulation" is his own personal and irreversible removal—from the physical "seat" of his youth, but more fundamentally, from his youth itself. The poet's subjective experience of temporality is projected as the impossibility of objective pastoral retreat. Thus the truths of nature are seen to be an effect of the truths of culture—that is, of human nature.

In so far as the poet finds he *can* go home again, it's because he sympathetically *re*populates the landscape with the memories of those he mourns, even in the act of mourning them. The swain and his milkmaid, the village preacher, the village school-master: these are the objects of pathos by whose sympathetic recreation the poet would imaginatively reclaim the innocence of his childhood. Like Thomas Gray in *Elegy Written in a Country Church-Yard* (1751), to which much of *The Deserted Village* is an inspired allusion,

Goldsmith sadly clears the land of its rustic personages only to re-people it with figures of his own imagination. In both poems, the natural retreat therefore is found ultimately in poetic artifice, which retrieves what nature cannot. This amounts to a pastoral deviation that circles back to the first principle of pastoral, the indispensability of poetic culture to the experience of the natural. Looked at another way, however, the internalization of pastoral retreat amounts to a striking modernization. In naturalizing the inmost recesses of human artifice, it helps facilitate the uniquely modern conviction that the source of normative value is to be found in individual subjectivity.

The most radical deviation from pastoral principles legitimated by eighteenth-century practice is exemplified by the poetry of Mary Leapor, daughter of a gardener to Northamptonshire gentry and herself a cook-maid. Although devoted to the depiction of the shepherd at song, the pastoral tradition had been equally devoted to the view that this rustic object of representation was by definition incapable of serving as its actual subject, its author. By the same token, the georgic tradition, especially, gendered nature as the fecund female object of cultivation and husbandry and the cultivating subject—the farmer, but by extension also the poet—as male. The emergence of pastoralists who were first of all rustic laborers and/or women revolutionized attitudes toward pastoral. It also helped articulate a contemporary revolution in the terms of status and gender categorization. Tle shape of this revolution can be sensed in the way it gets pastoralized in the *Tatler* and *Spectator* papers (1710–11).

In *Tatler,* no. 169, Steele undertakes to distinguish between two types of landholder:

> The Truth is, there is no Man who can be said to be Proprietor of an Estate, but he who knows how to enjoy it. Nay, it shall never be allowed, that the Land is not a Waste, when the Master is uncultivated. Therefore, to avoid Confusion, it is to be noted, that a Peasant with a great Estate is but an Incumbent, and that he must be a Gentleman to be a Landlord. . . . Who, that has any Passion for his native Country, does not think it worse than conquered, when so large Divisions of it are in the Hands of Salvages, that know no Use of Property but to be Tyrants; or Liberty, but to be unmannerly. A Gentleman in a Country Life enjoys Paradise with a Temper fit for it; a Clown is cursed in it with all the cutting and unruly Passions Man could be tormented with when be was expelled from it.[16]

Steele goes on to characterize the "Country Gentleman" in paternalist terms very close to those of Dryden's *beatus ille;* and he concludes that "when a Man in a Country Life has this Turn, . . . he lives in a more happy Condition than any is [sic] described in the Pastoral Descriptions of Poets. . . ."

The lines are clearly drawn. On the one side stands the savage clown or peasant mere-incumbent who works the land as though he has already Fallen from it; on the other stands the cultivated gentleman landlord, who administers a prelapsarian benevolence, utility, and pleasure. The difference seems as absolute as that between brutish nature and refined culture. And yet Steele's ease belies the difficulty of his project, which aims to establish a sharp boundary between social roles that are uncomfortably comparable. Despite the language of gentlemanliness, nothing so definitive as gentility or rank separates the two types. So, both find their recent origins in the "peasantry," and the "country gentleman" is distinguished only (perhaps) by the amount of time that has elapsed since his upward mobility, and by the degree of his acculturation. Steele uses the increasingly vestigial markers of status—in alliance with pastoral tropes—to justify one mode of life by distinguishing it from the phantom otherness of itself. And he divides a social category that the emergent language of class will soon conceive as a unit, to be set over against the not-yet-visible category of the rural proletariat.

In *Spectator*, no. 15, Joseph Addison undertakes a similar task in gender definition. The paper establishes a contrast between two married women, Aurelia and Fulvia. Aurelia is content with the simple, "solid and substantial Blessings" of a natural and rural existence, delighting "in the Privacy of a Country Life...."[17] She and her husband, sharing all pastoral virtues and offices, form an integrated domestic unit: "Their Family is under so regular an Oeconomy, in its Hours of Devotion and Repast, Employment and Diversion, that it looks like a little Common-Wealth within it self." Fulvia, by contrast, is "more attentive to the superficial Parts of Life...." Divided from her husband, she considers him "her Steward, and looks upon Discretion, and good House-Wifery, as little domestick Virtues, unbecoming a Woman of Quality. She thinks Life lost in her own Family, and fancies her self out of the World when she is not in the Ring, the Play-House, or the Drawing-Room...."

Again, the lines seem clearly drawn between the natural and the artificial, between positive and pejorative gender norms. But Addison's paper exists to document the paradoxical fact that women in general have what he calls a "Natural Weakness of being taken with Outside and Appearance." How does the contradictory maxim that it's natural for women to be artifical complicate the dichotomy between Aurelia and Fulvia? Addison uses pastoral to conflate, in Aurelia, virtues that partake of opposed institutions. On the one hand, she looks forward to a stabilized domestic *ideology,* that more or less strictly divides public from private, male from female employments. On the other hand, Addison's vision of the family as a little commonwealth looks back to a still-influential patriarchalist ideology that integrates male and female employments within a unified domestic *economy*.[18] Aurelia's apparently coherent naturalness is compounded of antithetical norms of the natural that, when juxtaposed, disclose the relativity, the cultural contingency, of each other's version of the natural.

When the customary objects of pastoral representation become also its authorial subjects, the contemporary revolution in status and gender categorization becomes quite explicit. The century's most celebrated and poignant case of such mobility is Stephen Duck, the Thresher Poet, whose first poem, *The Thresher's Labour* (1730), goes a great distance toward accommodating pastoral to the innovative representation of class conflict. Like Swift, Duck undertakes what looks like an "illicit," *anti*-pastoral deviation that nonetheless also can claim the status of a "lawful" *neo*-pastoral. But if Swift's deviation is spatial, Duck more radically deviates into the very voice and subjectivity of the pastoral object:

> Nor yet, the tedious Labour to beguile,
> And make the passing Minutes sweetly smile,
> Can we, like Shepherds, tell a merry Tale;
> The Voice is lost, drown'd by the louder Flail.
> But we may think—Alas! what pleasing thing,
> Here, to the Mind, can the dull Fancy bring?
> Our Eye beholds no pleasing Object here,
> No chearful Sound diverts our list'ning Ear.
> The Shepherd well may tune his Voice to sing,
> Inspir'd with all the Beauties of the Spring.
> No Fountains murmur here, no Lambkins play,
> No Linnets warble, and no Fields look gay;
> 'Tis all a gloomy, melancholy Scene,
> Fit only to provoke the Muse's Spleen.[19]

Within this viewpoint, the poet's task balances between the realist repudiation of pastoral, and the realist ambition to make pastoral honest. Demonstrating this equilibrium, Duck radically reconceives the ethical opposition between the rustic shepherd and the corruptions of artifice, between country and city values, as a fully embodied exploitation of wage labor by employer. Focused on "the Profits of the Year," the farmer imposes on his workers a modernizing system of labor discipline that subjects both work and time to the strict quantification of "Day-works" (ll. 16, 27):[20]

> Divested of our Cloathes, with Flail in Hand,
> At proper Distance, Front to Front we stand:
> . . . .
> Down one, one up, so well they keep the Time,

> The CYCLOPS' Hammers could not truer chime;
> ....
> Week after Week, we this dull Task pursue,
> Unless when winn'wing Days produce a new:
> A new, indeed, but frequently a worse!
> The Threshal yields but to the Master's Curse.
> He counts the Bushels, counts how much a Day;
> Then swears we've idled half our Time away. . . .
> (ll. 29–30, 38–39, 68–73)

Later, at corn harvest, the reapers are followed hard upon by "our Master":

> . . . and if he spies
> One charitable Ear, he grudging cries,
> 'Ye scatter half your Wages o'er the Land.'
> Then scrapes the Stubble with his greedy Hand.
> (ll. 242–45)

In this way, Duck makes palpable the social conflict that is customarily only tacit within pastoral and georgic opposition. In the process, he sidesteps the hierarchical and essentializing categories of social status in favor of the pragmatic dynamics of class oppression. But the reconception doesn't quite work. Balanced between anti- and neo-pastoral, Duck is also balanced between the embeddedness of the innocent pastoral object and the detachment of the knowing pastoral subject. In so far as he speaks with the distanced voice of the artful poet, he also runs the risk of seeing with the distanced eye of the cultivating employer. The issue comes to a head as Duck observes and records the spectacle of female labor. It's introduced, perhaps fatally, as a spectacle, a change of "scene":

> Soon as the rising Sun has drank the Dew,
> Another Scene is open to our View:
> Our Master comes, and at his Heels a Throng
> Of prattling Females, arm'd with Rake and Prong;
> Prepar'd, whilst he is here, to make his Hay;
> Or, if he turns his Back, prepar'd to play:
> But here, or gone, sure of this Comfort still;
> Here's Company, so they may chat their Fill.
> Ah! were their Hands so active as their Tongues,
> How nimbly then would move the Rakes and Prongs!
> ....
> Till by degrees so high their Notes they strain,
> A Stander by can nought distinguish plain.

So loud's their Speech, and so confus'd their Noise,
Scarce puzzled ECHO can return the Voice.
(ll. 160–69, 178–81)

The issue is inseparably one of place and one of voice. Within the context of Duck's radicalized pastoralism, the speaking thresher should find a class ally in the women, who enforce custom and resist the regimentation of the work week by setting their "tongues" against their "hands," their "play" against their work, their *otium* against their *negotium*. However, the thresher's posture as poet momentarily leads him instead to speak for, and to identify with, the employer—to transform the nascent pastoral opposition between natural laborer and artful owner into one between cultivating men and unproductive women. The artful detachment of the voice of the "stander by" renders the speech of the women unintelligible. By the same token (as Mary Collier implied nine years later[21]), the plain evidence of the women's laboring productivity is to Duck quite invisible (see ll. 202–3).

When Duck genders his innovative pastoral critique of agrarian employment, he divides laboring men from women in a way that cuts across, and vitiates, his critical class division. But the detached male speaker can also be turned to proto-feminist ends in pastoral. In narrating her autobiographical *Adventures of Rivella* (1714), Delarivier Manley impersonates a male biographer who consistently champions a private retreat from the world, preferably rustication with himself, as the only way Rivella's damaged reputation might be protected from further public exposure. At one point, the narrator declares that "I who knew *Rivella*'s Innocency, beg' d she wou'd retire to my Seat in the Country . . . ." (40).[22] In refusing this offer, Rivella envisions a very different version of pastoral retirement: "She told me her Love of Solitude was improved by her Disgust of the World; and since it was impossible for her to be publick with Reputation, she was resolv'd to remain in it conceal'd . . . 'Twas in this Solitude, that she compos'd her first Tragedy . . ." (41).

Like Boswell, Rivella locates the normative rural value of solitude in the City. But by "solitude" she also means using anonymous publication to protect her reputation while remaining in the public sphere. To her narrator, female honor depends upon not urban publication but rural domestication, and late in the story he rewrites her history to make it conform to this model, sending her into the country and away from publication after the possibility of marriage to another man has fallen through (107–8). Yet in fact, this passage glosses over the fact that it was then that Manley published her first scandalous and highly popular *roman à clef*. After the second is published and she narrowly evades prosecution for it, Rivella's narrator claims that "she now agrees with me, that Politicks is not the Business of a Woman, . . . and has accordingly set her self again to write a Tragedy for the Stage" (117). In fact Manley continued to publish political works in the transparent guise of private romance, a formal masquerade that recalls the public privacy of her urban anonymity. Indeed, *The Adventures of Rivella* is one such publication, which makes a strong claim to redeem Manley's honor in a way her male narrator thinks is possible only through rustication with a man. By this means, the natural virtue of female retirement persists as a pastoral fiction that veils a radical revaluation whereby female honor becomes accessible through the cultivation of publicity.

From one perspective an anti-pastoral, Manley's ingenious exercise is also intelligible as a neo-pastoral feminization of the form. I'll conclude with a rather different example of this sort of experiment. Early on in her correspondence, the twenty-one-year-old Lady Mary Pierrepont conceives marriage to Edward Wortley Montagu as a "retirement" from "Town" and "the World."[23] And in the face of Edward's diplomatic ambitions, Lady Mary easily converts pastoral to macro-pastoral convention: "If we retire into the country both your fortune and Inclination require a degree of privacy. . . . but . . . at Naples we may live after our own fashion. For my part, as I design utterly to forget there is such a place as London, I shall leave no directions with nobody to write after me. People that enter upon a solitude are in the wrong if they do not make it as agreable as they can. . . . The Scheme I propose to my selfe is living in an agreable Country, with a Man that I like, that likes me, and forgetting the rest of the world as much as if there was no other people in the world, and that Naples were the Garden of Eden" (August 6, 11, 1712). A lifetime later, Lady Mary finds herself actually living in Italy, conceiving her country estate there as an Edenic garden where the "Solitude" of horatian "retreat" entirely depends upon her being in a single state, unmarried (Lady Mary to Lady Bute, July 10, 1748; January 28, March 6, 1753). The blessings of pastoral retirement have remained vital in validating woman's lot as "natural"; but the state of matrimony has shifted from embodying, to hindering, those blessings.

Of course, the malleability of pastoral topics is nowhere so evident as in Lady Mary's celebrated Turkish Embassy letters. The disparate facets of her social identity here compose a contradictory chain each of whose links partakes of both "nature" and "culture" by turns. Lady Mary idealizes Turkey in part because she identifies with the feminized alterity of a nation that treats women with such apparent respect. From this perspective, the familiar local relation between English men and women, between artifical constraint and the natural need for liberty, is analogous to the macro-pastoral relation between England and Turkey, where liberty flourishes. However, two factors complicate this Turkish identification. The very idealization on which her orientalism is based suggests that Lady Mary is first of all an *English* woman, exoticizing the macro-other so as to identify with its naturalized otherness. Moreover, as a woman, Lady Mary ultimately sympathizes not with "Turkey" the macro-other, but with Turkish women, the local other *within* that macro-other. In this context, their liberty is a victory won over Turkish *men*, and it is attributed, characteristically, both to the naturalness and to the artifice of women—in the baths, to their "being in the state of nature, that is, in plain English, stark naked . . ."; in the streets, to the "perpetual Masquerade" of their total concealment. Yet both sorts of liberty presuppose aristocratic status. Lady Mary's insistence that they don't—that in the baths as on the streets, "there is no distinguishing the great Lady from her Slave"—only confirms what is elsewhere evident enough, that in both England and Turkey, when she says "women," Lady Mary means "noblewomen" (Lady Mary to Lady ——, Lady Mary to Lady Mar, April 1, 1717). All this is only to say that Lady Mary's Embassy letters convey the truth that personal "identity" is an unstable compound of elements—gender, social status, nationality—each of which makes its exclusive claim to a determinant naturalness in the face of simultaneous and contradictory claims by all others.

Let me end with a few remarks on the significance of pastoral experiment in eighteenth-century England. I've chosen to describe this experiment in terms of a proprietary survey, or as an ongoing effort to adjudicate the "lawfulness" of "deviations" from the pastoral norm. But pastoral has always been a tool for thinking beyond its own strictest limits, for challenging its own conventionality. The first pastoral deviation was from the *Eclogues* to the *Georgics*, a radical shift that pushed back the frontiers of culture by rethinking industrious cultivation as consistent with natural ends. It is therefore, as it were, "in the nature" of pastoral to survey, and to resurvey, the frontiers of culture, a dynamic process whose disorienting effects can be felt both as a naturalization of what before was deemed culture, and as a culturalization of what up to now was seen as nature. During the eighteenth century, the aggravation of this dynamic owes, paradoxically, to the unprecedented stabilization of "nature" and "culture" as interdependent categories whose very distinctiveness requires the constant vigilance of experimental conflation.

The spatial figure of a cultural "frontier" is persuasive because pastoral is first of all a discourse of shifting spatial relations. In the eighteenth century, pastoral undertakes to mediate negotiations that are underway in a number of locales—between country and city, but also *within* both country and city, as well as between nation and nation, metropolitan and colony, hemisphere and hemisphere. In supplying a measure for all these interlinked relationships, the opposition between nature and culture renders each of them intelligible even as the intelligibility of each dissolves into that of its greater or lesser version. The language of the frontier becomes figurative when we recall that pastoral is nonetheless also, and finally, about people as much as places. In the eighteenth century, pastoral intimately assists in the emergence of modern discourses that all depend, each in their own way, on a more definitive autonomization of categories that traditionally had been held in suspension: discourses of imperial politics and cultural difference; of national diplomacy and foreign policy; of class conflict; of sexuality and gender politics; of personal identity and its formation. If macro-pastoral names the insight that the sliding scale of pastoral norms can be externalized to the international level, micro-pastoral names the discovery that the human mind, that individual human development, are internal landscapes responsive to pastoral cognition.

What happens to pastoral in the modern world? On the most immediate level, pastoralism as a discipline of poetic technique can be said to die after 1800 only to be reborn as the prosaic, and increasingly mandatory and compelling, discourse of environmentalism. On a broader level, however, my preceding remarks may suggest that the breakup of pastoral is only another way of conceiving the modern division of knowledge, whereby a previously unified discourse replicates its own congenital concern with division and unification by dividing into the several discourses of the social sciences—sociology, anthropology, psychology—through which modernity extends in other terms the age-old project of surveying the frontier of nature and culture. But this is perhaps too grandiose a vision of pastoral's modern legacy. And it also will be objected that pastoral poetry doesn't really die in 1800. Both the romantic poets and their heirs continue to write not only poetry they're content to *call* "pastorals," but also poetry that lacks the name yet bears the deep imprint of pastoral preoccupation—preoccupation both with the dream of a direct apprehension of nature, and with the inevitability of nature's subjective internalization and its imaginative construction.

These days, the term "romanticism" is used to designate both a period discourse and a more general opening out into modernity. The complex logic that links modern "romanticism" to the traditionality of "romance" is powerful and undeniable. Nonetheless, there may be some value in seeing the poetic revolution undertaken by Blake, Wordsworth, and Coleridge as a movement not from "romance" to "romanticism," but from "pastoral" to "pastoralism"—in seeing romanticism as the profound assimilation of pastoral inquiry through its deliberate yet increasingly imperceptible application to all experience. In this way, under the disarmingly effective guise of its anachronism and disuse, pastoral is stealthily elevated to the status of the modern master discourse. But this, too, is perhaps grandiose.

NOTES

1. *Guardian*, nos. 28, 32, April 13, 17, 1713, in *The Guardian*, ed. Alexander Chalmers, 2 vols. (London: Luke Hansard, 1806). Further citations refer to this edition.
2. Ibid., no. 30, April 15, 1713.
3. Ibid., no. 28, April 13, 1713.
4. *Tatler*, no. 9, April 28–30, 1709, in *The Tatler*, ed. Donald F. Bond, 3 vols. Oxford: Clarendon Press, 1987). Further citations refer to this edition.
5. *The Beauties of English Poesy. Selected by Oliver Goldsmith* (1767), in *Collected Works of Oliver Goldsmith*, ed. Arthur Friedman (Oxford: Clarendon Press, 1966), 5:322.
6. *Tatler*, no. 238, Oct. 14–17, 1710, ll. 61–63.
7. Tobias Smollett, *The Expedition of Humphry Clinker* (1771), ed. Lewis M. Knapp and Paul-Gabriel Boucé (Oxford: Oxford University Press, 1984), 89, 120–21.
8. *Boswell's London Journal 1762–1763*, ed. Frederick A. Pottle (New York: McGraw-Hill, 1950), 68–69, 96.
9. William Collins, "Ode on the Popular Superstitions of the Highlands of Scotland, Considered as the Subject of Poetry" (1788), in *The Poems of Gray, Collins and Goldsmith*, ed. Roger Lonsdale (London: Longman, 1969), ll. 30–32. Further citations to this edition will appear parenthetically in the text.
10. Samuel Johnson, *London*, in *The Yale Edition of the Works of Samuel Johnson*, vol. 6, ed. E. L. McAdam, Jr. and George Milne (New Haven: Yale University Press, 1964), ll. 7–10, 210–11, 257. Further citations to this edition will appear parenthetically in the text.
11. John Dryden, "To my Honour'd Kinsman, John Driden, of Chesterton," in *The Poems of John Dryden*, ed. James Kinsley, vol. 4 (Oxford: Clarendon Press, 1958), l. 3. Further citations to this edition will appear parenthetically in the text.
12. Anne Finch, Countess of Winchilsea, "The Petition for an Absolute Retreat," in *The Poems of Anne Countess of Winchilsea*, ed. Myra Reynolds (Chicago: University of Chicago Press, 1903), ll. 1–7. Further citations to this edition will appear parenthetically in the text.
13. Mary Leapor, "Complaining *Daphne*. A *Pastoral*," in *Poems Upon Several Occasions* (London, 1751), ll. 7, 10. Further citations to this edition will appear parenthetically in the text.
14. James Thomson, "Winter," in *Eighteenth-Century English Literature*, ed. Geoffrey Tillotson et al. (New York: Harcourt, 1969), ll. 424–29. Further citations to this edition will appear parenthetically in the text.
15. Oliver Goldsmith, "Dedication to Sir Joshua Reynolds," in *The Poems of Gray, Collins and Goldsmith*, l. 20. Further citations to this edition will appear parenthetically in the text.
16. *Tatler*, no. 169, May 9, 1710.

17. *Spectator*, no. 15, March 17, 1711, in *The Spectator*, ed. Donald F. Bond, 5 vols. (Oxford: Clarendon Press, 1965). Further citations refer to this edition.

18. On the transition from a domestic economy to a domestic ideology, see Susan Cahn, *Industry of Devotion: The Transformation of Women's Work in England, 1500–1660* (New York: Columbia University Press, 1987); and Bridget Hill, *Women, Work, and Sexual Politics in Eighteenth-Century England* (Oxford: Blackwell, 1989).

19. Stephen Duck, *The Thresher's Labour* (1730), ll. 48–61, published together with Mary Collier's *The Woman's Labour*, intro. Moira Ferguson, Augustan Reprint Society no. 230 (Los Angeles, Calif.: William Andrews Clark Memorial Library, 1985). Further citations to this edition appear parenthetically in the text.

20. On time and labor discipline see E. P. Thompson, *Customs in Common: Studies in Traditional Popular Culture* (New York: New Press, 1991), chap. 6.

21. See Mary Collier, *The Woman's Labour. An Epistle to Mr. Stephen Duck* (1739), ll. 61–62. The text cited in this essay appears in *The Meridian Anthology of Early Women Writers: British Literary Women from Aphra Behn to Maria Edgeworth, 1660–1800*, ed. Katharine M. Rogers and William McCarthy (New York: New American Library, 1987), 382–89.

22. Delarivier Manley, *The Adventures of Rivella; or, the History of the Author of the Atalantis* (London, 1714), 40. Further citations to this edition appear parenthetically in the text.

23. Lady Mary to Wortley, April 25, 1710, March 24, 1711, in *The Complete Letters of Lady Mary Wortley Montagu*, ed. Robert Halsband, 3 vols. (Oxford: Clarendon Press, 1965–67). Further citations to this edition appear parenthetically in the text.

Letters: Painted/Penned/Purloined

MARY SHERIFF

Throughout the eighteenth century, various myths—literary, scientific, moral—secured the cultural positions "male" and "female," and thereby established the relation of sexed bodies to letters and pictures. What interests me is how those relations were imaged in the visual arts, and how certain images may have presented to women opportunities for understanding otherwise their relation to writing and painting. My work with paintings made by women artists, and especially those of Elisabeth Vigée-Lebrun, has led me to these concerns. In particular, her painted and textual self-images suggest that this artist was an oppositional reader of images and myths, who used to advantage the opportunities for transformation. In her case, oppositional reading was a necessity; any woman who showed herself as artist challenged the prescriptions and prohibitions that made "woman artist" theoretically inarticulate and provided no norms for her representation.

Evaluating how a woman artist purloined and recast the prevailing images and myths cannot tell us whether other women did, indeed, read against the grain. It can, however, open the frontiers of that possibility and thereby enable us to imagine a history of resistance. But even if it could be shown that no woman in the eighteenth century read oppositionally, oppositional reading still suggests strategies for taking back the bodies of some painted women rather than discarding them as signifiers of a phallocentric and phallocratic regime. I propose these strategies not to replace cultural critique, but to complement it when the occasion arises. Oppositional reading steals a few images from the canon, reinscribes them, and returns them as subversive facsimiles whose message is that woman's exclusion from knowledge, power, and representation was not and is not in the nature of bodies and things.

As I am using the term, to be "oppositional"—rather than merely willful, wishful, or fanciful—an interpretation must, with political purpose, analyze, occupy, and strategically redeploy the signifiers at work in a specific historical image. An oppositional reading is most effective when it moves into and cites the same discourses engaged by an image, both describing how the image is shaped by those discourses and looking for the subversive possibilities within them. A feminist oppositional reading constructs an interpretation that proceeds from a position theoretically inarticulate within prevailing norms (past and/or present), but actually occupied by women as historical subjects. Joan DeJean gets to the heart of the issue when she contests both normalizing the gaze as masculine and ceding to men the power it confers on them as representing subjects. She reminds us that the gaze does not belong to men just because they have claimed it. Nor does their claim mean that women have not wielded the gaze even though it has been forbidden them either by social convention or by excluding it from their proper "feminine" position.[1] Oppositional reading presumes both the possibility that women have stepped out of their place and the necessity for inscribing that possibility within our histories.

I do not propose that all paintings can or should be interpreted oppositionally; I want to explore instead the boundaries that enable and limit such interpretations. I take as my primary object of analysis an image that thematizes the relation between woman, painting, and lettering—Fragonard's *The Souvenir* (Figure 1)—and I suggest why this image is open to oppositional reading. In undertaking such a reading, I am indebted to recent feminist inquiry, such as Jane Burns's *Bodytalk: When Women Speak in Old French Literature*, and Jacqueline Bobo's *Black Women as Cultural Readers*.[2] I also borrow some of the strategies through which an eighteenth-century woman artist, Elisabeth Vigée-Lebrun, constructed her self-image by reoccupying and reimaging the prevailing myths and assumptions about art and the artist. Vigee-Lebrun's self-portrayals stand as my historical example of a woman's oppositional reading.[3] In contrast to Fragonard's painting, which I read as available for feminist appropriation, I pose Gabriel de Saint-Aubin's *The Private Academy* (Figure 4). In the specific way it signifies and immobilizes an excessively female female body, the Saint-Aubin begs for critique but limits our possibilities for imagining a reading that could empower the *pictured* woman. I end the essay by reflecting on an image that suggests the

Figure 1
J. H. Fragonard, *The Souvenir*, c. 1780
Photograph: Wallace Collection, London

power of women's interpretation in its very desire to control that power: Jacques-Louis David's *Marat Assassinated* (Figure 5). What interests me in this painting is David's refusal to materialize the body of Charlotte Corday—whom he indicates through her knife and letter—coupled with an appeal to women as audience for the work. When David presented his painting in a fête to honor Marat, he also represented the proper woman's response through the *citoyennes* of the Museum section. I hope to show that this image and the control of its reception are themselves compelling arguments for pursuing the practice of oppositional reading.[4]

Reading Letters

I begin my exploration with an image of a woman standing in an overgrown garden, rococo site of elite pastoral pleasures. Fragonard painted the image probably in the late 1770s; it is now called *The Souvenir*, although we know nothing of the title's genesis. The artist represents a young girl carving on a tree, an activity that confirms her place in the pastoral tradition. Among classical writers, Virgil, Ovid, and Lucian, all represented the practice, and later Ludovico Ariosto, Torquato Tasso, Jacopo Sannazaro, and, in France, Honoré d'Urfé preserved within the pastoral tradition the name or epigram carved on a tree. Such carvings were usually associated with love's loss, and they compensated abandoned lovers. The carving enlarges itself as the tree grows, and love persists through the carver's art aided by natural processes.[5] In the pastoral tradition women usually were the ones whose names were carved, but sometimes they also did the carving. Ariosto's Angelica writes on trees together with her lover Medaro, perhaps the only instance that such writing is a mutual celebration of love's consummation. And in *Jerusalem Liberata*, Tasso's Erminia, disguised as a knight, tells a shepherd that she has inscribed on trees the story of Tancred, her lost love.

Fragonard obviously does not "illustrate" any of these literary scenes, although his image cites the tradition. Signaling the loss of love that instigates art might, for example, account for the spaniel's depiction. Traditional symbol of faithfulness, the dog often functions as a contrast to (and recompense for) the lover who has betrayed his beloved, as in Fragonard's *If he were only as faithful!* (c. 1770; Malibu: J. Paul Getty Museum). On the other hand, the dog here could as easily function as an emblem of the *faithful* lover memorialized in art, a role Fragonard gave the spaniel in *Love Letters* (1772; New York: Frick Collection). Perhaps we could more easily interpret Fragonard's reading of the pastoral if we could identify the object lying beneath the bench. When Nicholas Delaunay engraved the painting in 1787 (Figure 2), he clearly marked that object as a letter. But like the faithful

Figure 2
Nicholas Delaunay, Engraving after J.-H. Fragonard, *Le Chiffre d'Amour*, 1787
Photograph courtesy Jerry Blow

pooch, letters can signal either the rupture of a love affair or its continuation.[6] And although Delaunay opens the possibility of seeing these marks as a letter, he is an unreliable guide to Fragonard's work. In his engraving, title, caption, coat of arms all suggest an interpretation of Fragonard's image appropriate for the specific individual—Madame de Polastron—named in the dedication. Looking at the area beneath the bench in the painting, the brushwork can as easily be seen as denoting a book. This sort of uncertainty about whether marks constitute one signifier or another is more particular to painting than to writing. Painting is not based on a limited differential code; no alphabet allows one to distinguish among marks in paintings.[7] Letter or book, the object lying under the bench cannot easily be read, and its vagaries cast into relief what the girl is carving—a letter of the alphabet.

Between Fragonard's painting and Delaunay's engraving we notice a redistribution of emphasis. Delaunay's carver has already completed and punctuated the first letter and is moving along to the next, but the letters themselves are not stressed. Fragonard's woman incises the letter's lower semicircle; she is in the process of making the letter despite the dot that appears to terminate it. Although it might seem logical to assume that one carves on trees as one writes, that is from left to right, here the young woman conflates design and writing as she has placed her stop before making the letter, the better to situate it in the upper center of the lighted area. Thus the painting highlights the letter S the young girl is designing and designating. Trying to find the story line, other interpreters have concentrated on what names the letter could signify; she has been said, for example, to be Julie carving the name of Saint-Preux.[8] I prefer to attend more closely to the letter itself, and to the process of carving or writing a letter.

We are by now familiar with the Enlightenment's particular concern with the origins of written and spoken language. As the cornerstone of mature writing, the alphabet was characteristic of "policed" societies, which according to Jean-Jacques Rousseau developed a written language superior to that of savage and barbaric peoples. The writing systems of these "others" were inferior—stuck in a more primitive state of development—because rather than analyze sound, they relied on a visual resemblance to the thing signified.[9] In this history the "primitive" character of the sign based on visual resemblance sustains both a positive and a negative reading; it belongs to a people closer to the natural state, but who are nonetheless not in nature, but in a primitive social order. There is no signification outside of society.

Although other writers would vary the scheme somewhat, it was widely acknowledged that both writing, in general, and alphabetic characters, or letters, in specific, developed from pictures. Just as pictures "resembled" and had their origin in natural bodies, so letters, too, contained primitive resemblances.[10] The alphabet thus retained something of both its pictorial character and motivated relation to objects and/or sounds. Take the S, for example, the letter Fragonard shows the girl carving. The S is doubly motivated. Many who wrote about writing's origin related both its shape and sound to the snake. Emphasizing the connection between scripting and drawing some concentrated on the serpentine shape of the letter; others shifted the focus to sound and the S as an onomatopoeia for the snake's hiss, or the sound of breath, in general.[11]

Fragonard's landscape provides an ideal setting for exploring this natural sign. The garden is constructed in a picturesque mode, which operates by confusing a natural artifice—or an art created by nature that is merely copied by the image maker—with an artificial naturalness—a naturalness imagined and feigned by the artist.[12] We see the picturesque at work where nature has obligingly configured itself into artful frames: first, in the oval shape formed by the overarching tree and young girl's bended arms; and then in a lighted cartouche cast on the beech bark and framed by foliage. With many other rococo scenes, Fragonard's image uses the picturesque mode to signal a pastoral setting, an edenic setting promising in its landscape to reconcile the naturally given and the culturally wrought. In this impossible setting, letters resemble things as much as art resembles nature.

If in this setting we concentrate on S as a letter that originated in a resemblance, we can suggest that *The Souvenir* enacts a particular reading of the pastoral tradition, for now Fragonard's image reveals a woman in a garden standing near a tree on which she is representing the shape and sound of a snake. She thus reminds us of her—indeed of all women's—descent from Eve, and that the so-called Fall of man even as late as the eighteenth century was associated with the beginning of human language as representation. This interpretation turned on the idea that before the Fall, Adam and Eve could communicate through silence or through simply seeing one another's thoughts.[13] Eve's seduction by the snake and her taking its position as seducer of Adam, brought with it both language and lust—and we should not forget the phallic associations also attached to the snake in this story.

Read allegorically, this myth of transgression suggests the origin of language as its birth into materiality; communication "falls" out of a pristine and original state of transparency. At the same time, sexuality and lust—imagined as knowledge of the material body—degrade human dignity. Eve stands at the nexus of language, seduction, lust, and the Fall—between Enlightenment theorizing about the origin of language and the biblical story that was never totally discarded. The daughter of Eve we see in *The Souvenir* reminds us of this position; carving nature's matter, she encodes the truth of her own seduction into language by showing us not the snake itself, but its sign. Clearly here I am not reading oppositionally, but tracing a particular view of woman that seems implicated in this picture. More remains to be seen before suggesting how another interpretation might displace this reading.

As serpent and serpentine line, the S-shape was frequently associated with woman's body throughout the eighteenth century. William Hogarth perhaps most overtly brought these associations to bear on Eve in the frontispiece of his *Analysis of Beauty*, which quotes John Milton's *Paradise Lost*—"So vary'd he, and of his tortuous train/ Curl'd many a wanton wreath, in sight of Eve,/ To lure her eye."[14] If in this statement Eve is seduced by the snake's motion and infinite variety, later in the text Hogarth noticed how Cleopatra seduced Anthony through the same gambits of constant change and varied diversion, thus transferring to woman the snake's seductive charm.[15] Interest in the serpentine line was hardly unique to Hogarth; indeed this particular line dominated the ornamental and pictorial structures of the visual arts throughout Europe well into the second half of the century. Abstracted from the observation of nature, this line represented the utopic reconciliation of all contradictions. It was at once still and moving; concave and convex; the same, yet varied. And like the letter, it encoded a natural resemblance.

Although historically the serpentine line was associated with both male and female bodies, in *The Souvenir*, Fragonard reveals it as the basis of the female form. Indeed, the female figure is rendered in a series of curves and countercurves, as both her back and her bosom flow in and out, and an S-curve articulates the relation between her hair and arms. The line the woman carves thus again pictures itself as a motivated sign—a sign of woman's body and a sign of artifice. The serpentine female figure slides along a signifying chain whose links include the serpent, Eve, Woman, Beauty, and Artifice. This chain reinforces connections expressed elsewhere, for when it lurked unseen in the flowers, the serpent could be taken as a rhetorical figure for beauty's danger. In 1783 the lurking serpent appeared in a poem praising the works of Vigée-Lebrun. The poem absorbs her art into a tale that describes how the narrator's desire is aroused by the beautiful goddesses she depicts. He says of her Venus in the painting *Venus Tying the Wings of Cupid:* "But without rival, here the queen of Cythera/ Makes her sweetest treasures shine/ What charms! on so beautiful a body." Continuing, the narrator seeks divine protection from beauty's danger, which earlier in the poem led him to challenge Jupiter's sovereignty. He implores the gods: "Keep us from fixing a reckless gaze./ We are afraid of again going astray/And, fearing the serpent, we avoid the flowers." The narrator's next move, however, typifies a strategy for both praising women artists and securing them in a "feminine" position. Collapsing the distinction between the artist and the art object, he finds the painter, like her images, dangerous beauty, seductive coquette: "Triumph lovely enchantress,/ Who, giving spirit to paint/ Makes the canvas so formidable/ And seems to trifle with hearts!"[16]

This critical gesture finds an analog in Fragonard's painting as the woman carving the initial and making art is herself figured within the image as a work of art. Notice how the young girl's upper body is rendered in profile, as if she were a silhouette, and how the profile appears generated by the light, as her dark form is posed against a brightened ground. To emphasize her pictorialization, the figure's upper body seems framed in an oval formed by the bending over of the tree limb and the bend of her elbows. She is like a portrait miniature, perhaps one made as a token for the lover whose name she inscribes on a tree. The particular nature of her pictorialization, moreover, suggests that painting's originary myths also structure Fragonard's image.

One pertinent myth located the origin of painting in a silhouette portrait made by tracing a shadow. This myth was reported by Pliny the Elder and interpreted in French paintings throughout the 1770s.[17] The central figure is the Greek maiden Dibutadis who invents painting by tracing the shadow of her lover's profile on a wall. Fixing the resemblance is suggested to her when she notices the natural effect of light, and she is moved to action by her desire to preserve the likeness of a lover about to depart for some distant shore. Like letters written on trees, portraits compensated lovers for the absence of the beloved. Fragonard's image connects to Dibutadis's story in suggesting the natural origin of painting in the shadow and in showing us a profile portrait. His woman's activity, however, suggests that drawing, although dependent on nature, is more than a mere copying of the natural. In tracing the S she renders the profile of her body in an abstracted form. She also associates drawing with another sort of signifying code, the alphabet, believed to be an abstraction of resemblances.

If the relation between painting and writing is thematized in the image, the artist's signature, which appears as if carved into the stone of the bench, can also be viewed within this matrix.[18] The artist's signature on a painting is relentlessly peculiar. Sometimes the signature remains an alien presence that disrupts the illusion.[19] Sometimes it is turned into a pictorial element through a *trompe l'oeil* effect. In the second case its inscription signifies as both writing and painting, and the alphabet is destabilized in reference to the more primitive pictorial sign, since writing is also seen to have a pictorial character that varies with the individual hand.

Fragonard did not sign many paintings, and his signature is never consistent. But he did play with the signature as in his fantasy portrait of an old man (Musée Jacquemart-André), in which his signature is made as an initial wrought on the brooch. Now if we look again at the signature on *The Souve-*

nir, another possible reading emerges, especially in relation to how the signature is enframed by the shawl thrown picturesquely over the bench. Notice the first letter of the signature, the F. In the italic script used throughout Europe at this time, the F and the S are very close to one another in appearance. As we have noted, the young woman is still working on her letter, still completing the lower curve. What if we imagine that she will stretch out the curve and then cross it, making the F out of the S?

But perhaps I am stretching things a bit too far. It is enough to note the relation between the S she carves and the F Fragonard has left on the bench to see that both originate in serpentine lines. Which reminds us that the serpentine line itself is a sort of artist's signature. In his *Self-Portrait with Pug Dog*, Hogarth showed that line drawn like a signature on his palette. He also conceptualized it in his treatise as the signature of Apelles, who when he wanted to leave his name for the artist Protogenes to read, left not just any line, but the most perfect serpentine one.[20] Thus considered, it hardly matters if the S will be crossed to make an F. Either way, it stands as the artist's signature, as the line that means art. But it is a signature that any artist can adopt or inhabit, be he Apelles, William Hogarth, or Fragonard. This signature calls into question the singularity of that other one, suggesting that as a pictorial imitation it too can be forged.

Although the artist can claim authority over an image, the image, as we know, cites other images—here of the pastoral, the picturesque, the serpentine, the originary legends of writing and painting. My point is that since painting is an act of citation (and interpretation), it depends on a sharing of cultural materials, and these cultural materials are shared by men and women, although men and women may cite differently, or from different positions in the social order. As Judith Butler has shown in another context, citation, even when it is culturally mandated, presents the opportunity for subversion and for challenging normative paradigms.[21] Citation can produce the unreliable facsimile.

Woman-Eve-Dibutadis—these are among the cultural models that secure originary myths of language and art and constitute allegories of the artist and artifice. That an image of the female sex stands in such a position, even though she be fictive and allegorical, particularly opens these myths and images to subversive citation by women. I want to return to the Dibutadis myth as it was cited in a 1790 self-image by Vigée-Lebrun, which shows her at the easel sketching from memory the portrait of Marie-Antoinette (Figure 3). Vigée-Lebrun undertook the work at her own initiative making it for the Grand Duke of Tuscany to hang in his gallery of self-portraits honoring celebrated artists who had traveled to Florence. I want to discuss this painting by focusing on the oppositional reading through which Vigée-Lebrun reworked images and myths.

Figure 3
Elisabeth Vigée-Lebrun, *Self-Portrait*, 1790, Florence: Uffizi
Photograph: Art Resources

Reading to the Letter or Literalizing Allegory [22]

Literalizing allegory undoes the reduction of woman to sign for man's art by inhabiting or particularizing the idealized allegorical women who embodied qualities that real women theoretically could not have or activities from which the culture theoretically or actually barred them. Painting as idea and activity could be reinhabited not simply because the allegory of painting showed the art (itself gendered feminine) as a young woman. More importantly, the category artist was thought occupied by men who shared physical characteristics with woman—notably sensitive sense organs. Reoccupying the category can nullify the gesture of denouncing in women a "feminine" quality that is then exalted and reclaimed for certain men.

Inhabiting allegorical figures, especially those like Dibutadis who were both named and derived from literary texts, allowed women to inscribe themselves in a history of "great women." There were such histories available in the eighteenth century, many of them extending the biographies of *femmes fortes* that circulated earlier. These histories and biographies often included women known from literary texts, such as the biblical Judith or the Amazons spoken of by ancient writers. No distinction was made between women known through other sorts of historical records to have actually lived and women whose existence outside these texts could not be verified.[23] Men, too, moved in and out of historical and literary exemplars, making the distinction between real and fictional characters meaningless in constructing a history of heroic or ideal predecessors.

In her self-portait, Vigée-Lebrun figures herself as Dibutadis by including what is not a typical inclusion in a self portrait—the artist's shadow, shown as the shadow of her arm and hand. Rarely, if ever, in self-portraits of this period does a shadow take on the specific, clear articulation that Vigée-Lebrun gives it. All references to the Dibutadis legend, however, had to be carefully crafted because various interpretations coexisted in the cultural materials available to her. Since Pliny and Quintilian, tracing shadows was considered a degraded activity in which "nature was the artist" and the artist a mere copyist. Yet French academicians reinterpreted the shadow so they could make Dibutadis the emblem of painting's origin. Claude-Nicholas Cochin's image of Dibutadis etched by Antoine-François Prévost in 1769, carries this caption: "Draw in your mind, that is the primary canvas." In Cochin's image, Dibutadis appears to be tracing the shadow, as she does in all standard renderings of the story. On the other hand, the caption exhorts the artist not to trace the outline of objects on some physical surface, but to draw it in the mind. Image and text do not seem so different, however, if we understand the shadow as a simultaneous memory, physically separate but temporally congruent with the object it recalls. In this sense, the shadow parallels—and can be taken to figure—drawing in the mind. Mental images produced at the moment of sensation are also simultaneous memories, but unlike shadows they can be recalled by the artist's imagination in the absence of objects.

Although the image of the mythical Dibutadis could, without contradiction, carry a caption exhorting (male) artists to draw in the mind, real women were not thought capable of such imaginative art-making activity. Dibutadis instantiated in a real woman risks being considered a mere copyist, a tracer of shadows. This risk was evident in the commentary on the first Salon in which Vigée-Lebrun appeared in 1783. Dibutadis herself attended that Salon, at least in one critic's account, and for the critic who summoned her she functioned not simply as a commentator, but as the prototype for the woman-painter. When Salon visitors addressed this Dibutades as the inventor of painting, she named herself a mere copyist: "If I am an inventor then it is of the silhouette portrait for I have just heard called by that name a profile in black made by tracing the shadow of a young person. It is exactly the same procedure that love inspired in me." Dibutadis here discovers only a reproductive technique—she is mother of the mechanical physiognotrace.[24]

Returning to Vigée-Lebrun's self-portrait, notice that she does not appear to trace the shadow cast on the canvas. The work thwarts any suggestion that the woman artist merely copies, for projected on the canvas pictured in Vigée-Lebrun's self-portrait is a distinct shadow, which she does not trace, and the tracing of a memory that she cannot see. And here it is significant that she shows herself picturing from memory the image of Marie-Antoinette. She works from that other sort of shadow, a mental image whose fading is emblematized in the evanescent sketch hovering on the canvas.

The story of Dibutadis and her portrait was particularly useful to women because it posited the origins of art in a sentimental relationship. I want to draw a parallel between the importance of the sentimental portrait to women's art making and the epistolary model to women's writing. Elizabeth MacArthur has argued that women were allowed to generate stories through letter writing, and that love letters made writing acceptable for women, since in love woman's supposedly inferior intellect and sentimental nature could be an advantage.[25] But as MacArthur has argued for France, and Mary Favret for England, sentimental letter writing led eventually to women writers reimagining epistolary form and producing other sorts of writing.[26] The portrait's supposed association with love and with "natural" artifice made it a field of artistic activity that women could enter with some ease. But just as women imagined varied forms of epistolary writing, Vigée-Lebrun in her self-portrait reconceives and makes political Dibutadis's engagement with love.

Love prompts Dibutadis to preserve a shadow. Vigée-Lebrun's image suggests that her desire to remember Marie-Antoinette has instigated the portrait she draws. Love and loss are at the origin of painting, but in this case, prestige and power are also factors. Vigée-Lebrun positions herself as the great artist honored by the ruler's love, by the ruler's desire to be portrayed by her. Reaching into the imaginary of painting, she plays Apelles to the queen's Alexander, as she had at the Salon of 1783 in other discussions of her work. Power is here exchanged between two women as the artist uses her power of representation to memorialize a monarch.

Finally, the artist is able through her portrayal of royalty to position herself not as passive object for the desiring gaze, but as an active subject for whom being in the public eye is a measure of *gloire*. Although the artist shows herself making an image, she also poses as the focus of attention. The performing painter is the object to be looked at, a spectacle displayed in a spot light bright enough to cast onto the canvas her arm's clear, sharp shadow. The image recalls a story Vigée-Lebrun tells in her *Souvenirs*: "Toward the end of the exhibition [of 1783] there was a play at the Vaudeville.... Brongniart, the architect, and his wife, whom the author had taken into his confidence, had reserved a box in the front and came to find me on the opening day to take me to the spectacle. As nothing prepared me for the surprise that awaited me, you can imagine my emotion when Painting arrived, and I saw the actress who represented her imitate me in a surprising manner in painting the queen's portrait. At that moment everyone in the parterre and in the boxes turned towards me and broke into applause."[27]

The anecdote suggests a play with the allegorical tradition. The unnamed actress represents Painting as a specific individual, Vigée-Lebrun, at work on a specific portrait. At a very basic level, in her self-portrait Vigée-Lebrun shows herself as Painting, recalling traditional depictions of the art as a female figure seated before an easel holding palette and brushes. But although the self-portrait preserves the allegory, it cannot be reduced to it. And although in this image the artist makes herself a visual spectacle, she is not presented as a passive object of the gaze. Far from it, she attracts the gaze to secure her position as representing subject. This strategy reminds us that because *everything* depicted in a painting is objectified as spectacle for the gaze, distinctions must be made in terms of how figures function within the fictional situation created by the image. The theoretical structure that posits the gaze as male and fixes woman in the feminine position as its object has unfortunately led to many oversimplifications of the viewing situation, especially when there is a woman in the picture.

The Possibilities and Limits of Oppositional Reading

Keeping in mind the woman in the picture, I turn back to Fragonard's image. First I propose that in reading this painting we now take the image literally as a representation denoting not an allegory, but a woman. This is, to be sure, to read the image perversely, but the image allows such reading since it posits art not only as an abstraction but also as a copy. For now the woman will remain nameless. I am interested first in the issue of the objectifying gaze. We have seen that she is pictorialized twice, as silhouette and as serpentine line. Do these aspects of the work inexorably pin her in the position of passive feminine object, or is there another way to read them, a way perhaps not expected by the image maker but allowed by the painting?

First consider the serpentine line. Fragonard clearly attaches it to the female body, connecting it with artifice and beauty. For women, signifying beauty becomes problematic in a culture for which beauty (or beauty as signifier of reproductive capacity) defines woman's value and use. Eighteenth-century France was such a culture. To signify beauty is not necessarily problematic if the object that carries those meanings is neither reduced nor limited to them. I am suggesting that Fragonard's image is open to an interpretation that disrupts this limitation and reads the normative cultural texts otherwise. To make the point more clearly, I want to introduce another work, which is an extreme case of the opposite effect—Gabriel de Saint-Aubin's *Private Academy* (Figure 4), an image that encodes many of the same themes as Fragonard's *The Souvenir*.

Saint-Aubin shows us an artist drawing from "nature" with his model posed so that the artist can exploit and master the serpentine line of her body. Her right arm is locked behind her back and hidden by the curve of her hip; her right breast seems to point upward and to continue the profile line of her right side. Behind the woman is another rococo aesthetic form based on serpentine lines—the fireplace, whose profile Saint-Aubin further likens to the body. Here Saint-Aubin follows François Boucher's painting of a woman tying her garter (*La Toilette*, 1742; Lugano: Thyssen-Bornemisza Foundation) in which the woman's splayed-out legs are mirrored by the curved hips and legs of the furnishing. Saint-Aubin pushes the association between woman's body and fireplace by visually rhyming the cartouche at the center of the mantle with the model's pubic triangle. He asks us to look there, between the jambs of the fireplace. Indeed, the broad surface of her body is articulated in eroticized zones—pubic area, navel, nipple, mouth. These rounded and open body parts mark this woman more forcefully than the serpentine line, especially as she is positioned before the gaping hole of the fireplace.

The image secures the female position as passive object of representation in relation to the male body, whose sexuality is also imaged in "resemblances" to his organs. These are particularly telling symbols because they double as the instruments of representation—the brushes placed in the thumbhole of

Figure 4
Gabriel de Saint-Aubin, c. 1778 *The Private Academy* (engraving)
Photograph: Bibliothèque Nationale de France, Paris

the palette resting on the mantle and the dark pen held by the artist as he draws. These are the tokens that she lacks. The image reminds us that although he did not theorize a castration complex, Rousseau, like Sigmund Freud, founded sexual differentiation and social role on the sexual organ. In his *Letter to d'Alembert* (1758) Rousseau invoked the most conventional notions of sexual difference. The union of the sexes requires each to take the appropriate role of attacker or defender. A reversal of this natural scheme would be disastrous because the success of the sex act depends on male arousal.[28] From this difference follows man's and woman's position in the social order. One can gauge the consequences of Rousseau's argument by turning to Pierre-Jean-George Cabanis's 1805 treatise *On the Relations Between the Physical and Moral Aspects of Man*. There the physiologist singles out this same passage from Rousseau and concludes that "From this first difference relative to the particular aim of each of the two sexes . . . derives the difference between their inclinations and their habits."[29]

The serpentine line in Fragonard's image, on the other hand, does not represent the body as a part, and this observation allows us to reread the line and its history. The serpentine line was allegedly found in the male figure—in an antique torso—by Michelangelo, who made it a feature of his art. It was picked up by his "followers" (the Mannerists); Giovanni Lomazzo, and later Hogarth, theorized its effects.[30] These writers conceptualized the line representing nature's beauty as originating in the male body. Two observations follow: first, manliness is not reduced to beauty since man is also the perceiver and recreater of beauty; and second, beauty is a positive sign for the nobility of the human body, which is here signaled by the body's outline and *not* by the male sexual organ. Both of these observations will eventually help our rereading.

The serpentine line, as we have seen, is a sign for art's transmission through tradition, as well as an indication of art's distance from and reliance on nature. A woman who draws the serpentine line not only reminds us that the human body is the basis for art's beauty, she also places herself in a tradition of artists. Here a 1767 portrait drawing of Angelica Kauffman by Nathaniel Dance is significant; the work posits her lineage, as she, like Michelangelo, studies and draws the antique torso.[31] Similarly, Fragonard's woman can be seen as inhabiting the signature of Apelles, of Michelangelo, of Hogarth, of Fragonard.

Saint-Aubin, on the other hand, gives his female figure no way of identifying with the means of representation envisioned as natural signs for male genitals and attached only to the artist who represents. In Fragonard's image the invisibility of the male body limits the possibilities for suggesting a single differential element according to which two sexed positions are defined. In

Saint-Aubin's image, the male figure seated directly over the artist's signature functions as artist and surrogate viewer. He abets the viewer's appropriation of the female form and suggests the viewing position is masculine territory. Fragonard has the spaniel sitting in the viewer's seat, on the bench positioned directly over the artist's signature, and thus the signature functions as label associating our mutt and artist. The spaniel produces art by seeing it, by seeing what is already made by nature, but it is difficult to imagine this figure as wielding an appropriating gaze. As replacement for the absent lover, the spaniel is faithfulness itself, a faithfulness that is adoring and subservient—which brings me to the second aspect of this woman's pictorialization.

Although symbolizing the sexual organs may seem the key difference here, equally important is the relationship within which the female figure is presented. The male figure is not seen in Fragonard's image, but given the conventions of heterosexual love, his role is implied not only by the spaniel, but also by the pictorialization of the woman as a sentimental portrait. Fragonard plays on the love relation and its supposed reciprocity; love shared or exchanged, places the lovers on equal footing. In the imaging of love exchanged, the one who acts as model for the other is not simply objectified since the portrait pertains to a specific individual, whose picture, like her person, has emotional power over the portrayer.

In Saint-Aubin's image the social relation of artist to model would adhere if the model were clothed or less overtly sexualized. As Candace Clements has shown, it was indeed a practice for male artists to draw female models in private studios.[32] Outside the sentimental scene, the artist-model relation is patently unequal whatever the sex of those occupying the positions. Modeling was the sort of labor no one really wanted to do; like prostitution, it was morally corrupting and degrading. Saint-Aubin's image eroticizes the model's labor. However, this woman is hardly co-partner in the aesthetic enterprise. She is its raw material, and with the thrown drapery visually paralleling her, she is the object of a drawing exercise. The artist does not want a portrait of his beloved, but an image of his talent; the nameless model is disposable; she will drop out of the picture. This is not necessarily the case for the woman who stands in Fragonard's image.

What can we call this woman? What name can we give her? The Dibutadis theme is implied in the work, and although we could see her in this light, she does not trace her lover. A better match might be Erminia, the shepherdess who carves in Tasso's *Jerusalem Liberata*. In that story Erminia appears cross-dressed as a knight, suggesting that as poet she assumes a role not typically feminine. Disguised as a man, but with visor raised to show her womanly face, Erminia tells a shepherd how she wrote the story of her love for Tancred in the bark of trees. She then calculates the effect that her story will have on other readers. Because her own rereading of her story provoked her tears, Erminia anticipates that other lovers reading the story will respond similarly. Perhaps we see in Fragonard's image not Erminia, but another lover who, having read Erminia's story enacts her pity by emulating the woman poet. The image will sustain this reading, which sets up the transmission of art as woman's business. The modern Erminia inserts herself into a history of women poet/carvers, just as she insinuates herself into a lineage of those who make serpentine lines. Moreover, these women who carve, or draw, or write their love also emulate those women who found in writing a way to revise the tradition of the deserted mistress who has a passionate death. Elizabeth MacArthur shows, for example, how in the *Lettres portugaises* the woman realizes that her death and emotions are only "textual" and that she can transform and control them by writing her own story.[33]

The choice of death or writing brings me to consider another aspect of Fragonard's image. In paintings, women with knives often turn the weapon on themselves—as Lucretia did. Or someone else, perhaps the father, is wielding the weapon for them, as in images of Virginia. In their silent rhetoric, these women recall the Levite's concubine whose dismembered body Rousseau used as an example of mute eloquence in his *Essay on the Origins of Languages*. The incident is drawn from the book of Judges; following his concubine's gang rape and subsequent death, the Levite cuts her body into twelve pieces, sending one to each of the tribes of Israel to move them to revenge. In his later *Levite d'Ephraim*, astutely analyzed by Judith Still, Rousseau adds an opening canto telling of the love between the Levite and his concubine and a conclusion that focuses on one girl, Axa, who sacrifices herself for her father and for the social good. Still argues that because Axa's gesture is imitated by her peers, Rousseau articulates a code of feminine virtue that constructs women as subjects manipulated into choosing to sacrifice themselves.[34]

What strikes me about Fragonard's work is how different is the relation it posits between women and knives and women and language. The knife here becomes woman's writing implement; it is not turned on herself. She is not the signifying material dismembered by the Levite's knife, and the serpentine line traces her body in a continuous profile. Moreover, the gestures she makes with the knife are deliberate and careful, suggesting that she controls any emotion she might feel in the process of representation. Hers are not the unreasonable gestures of a jealous Medea, or of a lustful Eve unable to restrain herself.

As a final possibility for reading Fragonard's painting, I'd like to return to Eve. No philosophe, not even Rousseau, wanted to go back to a prelinguistic state. Language, after all, was what distinguished man from the animals. Indeed the alphabet was conceptualized as the dawn of Western Civilization, an era even more paradisical than that of the mythical Eden. Which brings me to the Enlightenment's reinterpretation of Eden's loss as a fortunate fall. Among others, Johann Gottfried Herder and Immanuel Kant imagined the Fall as figuring a transition in human history that should be seen as gain. But in this version of the story Adam takes the lead; he perceives that the fruit of the tree is desirable as source of wisdom. In a brave and spontaneous gesture, he takes the fruit and with it grabs the possibilities of a fully human existence. And what about Eve? Well, Eve falls out of the picture.[35]

Fragonard's image allows us to keep woman in the picture, and we can read this work as a representation of how material nature was transformed into culture when Eve heeded the snake, and perceived the fruit as desirable, as a source of wisdom. About a hundred years after Fragonard's image, the artist Mary Cassatt would rewrite the story of Eve as an allegory of woman's knowledge in her paintings for the woman's pavilion at an international exposition. We can repeat Cassatt's gesture by reinterpreting Fragonard's painting, taking it as showing the enlightened Eve, or what Eve might have been had women rewritten the myth of the Fall during the Enlightenment. As she stands in the garden, she stands in the light, the period's own symbol for the dawning of reason. But light, as we know, can barely sketch of itself; its effects are fleeting in contrast to the greater permanence of the story/image she is carving on the tree. What this Eve writes is her position as subject of knowledge and representation, and her S stands for "savoir." Eve, like Adam, can name things, can say what they mean, if she, too, has access to Savoir. Controlling women's access to Savoir has a long and shameful history that continues throughout the world today.

Coda: Controlled Reading

The final image I want to consider highlights the relation between the control of women and control over their interpretation of images: Jacques-Louis David's *Marat Assassinated* (Figure 5). I have chosen this painting because we have a detailed account of its presentation to the public; because it includes many of the elements—letter, signature, knife—found in Fragonard's *The Souvenir*, and because it does not show the female body. Feminist interpretation has often turned on considering how the female body is objectified when materialized in paint; I suggest that a refusal to materialize the female body can also be a strategy to control the meaning of an image in relation to concepts of "woman." Analyzing David's *Marat* redirects my argument toward considering how artists tried to control the range of pos-

Figure 5
J.-L. David, *Marat Assassinated*, 1793, Musée Royale des Beaux-Arts, Brussels
Photograph: Art Resources

sible meanings, often to the disadvantage of the woman reader. It is not simply fortuitous that the image I have chosen to engineer this redirection was produced during the French Revolution. As Erica Rand has argued, David's art purposefully stripped women of political power. Responding to a cultural imperative to limit women's participation in public debate, David uses his portrait of Marat to argue for both the limitation of woman's social role and the need to control her interpreting power.[36] This is by no means to say that David's image cannot and should not be read oppositionally. In fact, Mary Favret offers a reading I would term oppositional at the opening of her *Romantic Correspondence*.[37] Nor is my point here to contend that David was more misogynistic than Fragonard (only historical research could produce such a claim). Rather I argue that David's image is anxious to control woman's response, and that we can use that anxiety as a mandate for oppositional reading.

Other art historians, and in particular Dorothy Johnson, have read the painting astutely in terms of David's career, and in relation to politics and language.[38] My interest in the work is more limited. I am concerned with how particular aspects of the image interact with women's responses as represented in the funeral of Marat and the fête that first presented David's image. Lynn Hunt and Nicholas Mirzoeff have specifically drawn attention to the role Marat's funeral offered women. Responding to an orator's pleas to "Let the blood of Marat become the seed of intrepid Republicans," women swore to populate the earth with as many Marats as possible.[39] Later at the procession orchestrated around David's painting, *citoyennes* marched as mothers holding the hands of their children. All these women represented the proper response to Marat's sacrifice—and Corday's action.

Can we read the suppression of Corday's body as implicated in this desire to control women's response? Two sorts of bodies in this period were ritually shown to the public—the bodies of criminals, that is, the executed, and the bodies of martyrs or heroes. Marat's body was subjected to such display, and David's display of the painted body repeats the ritual. As Rousseau's Levite knew, showing the body made for effective rhetoric. During the time that David was making his image, there was a very mixed public response to Corday, whose body—including her guillotined body—was a focus of attention, curiosity, sympathy, and disdain. Elizabeth Kindleberger has recently interpreted the varied and contradictory assessments and images of Corday that circulated at the time, and has shown that responses to Corday are not easily divided along royalist/revolutionary lines.[40]

David does not risk showing Corday; instead, he represents her figuratively through the handwriting on the note that names her and the bloody knife that she held. Given that Corday was a focus of public attention, materializing her body in paint would have compromised the artist's imagined control over audience response, as well as his control over the "truth." As painted, the image suggests that truth can be found only on Marat's body. Notice the underlining of the name Marat in Corday's letter. Visually, this underscoring parallels and emphasizes the mark of Corday's knife, also a straight line. This writing on the body locates truth, one *sees* the proof of Marat's assassination on his body. Indeed, David relies on visible truth throughout this work; as a natural sign for bodies, painting was thought tied to nature's truth. And besides the fact of Marat's stabbing, what David shows as true is Marat's poverty and generosity: we see his patched linen; the small amount of money he is able to give one who is poorer than he; his bare surroundings; his rude writing desk.

In the presence of these objects, Corday's note does not lie. In fact, as Erica Rand has pointed out, David "de-politicizes" Corday by not including the letter that falsely claimed to warn Marat of a conspiracy.[41] In the note David shows, Corday speaks the truth to Marat—it *is* enough that someone has known misfortune to have the right to Marat's benevolence. Corday has not lied, but she has played with language. Depicted as if inscribed in her personal hand, her words have a double meaning. Marat understands them one way, she intends them another. The note reminds us of this woman's, and perhaps of all women's, danger to public discourse.

Many have already discussed the relation between this message, which Marat holds, and the other one that he has written, the one that offers money to the poor widow whose sons have died for the fatherland. David shows the money beside the note; in representing the assignats visibly the viewer is made to see that Marat is writing the truth.[42] The pictorial sign here guarantees the truth of the written one. It is not only that David contrasts two women—one a deceitful aristocrat, the other a poor widow. The first distinction is between the opacity and deceit of Corday's writing and the transparent truth of Marat's. The second is between the woman who enters the public arena, whose words and actions have killed Marat, and the woman who has done her reproductive duty, who has produced sons. But more, she seems to have fulfilled in advance the promise made by women at Marat's funeral; she has peopled the earth with intrepid Republicans, with other Marats who like him are martyred for their country. The mother enters the public discourse only through her sons, neither her speech nor her writing are represented. She contrasts with the deceitful woman whose political motive David may have tried to suppress even as he showed the aftermath of her political act.

If within the painting we read the note from Corday and the message of Marat, it is still *David* who speaks Marat's image. The signature and dedication tells us as much. Nevertheless, David's signature is not a personal one, it is not his handwriting, which we can see on many other of his paintings. Here his signature is carved in the mode of those illustrious men, the ancients; it resembles their public inscriptions and is associated with their authority. David here pretends to speak not with his voice, but with the voice of ancient and eternal truth. If this is the case, what strikes me is that Marat has been fooled by the truth that David tells, the truth Marat would like to believe: that he *was* the poor friend of the people, that his benevolence extended to all the unfortunate. Marat has been captured by a certain image of himself, by the very image of truth that David recalls and projects. (It is here that an oppositional reader might also put pressure on this image.) In David's image, Corday does not capture Marat. Rather she is used to facilitate an exchange of power between two men; she guarantees the same old pact between the Hero and the Artist. Between Alexander and Apelles, Louis XIV and Charles Le Brun, and later between David and Napoleon. Each validating the other's position in an ongoing exchange of power disguised as truth.

David's image of Marat suggests that control of both women and women's interpreting is necessary for the social good. Like the speeches at Marat's funeral, David's display urged women to a particular kind of virtue, a self-sacrifice of the desire to define the "public interest" to which they were called to offer up their autonomy. For me, David's *Marat* is finally less about truth and more about power. As much in the controlled circumstances of its public presentation as in its visual rhetoric, David's image indicates who is empowered to speak, who is empowered to make, or if you prefer, to find the truth. This power was invested in the subject who took the cultural position deemed "natural" to the male sex. In David's image only men are shown as telling the truth, as saying what they mean, through writing and painting.

Whether they guaranteed it with the authority of religion or history, or fixed it with the truth of castration, men have claimed the power of truth and with it the right to name, to categorize, and to produce meaning. As contemporary viewers, we sacrifice our potential for subverting this received truth when we tether our interpretations to what we imagine visual images meant only for those viewers who controlled the making, receiving, circulating, and interpreting of images. My point is not to deny that such readings are valid nor to deny the control that certain men had over image making. I claim only that this control could not have been total. My claim is central to a practice of oppositional reading as I envision it; feminist viewers need not feel compelled to validate the mainstream interpretation of an image, nor to restrict themselves to strategic critique. Above all, I insist that we are not obliged to advance the interests of some elusive historical accuracy that limits our collective and individual power to name what we are and to say what we mean.

NOTES

I am grateful to Ann Bermingham, Keith Luria, Nicholas Mirzoeff, and James Turner for their comments and suggestions on this material, and thank my research assistants Hollye Maxwell, Erica Rockett, and Michael Yonan for their help. I am indebted to Dena Goodman for sharing with me her intellectual passion for the letter.

1. Joan DeJean, "Looking Like a Woman, The Female Gaze in Sappho and Lafayette," *L'Esprit Créateur* 28 (Winter 1988): 35.

2. E. Jane Burns, *Bodytalk: When Women Speak in Old French Literature* (Philadelphia: University of Pennsylvania Press, 1993) and Jacqueline Bobo, *Black Women as Cultural Readers* (New York: Columbia University Press, 1995). Both these authors are colleagues and have had a direct personal influence on my thinking.

3. Here I assume that a painting which engages and reworks other images and stories can be viewed as a reading or interpretation of them. Elisabeth Vigée-Lebrun's self-images are a major concern of my recent book, *The Exceptional Woman: Elisabeth Vigée-Lebrun and the Cultural Politics of Art* (Chicago: University of Chicago Press, 1996).

4. Mary Favret opens her book, *Romantic Correspondence: Women, Politics, and the Fiction of Letters* with a consideration of David's image. Favret argues in relation to the image that "the very idea of the letter, in David's painting and elsewhere, produced representations that threatened to disrupt the sentimental tradition which promoted it" (New York: Cambridge University Press, 1993), 1.

5. Rensselaer Lee, *Names on Trees: Ariosto into Art* (Princeton: Princeton University Press, 1977), 9–11.

6. For an example of its continuation, see Nicolas Lavreince, *The Love Letter* engraved by Nicholas Delaunay. For the letter that signals rupture, see *L'Amant Regretté* dedicated to Madame de Gondolini and produced by the engraver Dennel.

7. Here I am indepted to the theories of Nelson Goodman, *Languages of Art* (Indianapolis: Hackett, 1976).

8. See, for example, Georges Wildenstein, *The Paintings of Fragonard* (New York: Phaidon, 1960), 284. There the identity of the woman is alternatively Julie and Angelica.

9. Jean-Jacques Rousseau, *Essay on the Origin of Languages*, trans. John H. Moran and Alexander Gode (New York: Frederick Ungar, 1966), 16–19. Writing, of course, was a major concern of Jacques Derrida in *Of Grammatology*, trans. Gayatri Spivak (Baltimore: Johns Hopkins University Press, 1976). Barbara Stafford focused on the various relations between art and the origin of language in *Symbol and Myth: Humbert de Superville's Essay on Absolute Signs in Art* (London: Associated University Presses, 1979), 133–47.

10. One of the most interesting writers on this subject is Rowland Jones in his *Hieroglyfic* (London, 1768; reprint, Menston, Eng.: Scolar Press, 1972).

11. On the serpentine "S," see Jones, *Hieroglyfic*.

12. For further discussion, see Mary Sheriff, *Fragonard: Art and Eroticism* (Chicago: University of Chicago Press, 1990), 82–92.

13. See, for example, the preface to Jones's *Hieroglyfic* and Derrida, *Of Grammatology*, 280–313. Also, John Phillips, *Eve, The History of an Idea* (New York: Harper and Row, 1984).

14. William Hogarth, frontispiece, *The Analysis of Beauty*, ed. Joseph Burke (Oxford: Clarendon Press, 1955), 1. Further citations will be from this edition.

15. Hogarth, *Analysis*, 15.

16. M. de Miramond, *Vers à Madame Le Brun, de l'Académie Royale de Peinture, Sur les principaux Ouvrages, dont elle a décoré le Sallon cette année*, 1783, Collection Deloynes, 308. For a more extended discussion of this poem, see Sheriff, *The Exceptional Woman*, 131–41.

17. For the story of Dibutadis, see *Elder Pliny's Chapters on the History of Art*, trans. K. Jex Blake (Chicago: Argonaut Publishers, 1968), 336. Pliny includes the story not as an example of the origin of painting, but as an example of the origin of clay sculpture, since Dibutadis's father Butades, takes her drawing and forms from it a clay model, which he dries and bakes. Recent considerations of Dibutadis include: Gary Apgar, *Visualizing Voltaire* (New Haven: Yale University Press, forthcoming); Ann Bermingham, "The Origins of Painting and the Ends of Art: Wright of Derby's Corinthian Maid," in *Painting and the Politics of Culture*, ed. John Barrell (Oxford: Oxford University Press, 1992), 135–65; Jacques Derrida, *Memoirs of the Blind: The Self-Portrait and Other Ruins*, trans. Pascale-Anne Brault and Michael Naas (Chicago: University of Chicago Press, 1993), 49–51; Nicholas Mirzoeff, "Body Talk: Deafness, Sign, and Visual Language in the Ancien Régime," *Eighteenth-Century Studies* 25 (1992), 561–85; and Richard Shiff, "On Criticism Handling History," *Art Criticism* 3 (1988): 60–77. Examples include Joseph-Benoit Suvée, *Butades or the Origin of Drawing* (1791; Bruges, Groeningmuseum); Jeans-Baptiste Regnault, *Dibutadis Tracing the Portrait of Her Shepherd, or the Origin of Painting*, (Versailles: Musée du château); Alexander Runciman, *The Origin of Painting* (1771; Scotland: Pencuick House), and Joseph Wright of Derby, *The Corinthian Maid*, 1783–84 (Washington: National Gallery of Art). Perhaps most significant for my purposes is the example by Regnault that was an overdoor for the Salon des Nobles de la Reine at Versailles, and hence in Marie-Antoinette's apartments.

18. Wildenstein suggested the signature might not be "autograph"; however, the signature appears in both the painted and engraved versions of the image.

19. In such cases, the signature is merely written on the surface of the painted canvas rather than worked into the illusion of the image. See, for example, Jean-Etienne Liotard's *Portrait of Young Girl Reading a Letter* (Amsterdam: Rijksmuseum).

20. Hogarth, *Analysis*, 16–17.

21. Judith Butler, *Bodies That Matter* (London: Routledge, 1993). I discuss Butler's theorizing of citation in reference to women artists in *The Exceptional Woman*, 203–7.

22. This section theorizes a more particular argument in Sheriff, *The Exceptional Woman*, 227–39.

23. Examples include: Abbé Guyon, *Histoire des Amazones Anciennes et Modernes*, 2 vols. (Paris: Jean Villette, 1740); Pierre Le Moyne, *La Gallerie des*

Femmes Fortes (Paris: Charles Angot, 1760); and Riballier [?], *De L'Education physique et morale des femmes* (Brussels and Paris: Chez les Frères Estienne, 1779).

24. The Greek maiden was one of many fictive Salon visitors invented by critics in the 1770s and 1780s. she appears in a pamphlet entitled, *La Morte de trois mille ans au salon de 1783*, 1783 Collection Deloynes, 286. For a discussion of this pamphlet and Dibutadis's appearance at the Salon, see Sheriff, *The Exceptional Woman*, 73–74.

25. Elizabeth J. MacArthur, *Extravagant Narratives: Closure and Dynamics in the Epistolary Form* (Princeton: Princeton University Press, 1990), 19, 69–70, 145.

26. MacArthur, *Extravagant Narratives*, and Favret, *Romantic Correspondence*.

27. "Vers la fin de l'exposition on fit une petite pièce au Vaudeville, qui, je crois, avait pour titre: *La réunion des Arts*. Brongniart, l'architecte, et sa femme, que l'auteur avait mis dans sa confidence, firent louer une loge aux premières et vinrent me chercher le jour de la premières représentation pour me conduire au spectacle. Comme je ne pouvais nullement me douter de la surprise qu'on me ménageait, vous pouvez juger de mon émotion lorsque la Peinture arriva, et que je vis l'actrice qui la représentait me copier d'une manière suprenante, en peignant le portrait de la Reine. Au même instant, tout ce qui était au parterre et dans les loges se retourna vers moi en applaudissant à tout rompre," Elisabeth Vigée-Lebrun, *Souvenirs*, ed. Claudine Hermann, 2 vols. (Paris: Des Femmes, 1986), 1: 66.

28. Jean-Jacques Rousseau, *Lettre à Mr. d'Alembert sur les spectacles*, ed. M. Fuchs (Geneva: Droz, 1948), 112.

29. Pierre-Jean-Georges Cabanis, *On the Relations between the Physical and Moral Aspects of Man*, trans. Margaret Saidi, ed. George Mora, 2 vols. (Baltimore: Johns Hopkins University Press, 1981), 1:234.

30. Hogarth, *Analysis*, 5–6.

31. For an illustration of this work, see Wendy Wassyng Roworth, "Anatomy is Destiny: Regarding the Body in the Art of Angelica Kauffman," in *Femininity and Masculinity in Eighteenth-Century Art and Culture*, ed. Gill Perry and Michael Rossington (Manchester: Manchester University Press, 1994), 48. Roworth offers a different reading of the protrait.

32. Candace Clements, "The Academy and the Other: *Les Graces* and *Le Genre Galant*," *Eighteenth-Century Studies* 25 (1992): 469–94.

33. MacArthur, *Extravagant Narratives*, 92.

34. Judith Still, "Rousseau's *Lèvite d'Ephraïm*: The Imposition of Meaning (On Women)," *French Studies* 43 (1989): 12–30.

35. Phillips, *Eve*, 75–83.

36. Erica Rand, "Depoliticizing Women: Female Agency, the French Revolution, and the Art of Boucher and David," *Genders* 7 (1990): 47–68.

37. Favret, *Romantic Correspondences*, 1–11.

38. There is a vast literature on this image, and several writers consider at length the issue of writing. Recent considerations include Erica Rand's essay cited above, Dorothy Johnson, *Jacques-Louis David: Art in Metamorphosis* (Princeton: Princeton University Press, 1994), 100–109, and T. J. Clark, "Painting in the Year Two,"

Representations 47 (1994): 13–64. Clark makes truth, transcendence, and contingency his key terms.

39. Lynn Hunt, *The Family Romance of the French Revolution* (Berkeley: University of California Press, 1992), 76. Nicholas Mirzoeff, *Bodyscape: Art, Modernity, and the Ideal Body* (London: Routledge, 1996), 75–80. Clark, likewise, considers this material, "Painting in the Year Two," 13–15.

40. Elizabeth Kindleberger, "Charlotte Corday in Text and Image: A Case Study in the French Revolution and Women's History," *French Historical Studies* 18 (1994): 969–99.

41. Rand, "Depoliticizing Women," 56–57.

42. Clark especially stresses the assignat as writing that stands for property.

"Opposition Augustanism" and Pope's *Epistle to Augustus*

THOMAS KAMINSKI

The term "Augustan" has suffered many indignities in recent years, especially since the publication of Howard Weinbrot's *Augustus Caesar in "Augustan" England*. Many scholars have declared the term ambiguous or useless, and many more have simply abandoned it silently. Much of the antagonism to "Augustan" can be traced directly to Weinbrot's work, in which he demonstrates that the "tradition of Augustus as usurping tyrant" was wide spread in the eighteenth century and was founded on the writings of Tacitus and other ancient historians.[1] This point is in fact beyond dispute. But I wish to suggest that the verdict of the ancient historians, on which Weinbrot based so much of his argument, represented only one aspect of the "Augustan myth." Several of the post-Augustan Roman poets, especially Martial and Juvenal, depicted the court of Augustus as a place of benevolent patronage, and this depiction not only survived the vigorous attempts of seventeenth- and eighteenth-century historians to pull down Augustus's beneficent image, but actually became one of the bases of opposition attacks on George II and his minister, Sir Robert Walpole. In fact, the work of Martial and Juvenal contributed to the development of what I call "opposition Augustanism," which formed the basis of Pope's criticism of his monarch and society in the *Epistle to Augustus*.

We must begin with the ancients. Within a hundred years of the death of Horace, Roman writers had begun to speak of the decline of letters, in which they included oratory as well as poetry. For Tacitus, the decline in oratory seemed traceable to the end of the Republic.[2] But why were there no more Vergils? To explain this, Martial and his contemporaries pointed to the decay of patronage.[3] Conditions for writing poetry were no longer what they had been under Augustus. No one valued genius anymore, they argued, and one does not write *Aeneids* on an empty stomach. We find this theme over and over in Martial. Take, for example, *Epigrams*, 1.107.1–6.

> Saepe mihi dicis, Luci carissime Iuli,
>   "Scribe aliquid magnum: desidiosus homo es."
> otia da nobis, sed qualia fecerat olim
>   Maecenas Flacco Vergilioque suo:
> condere victuras temptem per saecula curas
>   et nomen flammis eripuisse meum.[4]

> [Often you say to me, dearest Lucius Julius, "write something great. You're lazy." Give me such freedom from care as Maecenas once provided for his Horace and his Vergil; then I should try to compose works to live through the ages and to snatch my name from the flames.]

In the eighth book of *Epigrams*, we find Martial telling his friend Flaccus, "Let there be Maecenases, and Vergils will not be wanting."[5] When Nerva succeeded Domitian to the imperial throne, Martial hoped for a return to an Augustan age of patronage. In book 11 of his *Epigrams*, he boasts that his poems are wildly popular: they are read by all classes at Rome; the centurion on station along the Danube thumbs his book; even remote Britain sings his verses. And yet,

>   quid prodest? nescit sacculus ista meus.
> at quam victuras poteramus pangere chartas
>   quantaque Pieria proelia flare tuba,
> cum pia reddiderint Augustum numina terris,
>   et Maecenatem si tibi, Roma, darent!
>   (*Epigrams*, 11.3.6–10)

> [What does it get me? My purse does not know it. But what everlasting pages I might write, what battles I might blare with Pierian horn, if, now that the gods have returned Augustus to the world (i.e., in the person of Nerva), they would also give you, Rome, a Maecenas!]

Even an emperor, however wise and good, needs men of taste to encourage poets.

By far the greatest work expounding this theme is Juvenal's Seventh Satire. It is a scathing attack on the Roman nobility, who lavish money on charioteers and musicians but neglect literature. Even Juvenal, renowned during the eighteenth century for his defense of liberty and his hatred of tyrants,[6] returns to the age of Augustus to find patrons who appreciated literary merit:

> quis tibi Maecenas, quis nunc erit aut Proculeius
> aut Fabius, quis Cotta iterum, quis Lentulus alter?
> tum par ingenio pretium, tunc utile multis
> pallere et vinum toto nescire Decembri.'

> [Who will now be a Maecenas or a Proculeius to you, or a Fabius? Who will be another Cotta, a second Lentulus? Then the reward was equal to the genius; then many found it advantageous to grow pale and abstain from wine all through December (i.e., to absent themselves from pleasure, even during the Saturnalia, in order to study and write).]

Under Augustus merit was recognized. Vergil, Horace, and Ovid[8] had patrons who provided them with *otium*, the productive leisure necessary for genius to operate at its full. But the people of wealth and rank no longer have the taste or judgment to support men of ability; instead, they prefer to squander their money on trivial entertainments.[9] For Juvenal and Martial, this neglect of genius is a clear symptom of the decadence of their society. The ancients themselves, then, had created a mythic Augustan court in which noble patrons recognized and rewarded literary merit; even the "republican" Juvenal helped propagate it.

In addition to the myth of enlightened patronage, Augustanism also rested on a vision of literary progress that was articulated by Horace in both the original epistle to Augustus and the *Ars Poetica*. Horace had detailed the progress of Roman taste from crude amusement at rustic singing contests to a new standard of refined literature based on Greek models.[10] Implicit in this concept of literary progress was a presumed increase in the sophistication of Roman society, at least at the highest level. Horace himself claimed to disdain popular approval, writing, he tells us, for a small, cultivated audience capable of appreciating true poetic craftsmanship.[11] His emphasis on technical perfection and his appeal only to a highly sophisticated audience lie at the root of all that we should properly call Augustan.

This Horatian view of literary progress, along with the idealized world of enlightened patronage depicted by Martial and Juvenal,[12] contributed greatly to the development of the Augustan myth in the seventeenth century, in France as well as in England. As Domna Stanton has shown, the *honnêtes gens* of the age of Louis XIV emulated the courtiers of Augustus's reign,[13] and the poets of the age sought to win their favor with urbane, polished verse. At the Restoration, Charles and his courtiers transported across the Channel a set of assumptions about the proper nature, function, and value of literature in society that formed the basis of what came to be known in the eighteenth century as "polite letters." The origin of this phenomenon is quite complex, including among other influences the poetic "reforms" of Malherbe at the very beginning of the seventeenth century, the attempts of the *précieux* circles in France to purge language of its grossness and to reform French manners, and the triumph of "classicism" in French poetry; but even a cursory examination of writers from Guez de Balzac through John Dryden shows that the ideology of "polite literature" rests, at least in part, on the literary and social ideals of the court of Augustus as reimagined by French and English authors during the seventeenth century.[14]

By the time of Dryden's poetic maturity, these ideas had taken firm root in England. In the world of "polite letters," correctness of manners, of expression, and of taste had all become intertwined, resulting in a literature that embodies stylistic *polish* (the root of "polite") and that is consistent with social decorum. As these values became the common currency of literary discourse, they lost much of their aristocratic air, but they maintained their emphasis on polish and their close contact with societal refinement. By the time of *The Spectator*, these impulses had become so totally assimilated into English literary culture that Addison could use them as the basis for his attempt to improve both the taste and the morals of his countrymen. Under this guise, literary Augustanism, far from following the ups and downs of Augustus's reputation, held its place firmly until it was undermined by the rising tide of "sensibility" and finally overwhelmed by Romanticism.

In this defense of literary Augustanism, I do not deny the politically charged nature of the term; I simply wish to give a more nuanced understanding of its complexities. Let me make a brief digression into Dryden's career to show what I mean. As Weinbrot and others have made clear, Dryden's early praise of Charles as a new Augustus had dangerous implications, for while Charles was busy reforming English manners, Louis XIV, another putative Augustus, was increasing autocratic rule in France. Nevertheless, circumstances prevented the aesthetics of refinement from becoming too tightly bound up with the English monarchy and thus coming in conflict with English liberty. After the death of Charles II and the flight of his brother, and after Parliament had asserted its right to determine the royal succession, Dryden, stripped of his honors, quickly demonstrated that his literary values were not in fact governed by royal favor, especially when royalty itself had, in his opinion, lost the qualities of dignity, refinement, and taste. Dryden turned his poetry against the hated William, but he did not abandon his social, moral, or aesthetic principles. Rather, he suggested that the Court as currently constituted lacked both moral values and social refinement.[15] And so the first great exemplar of "polite letters" in English became the first "opposition" Augustan—that is, the first author who implied a direct linkage between his taste, his morals, and his politics, and who then criticized the court for betraying or neglecting those values.

Throughout William's reign and well into the eighteenth century, Whig historians continually assaulted Augustus's character, but they discredited only one aspect of the Augustan myth. The blend of social and literary values implicit in the myth of the Augustan court—that a refined society requires and supports a highly polished literature—continued to attract men of letters. In fact, the political situation of the 1720s and 1730s gave many writers cause to embrace the myth of an Augustan age of benevolent patronage, despite the increasing disrepute that was to stain the character of Augustus. The opposition poets and journalists of the day often pointed to Walpole's neglect of literary merit as a primary symptom of the moral and intellectual bankruptcy of his administration. They repeatedly invoked the ideal of the Augustan court as the antithesis of Walpole's disdain for literary men.[16] In the party press, the myth of Augustan patronage existed side by side with the image of Augustus as a tyrant who destroyed Roman liberty and crushed free expression. *The Craftsman* could at one time criticize the Walpole administration for its neglect of men of genius, citing the Augustan court as a positive example, and at another attack the administration for its assaults on English liberty, using Augustus as a model of tyranny.[17] The myth of the Augustan court, then, was a flexible tool, one that allowed political writers to turn the past to use.

I wish now to turn to Pope's *Epistle to Augustus* and show how the complicated blend of literary, social, and political values that I have just described informs the text that has long been the most contested territory in all of the disputes about Augustanism. To begin with, the scope of many modern analyses of Pope's *Epistle*, especially those that concern themselves with the comparison between George II and Augustus, is much too narrow. Weinbrot, for instance, argues that "Pope gains authority by dissociating himself from Augustan—Horatian and Georgian—courtly values, and by associating himself with the opposition in general and Swift in particular."[18] There can be no doubt about Pope's opposition stance and his attempt to associate himself with Swift, but we must beware of oversimplifying the nature of "Augustan courtly values," especially since enlightened patronage was repeatedly associated with the Augustan court. By the time Pope wrote his *Epistle*, both the threat to freedom from a despotic government and the neglect of genius by an ignorant and depraved court had become integral parts of the attack on public corruption, the dominant theme of the opposition to Sir Robert Walpole. Opposition authors depicted themselves as an embattled minority maintaining the value of liberty against an increasingly despotic government, and the importance of "taste" against the vulgarity and corruption of Walpolean society.

As the *Epistle* itself makes clear, Pope finds Horatian *literary* values completely in accord with his opposition stance. He reviews English literary history and dispenses praise and blame in much the same manner that Horace had, and, again following Horace, he seeks to reaffirm the poet's proper place in society. In addition, Pope's imitation repeatedly calls to mind, through its irony, Martial's and Juvenal's nostalgia for an age in which a social elite supported genius and in which literary men adorned the court. If we fail to recognize how Horatian literary values combine with post-Augustan nostalgia to form the classical contexts for Pope's poem, we will find only a handful of passages in the *Epistle* that carry any real political bite. (Perhaps that is why most of the "anti-Augustus" readings of the poem concentrate on its opening and little more.) But Pope's opposition Augustanism has a broader intent. George, his minister, and the overall corruption of the Walpolean system represent a threat to all decency. In response to this threat, Pope maintains the importance of a refined taste (a notion fraught with moral implications throughout Pope's work)[19] and stresses the poet's duty to speak the truth without flattering the great. In this way, Augustan values, far from being the target of Pope's attack, represent the very ideals that he wishes most vigorously to uphold.

The genius of Pope's poem lies in the nimble-footed way he adapts Horace's content. When Horace directly praises Augustus, Pope ironically praises George. (There is, of course, nothing new in this assertion, but it requires defense and reaffirmation, for Howard Weinbrot has argued just the opposite—that Pope is not contrasting George Augustus with his namesake but identifying the two.)[20] Even so, we must not fall into the unhistorical trap of assuming that Pope's irony would have been immediately obvious to everyone. For the praise accorded George fits comfortably within the tradition of courtly panegyric that approached its nadir in the works of such poets as Eusden, Welsted, and Cibber. Let me make a brief digression into contemporary panegyric to give some context to Pope's language.

In 1727 Richard Savage published *A Poem, Sacred to the Glorious Memory of our Late Most Gracious Sovereign Lord King George.*[21] Like all of Savage's poems to or about great personages, this poem constituted an implied appeal for support. It consists of hyperbolic praise of the recently dead George I, and thus provides a useful example of the normal excesses of royal panegyric:[22]

> Was there a Glory, yet to Greatness known,
> That not in *Brunswick*'s Soul superior shone?
> . . . .
> But, Oh!—what Love, what Honour shall he claim,
> Whose Joy is Bounty, and whose Gift is Fame?
> He (truly great!) his useful pow'r refines,
> By him discover'd *Worth* exalted shines;
> Exalted *Worth*, th' enlivening act, repeats,
> And draws *new Virtues* from obscure retreats.
> (ll. 53–54, 69–74)

Readers of the opposition press should certainly be astonished by such praise, for what have we here but enlightened patronage flowing from George's bounty? And then there is his military might:

> *Nations* were ballanc'd by his guardian skill,
> Like the pois'd *Planets* by the all-pow'rful Will.
> . . . .
> By GEORGE the *Austrian Eagle* learns to tower,
> While the proud *Turk* shakes conscious of her power;
> But when her Menace braves our envied shore,
> She trembles at the *British Lyon*'s Roar;
> Trembles, though aided by the force of *Spain*,
> And *India*'s wealth!—'gainst *Brunswick*, All how vain!
> (ll. 79–80, 83–88)

In the modern world we have come to think of all such praise as ridiculous, but we must remember that Savage was merely conforming to the expectations of a monarchical system in which such effusions could earn the writer a pension. And although the language is excessively agitated, the images hackneyed, and the emotion artificial, Savage has engaged an important contemporary issue: he credits George with achieving the "balance of powers," a much sought-after goal in eighteenth-century diplomacy.

Compare now the opening of Pope's *Epistle to Augustus*:

> While You, great Patron of Mankind, sustain
> The balanc'd World, and open all the Main;
> Your Country, chief, in Arms abroad defend,
> At home, with Morals, Arts, and Laws amend;
> How shall the Muse, from such a Monarch, steal
> An hour, and not defraud the Publick Weal?[23]

We find here many of the same topics addressed by Savage—the balance of powers, military readiness, moral perspicacity—but Pope's praise, modeled of course on Horace's, lacks the emotional excesses of Savage's. Within the conventions of courtly panegyric, conventions that take hyperbole for granted, the opening of Pope's poem seems moderate and restrained. There is no reason to assume that his contemporaries would find such a passage exaggerated, ironic, or patently insincere. Similarly, many modern readers find it obviously ludicrous that Walpole's master should be addressed as "Great Friend of Liberty!" (l. 25), but this response ignores the fundamental political realities of Pope's day: the Hanoverian succession came about because of the perceived threats to English liberty from a Catholic Stuart monarch. Few Whigs, not even those members of the opposition seeking to topple Walpole, would hesitate to attribute such a character to a king who subscribed to the Revolution settlement. The most important thing to realize about the poem's irony, then, is that it would not have been immediately obvious to Pope's original readers. And the truest sign of Pope's subtlety is that he never gives the game away, never winks to his audience to tell them that he is not sincere: he trusts right-minded readers to recognize the absurdity of praising the new Augustus.

Throughout the poem the political irony functions in this subtle, sophisticated manner. Horace's poem is largely an indictment of contemporary Roman taste, a complaint that modern genius goes unappreciated while the crudeness of older writers receives public applause. Pope follows Horace point by point, but as he reworks the material, he colors Horace's criticisms with opposition laments over public corruption. Buttressed by the social criticism he found in Martial and Juvenal, especially their complaints over the neglect of authors and the public enthusiasm for trivial entertainments, Pope turns Horace's criticism of an unsophisticated literary taste into a broader indictment of the decline of societal values generally.

Horace argues, for instance, that just because the oldest Greek authors were the best, the same need not be true of the Romans (*Epistles*, 2.1.28–33). Pope picks up the broad issue of the society's comparing itself with its forerunners, but he turns it into a censure of public amusements:

> Tho' justly Greece her eldest sons admires,
> Why should not we be wiser than our Sires?
> In ev'ry publick Virtue we excell,
> We build, we paint, we sing, we dance as well,
> And learned Athens to our Art must stoop,
> Could she behold us tumbling thro' a hoop.
> (ll. 43–48)

This last couplet has no analogue in Horace; Pope singles out the despicable sort of arts in which his society outstrips the ancients.

Horace himself often sneers at public displays, and Pope had little trouble turning such passages into opposition indictments of declining values. When Horace laments that even the Roman knight no longer takes pleasure in the language of a play, that his eyes, unfixed (*incertos*), enjoy the empty shows of modern spectacle (ll. 182–88), Pope evokes opposition charges of corruption at court:

> What dear delight to Britons Farce affords!
> Farce once the taste of Mobs, but now of Lords.
> (ll. 310–11)

In their tastes Lords are now indistinguishable from the mob. In opposition circles it was indisputable that the bad taste of the court reflected the collapse of public morality. One might also wonder whether the most obvious farce entertaining the Lords was not the court itself.

Throughout the poem, Pope adds similar suggestive comments. If, for instance, one should question the perfection of Shakespeare's art,

> How will our Fathers rise up in a rage,
> And swear, all shame is lost in George's Age!
> (ll. 125–26)

All shame, of course, *is* lost in George's age—though not because an enlightened critic like Pope finds occasional bombast or other excesses in Shakespeare. And when Pope lists some of the poet's contributions to society, he adds the following demurral not to be found in Horace:

> I scarce can think him such a worthless thing,
> Unless he praise some monster of a King,
> Or Virtue, or Religion turn to sport,
> To please a lewd, or un-believing Court.
> (ll. 209–12)

The lines in fact are innocent; they attack servile flattery and impiety. There is nothing here to anger an adherent of the present royal family, no direct suggestion that this court is either lewd or unbelieving. Indeed Pope further deflects any seditious implications by immediately following this passage with a sigh for Dryden, who could not survive Charles's court without taint. But friends of the opposition were always ready to read their own sentiments into such lines, a fact that Pope could count on, and such readers were quick to despise both the king and his laureate.

And yet, all the satirical attacks on George Augustus and his court make up only a small portion of the poem. Just as Horace's subject was not Augustus himself but the state of letters in Augustan Rome, so Pope's subject is not George but the state of letters in Georgian England. Critics who focus on the obvious political references in the poem or who expect irony to be Pope's only satirical technique here are likely to ignore his equally subtle handling of the gradual progress of taste and sophistication, now threatened with decline because of public corruption. One of the clear thrusts of Horace's poem is that Augustan Rome had progressed greatly over earlier ages in literary sophistication. Earlier writers had often been slovenly—their style old-fashioned, their measures harsh, their expressions flaccid.[24] Horace and his contemporaries, though, had developed a new style, disciplined and decorous in diction, expression, and meter. But most modern readers, Horace complains, lack the taste to recognize these achievements, preferring old works simply because they are old, willfully blind to their imperfections. Fortunately, though, Augustus himself has recognized the merit of Vergil and Varius and rewarded them appropriately (ll. 245–47). In the end, then, Horace praises not the broad, general progress of his society, but the special sensibility of its elites. And so the circle of authors and connoisseurs that Maecenas gathered around himself—certainly the true audience of the original poem—could share the smug satisfaction of knowing that their sophistication lifted them above the naïveté or vulgarity of contemporary taste.

Pope had little problem rewriting English literary history according to this model, for the development of "polite letters" was generally perceived as a triumph over native English crudity.[25] In the *Epistle*, Pope simply makes this explicit. The poets of former ages, we are told, were often careless, lacking the polish necessary truly to please a refined age. Shakespeare "grew Immortal in his own despight" (l. 72). As for the other giants of the Renaissance:

> Spenser himself affects the obsolete,
> And Sydney's verse halts ill on Roman feet:
> Milton's strong pinion now not Heav'n can bound,
> Now serpent-like, in prose he sweeps the ground,
> In Quibbles, Angel and Archangel join,
> And God the Father turns a School-Divine.
> (ll. 97–102)

Each of these authors shows a failure of taste, a tendency to indulge an antiquated, affected, or inappropriate style.[26]

Pope asserts his Augustan values most clearly in his development of Horace's famous conceit,

> Graecia capta, ferum victorem cepit. (1. 156)
> [Captive Greece her rough conqueror subdued.]

The influence of Greek culture had provided Rome its first impetus towards refinement; the English too had learned politeness from a foreign source:

> We conquer'd France, but felt our captive's charms;
> Her Arts victorious triumph'd o'er our Arms:
> (ll.263–64)

The violence here done to political history was hardly a matter of concern for an imitative poet; he could rely on the chauvinism of his readers to approve the ingenuity of his imitation and to forgive any exaggeration. And Pope redeems the distortions of this couplet with his splendid depiction of the gradual progress of aesthetic refinement:

> Britain to soft refinements less a foe,
> Wit grew polite, and Numbers learn'd to flow.
> Waller was smooth; but Dryden taught to join
> The varying verse, the full resounding line,
> The long majestic march, and energy divine.
> Tho' still some traces of our rustic vein
> And splay-foot verse, remain'd, and will remain.
> Late, very late, correctness grew our care,
> When the tir'd nation breath'd from civil war.
> Exact Racine, and Corneille's noble fire
> Show'd us that France had something to admire.
> Not but the Tragic spirit was our own,
> And full in Shakespear, fair in Otway shone:
> But Otway fail'd to polish or refine,
> And fluent Shakespear scarce effac'd a line.
> Ev'n copious Dryden, wanted, or forgot,
> The last and greatest Art, the Art to blot.
> (ll. 265–81)

Uneven though this progress was, we can see clearly the direction in which literature has been striving—towards polish, smoothness, correctness. If the English temperament has had a flaw, it was in the refusal of its native vigor to surrender totally to refinement, but then the Romans had balked in much the same manner. But even that, we may infer, has been remedied. Pope, like Horace, views the past largely as a prelude to the new age of polite literature, a literature that has finally overcome its native awkwardnesses and whose achievements can be estimated from the poem before us.

And yet, despite Pope's clear advocacy of polish and decorum, despite his confident assertion of the triumph of "polite letters," the *Epistle to Augustus* resonates with a number of different overtones from Horace's original; for the literary, social, and historical contexts of Pope's poem differ greatly from those of its source. To begin with, Horace's view of Roman literary history as a long climb from barbarism to sophistication, however colored it may be by his dominating aesthetic assumptions, follows no preestablished pattern. We read his poem without reference to a base text. But Pope and his contemporaries had read not only Horace, but Martial and Juvenal as well; they knew that the progress celebrated by Horace had been followed by an inevitable decline. Pope also could not close his mind to the political attacks on Augustus as tyrant; he undoubtedly would have known the historians' argument that the undermining of Roman liberty had caused both social and literary decay. As a result, all of the opposition concerns about public corruption also lay behind this poem. One could not talk of progress, of politeness, of sophistication, without a sense that all was endangered. Poetry perhaps had achieved refinement, but could this refinement survive? A corrupt court, a debauched king, a minister who despises genius and puts his trust in the power of money to accomplish all things—can these provide the necessary encouragement to letters? We find ourselves, then, towards the end of the poem, directly confronting the problem of patronage in a corrupt age. Horace had counseled Augustus to beware the praise of fools: a foul poem can besmirch glorious deeds (ll. 235–37). But what of the world of George and Walpole, where there are no deeds deserving a poet's song, and where all praise must redound disgracefully upon both the court and the poet?

> A vile Encomium doubly ridicules;
> There's nothing blackens like the ink of fools;
> If true, a woful likeness, and if lyes,
> "Praise undeserv'd is scandal in disguise:"
> Well may he blush, who gives it, or receives
> (ll. 410–14)

Indeed, the entire system of patronage had become impracticable, for what man of taste was there in power, and what encomium was now possible? The hireling scribblers whom Pope had pilloried a decade earlier in the *Dunciad* might praise such a king and his minister, but wit and sense were forced to hold their tongues—or resort to irony.

In addition to its ironic attacks on the Hanoverian Court, Pope's *Epistle to Augustus* offers a vindication of "polite letters," a vindication directly modeled on Horace's own and one that might readily be called a defense of literary Augustanism. Pope exalts such values as polish, correctness, decorum;

and like Horace he ties them to the progress of civilization. But that progress is seen to be threatened by the political corruption pervading society. Insofar as the political situation of the 1730s put pressure on Pope to oppose all cooperation with tyrannical regimes, a number of his comments might be acknowledged to reflect unfavorably upon Horace himself;[27] but for the most part the poem represents Pope's appropriation of Horace as a vehicle for recounting the development of English letters and for suggesting the difficulties encountered by a poet of integrity and genius in maintaining moral and aesthetic principles in the face of societal corruption. Pope in fact is always an Augustan, whether praising Queen Anne or damning George Augustus. His values do not change in the years between *Windsor Forest* and the *Epistle to Augustus*; rather, a new government has been installed that treads those values under foot. As Weinbrot has noted, Pope's satires of the late 1730s were perceived as being "in the Juvenalian camp";[28] it is no wonder. Horatian satire, with its avuncular tone and its injunctions against various kinds of folly, is an inappropriate response to the corruption that, in the view of the opposition, was overwhelming English society. George Augustus and his minister had rejected all values—moral, social, and aesthetic. Nevertheless, Juvenalian fury at corruption does not call for an abandonment of Augustan values, for those values are among the worthwhile aspects of civilization that Pope wishes to sustain.[29] To read this poem as anti-Augustan seems to me totally misleading; its true character is that of "opposition Augustanism," the attempt to invest "polite literature" with social and moral significance, and then to criticize the court or the government for neglecting or betraying those values.

NOTES

1. Howard Weinbrot, *Augustus Caesar in "Augustan" England* (Princeton: Princeton University Press, 1978), 7ff.
2. Tacitus argued that political debate under the Republic, in which both personal prestige and public policy were at stake, had honed the skills of the disputants. The empire had brought sloth along with its relative peace, and the incentives to rhetorical brilliance dissipated: see *Dialogus de Oratoribus*, sections 25–28, 36–41.
3. As Weinbrot, *Augustus Caesar*, notes (68–79), many eighteenth-century commentators argued that the decline in Roman poetry had the same roots as the decline in oratory—the destruction of Roman freedom under the Empire. But this was not Martial's explanation.
4. The Latin texts of Martial are from the Loeb edition, ed. Walter C. A. Ker, 2 vols. (London: Heinemann, 1925); the translations are my own.

5. Martial, *Epigrams*, 8.56.5: "Sint Maecenates, non derunt, Flacce, Marones." Hereafter cited in the text.

6. Weinbrot, *Augustus Caesar*, 150–81.

7. Juvenal, *Satires*, 7.94–97, ed. John Ferguson (New York: St. Martin's, 1979), 54.

8. Fabius and Cotta were both patrons of Ovid. Juvenal does not mention Augustus's banishment of Ovid, which deprived him of the freedom from care supposedly needed to write great poetry.

9. Both Martial and Juvenal complain repeatedly about the large amounts of money paid to charioteers and musicians while men of letters go hungry: see Martial's *Epigrams*, 3.4, 5.56, 10.74; and Juvenal's *Satires*, 7.112–14, 175–77.

10. See Horace, *Epistles*, 2.1.139–67, 2.3.258–94.

11. See Horace, *Satires*, 1.10.72–92. This satire constitutes Horace's most direct tribute to the coterie of readers he claims to write for and his most explicit defense of the superiority of Augustan craftsmanship.

12. These two elements of the Augustan myth are of course directly related: Horace had first proposed the circle of Maecenas as a fit audience for a truly sophisticated poet, and a century later the finest authors could find no counterpart in their own society. Thus the social aspect of the Augustan myth was created in part by Horace himself.

13. Domna Stanton, *The Aristocrat as Art* (New York: Columbia University Press, 1980), 14–18. Stanton quotes Guez de Balzac on the court of Augustus: "Everything was polished and refined during that reign, everyone was learned and ingenious in the court, from Augustus to his valets." And Saint-Evremond described Maecenas as "a winning man whom urbane and witty individuals tried to win over. . . . His tastes determined those of others; . . . they strove to adopt his manner and to imitate his personality as best they could" (Stanton, *Aristocrat*, 15).

14. The *locus classicus* for recognizing the relation of "polite literature" to Horatian values in England is Dryden's "Defence of the Epilogue to *The Conquest of Granada*." For a full discussion of these issues, see my article, "Rehabilitating 'Augustanism': On the Roots of 'Polite Letters' in England," *Eighteenth Century Life* 20, no. 3 (November 1996): 49–65.

15. As James Winn has noted, in the "Discourse Concerning Satire" Dryden guardedly praises Louis XIV for his patronage of the arts, comparing him to Augustus and clearly implying William's failure in this area. In addition, Dryden refused to dedicate his *Virgil* to the king, choosing instead three dissident lords who had refused to swear oaths to William: see *John Dryden and His World* (New Haven: Yale University Press, 1987), 459, 484–92. Numerous recent critical essays have detailed the satire on William and his court concealed in Dryden's late translations and other works.

16. See Bertrand Goldgar, *Walpole and the Wits* (Lincoln: University of Nebraska Press, 1976), 8–19.

17. Goldgar, *Walpole and the Wits* (11, 14–15), quotes several passages from *The Craftsman* and *Fog's Weekly Journal* in which the court of Augustus is praised

for its patronage of men of letters; Weinbrot, *Augustus Caesar* (109–17), offers numerous contrary examples.

18. Weinbrot, *Augustus Caesar*, 189. Malcolm Kelsall starts from a similarly narrow premise in his article "Augustus and Pope," *Huntington Library Quarterly* 39 (1976): 117–31. After noting that Augustus is "likened to divine or heroic figures" at the beginning of Horace's poem, Kelsall asks whether one can "accept without qualification that the Latin supplies the ideals which Pope wished accepted in England" (120). The obvious answer is "no." In imitations of this sort, nothing is ever accepted "without qualification." Readers always assume that the material is being ingeniously adapted to fit new, modern contexts; that is, such poems are read *mutatis mutandis*, with the appropriate changes being made. The question is not whether Pope wanted a usurping tyrant glorified like an ancient "hero" on the English throne, but whether he would not have preferred a monarch who surrounded himself with men of taste and genius to the monarch he had.

19. Pope had already examined the moral implications of taste in his two essays "Of the Use of Riches": the *Epistle to Burlington* (1731) and the *Epistle to Bathurst* (1733).

20. Weinbrot, *Augustus Caesar*, 188–89, 200.

21. *The Poetical Works of Richard Savage*, ed. Clarence Tracy (Cambridge: Cambridge University Press, 1962), 82–87.

22. This poem also reaffirms that the name "Augustus" continued to function as a vehicle for praise at this time, for Savage addresses the new king, George II, by this name. For this and other contemporary examples of the laudatory use of the name, see Howard Erskine-Hill's impressive defense of "Augustanism," *The Augustan Idea in English Literature* (London: Edward Arnold, 1983), 243.

23. For the *Epistle to Augustus*, see the Twickenham Edition of the Poems of Alexander Pope, vol. 4, *Imitations of Horace*, ed. John Butt, 2nd ed. (London: Methuen, 1953), l95ff. (All subsequent references will be noted by line number in the text.)

24. See Horace, *Epistles*, 2.1.63–68.

25. Pope was not the first English author to attempt to rewrite literary history along Horatian lines. Dryden had taken a very similar position in both the "Defence of the Epilogue" and the poem "To My Dear Friend Mr. Congreve." In fact, Dryden's adoption of the Horatian pose is in every way more convincing than Pope's, for Pope was writing in the wake of Waller and Dryden, authors whose poetry had long before given England a claim to "polite letters," and Dryden was proclaiming a major stylistic break with the past at a time when an older generation could still remember with fondness the "irregular" dramatists and lyric poets of their youth.

26. In his determination to follow Horace and to establish a similar progress from crudeness to elegance in English letters, Pope can be distressingly unfair. The comment on Sidney's "Roman feet" refers to his quantitative experiments in the *Arcadia*, hardly a balanced estimate of Sidney's poetic technique. And Pope attributes to Ben Jonson the same unconcern for his future reputation that he had remarked in Shakespeare (11. 69–74). Even restricting Pope's comment to Jonson's

"dotages" (as Pope himself does in a note to 1.69) hardly saves it from gross misrepresentation of a poet who carefully sought to preserve his works for posterity.

27. Weinbrot, *Augustus Caesar*, especially 200–12, suggests that Pope carefully distanced himself from Horace and in fact satirized him as an official toady. On the whole I find his argument unconvincing, largely because it focuses on subtle readings of several political passages and ignores the great bulk of the poem where Pope clearly aligns himself with Horace's literary views and values. An eighteenth-century reader may indeed have felt that Horace, despite the distaste for flattery expressed in this and other epistles, went too far in his praise of Augustus and was thus implicated in his own criticism of those who flatter the great; but as has often been noted, Pope insulated Horace from at least some of this criticism by the statement with which he concludes the "Advertisement" prefixed to the poem: "We may farther learn from this Epistle, that *Horace* made his Court to this Great Prince, by writing with a decent Freedom toward him, with a just Contempt of his low Flatterers, and with a manly Regard to his own Character" (Twickenham Edition, 4: 192).

28. Weinbrot, *Augustus Caesar*, 181.

29. If Pope's *Epistle* is Juvenalian, it is so only by its political implications, not by its form or style.

Phillis Wheatley, the Aesthetic, and the Form of Life

FRANK SHUFFELTON

I

In a frequently admirable attempt to rescue the "Letters of the Early Republic" from persistent neglect, Michael T. Gilmore in the new *Cambridge History of American Literature* rejects criticism of American writing between 1790 and 1830 for its failure to live up to post-Romantic aesthetic criteria. His defense, nevertheless, concedes the point to those aesthetically grounded critics who would supposedly hold all literature up to a single, universal standard of evaluation and hence find early American literature wanting. His argument instead aims to privilege the literature of the early republic for its ideological work over its aesthetic enterprise. This literature is interesting, he urges, as "the product of a historical formation dominated by republicanism, communalism, and a pre-industrial agrarian economy," whereas "the privileging of the aesthetic as something desirable purely for its own sake was itself the product—at least in America—of a historical configuration that postdated the early national period."[1] His introduction of a base and superstructure model immediately limits consideration of the ways in which aesthetic experience might subvert or transform any given "historical formation." Furthermore, the identification of the aesthetic with "the privileging of the aesthetic as something desirable purely for its own sake," later called "the Romantic-modernist ideal," is more misleading than helpful because the modern aesthetic arose in the "historical formation" that preceded the early republic rather than in the era succeeding it.

Paul O. Kristeller demonstrated four decades ago that aesthetics, considered as the incorporation of "the comparative and theoretical treatment of the fine arts as a separate discipline into the system of philosophy," did not emerge until the end of the eighteenth century in Germany, and he concluded that "the modern system of the fine arts is thus pre-Romantic in its origin, although all Romantic as well as later aesthetics takes this system as its necessary basis."[2] The key texts and dates here are undoubtedly Alexander Baumgarten's *Aesthetica* of 1750, which coined the term, Gotthold Ephraim Lessing's *Laokoon* of 1768, and Immanuel Kant's *Critique of Judgement* in 1790. Because the eighteenth-century German "historical configuration" that produced aesthetics was, arguably, as substantially preindustrial and communal as that of the early American republic, Gilmore's historical materialist argument does not seem to be particularly cogent. Germany and America were certainly differently situated, but one sign of that difference was the emergence of a philosophical articulation of the aesthetic idea as opposed to the poetic articulation that was perhaps more favored by writers in the English vernacular.

More important, aesthetics in this modern sense grew out of critical engagement with a discourse about the experienced pleasures of art that is at least as old as Plato and Aristotle, a tradition aware from the very beginning that aesthetic experience could either subvert or support ordering ideologies or historical formations. The discourse of the beautiful and the pleasures of the imagination available to Baumgarten and his successors included texts in English and French by Addison, Shaftesbury, Hume, Dubos, Batteux and others, so that if the science of aesthetics first appeared in Germany, the materials out of which it was constructed were far more widely available, many even in America. Equally, aesthetics grew out of engagement with the problematic art of its own era (styled by historians as early modern in distinction to Gilmore's "pre-modern"), an era in which the vernacular literatures displaced those of the classics as compositional norms. Benjamin Franklin learned to write by imitating the *Spectator*, not Cicero, and he acquired an archetypically modern self-consciousness about language and self-representation in so doing. Simultaneously, the concept of originality emerged in this same era. Edward Young's *Conjectures on Original Composition* (1759) appeared in the same decade as Baumgarten's *Aesthetica*. In other words, by the time of Kant's third critique the arts were already modern, even if not yet Romantic, and if the modern system of the arts was first constructed in Germany, it was intended to reflect on a literature widely current in the Atlantic civilization, not excepting whatever literature was produced on its westem fringes.[3]

Above all, as Luc Ferry has recently argued, the concept of aesthetics appeared simultaneously with a subjectivization of the world marked by the appearance of the modern concepts of individualism and democracy. Against a radical vision of subjects reduced to Leibnizian monads, it is the beautiful, says Ferry, "which at the same time brings us together the most easily yet the most mysteriously." Aesthetics in his reading becomes the ground for an intersubjectivity already implied in Kant's antinomy of taste and now increasingly important for us who "no longer live in an a priori common world."[4] To ignore the question of the aesthetic in early American writing risks missing what might have been most important for its creators, the commitment to pleasures of the imagination that made social life possible, and it risks missing what that literature might have to say to us. To read early American literature only as an ideological performance underestimates its full power as an imaginative, imagined form of life that arises out of and stands against the daily experience of its creators and audiences. I am invoking here Wittgenstein's well-known observation, "To imagine a language means to imagine a form of life," because it allows space for both imaginative subjects and objective social fomns. Furthermore, I would like to reflect this upon Phillis Wheatley, who brilliantly imagined a new language for herself in a new world, and whose writings delivered pleasure and consolation to herself and to the citizens of Boston who were both its occasions and first readers in the 1770s and 1780s. While her writing is clearly implicated in discourses of empire, of freedom, and of redemption, its mastery of feeling and estrangement finally matter more than the political messages ideological critics have decoded. Her complex structuring of feeling, the experience of the subject that grounds the aesthetic dimension of poetry, may in fact have a more profound political import than her more overtly ideological statements.

II

When Phillis Wheatley's *Poems on Various Subjects, Religious and Moral* appeared to British and American audiences in 1773, they were introduced by several pages of legitimating statements; some, like the dedication to the Countess of Huntingdon, were thoroughly conventional, but others announced a radically new literary and cultural presence, especially the attestation "To the PUBLICK" signed by eighteen of colonial Boston's leading inhabitants. This document and the letter from the author's master, John Wheatley, established that Phillis, identified on the title page as a "Negro Servant," was not merely another pastoral voice from the lower orders but "a Slave in a Family in this Town," a person in a situation very different from that of faddishly popular Thresher Poets and Milkmaid Poets. Equally important, "To the PUBLICK" also implied a complex performative understanding in which Wheatley's poems would operate, an understanding that was more radical than perhaps any of the signers recognized.[5]

For most of these men—and they were all men—, it would be one of the few times in the 1770s that they would agree on anything in public. Thomas Hutchinson and Andrew Oliver, the governor and lieutenant-governor, were already becoming the most hated men in Massachusetts, and those who did not despise them feared John Hancock. The revolutionary violence of the coming years would send Tories like Hutchinson, Oliver, and Joseph Green into exile, place Mather Byles under house arrest, and embitter conservatives like Harrison Gray. For the moment, however, they could come together to advance the publication of "the Writings of PHILLIS, . . . a young Negro Girl, who was but a few Years since brought an uncultivated Barbarian from *Africa*." They were for the moment able to overcome their suspicions and jealousies precisely because Phillis was not a "Barbarian" but an accomplished practitioner of what David Shields has recently described as "British-American Belles Lettres, . . . a mode of writing that subordinated the traditional tasks of edification, revelation, and memorialization to the work of stimulating social pleasure."[6] Any doubts on this matter would be swept away by a consideration of Wheatley's first poem, "To Maecenas," that immediately invoked a parallel to Horace, the ultimate classic exemplar for all practitioners of belles-lettres. Horace began his own *Odes* with an address to Maecenas, but as Cynthia J. Smith has astutely observed, where Horace sought material support from a real patron, Wheatley apostrophized an interpellated figure as "a sympathetic reader, perhaps even as a critic." Invoking a "shared sensibility," Wheatley praised not so much Maecenas as the pleasures of reading "o'er what poets sung, and shepherds played."[7] Thomas Hutchinson and John Hancock, Mather Byles and Charles Chauncy could sink their political differences in the common pleasure of reading Homer, Virgil, and, now, Phillis Wheatley.

Belles-lettres, or polite letters as it was usually translated, was a trope that offered Wheatley's attestors a safe ground because its traditional association with the virtues of sociability normatively precluded expressions of political rancor. As Shields explains, "Polite letters were ideally expressions of the sensus communis that communal spirit of candid friendliness that Shaftesbury identified . . . as the soul of genteel society."[8] Politics might well enter into the conversation that was of the essence of sociability, but the Tuesday Club of Annapolis demonstrated in its eighth law of club behavior how "candid friendliness" should deal with political topics: "That if any Subject of what nature soever be discussed, which levels at party matters, or the administration of the Government of this province, or be disagreeable to the Club, no answer Shall be given thereto, but after Such discourse is ended, the Society Shall Laugh at the member offending, in order to divert the discourse."[9] Polite letters ultimately aimed at advancing civility, and politeness typically dealt with politics either by surrounding it with silence or by masking it with laughter or sentiment.

The community of belles-lettres thus provided what Jürgen Habermas has called an "ideal speech situation . . . neither an empirical phenomenon nor mere construct, but rather an unavoidable supposition reciprocally made in discourse."[10] Neither so egalitarian nor so apolitical as it claimed, the conversational sensus communis was not simply a counterfactual myth. It was widely and frequently practiced in clubs, salons, drawing rooms, and taverns, and this practice marked the appearance of a form of life that centrally supported the Enlightenment's project of emancipation as well as the work of the empire. The belletristic moment of the attestation pretended that Thomas Hutchinson and John Hancock were not conniving at each other's political ruin, and it further upheld the fiction that Phillis Wheatley's status as a slave was no hindrance to her sharing with Maecenas "softer language, and diviner airs."

In spite, however, of the pretense of agreeability implied in the gentlemen's attestation, their statement underlined the fact that both they themselves and Wheatley's *Poems* were inescapably connected to a politics of empire. Archibald Bell, her London publisher who had requested this testimonial, occupied an imperial center that was at once the arbiter of manners in the English-speaking world and the center of imperial political and economic control. The Boston attestors played a familiar role by authenticating provincial facts for this center, and their report from the margins of the Atlantic world reinscribed the imperial order.[11] Royal appointees Hutchinson and Oliver appended their titles to their names, and the attestors who enjoyed appointment to the governor's Council were distinguished with the prefix "Honorable." If the attestors came together supposedly in the interest of polite literature, the relationship of their names on the page traces out power and hierarchy. "PHILLIS" herself is more deeply enmeshed in this power, since she was "but a few Years since, brought . . . from *Africa*, . . . and now is, under the Disadvantage of serving as a Slave in a Family in this Town." She has been an object of the commerce that is both the cause and the purpose of this empire, and in a very real sense she is still an object of exchange, offered up as a commodity for the conversation of imperial polite letters. In this regard her race and political status are not discreetly masked by belletristic fictions, as was Hancock's politics, but become marked qualifications for her participation in the trans-Atlantic community of letters. The portrait, requested by the Countess of Huntingdon, is circled with the inscription "Phillis Wheatley, Negro Servant to Mr. John Wheatley, of Boston." Each of the prefatory documents—title page, dedication, publisher's preface, letter from John Wheatley, attestation—refers to her status as Negro, servant, or slave, leaving no doubt that *Poems on Various Subjects* was in effect one more trophy of empire, another marvel from the New World.

Nevertheless, if the attestation reinforced the hegemonic relationship between imperial center and margins, it also indicated the potential for recapture of personal and social power within an imperial system, particularly when, like the first British empire, it wrapped itself in the myths of belles-lettres.[12] In an empire legitimating itself through mercantilist visions of exchange that would make wealthy both center and provinces, belle-lettrists' faith in conversation as "the fundamental Principle of Society" was the ultimate economics. More important, the world of Anglo-American polite literature in the years between the Glorious Revolution and the American Revolution coincides with the Habermasian "public sphere in the world of letters," where "the subjectivity originating in the interiority of the conjugal family, by communicating with itself, attained clarity about itself" The great achievement of the Enlightenment as Habermas describes it was the functional conversion of the public sphere in the world of letters into a public sphere in the political realm where "private people making use of their reason" might criticize public authority.[13] By the time the woman we know as Phillis Wheatley arrived in Boston the public sphere in literature, in spite of its belletristic pretensions to the contrary, had become identified with the public sphere in the political realm. Participation in the one necessitated participation in the other, so much so that scholars using Habermas's extremely useful notion tend to refer simply to *the* public sphere, undervaluing the distinctions implicit in its historical emergence.

It seems entirely appropriate, then, that the attestors who placed their names at the head of Wheatley's 1773 *Poems* seem to be also represented in its final pages with a sort of conversational riposte to the intervening poems. The next to last poem, titled "A Rebus, by I.B.," is *not* by Phillis but is probably by James Bowdoin, an attestor who was an important merchant of the period; both a patriot leader and a scientific virtuoso, he would eventually become governor of Massachusetts in 1785 as well as the first president of the American Academy of Arts and Letters.[14] Wheatley saves the last word for herself with "The Answer to the *Rebus*, by the Author of These

Poems" in which she identifies Quebec as the hidden figure in the rebus. General James Wolfe's capture of Quebec was regarded as a triumph of British imperial power and virtue, an heroic enterprise in which troops of both the home country and the colonies took part and which sealed the future of North America as an English-speaking (and Protestant) empire. The subsidiary figures that contribute to solving the rebus are variously typological and scriptural, imperial, local, and classical: "the *Quail* of most inviting taste/ Fed *Israel's* army in the dreary Waste," the Unicorn from "*Britain's* royal standard," the Emerald "Among the gems which regal crowns compose," Boston ("a town, polite and debonair,/ To which the beaux and beauteous nymphs repair"), "*Euphorbus* of the Dardan line," and "*C [hatha]m* zealous to support our laws" (111). This richly imbricated set of figures compasses the idealized self-image of the British Empire in 1773, but its references to the old Puritan trope of liberation and mission and to William Pitt also recognize the stresses that threatened to shatter the ideal. Wheatley's concluding quatrain could be read on either side of the Atlantic in 1773 with different degrees of self-congratulation or apprehension:

> *Quebec* now vanquish'd must obey,
> She too must annual tribute pay
> To *Britain* of immortal fame,
> And add new glory to her name.

Conventions of polite letters subdue political anxieties here, even if they do not entirely dispel them. Wheatley herself, not yet emancipated, might be presumed to have had her own ironic take on the image of a vanquished Quebec forced to pay tribute to British glory, even as her testimonial to empire brought her into its conversational circles.

Phillip M. Richards has described Wheatley's participation in the public sphere as playing a significant role in what he calls "the romance of America," but her emergence into the public sphere was authorized by an earlier romance of British empire.[15] This is also a distinction worth maintaining. Inclusion and expansion are sustaining principles of empire, the structural inclusion of diverse subjects and the expansion of legitimating mythologies to enfold them. The British imperial literary public sphere as figured in belles-lettres shaped myths of conversation between the center and the provincial margins, between colonizers and colonized, that depended upon cultural difference. This empire legitimated itself by transforming dissimilar cultures, and thus always needed convertible and conversable subjects who could confirm its successes. Public spheres in later nation states, however, became susceptible to a logic of exclusion, to the formation of national identities by rejecting alien others. The imperial literary public sphere encouraged a trans-

Atlantic conversation of sociability and civility among its subjects, but to do so it necessarily extended to them the dialogic equality that was the idealized and practical basis of belletristic friendship.

III

Converted from her extra-imperial beginnings as "an uncultivated Barbarian," Wheatley was peculiarly able to affect the romance of America because she had first gained her voice within this ideal speech situation of British-American letters. Her *Poems on Various Subjects* obviously carried on the conversation of empire in poems addressed "To the King's Most Excellent Majesty, 1768," "To Captain H——D, of the 65th Regiment," and "To the Right Honourable William, Earl of Dartmouth." Nevertheless, the support necessary for their publication came from the many poems that were, as promised in the title, religious and moral. She seems to have specialized in grief; there are fourteen elegies plus a translation from Ovid's *Metamorphoses* of "Niobe in Distress for Her Children Slain by Apollo," to say nothing of three poems to people who have narrowly escaped disaster or are seeking to recover their health. These are not so much the signs of a melancholy or morbid temperament in Wheatley as of the form of life her poetry assumed in pre-revolutionary Boston. Discussing the connection between printed texts and manuscripts in the public sphere, David Shields makes an important point: "before print there was writing; after printing there was writing."[16] Wheatley's poems circulated in manuscript and in broadsides and pamphlets before they appeared in a bound volume, and we must recognize this as an essential function of her participation in the public sphere.

A number of Wheatley commentators have fastened upon the more obviously political poems, particularly the poem to Dartmouth with its powerful lines expressing a black presence under the sign of slavery, as evidence for her significance in the American revolutionary public sphere.[17] But when societies effectively transform themselves, significant changes are required on the level of individual moral-practical consciousness as well as on the structural political level. Social development requires the mastery of new forms of moral imagination as well as new political institutions.[18] Wheatley's poems performed new imaginative possibilities that gave pleasure to many people of Boston, as evidenced by Deborah Cushing's letter of 1774 to her husband: "I rote you by Mr. Cary and sent you one of Phillis Whetly's books which you will wonder att but Mrs. Dickerson and Mrs. Clymer and Mrs. Ball with some other ladies ware so pleased with Phillis and her performances that they boight her books and got her to compose some pieces for them which put me in mind of Mrs. Vanhorn to hume I thought it would be very agreabel."[19] Undoubtedly, the novelty of an African woman poet provided some of the pleasure here, but where novelty might be appreciated at a distance as an act of the understanding, Mrs. Cushing and her friends apparently found a more sensible pleasure in conversing directly with each other and with Wheatley as they shared the pleasures of the imagination.

If the moral-practical consciousness of Deborah Cushing's friends was touched upon this occasion, Wheatley seems to have made a much greater impact with her elegiac poetry, which engaged with more powerful emotions than those proper to the sociability of the tea table. On September 22, 1772, for example, John Andrews, a successful Boston merchant, wrote to his brother-in-law in Philadelphia, William Barrell: "The 3d instant I wrote you by the post, acquainting you with the death of little Charles. Ruthy has inclos'd you by this copy a poem by P. Wheatly, addressed to the father on this melancholy occasion; and wch I think is a masterly performance."[20] Charles Eliot was Andrews's nephew, and his mother was sister to both Ruth Andrews and William Barrell. Wheatley's poem, which survives in two manuscript copies, was revised and published as "A Funeral Poem on the Death of C. E. an Infant of Twelve Months." It thus migrated from the edges of the public sphere, where it was bound by intimate relationships, to a clarified public subjectivity; it moved from a private scene defined by kinship and shared grief to a communal vision of conversation and power in which the slave becomes masterly.

This elegiac ode is structurally and thematically in many ways typical of most of Wheatley's elegies, which use a half dozen or so of basic conventions. Here, the poem opens with a vision of C. E. winging his way to heaven "Through airy roads," offers a Miltonic view of the "universal whole," and pictures his welcome by angelic companions and his responsive raptures. The second stanza consoles his parents, and the three-line final stanza exhorts the readers, "To yon bright regions let your faith ascend, / Prepare to join your dearest infant friend/ In pleasures without measure, without end." These features of the elegy offer a highly conventional message of Christian consolation, but Wheatley's freshly imagined perspective enlivens and transforms them into an expression that is at once personal and public. She frequently gives voices to departed spirits in her elegies, a practice that is unusual in the form and that calls into question the usual dismissal of her as merely an imitator of Alexander Pope. Her models for this practice are more clearly John Milton and Edward Young, drawing lines of affiliation simultaneously to her Protestant gravity and to her modern sensibility.

More important, her construction of dialogues between the living and the dead points to aesthetic influences more powerfully mysterious and estranging than "Il Penseroso" or *Night Thoughts*. As Gregory Rigsby pointed out in a pioneering essay, Wheatley's heaven is in significant ways unlike the traditional Christian abode with God in which all souls are treated equally and objectively by a divine subject. Her heaven reflects African concepts of the dead; it is "the topmost rung of the hierarchial ladder—the seat of the ancestors"—where human subjects find the culmination of their earthly stations. Men typically find themselves in seats of power, women amidst virtue and bliss find love's fulfillment, and children find the affection and attention that surrounded them here.[21] In one of her elegies which did not contain heavenly voices, Wheatley seemingly felt the need to emphasize her Africanness as the source of a peculiar authority. In "To His Honour the Lieutenant Governor, on the Death of His Lady, March 24, 1773," she herself took on the task of directly addressing Andrew Oliver, telling him, "Nor canst thou, *Oliver*, assent refuse/ To heav'nly tidings from the *Afric* muse" (107).

Wheatley's Africanized view of heaven was equally a modern perspective, in that it was a heaven of human subjects finding the possibility of their voices for the first time. While little Charles Eliot's heaven is "The seat of saints, of seraphs, and of God," the latter is scarcely in evidence. On the other hand, the infant Charles enjoys an enlarged subjectivity that allows him to speak both to seraphs and saints and to those he left behind on earth. For Charles death is the occasion of the ultimate sublime experience, an aesthetic event that becomes for him the topic of a heavenly conversation: to the angelic welcome,

> The raptur'd babe replies,
> "Thanks to my God, who snatch'd me to the skies,
> "E'er vice triumphant had possess'd my heart,
> . . . .
> "But soon arriv'd at my celestial goal,
> "Full glories rush on my expanding soul."

Charles's "expanding soul" is a "representation of limitlessness" characteristic of the sublime, but for those he has left behind his loss is "an outrage on the imagination" that is equally an aspect of the sublime.[22] But because in Wheatley's poem he achieves his full subjectivity, deploying the speech that a twelve-month-old infant had not acquired, Charles reorders the stormy emotions raised by his death. Torn from his parents, the enraptured infant is simultaneously presented to them as a figure of Wheatley's imagination, and as "the happy subject of my song," he can speak to their grief. In the second stanza Wheatley asks the parents, "why this unavailing moan?/ . . . Say would you tear him from the realms above/ By thoughtless wishes, and preposterous love?" When the poet's reasonableness fails to comfort the heartsick parents, she asks what would happen if they tried to recall to this world "The heir of bliss?" "Methinks he answers with a smile severe,/ "Thrones and dominions cannot tempt me there." Although the voice of the child, now double-edged with the ironic power of the sublime, cannot quench their grief, their formerly animal-like moans and groans now assume the measured, fully human voices of complaint and longing.[23] Wheatley's poem opens a conversation among poet, child, and parents, which, if it will not be concluded on this side of the "purer regions of celestial light," constructs a new family relationship based upon sensibility and imagination. The power of this poem lies not in any didactic intention—the poet's attempt to teach a lesson in fact fails to contain the grief over the child's death—but in its process of dramatizing voices in a significant, if open-ended, conversation. Its process, not its content, thus encourages the appearance of a new moral-practical consciousness, a newly imagined form of life that opens out from the kinship of Eliots, Andrewses, and Barrells to a larger Atlantic, human community into which they, along with poet Phillis, are implicated.

In the process of constructing her elegiac conversations, she does not tamely suppress her Africanness beneath European forms; rather, she makes that Africanness become constitutent of a new identity, an American identity. Wheatley's elegiac strategy of speaking and giving responsive voices to those who are not there, to what the Eliot parents see in the end are "Phantoms," serves more ends than merely consoling the bereaved. By imagining the feelings of subjects enormously distant from each other, she does some of the cultural work of imperial ideology, imagining space as the grounds for the ultimate benevolent exchange of sensibility. Speaking as a survivor of the middle passage, however, she also serves the needs of her own moral-practical consciousness through a sublime transformation of outrage and grief into spaces of freedom and hope. She is herself, like little C. E., a speaking child who has been lost, "snatch'd" as she puts it, and with a ventriloquized, colonized voice, she perhaps reaches out to parents who are not there for her. Whether she is writing as a public poet or out of suppressed memory, however, Wheatley's deeply felt need to give aesthetic structure and meaning to human feeling precedes and is a necessary part of the historical formation in which her "*Afric* muse" hopes to find herself.[24] Or, as Alexander Baumgarten might have recognized, her attempt to give sensual perfection to her language served ultimately the quest of the individual in her specific diversity and richness to imagine a sustainable form of life.[25]

NOTES

1. Michael T. Gilmore, *Cambridge History of American Literature: Volume I 1590–1800*, ed. Sacvan Bercovitch (New York: Cambridge University Press, 1994), 1: 542–43, 541.

2. Paul O. Kristeller, "Modern System of the Arts," in *Essays on the History of Aesthetics*, ed. Peter Kivy (Rochester: University of Rochester Press, 1992), 62.

3. On the change in compositional norms, see Walter J. Ong, *Rhetoric, Romance, and Technology* (Ithaca: Cornell University Press, 1971), 255–83. On the modernity of the eighteenth century, see Frank Shuffelton, "The Discourse of Modernism in the Age of Jefferson," *Prospects* 15 (1990): 23–37. Also Martha Woodmansee offers a well-historicized account of the growth of the aesthetic idea in the changing eighteenth-century literary marketplace in *The Author, Art, and the Market: Rereading the History of Aesthetics* (New York: Columbia University Press, 1994).

4. Luc Ferry, *Homo Aestheticus: The Invention of Taste in the Democratic Age*, trans. Robert De Loaiza (Chicago: University of Chicago Press, 1993), 25, 246.

5. "To the PUBLICK" is quoted from Julian Mason, ed., *The Poems of Phillis Wheatley* (Chapel Hill: University of North Carolina Press, 1989), 48. Future citations from Wheatley will be from this volume and will be cited parenthetically in the text.

6. David S. Shields, "British-American Belles Lettres" in *Cambridge History of American Literature* (Cambridge: Cambridge University Press, 1994), 1: 309.

7. Cynthia J. Smith, "Phillis Wheatley's Invocation of an Idealized Reader," *Black American Literature Forum* 23 (1989): 583. On Wheatley and classical literature, see also John C. Shields, "Phillis Wheatley's Use of Classicism," *American Literature* 52 (1980): 97–111.

8. David S. Shields, "Belles Lettres," 315.

9. Elaine G. Breslaw, ed., *Records of the Tuesday Club of Annapolis, 1745–56*, (Urbana: University of Illinois Press, 1988), 7–8.

10. Quoted by Thomas McCarthy, *The Critical Theory of Jürgen Habermas* (Cambridge: MIT Press, 1978), 310.

11. See Alison Gilbert Olson, *Making the Empire Work: London and American Interest Groups, 1690–1790* (Cambridge: Harvard University Press, 1992), for an examination of the role of interest groups in maintaining connections between the imperial center and periphery.

12. See David S. Shields, *Oracles of Empire: Poetry, Politics, and Commerce in British America, 1690–1750* (Chicago: University of Chicago Press, 1990), for an authoritative description of the role of belles-lettres in the eighteenth-century British American world.

13. Jürgen Habermas, *The Structural Transformation of the Public Sphere: An Inquiry into a Category of Bourgeois Society*, trans. Thomas Burger (Cambridge: MIT Press, 1989), 51.

14. I follow Julian Mason's annotation of this poem in identifying James Bowdoin as its probable author, *The Poems of Phillis Wheatley*, 110.

15. Phillip M. Richards, "Phillis Wheatley, Americanization, the Sublime, and the Romance of America," *Style* 27 (1993): 216.

16. David S. Shields, "The Manuscript in the British American World of Print," *Proceedings of the American Antiquarian Society* 102 (1993): 404.

17. John Shields, "Phillis Wheatley's Struggle for Freedom in Her Poetry and Prose," in *The Collected Works of Phillis Wheatley*, ed. John Shields (New York: Oxford University Press, 1988), 229–70.

18. Jürgen Habermas, *Communication and the Evolution of Society*, trans. Thomas McCarthy (Boston: Beacon, 1979), 147–48.

19. Deborah Cushing, quoted in David Grimsted, "Anglo-American Racism and Phillis Wheatley's 'Sable Veil,' 'Length'nd Chain,' and 'Knitted Heart,'" in *Women in the Age of the American Revolution*, ed. Ronald Hoffman and Peter J. Albert (Charlottesville: University Press of Virginia, 1989), 389.

20. John Andrews quoted in William H. Robinson, *Phillis Wheatley: A Bio-Bibliography* (Boston: G. K. Hall, 1981), 13.

21. Gregory Rigsby, "Form and Content in Phillis Wheatley's Elegies," *CLA Journal* 19 (1975): 251–52. Rigsby lists on p. 250 six elegiac conventions used by Wheatley. For African beliefs about heaven and their survival in New England, see also William D. Piersen, *Black Yankees: The Development of an Afro-American Subculture in Eighteenth-Century New England* (Amherst: University of Massachusetts Press, 1988), 151–52.

22. Immanuel Kant, "Analytic of the Sublime," in *Critique of Judgement*, trans. James Creed Meredith (Oxford: Clarendon Press, 1928), 90–91.

23. For Wheatley's use of the sublime, see John C. Shields, "Phillis Wheatley and the Sublime," in *Critical Essays on Phillis Wheatley*, ed. William H. Robinson (Boston: G. K. Hall, 1982), 189–205; see also, Anita Silvers, "Pure Historicism and the Heritage of Hero(in)es: Who Grows in Phillis Wheatley's Garden?" *Journal of Aesthetics and Art Criticism* 51 (1993): 475–482.

24. See Norman Grabo, "And if it is art alone that structures and expresses the nature of human feeling, determining both the direction and the extent of intellectual progress, the intellectual historian is going to have to take greater account of the symbolism of artistic form than he yet has." "The Veiled Vision: The Role of Aesthetics in Early American History," in *The American Puritan Imagination*, ed. Sacvan Bercovitch (New York: Cambridge University Press, 1974), 24.

25. Ferry, *Homo Aestheticus*, 73.

"Struggling Manfully" through Henry Fielding's *Amelia:* Hysteria, Medicine, and the Novel in Eighteenth-Century England

GLEN COLBURN

Henry Fielding's modern readers have "struggl[ed] manfully" (to borrow a phrase from *Amelia*'s opening chapter) to explain how the author of two comic masterpieces such as *Joseph Andrews* and *Tom Jones* could have produced such a sentimentalized failure as *Amelia*. The critical consensus in the 1960s and 1970s was that an incoherent, near-hysterical emotionalism in *Amelia* negates or interferes with the formal achievements that make Fielding's earlier novels more satisfying.[1] Like Robert Alter, most critics were inclined to attribute the novel's "shrill hortatory tones" to the "unfortunate intellectual fashion" of "the cult of sensibility," with its preference for "mysterious and limitless penumbras of experience, vaguely apprehended," rather than "a lucid vision of familiar reality."[2] Critics since the mid-1980s, less interested in the novel's formal flaws *per se* than in the ideological implications of those flaws, have agreed with Terry Castle that the novel's "generic fluctuations" manifest significant "inconsistencies at a deeper level." Yet these later critics, struggling to decide whether *Amelia*'s inconsistencies betray reactionary or progressive tendencies, do not entirely agree about what the "disturbing oscillations in tone, peculiarities of plot and character, [and] general thematic confusion" signify.[3]

The critical reputation of *Amelia* raises important questions. Are we to dismiss the novel as a literary failure because of its melodramatic pathos, or is it an important text that should be studied for its representation of the social and political contexts in which it was produced? And if *Amelia* is an important novel, should we consider it an essentially progressive or reactionary text?

I propose to address these questions by comparing two ostensibly disparate kinds of discourse: *Amelia* and contemporaneous medical treatises about hysteria.[4] The point of such a comparison is to demonstrate that *Amelia* is a "hysterical" text in two senses. It is *about* hysteria, but it also *is* hysterical. That is, like the medical treatises it echoes, the novel succumbs discursively to the disorder that it seeks to diagnose. An examination of this discursive hysteria demonstrates that in both *Amelia* and treatises on hysteria, an ostensibly enlightened and reformist rhetoric is a vehicle for precisely those traditional, patriarchal biases we would expect the rhetoric to reject or transcend.[5] Like the medical treatises, *Amelia* is simultaneously progressive and conservative, rational and irrational; it both reaffirms traditional ideas and embraces a new ideology.[6] Though the novel is, as earlier critics have insisted, formally incoherent, its emotional excesses and self-contradictions reflect an epistemology that may indeed inform a popular "cult of sensibility," but that also is more profound than a mid-century "intellectual fashion."[7] It is the epistemology of the "new mechanical philosophy," associated with Robert Boyle and Sir Isaac Newton, and popularized in the eighteenth century by Whigs of moderate religious persuasions who dominated England's political, educational, and religious institutions.[8]

A brief examination of hysterical episodes in *Amelia* serves two purposes: it illustrates Fielding's familiarity with contemporary medical accounts (or at least with popular disseminations of their ideas), and it demonstrates that the episodes have a thematic function. The most explicit allusion to hysteria in the novel—Booth's account of Amelia's succumbing to the "Fatigues" of nursing him after he was wounded in the siege of Gibraltar—includes a diagnosis that could almost be taken verbatim from the period's medical treatises. Booth tells Miss Mathews that Amelia's exertions "added to the Uneasiness of [her] Mind, overpowered her weak Spirits, and threw her into one of the worst Disorders that can possibly attend a Woman." Amelia, Booth says, suffered from a "Disorder very common among the Ladies, and our Physicians have not agreed upon its Name. Some call it the Fever on the Spirits, some a nervous Fever, some the Vapours, and some the Hysterics."[9] Booth's description accurately reflects mid-century medical views on hysteria. Not only did physicians seldom agree about its name, but they also disagreed about its etiology, diagnosis, and prognosis.[10] At the same time, most medical texts written before 1750 agreed that "weak spirits" were the primary cause of hysteria. As Booth indicates in calling Amelia's "Distemper" a "Compilation of all Diseases together" (122), physicians also agreed that its protean nature made hysteria difficult to diagnose because its many possible physical symptoms—gastro-intestinal discomfort, choking sensations, dizziness, fever, heart palpitations, hot and cold flashes, convulsions, fainting, numbness, anatomical rigidity and distortion—imitated the symptoms of other disorders. They further agreed that the physical symptoms were accompanied by particular mental or emotional symptoms, some of which Booth may be referring to when he mentions Amelia's "violent Fits," her "almost Madness," and her barely "recover[ing] her Senses" (122): fickleness, peevishness, manic mood swings, episodes of delirious ravings or incoherent talk, and paranoia.

Hysterical reactions occur often enough in the novel to raise suspicion that they have a thematic role. Indeed, the pervasiveness of these scenes seems intended to confirm George Cheyne's claim in 1733 that hysteria has become "the English Malady."[11] Miss Mathews repeatedly indulges in emotional outbursts, and her sudden leaps from "bewitching Softness" to "Fury" (43) manifest the hysteric's tendency to oscillate wildly between opposing emotions.[12] The melancholic Mrs. Bennet-Atkinson recounts her "long ill State of Health" (303), the consequence of her first husband's dying shortly after he, too, had suffered a hysteric fit.[13] Amelia's "gentle Spirits" are repeatedly "overpowered" by "contending Passions" (23) that leave her "a lifeless Corpse" (104). Such episodes are not necessarily (or not simply) evidence that Fielding has succumbed to maudlin sentimentality in writing *Amelia*. Their frequency indicates that Fielding intends them to be evidence of a larger social disorder, which might be characterized as a cultural hysteria.

Fielding's diagnosis in *Amelia* of a hysterical society corresponds to the social vision expressed in contemporary medical treatises, and it is here that these seemingly different kinds of discourse—literary narrative and medical analysis—begin to converge. Though physicians disagreed about the exact cause of hysteria, most were inclined by mid-century to locate its origin in a weakness of nerves.[14] By extension, the analogical character of eighteenth-century scientific thinking encouraged physicians to believe that "[n]eurological chaos in the body merely mirrored the social disorder of the time."[15] Like other natural philosophies of the period, medicine had inherited from the seventeenth century a tendency to see the world as a network of isomorphisms. If, as Margaret Jacob has noted, a common theme of the period's natural philosophy was the resemblances between the "world natural" and the "world politick," a corollary theme for medical science was the resemblances between the body physical and the body social.[16]

These resemblances would have appeared particularly compelling to medical theorists of hysteria because hysteria was (and continues to be) a controversial medical category rather than a discrete disease with a definitive etiology.[17] Susan Sontag's reflections on the social significance of disease help to explain how the mystery about the origins of hysteria allowed eighteenth-century writers to apply *hysteria* metaphorically to the culture:

> The notion that a disease can be explained only by a variety of causes is precisely characteristic of thinking about diseases whose causation is not understood. And it is diseases thought to be multi-determined (that is, mysterious) that have the widest possibilities as metaphors for what is felt to be socially, or morally, wrong.[18]

It is not surprising, then, to see Edward Strother claiming in 1725 that hysteria is epidemic because of social fashions that encourage "feast[ing] Luxuriously," indolence, and "the immoderate use of" tea and coffee.[19] Similarly, George Cheyne claims in 1733 that the causes of hysteria include "Intemperance, want of due Exercise, rioting in sensual Pleasures, [and] casual excessive Evacuations of any Kind," abuses made fashionable by a society that values "continu'd Luxury and Laziness."[20] In most cases, physicians trace the increased incidence of hysteria to a general lack of nerve, that is, socially encouraged self-indulgence and unwillingness to restrain desires and passions.[21]

By mid-century, G. S. Rousseau suggests, not only had the nerve become the most important "linguistic trope . . . for philosophical and scientific analogy," but "the rhetoric of the nerve had invaded all the realms of English prose and poetry."[22] *Amelia*, like the medical treatises, therefore treats individual instances of hysteria as symptoms of a larger lack of nerve. In the opening chapter of the novel, the narrator rejects the "Invention which Superstition hath . . . attributed to Fortune": "if Men are sometimes guilty of laying improper Blame on this imaginary Being, they are altogether as apt to make her Amends by ascribing to her Honours which she as little deserves" (16). The problem, Fielding implies, is that people are willing neither to accept responsibility for the consequences of their actions nor to acknowledge that others' successes are the consequence of perseverance. They refuse to see that "Miseries" usually are the result of "quitting the Directions of Prudence, and following the blind Guidance of a predominant Passion" (16). Instead, they prefer to invoke occult forces such as "fortune" to account for their own failures and others' triumphs. Booth's character epitomizes the general problem, because his "Doctrine of the Passions" (109) allows him to believe that "every Man act[s] merely from the Force of that Passion which [is] uppermost in his Mind, and [can] do no otherwise" (32). Certainly, Booth is sometimes a victim of forces beyond his control. He is unjustly imprisoned by a corrupt justice, and his sister-in-law's fraudulent execution of Mrs.

Harris's will keeps Booth and Amelia in poveny. But Booth is equally responsible for his troubles because he believes himself unable to control his passions, even claiming that he cannot help himself because his heart is "combustible Matter" (69). In buying a coach that he cannot afford, he indulges what Dr. Harrison calls a "criminal Vanity" (165). His "love of Gaming" (36) leads him once to lose what little money he has (41) and later to go into debt more deeply than he can repay (432–33). He sometimes drinks intemperately and as a consequence acts rashly. In other words, Fielding shows that Booth's imprudent self-indulgence exacerbates his poverty and legal troubles, just as Strother and Cheyne claim that luxuries exacerbate hysteria.

Fielding's diagnosis of cultural hysteria agrees with the physicians' views not only in its identification of self-indulgence as the immediate cause, but also in its identification of pride as the original cause. Bernard Mandeville claims that hysteria persists because "Pride . . . makes the Physician . . . take up with the loose Conjectures of his own wandering Invention" and "makes [patients] in love with the Reasoning Physician, to have an Opportunity of shewing the Depth of [their] own Penetration."[23] The problem, according to Mandeville, is that the self-aggrandizing physician is too apt to give patients what they want to hear: deterministic explanations based on hermetic reasoning rather than the salutary prescription of self-restraint. Similarly, Booth's belief that "a larger Share of Misfortunes had fallen to his Lot than he merited" is "a dangerous Way of reasoning," Fielding says, because it is "liable to much Error from Partiality to ourselves; viewing our Virtues and Vices as through a Perspective, in which we turn the Glass always to our own Advantage" (31). Like Mandeville's hysterics, Booth misses the plain remedy to his plight because his pride suggests to him that he suffers unjustly through influences (the passions, fortune, fate, the malice of others) beyond his control.

Though the narrator of *Amelia* and writers of medical treatises pretend to diagnose cultural hysteria from a position outside or above that culture, these texts belong, of course, to the very culture they are diagnosing. Consequently, when *Amelia* and the medical treatises diagnose their culture as hysterical, they also implicate themselves in the disorder. Since both kinds of texts confront epistemological and moral crises that Michael McKeon has called "questions of truth" and "questions of virtue," McKeon's description of the novel as a cultural "mediator" can be applied to the period's medical treatises about hysteria: intended to "resolve . . . problems of categorial instability," each treatise "also inevitably reflects" the unstable disorder it addresses.[24] This textual "instability," which I will call discursive hysteria, arises in both the medical treatises and *Amelia* when the writers attempt to produce empirically accurate narratives that faithfully record observable, unique situations and yet also reveal an abstract, universal reality. To understand how the texts become hysterical, then, we need to examine the ways in which they determine "[w]hat kind of authority or evidence is required of narrative to permit it to signify truth to its readers."[25]

The "new science," the dominant discourse whereby eighteenth-century natural philosophers sought to signify truth, has been described by Margaret Jacob as a "synthesis of philosophy and experimental method" in which "the interaction of experiments and hypotheses produc[e] probable explanations, in the end laws of nature that [can] be applied to other phenomena, previously unexplored."[26] In the medical treatises of the period (like other texts of natural philosophy), this synthesis is labeled "history." Thomas Sydenham calls his treatise of 1682 a "short History of the Disease according to the true Phaenomena of Nature."[27] Similar claims for the presentation of "the history of diseases" can be found in John Purcell's treatise of 1702, Bernard Mandeville's treatise of 1704, and Peter Shaw's treatise of 1726.[28] But as Maurice Mandelbaum has suggested in his study of John Locke's conception of the 'historical' method," *history* is not a monolithic concept for the period. It may designate Sydenham's method, "which presumably did not seek explanations, even in the form of empirical hypotheses, but confined itself to rules of practice based on past observation," or it may derive from Boyle, "for whom 'a history' did not stand opposed to an experimental inquiry, but was a means of reaching or testing an empirical hypothesis."[29] The period's "natural histories," then, need not be simply compilations of observations. They may be carefully plotted, empirical narratives informed by an epistemological tension between two kinds of truth: observation of symptoms and hypotheses about causes.

Writers like Sydenham generally express the inductive side of this epistemological dialectic in polemical tones, with the consequence that they seem to be discounting any knowledge that does not derive directly from observation. Sydenham cites the authority of Francis Bacon for basing "a History or Description of Diseases" on observation and experience rather than relying on "every Philosophical Hypothesis that has inveigled [the medical] Writer's Mind."[30] Mandeville initially defines the empirical process as a dialectical process that balances "Experience made by the Senses" against "reasoning" about "the Causes of the Effects we find"; but then he cautions that since "no body can be sure that he is in the right, 'till after he has been convinced of the Solidity of his Reasoning by the same Experience, proving and confirming the said Reasoning with matter of Fact," we ought to have strong reservations about hypothesizing: "How little and precarious a Use at this rate Reasoning is of in Physick, if compared to the absolute Necessity of Experience."[31] Shaw warns that his readers are "not to expect any hypothetical reasoning, or solutions of phaenomena; but naked matter of science, delivered in plain and simple language," and he claims that "uncertain reasonings, and a studied style . . ., instead of instructing us in the cure of diseases, will rather teach us to harangue upon them."[32] Richard Manningham, too, claims that "a true and proper Use of our Knowledge in Philosophy, and the Animal Oeconomy, with regard to the Practice of Physic," consists in "reason[ing] on real Facts, grounded on repeated Experience and Observation; which ought never to give Way to Speculation or theory, upon any Account whatever. For, as the great Newton justly observes, whatever is not deduced from Phaenomena, is Hypothesis."[33] To judge from Manningham's language, direct experience has acquired such priority over theoretical speculation by mid-century that the very word *hypothesis* has negative connotations.

Like these physicians, Fielding polemically advocates an inductive methodology in the opening chapter of *Amelia*. Having suggested that it is an "Absurdity" to attribute "the ordinary Phenomena" of life to "Fortune" when we may account for them "by natural Means," the narrator defines the purpose of *Amelia*:

> By examining carefully the several Gradations which conduce to bring every Model to Perfection, we learn truly to know that Science in which the Model is formed: As Histories of this Kind [i.e., *Amelia*], therefore, may properly be called Models of Human Life; so by observing minutely the several Incidents which tend to the Catastrophe or Completion of the whole, and the minute Causes whence those Incidents are produced, we shall best be instructed in this most useful of all Arts, which I call the Art of Life. (17)

Though Fielding acknowledges that the ultimate goal is to uncover causes, the language here clearly privileges the inductive side of empiricism: "Histories of this Kind" are produced by the "natural Means" of "examining carefully" the "ordinary Phenomena" of life, and it is an "Absurdity" to explain consequences by reference to an occult power such as "Fortune." The passage implies that even "minute Causes" are accessible to observation. The tone is, as John Bender has astutely pointed out, that of "a scientist" recording his observations in a "laboratory."[34]

In literary terms, to quote J. Paul Hunter, "we are tempted by Fielding's subject and method to apply "'realistic' criteria" because, unlike *Joseph Andrews* and *Tom Jones*, "*Amelia* does not claim to be a comic history. Its title page makes no generic claim. But its pages claim to cope with suffering and evil."[35] Whereas the preface to *Joseph Andrews* invokes classical history as a literary model and the first two chapters of *Tom Jones* claim an authorial right to create a highly selective and overtly manipulated narrative, the opening chapter of *Amelia* claims that the subsequent narrative consists in "ordinary Phenomena" observed "minutely."[36] Even Fielding's claim to construct an "Art of Life" in *Amelia* does not clearly separate the novel as a discursive artefact from medical treatises, for the language Fielding uses to describe the purpose of his empirical "Model" echoes Mandeville's inductive prescription for "restoring the glorious Art" of medicine and Shaw's for showing "the whole art [of medicine] to better advantage."[37] The point is not that *Amelia* is "realist" fiction in the same sense that *Pamela* or *Robinson Crusoe* are, but that Fielding polemically legitimates his narrative by adopting the dominant discourse of his time—the language of empiricism.[38] If Amelia in fact contains many anti-realist elements characteristic of Fielding's earlier novels, one can still make the case that *Amelia* is an empirical narrative, because its narrative intrusions are much like the deductive reasoning physicians interject into their narratives.

Diagnosis of hysteria requires an hypothesis, because physicians must identify a cause in order to prescribe a cure even though they cannot directly observe the cause. Thus, many treatises contain defenses of deduction that are as polemical as other treatises' advocacy of induction. Purcell claims that the most inductively oriented physicians, including Sydenham, "all . . . had their Hypotheses. . . . For how possibly shall any reasonable Man judge from such and such Symptoms, the Method in Curing ought to be this or t'other, unless he has an Idea in the Causes and Manner of their Production?"[39] Edward Strother agrees with Purcell that Sydenham was mistaken in relying on experience alone and "spurn[ing] all Hypotheses: We may pretend to reject a Rationale, but then how shall we act?"[40] In other words, medical histories must be informed by a plot whereby observable symptoms are temporally connected to a cause. The empiricism of these treatises creates an uneasy balance between inductive and deductive methods, made manifest when the adamantly speculative Purcell acknowledges that "the Experimental and Practical" is "the more sure and useful part of Physick" while stressing "the indispensable necessity, as well as benefit of the Speculative, wherein chiefly the Judgment of a Physician consists."[41]

The tension between "more sure and useful" observation and "indispensible" speculation makes it impossible for even the most inductive minded physician to avoid deductive leaps that shape what he sees. Part of the problem, as Sydenham confesses in exasperation, is that the "Diagnostick" of "Hysterick Diseases . . . is very obscure, and more difficult than other Diseases that afflict Mankind," because hysteria presents a "disorderly Heap of Phaenomena," which are not only "very various, but also so irregular, that they cannot be contain'd under any uniform Type."[42] Consequently, a discrepancy arises between theory and practice. In theory, Shaw claims, "proper methods of treat[ment]" depend on "a history of the Disease" consisting of "one standard example, which takes in all the more common symptoms of the Distemper; without regarding those that may happen of an extraordinary nature"; in practice, he acknowledges, because "the several symptoms . . . are different in different subjects, we must of necessity prescribe to particular cases."[43] The ambiguous nature of hysteria forces physicians to fall back on speculation about unseen realities of physiology despite their claims for purely inductive empiricism. Thus, Sydenham acknowledges that he does not simply describe what he observes; he selectively describes "peculiar and perpetual Phaenomena apart from those which are accidental and adventitious."[44] This method amounts to an emplotment of hysteria. Sydenham creates a narrative in which "Procatar[c]tick, or external Causes of this Disease"—such as "violent Motions of the Body, or, which is much oftener, violent Perturbations of the Mind from some sudden Assault, either of Anger, or Grief, or such like Passions"—are distinguished from "internal efficient Causes," which consist in "a Confusion of Spirits" and an "unequal Distribution which is altogether contrary to the Oeconomy of Nature."[45] Mandeville, too, distinguishes "Procatarctick Causes" from the efficient cause, which is "Disorders . . . of the Chylifications" that weaken the "Animal Spirits."[46] Manningham makes a similar distinction, claiming that hysteria "proceeds from a vitiated and impoverished State of the Blood, with a Diminution of its Quantity, not affording a due Secretion of the animal Spirits in the Brain," and that this "immediate Cause . . . may be owing to innumerable antecedent Causes; such as Grief, great Sollicitude, Watchings, intense Thought and Study; taking Cold; undue and profuse Evacuations, with the like."[47] All three writers expressly and polemically subordinate hypotheses to observation in the introductions to their treatises; yet all three also construct plots for their "histories" in which the cause of hysteria is traced to an entity that can only be hypothetical: "animal spirits."

The discrepancy between inductive theory and deductive practice indicates that a primary function of the word *history* in these treatises is rhetorical. In calling their treatises "histories," physicians distinguish in theory their empirical narratives from competing narrative models such as "romance," but the two types of narratives agree in practice.[48] Physicians may disagree about the relative importance of hypotheses as opposed to observation. They may differ in the exact natures of their hypotheses.[49] They may disagree about whether the body is animated by external or internal forces.[50] But most of them concur in accepting the "new mechanical philosophy" because, as Margaret Jacob has shown, it harmonizes with their political and religious views: "The ordered, providentially guided, mathematically regulated universe of Newton gave a model for a stable and prosperous polity, ruled by the self-interest of men."[51] So strong is this tendency that even apparent anti-Newtonians, such as Mandeville and Cheyne, draw on mechanistic imagery to describe the operations of the body. Mandeville characterizes "the Soul as a skilful Artificer" and "the Organs of the Body" as "her Tools":

> for as the Body and its most minute Spirits are wholly insignificant, and cannot perform that Operation, which we call Thinking, without the Soul, more than the tools of an Artificer can do any thing without his Skill, so the Soul cannot exert herself without the Assistance of the organick Body, more than the Artificer's Skill can be put in execution without the Tools.[52]

Cheyne writes that "the Human Body is a Machine of an infinite Number and Variety of different Channels and Pipes," all governed by "the Intelligent Principle, or Soul, resid[ing] somewhere in the Brain."[53] Though they may disagree about whether external or internal forces activate the human body, most physicians conceive of the body itself through images of a machine.

Like the medical writers, Fielding characterizes his narrative as a "history," implying that *Amelia* possesses the objectivity of natural histories' simple compilations of observations. But Fielding is no more interested in mere description of individuals than are the physicians. Fielding professes a "strict Adherence to universal Truth" in his depictions of individual characters (73), just as physicians assume a universal truth about hysteria when they propose a general etiology to explain individual cases of hysteria. Both Fielding and medical writers postulate a hypothetical uniformity beneath the observed variations. In *Amelia*, as in the medical treatises, this uniformity is supplied by an assumption that human reactions are explicable in mechanistic terms.

Fielding's mechanistic hypothesis emerges in the second chapter, following the opening chapter's defense of an inductive approach to moral questions. "It will probably be objected," the narrator says of his portrait of the corrupt Justice Thrasher and London's unjust legal system, "that the small Imperfections which I am about to produce, do not lie in the Laws themselves, but in the ill Execution of them." The narrator then remarks that such a view is "no less an Absurdity, than to say of any Machine that it is excellently made, tho' incapable of performing its Functions" (11). Like the physicians, Fielding polemically advocates apparently opposing positions. In the first chapter, it is an "Absurdity" to hypothesize that human behavior is subject to invisible forces such as "Fortune." In the second, it is equally an "Absurdity" to reject the hypothesis that social conditions are explicable in mechanistic terms:[54]

> Good Laws should execute themselves in a well regulated State; at least, if the same Legislature which provides the Laws, doth not provide for the

Execution of them, they act as Graham would do, if he should form all the Parts of a Clock in the most exquisite Manner, yet put them so together that the Clock could not go. In this Case, surely we might say that there was a small Defect in the Constitution of the Clock. (19)

The passage implies a structural similarity between the behavior of human beings and the behavior of a machine, so that the individual volition Fielding celebrates in the first chapter is now diminished: injustice exists in the laws, not in the individuals who execute them, and individuals can be compelled to act justly by well-made laws. So strong is the attraction of the mechanistic hypothesis that it seems to lead Fielding into self-contradictions (an effect we will look at more closely in a moment), and the rest of the first volume of the novel is replete with descriptions that reinforce this mechanistic vision of human beings. The narrator describes Blear-Eyed Moll's mouth as a "large and long Canal, which Nature had cut from Ear to Ear" (28). He calls Miss Mathews's "large Flood of Tears" a "Vent" for her passions, adding that her iatrohydraulic ventings are "as critical Discharges of Nature, as any of those which are so called by Physicians" (42). Such descriptions imply the hypothesis that at least some of the "minute Causes" referred to in the first chapter are to be accounted for by understanding human beings as machines governed by natural laws.

If we consider the tensions between observation and hypothesis in empiricism to constitute a dialectic, then we are tempted to focus on the coherence that results from a synthesis of the opposing tendencies. This approach makes sense if we wish to assess the degree to which Fielding and the medical writers achieve their ideal of creating coherent narratives. But if we consider the tensions to constitute a dilemma, the focus shifts to the logical incoherence created at key moments in the texts by irreconcilable epistemologies. Bender, for example, claims that "Fielding is caught, intellectually and emotionally, between religious principles that seem to offer the only hope for moral responsibility in society and a skeptical, materialistic psychology that more persuasively accounts for reality."[55] Similarly, natural philosophers like Newton were caught between what Jacob calls "scientific rationalism" and "intense religious piety and millenarianism."[56] Another perspective from which to perceive the logical incoherence of these literary and medical narratives is offered by Peter Brooks: if plot is "the logic or perhaps the syntax of a certain kind of discourse, one that develops its propositions only through temporal sequence and progression," then "[t]o offer causality as the key character of plot may be to fall into the error of the *post hoc ergo propter hoc*."[57] The belief that there are causal connections between events, explicable in terms of providential laws guiding a mechanistic universe, is fundamental to the period's moral vision, yet this assumption clashes with the period's empirical ideal of writing narratives or histories that record unpoliticized, neutral observations. In order to appear coherent and truthful at the same time, then, such histories must conceal or downplay their *a priori* assumptions and pretend to be transparent recordings of observable phenomena. But the assumptions are so central to the period's notions of what is true that they cannot be contained; they surface at moments of narrative incoherence in the form of digressions, ellipses, periphrases, and other rhetorical devices. The narrators are no longer recording the truth as they see it but shaping what they (and we) see in order to make it conform to a preconceived truth. At these moments, the logic of the texts often becomes self-contradictory, their language often stridently polemical or even shrilly emotional. In short, the "bodies" of the texts become hysterical, and the ideological burden of the texts emerges at these "hysterical" moments.[58]

One major symptom of this discursive hysteria is self-contradictions, which arise from writers' attempts to conflate deductive, moral truths and inductive, physiological truths. Because hysteria was conceived of as a psychosomatic disorder, it involved physicians in speculations about the mental, emotional, and moral as well as physical states of their patients.[59] In other words, treatises about hysteria tend to blur the distinction between medical and moral inquiries, in a manner similar to Fielding's blurring of the distinctions between literary and empirical agendas in the opening chapter of *Amelia*. Mandeville, for example, prefaces his treatise with language befitting a spiritual physician when he links the Fall, disease, and the stagnation of medicine:

> When the crafty Tempter of Mankind, meditating their Ruin, attack'd our first Parents in their Pride, he shew'd himself profoundly skill'd in humane Nature; from which the Vice I named is . . . inseparable. . . . [A]s [pride] was destructive to unexperienc'd Adam, by bringing Sickness and Death upon him, so it has still continued to be no less pernicious to his forewarn'd Posterity, by principally obstructing the Progress of the glorious Art, that should teach the Recovery as well as Preservation of Health.[60]

Having begun as a spiritual physician diagnosing moral disorder, Mandeville prescribes a remedy: "the absolute Necessity of Experience."[61]

Mandeville's prefatory recommendation of empiricism, however, leads to self-contradiction. Though the preface blames the "sprightly talkative Age" for neglecting "the silent Experience of pains-taking Practioners," talk becomes therapeutic in the narrative itself.[62] As Roy Porter puts it, "Mandeville's dialogue bubbles with paradox" because the hysteric "Misomedon finally cur[es] himself—of his self-inflicted hypochondria—merely by pouring out his tale of woe to the sagely quiet Philopirio [the physician-protagonist of Mandeville's dialogue]."[63] There are other paradoxes in the treatise, most notably near its center, when Philopirio claims that disordered or weakened "animal spirits" in the nerves are the immediate cause of hysteria. Misomedon objects that since nerves are inaccessible to close observation, they may be "solid Bodies like Strings, or Cords made up of many lesser Strings," rather than the "hollow" vessels Philopirio assumes. Philopirio's rejoinder reinstates the very hypothesizing that Mandeville has rejected, even ridiculed, in the first half of the treatise: "Many things are true that admit of no Demonstration a *Priori*."[64] Though Philopirio has earlier rejected the use of figurative language, he defends his position here with similes: "We must consider the Soul as a skilful Artificer, whilst the Organs of the Body are her Tools."[65] He maintains this mechanistic view, even though he shortly thereafter reverses himself again, rejecting the belief that "all the Operations of the Body [are] mechanical." Though he believes that one cannot "undress Nature, and penetrate into the first Elements of her," the need to discern the invisible causes of hysteria leads him into speculation about those "first Elements," and it is not mere coincidence that the object he "undresses" is a "her."[66]

Once he has established his hypothesis about animal spirits through deduction, the way is prepared for Mandeville to reason analogically that women are inferior to men. He claims that women suffer from hysteria more often and more severely than do men because "Women are not of that robust Constitution as Men are," but his physiological observation immediately becomes a pretext for ostensibly objective assertions about less tangible qualities: "they are sooner offended by, and more impatient of, Heat, Cold, and other Injuries; they have not that Constancy, Resolution, and what we call Firmness of the Mind." Mandeville appears rational and unbiased in allowing that women's "Immortal Substance is without doubt the same with ours." He even appears complimentary when he allows women superiority in elegance, beauty, sensitivity, "Sprightliness of Fancy, Quickness of Thought and offhand Wit." But the conflation of a hypothesis about animal spirits with observations of female anatomy transforms woman's greater sensitivity into "less Constancy," her "Sprightliness of Fancy" into incapacity for "Assiduity of Thinking," and her "Delicacy" into "Imbecility of . . . Spirits"; this "imbecility" is in turn "conspicuous in all [women's] Actions, those of the Brain not excepted."[67]

The tension between inductive and deductive truths creates similar self-contradictions, with identical ideological implications, in the first volume of *Amelia*. In fact, the openings of the novel and Mandeville's treatise mirror each other, demonstrating how similar the two kinds of discourse can be structurally. As Fielding adopts the empirical language of science in a literary narrative to explain analytically the moral degeneration of his world, Mandeville adopts literary tropes and other narrative devices in his dialogic treatise to tell the story of medicine's decline. As Fielding proposes to substitute "minute" observation of "ordinary phenomena" for outdated theories about "fortune" in order to explain the causes of suffering, Mandeville proposes to substitue "the solid Observation of never-erring Nature" for "the witty Speculations of Hypothetical Doctors" in order to explain the causes of hysteria. Yet each confesses that simple experience and mere observation are inadequate. Mandeville acknowledges that "Nature [has] Recesses beyond the Reach of [human] Sagacity."[68] Fielding acknowledges that "nothing [is] more difficult than to lay down any fixed and certain Rules for Happiness; or indeed to judge with any Precision of the Happiness of others, from the Knowledge of external Circumstances" (161). Thus, the *Treatise* and *Amelia* confront a similar epistemological dilemma.

A significant thematic self-contradiction arises early in *Amelia* precisely because Fielding attempts to formulate "fixed and certain Rules for Happiness" in the first chapter while questioning the reliability of "the Knowledge of external Circumstances" in the narrative itself. Having discounted the occult influence of "Fortune" in human behavior, the narrator concludes in the opening chapter that "[t]o retrieve the ill Consequences of a foolish Conduct, and by struggling manfully with Distress to subdue it, is one of the noblest Efforts of Wisdom and Virtue" (16). Near the end of the novel's opening prison scenes, however, the narrator excuses "the Frailty of Mr. Booth" in succumbing to the charms of Miss Mathews on the very grounds that have been dismissed in the first chapter: "We desire . . . the good-natured and candid Reader will be pleased to weigh attentively the several unlucky Circumstances which concurred so critically, that Fortune seemed to have used her utmost Endeavours to ensnare poor Booth's Constancy" (154). To palliate Booth's guilt, the narrator invokes the "Fortune" that he has already ridiculed as a superstition.

This self-contradiction arises in conjunction with a reaffirmation of conventional gender ideals. Fielding's opening exhortation to "struggl[e] manfully with Distress" is not simply a restatement of the classical, stoic notion that virtue is primarily male.[69] The patrician ideal is given a new, apparently objective foundation when it is yoked in the opening chapter with the empirical language of the new science. But when it turns out that Booth is not "manful" enough to resist Miss Mathews's charms, the narrator falls back on a different definition of masculinity. First, the narrator confesses that he is "much more concerned for the Behaviour of [Booth], than of [Miss Mathews], not only for his Sake, but for the Sake of the best Woman in the World, whom we should be sorry to consider as yoked to a Man of no Worth or Honour."

The narrator explicitly disregards Miss Mathews's moral status, as if questions of worth and honor apply only to men and those *femmes couvertes*, their wives. Then, having invoked "Fortune" as an excuse for Booth, the narrator enumerates "the several unlucky Circumstances" conspiring against the hero:

> Let the Reader set before his Eyes a fine young Woman, in a manner a first Love, conferring Obligations, and using every Art to soften, to allure, to win, and to enflame; let him consider the Time and Place; let him remember that Mr. Booth was a young Fellow, in the highest Vigour of Life; and lastly, let him add one single Circumstance, that the Parties were alone together; and then if he will not acquit the Defendant, he must be convicted; for I have nothing more to say in his Defence. (154)

The narrator's legal defense of Booth shifts the gender of the jury. He begins with an appeal to the ungendered "Reader" and ends with an appeal to "he," as if only men will be "good-natured and candid" enough to recognize that "a young Fellow, in the highest Vigour of Life" cannot resist "a fine young Woman."

The self-contradictions and the accompanying assumptions about gender seem so obvious that one wonders how "enlightened" writers such as Fielding and Mandeville could have failed to recognize them. Certainly, Fielding could have created a Booth who remains faithful to his wife and thus could have avoided the necessity of hypothesizing about occult influences to exonerate a character with whom readers are meant to sympathize. Likewise, Mandeville could have avoided the diatribe against talkativeness and the hypothesis about animal spirits, which lead to self-contradictions in his treatise.

How, then, do we account for the writers' choices? I would suggest that the texts' hysteria is invisible to the writers (and perhaps to readers) because it arises from an analogical process of reasoning that science encourages us to consider a natural or neutral synthesis of empiricism's dialectical tensions. Robert Whytt's mid-century treatise is a particularly useful illustration of both the tensions embedded in the new science and the apparent obliviousness to the problems raised by these tensions, because Whytt's analysis of the nervous system moves dramatically away from his predecessors' writings and closer to the impersonal style and theoretical content of current medical anatomy. At the beginning of his chapter on general nervous disorders, Whytt asserts that hysteria "may arise from a fault either in [the nerves'] coats, their medullary substance, or in the brain and spinal marrow."[70] Two pages later, however, he qualifies his earlier claim, confessing that "[t]he subtility of these parts makes it often impossible for us, either before or after death, to discover, precisely, from what cause such diseases proceed"; and yet Whytt then immediately reverses himself again to claim that "how much soever we may be in the dark about the immediate causes of the diseases of the nerves, yet their effects may all be reduced to some change in that sensibility or moving power, which the nerves communicate to the different parts of the body."[71] Whytt asserts that though we cannot "precisely" identify a "fault" in the nerves as the cause, nonetheless the disorder's "effects may all be reduced to" a "change" that sounds very much like a "fault" in the nerves. What allows Whytt, like his predecessors, to claim a cause that he cannot actually verify is the analogical reasoning of the new science, which deduces that the outside mirrors the inside.[72] As Sydenham writes some eighty years before Whytt, "the inward Man" has "a [systematic] Fabrick of the Spirits" visible to "the Eye of Reason," just "as the outward Man is framed with Parts obvious to the Sense."[73]

The themes of *Amelia* are developed through a similar analogical reasoning that posits a correspondence between the "inward" or abstract and the "outward" or concrete. As I have already noted, Fielding compares the constitution to a clock in order to suggest that the laws governing the concrete object apply to the abstract concept. He relies on a similar objectification to explain Miss Mathews' emotional outbursts as "Vents" or "critical Discharges of Nature," even though he confesses uncertainty about whether they are expressions of "Sorrow or Shame; or . . . Rage" (42–43). As Whytt "reduces" hysteria to a disorder in the nerves even though he cannot explain "precisely" the connection between nerves and hysteria, so Fielding reduces the expression of emotion to the mechanistic process of venting or discharging even though he cannot say precisely what emotion causes Miss Mathews' discomfort. Fielding suggests, then, that abstractions related to human behavior are explicable in terms of the laws that govern a game or mechanism. To mid-eighteenth-century readers, trained by scientific discourse to take mechahistic metaphors for granted, Fielding's analogies would have the effect of making his reasoning seem "natural" or common-sensical—in other words, not reasoning at all, but self-evident truth.

The analogies may seem equally transparent to modern readers. As Ludmilla Jordanova has suggested, it is difficult to avoid acquiescing to science's "particular form of inferential thinking, that move[s] from visible indicators on a surface . . . to invisible traits inside the body."[74] The practical benefits of medical science seem to legitimate its methods. Moreover, modern literary criticism has institutionalized the practice of reading between the lines, making the legible text a signifier for an invisible signified. But if we take at face value Fielding's and medical writers' claims to empirical objectivity and if we suspend our tendency to explain away inconsistencies or to impose coherence on paradoxes, it becomes clear that at times the ordered, rational coherence of scientific methodology is overwhelmed by the emotional excess and chaotic particularity with which hysteria confronts it. Faced with an ineffable mystery, the methodology turns back on itself. It retreats into analogical reasoning that objectifies the body and thereby creates a causal explanation for otherwise inexplicable events.

Such objectifying analogies, whether in novels or in medical treatises, transform synecdoche into metaphor. They begin with the premise that the physical body is *part of* or *partially representative* of the individual and end in the conclusion that the physical body *is* the individual. This substitution of tropes has significant consequences for the medical treatises and *Amelia*. If the individual is identified with his or her body, then diagnosticians are more likely to equate physiological disorder in the body with moral disorder in the individual. This identification becomes almost inevitable if an empirical rejection of occult influences tends to make afflicted individuals somehow responsible for their condition. Once disease is no longer perceived as "an instrument of divine wrath," it becomes an expression of character or "a product of will," so that "judgment tends to fall on the individual rather than the society."[75] And if a disease is perceived as so epidemic that it signifies a broader cultural problem, then individuals, who are responsible for their own affliction, also become responsible for the social or moral ills the disease represents.[76]

Among the most significant consequences of this analogical reasoning for *Amelia* and the treatises is a putatively scientific reaffirmation of conventional attitudes about gender differences: what is perceived as the external, physical weakness of women becomes an internal, mental, and emotional weakness as well. Adopting what Manningham calls "the most natural and rational Method,"[77] Fielding and the physicians appear enlightened or liberal in their rejection of superstitions, such as the belief that human destiny is shaped by fortune or that women have inferior souls or that hysteria is caused by a wandering womb.[78] Nonetheless, both the medical writers and Fielding find what they consider "natural" reasons to reassert what they perceive to be women's "natural" inferiority to men.

Digressions are an important means by which writers convey their "natural" observations and, at the same time, digression is a major symptom of the discursive hysteria that arises from empiricism's dilemma. While digression allows Fielding and physicians to control their narratives, shaping observations to fit preconceptions, it also disrupts their narratives; digressions depart from the plot or topic or tone of the surrounding passages, often creating self-contradictions or recording discursively inappropriate emotions. In the first five chapters of *The English Malady*, for example, Cheyne offers empirical evidence for his hypothesis that the cause of "Disorders of the Nerves" is the "Weakness or Laxity of their Tone" brought on by "continu'd Luxury and Laziness."[79] This evidence consists in observations of the "Strength, Power and Springiness" of the "Fibres or Solids" in a healthy body; the observation that nervous disorders "happen only to the Rich, the Lazy, the Luxurious, and the Unactive"; and experiments confirming that the "Salts and Sulphurs" of "rich Foods" destroy "animal Fibres and Constitutions."[80] But Cheyne's hypothesis has a moral dimension, which becomes increasingly apparent as he warns that hysteria is a threat not only to "a strong Constitution, and firm State of Nerves" weakened by "Intemperance, want of due Exercise, rioting in sensual Pleasures, [or] casual excessive Evacuations of any Kind"; it is also a threat to the economy, which must provide "Materials for Riot, Luxury, and to provoke Excess."[81] Already, Cheyne has begun to digress from medical diagnosis to social indictment. The disruption of discursive expectations becomes even more pronounced when Cheyne launches into a digression on the decline of Western civilization. As proof of the connection between social mores and hysteria, Cheyne narrates a brief (and familiar) history of Western civilization, claiming that as the Egyptians, Greeks, and Romans

> advanced in Learning, and the Knowledge of the Sciences, and distinguished themselves from other Nations by their Politeness and Refinement, they sunk into Effeminacy, Luxury, and Diseases, and began to study Physick, to remedy those Evils which their Luxury and Laziness had brought upon them.[82]

Cheyne's wording in this digressive "history" links "Effeminacy, Luxury, and Diseases." His "history," then, becomes a pretext for condemning leisure activites that were particularly associated with women in the thought of the period: "Assemblies, Musick, Meetings, Plays, Cards, and Dice."[83]

In John Purcell's treatise, the digression in a chapter significantly titled "Mechanical Explanations of the Symptoms, and Accidents of Vapours" illustrates dramatically how the conflation of empiricist methodology and gender bias shifts the tones of a text. Explaining why women with vapours feel "the sensation of a Hard ball press'd against the outside of their Throats," Purcell begins scientifically enough:

> In the superior part of the Throat a Cartilage is situated exterior to the Gullet and Wind-pipe, from its figure representing a shield, call'd Cartilago Scutiformis or Thyroides; this makes an eminence or protuberance plain to be felt and seen in the Neck, which several Anatomists call Pommum Adami. . . .

Then the discourse suddenly shifts from mechanistic to religious imagery:

> or the Apple of Adam, from a vulgar superstitious notion, that when Adam eat the forbidden Apple it stuck in his Throat, and that God to perpetuate the memory of this his offence plac'd the like protuberance in the throats of all his posterity; which is not quite so apparent in Women, because, say they, the Crime of Eve was less; but a better reason is, because Woman being made for Beauty and Ornament, and to be, as the Scripture terms it, the Glory of mankind, such a visible protuberance in the Neck would have been unbecoming.

And then just as suddenly the style becomes "mechanical" again: "Outward of this Cartilage are situated a pair of muscles call'd Sterno-hyoide, these take their Origin from the Sternum. . . ."[84] Purcell proceeds as though the "mechanical explanation" and polite, religious digression were two parts of a coherent whole. He apparently assumes that from a "mechanical" view—that is, a modern, Newtonian view—women are "made for beauty and ornament." It seems clear that the enlightenment epistemology of eighteenth-century medicine can easily become an insidious vehicle for the period's assumptions about gender difference.

The language of Purcell's digression is discursively hysterical because, like the hysteric patient, it suffers from inexplicable and abrupt emotional shifts. Like Mandeville's prefatory allusion to the Fall and Cheyne's diatribe against luxury, Purcell's digression juxtaposes the language of science against the language of religion, the language of observable truth against the language of revealed truth. Such juxtapositions create ruptures in the bodies of texts intended to record empirical observations; they mark moments when the desire to contain hysteria by hypothesizing about its cause overcomes the desire simply to understand hysteria by observing and describing it.

If the digressions in the medical treatises betray a profound anxiety about questions of truth and virtue, then we ought to be cautious about claiming that the similar narrative gaps or incoherences in *Amelia* are merely the effects of faddish sentimentalism. These ruptures in the body of the novel mark moments of tension between Fielding's empirical recording of hysterical outbursts and his attempt to contain hysteria by explaining its causes. They also show that the novel shares eighteenth-century medicine's "enlightened" discourse and assumptions about gender.

The novel becomes hysterical when Booth describes Amelia's hysteria. His statements become fragmentary and disjointed, as if his language shares in the disorder about which he speaks: "A Disorder very common among the Ladies, and our Physicians have not agreed upon its Name." (120). Miss

Mathews's response articulates the once conventional view that hysteria is mere affectation or female peevishness: "I pity you, I pity you from my Soul. A Man had better be plagued with all the Curses of Egypt than with a vapourish Wife" (120). But Booth then responds in an apparently more liberal vein, "Pity rather that dear Creature, who, from her Love and Care of my unworthy Self, contracted a Distemper, the Horrors of which are scarce to be imagined" (120). Unlike his earlier works, in which Fielding "seems to allude to [hysteria] sceptically," as Martin Battestin points out, "the tenor of the present passage" indicates that Fielding "came to consider the distemper very real indeed."[85] Though this shift may indicate Fielding's greater sympathy for women suffering from hysteria, it is not necessarily a sign that Fielding's views on women have become less patriarchal. Each of the medical writers I have mentioned also considered hysteria "very real indeed," but they considered it real because they believed women to be inherently flawed. Booth's digression simply assumes that the "weak Spirits" of the female constitution make women prone to "almost Madness." He later betrays these assumptions when he attempts to explain his lack of "manly" resolve to Colonel James: "Pardon me, my dear Friend, these Sensations are above me, they convert me into a Woman; they drive me to Despair, to Madness" (333). Booth's apology links emotional excess and lack of self-control with "madness" and "woman," as if the close connections between those concepts can simply be assumed.

The same assumptions about natural female qualities shape digressive characterizations of women in the novel's prison scenes. For example, the narrator interrupts the story of Booth's imprisonment with a four-paragraph description of Blear-Eyed Moll. I quote but a small part:

> Her Eye (for she had but one) . . . was such, as [her] Nickname bespoke; . . . as if Nature had been careful to provide for her own Defect, it constantly looked towards her blind Side. . . . Nose she had none; . . . the Bone . . . was far beneath the Bones of her Cheeks, which rose proportionally higher than is usual. About half a dozen ebeny Teeth fortified that large and long Canal, which Nature had cut from Ear to Ear, at the Bottom of which was a Chin, preposterously short, Nature having turned up the Bottom, instead of suffering it to grow to its due Length. (27–28)

The narrator declares, "We have taken the more Pains to describe this Person for two remarkable Reasons; the one is, that this unlovely Creature was taken in the Fact with a very pretty Fellow; the other, which is more productive of a moral Lesson, is, that . . . she was one of the merriest Persons in the whole Prison" (28). In other words, the narrator admits that he has digressed in order to show all the ways that Moll "naturally" violates the ideal of womanhood; the "moral Lesson" his digression is meant to serve continues when Moll launches at Booth a "Volley of dreadful Oaths" (28). The emphasis on the agency of "Nature" implies that external ugliness naturally mirrors internal ugliness. Fielding's characterization of Moll draws on the metaphor of identity that we have seen in physicians' analogical reasoning: Moll is spiritually repulsive because she is physically so, just as (according to physicians) all women are internally weaker than men because they are externally so.[86]

In contrast to Moll, as Smallwood points out, women in other digressive or extraneous episodes—such as the pretty, innocent-looking young prostitute who "damn' d [Booth's] eyes" (33) as she passed—seem to undermine the "romantic image of womanhood in which physical and moral beauty infallibly go together."[87] The operative word is *seem*: these physically attractive women—Miss Mathews, the nameless young prostitute, Betty Careless—reaffirm one part of the "romantic image of womanhood" while they undermine the other. They are presented as moral transvestites, repugnant because they put on the stereotypically masculine behaviors of cursing, drinking, smoking, and physical violence. Thus, while these portraits deny that physical and moral beauty always accompany each other, they reinforce the romanticized equation of female modesty and delicacy with moral beauty.

The discrepancies between the outside and inside of female characters are related to a central assumption of the anti-feminist tradition, which is also reaffirmed by treatises on hysteria: the belief that women are inherently changeable or fickle; in other words, the belief that women are, like hysteria itself, protean. *Amelia* dramatizes the assumption in a digression intended to remind readers that female assertiveness and virtue are incompatible. Having recounted Miss Mathews's hysterical exultation at the news that her unfaithful lover has died from a wound she gave him, the narrator pauses:

> But before we put an End to this, it may be necessary to whisper a Word or two to the Critics, who have perhaps begun to express ... Astonishment ... that a Lady, in whom we had remarked a most extraordinary Power of displaying Softness, should the very next Moment after the Words were out of our Mouth, express Sentiments becoming the Lips of a Dalila, Jezebel, Medea, ... or any other Heroine of the tender Sex. (44)

The narrator self-consciously interrupts his narrative; he suspends the empirical description of Miss Mathews in order to answer the potential objection that the narrative is not realistic because it violates the critical dictum of conservation of character. In order to justify his narrative model, he invokes a historical list of termagants, drawing on the precedent of anti-feminist, classical tradition. But he goes further. Like a physician, he cites personal observation to give his hypothesis an empirical foundation.

As proof that the portrait of Miss Mathews is realistic, the narrator recounts having seen a woman lie "in Bed with a Rake at a Bagnio, smoking Tobacco, drinking Punch, [and] talking Obscenity" one morning, then having seen her put on an "Appearance of Modesty, Innocence and Simplicity" at the theater a few nights later (47). In order to demonstrate that a pretty young woman may "abandon" her feminine character, the narrator offers personal observation, but in doing so raises another difficulty for the narrator. Now, he must frame an excuse for his own presence at the brothel: "remember, Critic, it was in my Youth" (47). In the very act of dismantling one gender myth, the narrator reasserts the sexual double standard that allows young men to draw observations from a brothel, and he does so under the pretext of offering empirical evidence. Thus, Fielding relies on empirical methodology—like a male physician observing his hysterical female patients—to support the anti-feminist belief that women are, as Sydenham says of hysteria, "very various" and "so irregular, that they cannot be contain'd under any uniform Type" (307).

Drawing on such assumptions about the nature of and appropriate roles for women, volume 1 of *Amelia* sets up a series of gender inversions that represent the degenerate, disordered world with which characters must contend. These gender inversions become a recurrent source of conflict in the novel, providing the energy of the plot. Especially important are the inversions that involve the protagonists: Amelia is a heroine who struggles more "manfully" with distress than does Booth. To use the language of Mandeville and Cheyne, Booth lacks "manful" resolution and his self-indulgence in luxuries is "effeminate." His stereotypically "female" qualities embroil the Booths in the difficulties that occupy most of the novel. In this world turned upside down, Amelia can cope with the difficulties only by abandoning her own "natural" female qualities. Thus, Booth praises the "Magnanimity of Mind" with which Amelia bore the injury to her nose by invoking qualities that contemporaneous medical texts would have defined as masculine. He speaks of her "Dignity" and "Resignation"; he even compares her stoicism to "the firmness of Soul in a Man" (67).

The novel, then, is emplotted much like the narratives in medical treatises, in which prescription invariably follows description. Having identified the social disease as hysteria, *Amelia* then proceeds to the cure. Given the gender ideals implied by the novel, the happy resolution necessarily entails the protagonists' return to normal gender roles so that the hysterical excesses threatening both the novel and society are contained or "cured." This process of normalization begins with the scene in which Atkinson confesses his love for Amelia, where the narrator pauses momentarily for yet another digression:

> To say the Truth, without any Injury to her Chastity, that Heart which had stood firm as a Rock to all the Attacks of Title and Equipage, of Finery and Flattery, and which all the Treasures of the Universe could not have purchased, was yet a little softened by the plain, honest, modest, involuntary, delicate, heroic Passion of this poor and humble Swain; for whom, in spite of herself, she felt a momentary Tenderness and Complacence, at which Booth, if he had known it, would perhaps have been displeased. (482–83)

Castle characterizes this incident as evidence that the masquerade episode has transformed the novel's allegorical mode into more "mimetic" fiction because Amelia appears transformed from an idealized "paragon" into a more "realistic" or "mixed" character.[88] Drawing on Tony Tanner's view of the novel as a "transgressive" genre, Castle suggests that Amelia flirts here with adulterous sensations. I would argue, however, that rather than transgression, this episode marks the beginning of Amelia's return to an ideologically feminized mode of action. Her heart, which has manfully "stood firm as a Rock," is "now a little softened." She experiences "a Confusion on her Mind that she had never felt before" (483). In other words, she has started to become what a woman ought to be from a medical perspective: softened, irresolute, and confused.

Atkinson plays an important role in this episode. Fielding describes Atkinson's "passion" in the language medical writers use to describe women. The sergeant confesses his love in a moment of hysteria, "a raving delirious Fit" (480). His "modest, involuntary, delicate" love figuratively emasculates him. Since, as the narrative constantly reminds us, Atkinson belongs to the laboring classes, we would expect him, according to the claims of medical treatises, to have the strong nerves and insensibility of his social class.[89] But the language of nerves is ambiguous or flexible enough to be adapted to any apparent contradiction of the natural order, and in fact the emasculation of Atkinson allows Fielding to imply that Atkinson's love is inappropriate. Amelia's weak feminine constitution requires masculine control, and Atkinson's weak nerves make him unable to provide such control. In other words, Fielding combines assumptions about class and gender in the apparently inconsistent characterization of Atkinson to imply a larger message: Booth's resumption of control over his wife and himself is necessary to forestall the dangerous encroachment of the lower classes and to restore the paternalistic social order.

Amelia's return to gender normalcy is completed in Booth's liberation from the bailiff's house. The scene emphasizes Amelia's "tender ... Fears" and "gentle Spirits"; the Booth's happy reversal of fortunes gives "so violent a Turn ... to [Amelia's] Spirits, that she was just able, with the Assistance of a Glass of Water, to support herself" (524). In the meantime, as Amelia becomes progressively more "tender," more dependent on her husband for "support," physically weaker, and thus more conventionally feminine, Booth has become more conventionally masculine. He rejects his former belief in the irresistible power of "Ruling Passions," then colludes with Doctor Harrison in keeping from Amelia the secret of her restored estate "lest it should overpower her" (525). Booth, in other words, has acquired a "manly" resolution and authority over his wife.

Shortly after having adopted this more masculine posture, Booth exercises his authority in an episode so apparently superfluous—that is, so "hysterical"—that I can account for it only by suggesting that Fielding includes it to emphasize the control his narrative has obtained over hysterical excess, to show that the prescribed return to appropriate gender roles has effected a cure. In the penultimate chapter of the novel, Booth recommends to Amelia that they accept Atkinson's offer of twenty pounds, even though Booth already knows, as Amelia does not, that her estate has been returned to her. Amelia responds, "You know I never contradict you, ... but I assure you it is contrary to my Inclinations to take this Money," and Booth rejoins, "Well, suffer me ... to act this once contrary to your Inclinations" (526). Booth then examines her feelings about living in poverty, and her responses illustrate what she calls her "Happiness of such a Husband" and her "Humility" (527). Booth's examination of Amelia's conscience resembles the method Purcell recommends to physicians in their dealings with hysterics whose "Blood has contracted several Vices" and whose "Appetites" are "deprav'd":

> these Persons are for the most part possess'd with some Passion or deep Concern, which cannot easily be effac'd out of their Minds, and which 'tis very hard to prevail with them to own, or if they do, to discover the true cause; this a Physician ought to examine well into, and endeavour by all means possible to find out; for as long as the Mind is deeply intent upon any one thing, the Spirits are detain'd in the Brain, and for want of them the fermentation of the Blood is lessen'd.[90]

Purcell advises physicians to conceive of themselves as priestly confessors, probing their patients' minds to discover the mental or emotional source of the "vitiated" blood. In a similar manner, Fielding's digressive episode seems intended to demonstrate that Amelia and Booth have become what Fielding's contemporaries would consider the perfect woman and man. Booth imposes his will and examines his wife's conscience; she professes her submission and humility.

My argument has focused on *Amelia* because claims about "hysteria" in a narrative are more often made about the narratives to which *Amelia* is supposedly superior, narratives that often are not granted the generic status of "novel" because they seem unlike canonical novels: romances, scandal chronicles, amatory novellas and other sorts of "popular fiction" produced largely by women in the early eighteenth century. I have tried to turn the conventional claim around, to suggest ways in which the production of a male, canonical novelist is hysterical. This claim might become the pretext for a larger argument that the early English novel is inherently hysterical because the period's dominant culture gendered the categories of "hysteria" and "novel" in response to the feminization of culture. In other words, physicians and novelists created bifurcations—female hysteria/male hypochondria, female romances/male novels—that allowed them to attribute masculine qualities to the desirable effects, feminine qualities to the undesirable effects of the same elements of modern civilization: increasing luxuries, increased leisure, and the production and consumption of novels.[91]

Let me conclude by outlining this larger argument. As G. S. Rousseau has noted, the "historical transformations and representations" of hysteria manifest the disorder's "protean ability to sustain the existence of a condition called hysteria without a stable set of causes and effects or, more glaringly, a category identifiable by commonly agreed upon characteristics."[92] Eighteenth-century physicians repeatedly complain that definition is difficult not only because the disorder varies from patient to patient, but also because it possesses an imitative capacity that allows it, as Sydenham writes, to "resemble almost all the Diseases poor Mortals are inclinable to" (302). Yet physicians' reactions to hysteria are not completely negative. Cheyne is merely repeating a commonplace when he notes that those afflicted by the "Misfortune" of "weak Nerves" have "the Advantage of . . . those of strong Fibres and robust Constitutions"; the former have a greater capacity for "the innocent Enjoyments of Life," particularly "intellectual Pleasures, . . . because the Organs of these Operations being in their own Nature delicate and fine, when wafted or scrap'd, (by Chronical Diseases not mortal) and thus communicated to their Posterity, these naturally subtil Parts thus become more fine and sensible."[93] As dire as the symptoms of hysteria might be, they are also considered a sign of refined taste, intellect, and manners.

Fielding and his contemporaries reacted to the novel in ways resembling the reactions to hysteria. Like hysteria, the novel had many names and could take many forms—romance, history, autobiographical narrative, collection of letters, found manuscript, and so on. The categorical indeterminacy and imitative capacity of novels provoked mixed reactions as much as those qualities in hysteria did. Some reactions, it is true, were purely negative, as the essayist's claim in the *Monthly Review* that London is "drenched and surfeited" with "useless books," or Richard Hurd, the Bishop of Worcester's claim that novels appeal to "a vitiated, palled, and sickly imagination—that last disease of learned minds, and sure prognostic of expiring Letters."[94] Most reactions, however, were mixed. The author of "An Essay on the New Species of Writing Founded by Mr. Fielding," for example, claims that the romances preceding Fielding's "new Species" were "nothing but Chaos and Incoherency."[95] Similarly, an essay in the *Monthly Review* complains that "[t]he Genius of Romance seems to have been long since drooping among us," degenerating into "buffoonry" or "obscenity" rather than serving its more legitimate "purposes of conviction and persuasion."[96] Very often praise of novels' didactic potential accompanies condemnation of a particular novel, as in a review of *Tristram Shandy*, which asserts that Sterne's sole "design" is "showing the author's wit, humour, and learning, in an unconnected effusion of sentiments and remarks."[97] In each case, the writer adopts a view something like that of the essayist in the *Monthly Review*, who cautions, "We must copy Nature, it is true; but Nature in the most perfect and elegant form in which conception can paint her."[98] In other words, critics advise a containment of disordered "nature," as physicians advise containment of the disordered hysteric.

A second striking similarity between the protean categories of hysteria and the novel is their feminization. Hysteria was considered preeminently a disorder of upper-class women. Sydenham's view that "very few Women" escape hysteria, as well as his suggestion that the group he refers to as "Women" does not include those "accustomed to Labour," is frequently repeated throughout the first half of the eighteenth century, entrenching both the belief that women are inherently prone to hysteria and the belief that the laboring classes inherently lack the sort of refinement that Cheyne remarks in hysterics.[99] Likewise, the novel was often characterized as women's writing in both senses of production and consumption, and this gendering of the novel entailed assumptions about social class. After condemning the "Chaos and Incoherency" of romances, the author of "An Essay on the New Species of Writing" claims that Fielding "persuaded the ladies to leave this Extravagance to their Abigails. . . . Amongst which Order of People, it has ever since been observ'd to be peculiarly predominant."[100] The reviewer of *Tristram Shandy* attributes the popularity of the novel to "a sort of *fames canina*" rather than "a natural appetite" (as physicians often attribute hysteria to depraved appetites in women) and he claims that its readers range "from the stale maiden of quality to the snuff-taking chambermaid."[101] Like physicians, who make hysteria a sign of refinement that demonstrates one's privileged social status and yet also a sign of female excess, critics make the novel an entertainment for socially privileged women and yet also an object of consumption among "abigails" and "snuff-taking chambermaids."[102]

The varying definitions of and reactions to the novel have continued into the present.[103] Rousseau's description of hysteria as "protean" echoes current descriptions of the novel as a genre; though we all agree that there is such a thing as the novel, it is—like hysteria—a "category" with no "fixed content" and few "commonly agreed upon characteristics."[104] As Walter Reed asserts, "a poetics of the novel proper is a highly problematic undertaking, attempting, as it must, to systematize the antisystematic and to canonize the anticanonical."[105] Like eighteenth-century medical theorists, reacting ambivalently to hysteria, twentieth-century theorists have interpreted the novel's generic indeterminacy as both a sign of cultural decline and a sign of progress.[106]

Perhaps debates about what constitutes the novel continue because we have inherited from the "enlightened" discourse of Fielding's age an assumption that the primary criterion of any judgment ought to be naturalness. Contemporary rhetoric of all sorts, regardless of the conservatism or liberalism of the writer or speaker, manifests the degree to which our discourse is informed by an assumption that the most "natural" is best: arguments that homosexuality is "unnatural" or "natural," that mothers have a "natural" maternal instinct, or that men are "naturally" competitive. A similar kind of thinking informs arguments that canonical literary works possess an organic or unpoliticized—that is, "natural"—superiority to the productions of popular culture.[107] It may be, then, that the debates about canon are sometimes so fiercely contested because we consider the "natural" to be a scientific given even as we adopt differing views about what is natural.

NOTES

I wish to acknowledge the invaluable advice of several people who read this essay at various stages: Catherine Ingrassia, Nancy Peterson, and Layne Neeper, as well as my colleagues in a 1994 NEH Summer Seminar, and the director of that seminar, John Richetti.

1. In *Occasional Form: Henry Fielding and the Chains of Circumstance* (Baltimore: John Hopkins University Press, 1975), J. Paul Hunter suggests that the novel asks for "extreme emotional reponses . . . without giving us grounds or even excuses for doing so" (201), and he sums up the difference between *Amelia* and Fielding's earlier novels as a "diminished vision of rhetorical possibility" (193). In *Henry Fielding and theAugustan Ideal Under Stress: "Nature's Dance of Death" and other Studies* (London: Routledge and Kegan Paul, 1972), Claude Rawson labels the "emotional rhetoric" of *Amelia* "strident and unearned" (96–97). Even

Martin Battestin, Fielding's staunchest champion over the past forty years, cannot avoid lamenting, in the general introduction to *Amelia*, ed. Fredson Bowers (Middletown Conn.: Wesleyan University Press, 1983), that the novel's narrative "voice, wavering between indignation and a maudlin sentimentality, no longer inspires confidence" (xv–xvi).

2. Robert Alter, *Fielding and the Nature of the Novel* (Cambridge: Harvard University Press, 1968), 157. For other discussions of the novel's "sentimentality," see Morris Golden, *Fielding's Moral Psychology* (Amherst: University of Massachusetts Press, 1966), 87–88, and Rawson, *Henry Fielding and the Augustan Ideal under Stress*, 131.

3. Terry Castle, *Masquerade and Civilization: The Carnivalesque in Eighteenth-Century English Culture and Fiction* (Stanford: Stanford University Press, 1986), 184. Castle takes the "general discontinuities" to be "important traces of [the] atavistic or antirationalist tradition." The novel, she argues, dramatizes the period's uneasy transition from "the organic metaphysics of earlier centuries and the archaic belief in the unity and wholeness of experience" to "the new rationalist ideology" (184–87). In contrast to Castle's reading of Amelia as an essentially conservative text, Angela Smallwood argues in *Fielding and the Woman Question: The Novels of Henry Fielding and Feminist Debate 1700–1750* (New York: St. Martin's Press, 1989), chaps. 8 and 9, for a progressive reading. Questioning the "masculine ethos" conventionally ascribed to Fielding's writings, Smallwood argues that *Amelia* sympathetically invokes ideals from "the rationalist-feminist polemic which dates from the late seventeenth century" (2). John Bender, whose position resembles Smallwood's, claims in *Imagining the Penitentiary: Fiction and the Architecture of Mind in Eighteenth-Century England* (Chicago: University of Chicago Press, 1987) that "the splits and contradictions that have preoccupied critics of *Amelia* since its original publication" are "symptoms of the novel's situation on the threshold of reformist discourse"; thus Bender, too, tends to read *Amelia* as an essentially progressive text in which "traditional ideas . . . remain superficially intact while undergoing sharp revision through restatement in the dominant discourse of empiricism" (181, 187).

4. The comparison of the period's novelistic and medical discourse is not unprecedented. In "Hypochondria and Hysteria," *The Eighteenth Century* 25 (1984): 141–74, John Mullan explores the connections between sentimentalism and medical descriptions of hysteria. Mullan also devotes a whole chapter of his *Sentiment and Sociability: The Language of Feeling in the Eighteenth Century* (Oxford: Clarendon Press, 1988) to the cultural resonances of these medical treatises' "construction of a body attuned to sentiment" and their "concentration on the gestural force of feeling," arguing that the treatises "do not merely share a vocabulary with novels of sentiment; they also represent a capacity for feeling as ambiguous in similar ways" (201). As will become evident, though I have profited a great deal from Mullan's study and I agree especially with Mullan's acute analysis of the "construction of femininity" in the medical texts, I disagree with Mullan's assertion that "discourses about nervous disorder . . . are not themselves disordered" (203). I

wish to complicate his claim that "figures of feminine susceptibility and delicacy are not invented for the purposes of any political protest or criticism" (224); and while I agree that the "ambiguous potential" of "heightened sensibility" to signify "either the defeat or the triumph of virtue" "renders difficult any attempt to relate descriptions of the body and its nervous disorders to any prevailing political or social concerns" (236), nonetheless I believe it is possible to make such a connection. More generally, I suggest that many elements of Mullan's analysis apply not only to sentimental novels, but also to the writings of distinctly non-sentimental novelists such as Fielding. In addition to Mullan's illuminating and groundbreaking work, Thomas Laqueur points out philosophical and ideological connections among "the realistic novel, the autopsy, the clinical report, and the social enquiry" (177) in his stimulating "Bodies, Details, and the Humanitarian Narrative," in *The New Cultural History*, ed. Lynn Hunt (Berkeley, Los Angeles, and London: University of California Press, 1989), 176–204.

5. My suggestion here echoes Londa Schiebinger's assessment *The Mind Has No Sex? Women in the Origins of Modern Science* (Cambridge, Mass.: Harvard University Press, 1989): "One might expect dramatic changes in the understanding of woman's place in society and nature during the tumultuous years of the scientific revolution" (8). Although her analysis of the period's anatomical studies supports Schiebinger's contention "that modern science—strident in its claims to replace the old—was curiously silent on the issue of gender" (8), I will be demonstrating that in the medical version of eighteenth-century science, there is a great deal of talk about gender.

6. Though I agree with Bender and Smallwood that the language of the novel is reformatory, I do not believe that this language undermines "traditional ideas" of gender; conversely, though I agree with Castle that the novel is reactionary, I do not believe that it betrays uneasiness about "the new rationalist ideology" (see n.3 above). Smallwood provides compelling evidence in *Fielding and the Woman Question* that Fielding may have intended his novels to reveal "relatively enlightened, liberal views on the woman question" (173), but I am pursuing a different angle, which in fact Smallwood recommends at the conclusion of her study: "[t]he way forward from here is in the direction of the blind side of Fielding's relation to contemporary ideologies of gender" (175).

7. On the connections between medical theories about hysteria and sentimentalism, see Mullan, "Hypochondria and Hysteria," *Sentiment and Sociability*, and G. S. Rousseau, "Toward a Semiotics of the Nerve: The Social History of Language in a New Key," in *Language, Self and Society: A Social History of Language*, ed. Peter Burke and Roy Porter (Oxford: Polity Press, 1991), 213–75.

8. The phrase "new mechanical philosophy" and much of what I have to say about this philosophy is taken from Margaret C. Jacob, *The Newtonians and the English Revolution, 1689–1720* (Ithaca, N.Y.: Cornell University Press, 1976), 18–19.

9. Fielding, *Amelia*, 119–20. Subsequent references, cited parenthetically in the text, are to the Wesleyan edition.

10. I follow current scholarly usage in making *hysteria* an umbrella term to signify what may have been a cluster of different but related nervous disorders designated by different names: spleen, vapors, hypochondria, hyp, febricula, hysteric fever, and so on. Certainly, as G. S. Rousseau points out, eighteenth-century writers tended to conflate the disorders: "Melancholy, madness, hysteria, hypochondria, dementia, spleen, vapors, nerves: by 1720 or 1730 all were jumbled and confused with one another as they had never been before" ("'A Strange Pathology': Hysteria in the Early Modern World, 1500–1800," 91–224 in *Hysteria Beyond Freud*, ed. Sander L. Gilman et al. [Berkeley and Los Angeles: University of California Press, 1993], 153).

11. George Cheyne, *The English Malady* (1733), with an introduction by Eric T. Carlson (Delmar, N.Y.: Scholars' Facsimiles and Reprints, 1976).

12. See also p. 59, where Miss Mathews "vented her Passions" in a harangue "full of Bitterness and Indignation," then "all at once put on a serene Countenance."

13. Though, as Booth suggests when he speaks of Amelia's disorder, physicians considered hysteria "common among the Ladies," they also agreed that a man might be susceptible to it, particularly if his profession or habits inclined him to intense study and a sedentary lifestyle. The bookish clergyman, Mr. Bennet, would then be precisely the sort of man susceptible to hysteria. Accordingly, Mrs. Bennet-Atkinson tells Amelia, after he discovered that he had contracted a venereal disease from his wife, "He entered the Room . . . Looking like a Fury . . . and with the Malice of a Madman, threw [a large book] at my Head, and knocked me down backwards. He then caught me up in his Arms, and kissed me with the most extravagant Tenderness; then . . . with his utmost Violence he threw me again on the Floor" (299). The allusion to madness and the wild emotional oscillations indicate a hysteric fit.

14. On medical controversies concerning hysteria during the eighteenth century and the gradual shift (in natural philosophy generally as well as medicine) from seventeenth-century humoral theory to early-eighteenth-century mechanistic theories and then to mid- and late-eighteenth-century materialist and vitalist theories, see Michel Foucault, *Madness and Civilization: A History of Insanity in the Age of Reason*, trans. Richard Howard (New York: Random House, 1965), 136–58; Steven Shapin, "Social Uses of Science," in *The Ferment of Knowledge: Studies in the Historiography of Eighteenth-Century Science*, ed. G. S. Rousseau and Roy Porter (Cambridge: Cambridge University Press, 1980), 93–139; G. S. Rousseau, "Mysticism and Millenarianism: 'Immortal Dr. Cheyne,'" in *Hermeticism and the Renaissance: Intellectual History and the Occult in Early Modern Europe*, ed. Ingrid Merkel and Allen G. Debus (Washington: The Folger Shakespeare Library, 1988), 192–230. For the broader philosophical context and implications of this shift, see John W. Yolton, *Thinking Matter: Materialism in Eighteenth-Century Britain* (Minneapolis: University of Minnesota Press, 1983), especially chapter 8, "The Physiology of Thinking and Acting" (153–189).

15. Rousseau, "'A Strange Pathology,'" 165. I will have more to say about this idea later in the essay.

16. In *The Newtonians and the English Revolution* Jacob writes, "Throughout the seventeenth century, thinkers of whatever philosophical or political persuasion

assumed that some sort of relationship, of varying degrees of causality or simply of intimacy, existed between the world natural and the moral and social relations prevailing or desired in the 'world politick'" (24). See also Margaret C. Jacob, *The Cultural Meaning of the Scientific Revolution* (Philadelphia: Temple University Press, 1988).

17. See Rousseau, "'A Strange Pathology.'"

18. Susan Sontag, *Illness as Metaphor* (New York: Farrar, Straus and Giroux, 1977), 60.

19. Edward Strother, *An Essay on Sickness and Health* (London, 1725), 37, 394.

20. Cheyne, *English Malady*, 16–17, 33–34.

21. As Rousseau has pointed out in "'A Strange Pathology,'" Thomas Sydenham intuited near the end of the seventeenth century that "hysteria imitates culture" (102). Though Rousseau suggests that subsequent physicians failed to follow through on Sydenham's hint, nonetheless they recognized a connection between social practices and hysteria.

22. Rousseau, "Toward a Semiotics of the Nerve," 224–25.

23. Bernard Mandeville, *A Treatise of the Hypochondriack and Hysterick Diseases. In Three Dialogues*, 3rd ed. (London, 1711), iv.

24. Michael McKeon, *The Origins of the English Novel 1600–1740* (Baltimore: Johns Hopkins University Press, 1987), 20. For the idea that hysteria is a "category" with no "fixed content," see Rousseau, "'A Strange Pathology,'" 92. I will return to this idea in the conclusion.

25. McKeon, *Origins of the English Novel*, 20. My discussions of concepts of "history," "questions of truth," and "questions of virtue" in the present essay owe a great deal to McKeon's fuller and more sophisticated analysis of the reversals and double reversals entailed in two parallel trends: the epistemological movement from romance to "naive empiricism" to "extreme skepticism" and the ideological movement from "aristocratic" to "progressive" to "conservative" morals.

26. Jacob, *Cultural Meaning*, 73, 3–4.

27. I am citing Thomas Sydenham's *An Epistolary Discourse . . . Concerning . . . Hysterick Diseases* as it appears in *The Whole Works of that Excellent Practical Physician, Dr. Thomas Sydenham*, 11th ed., translated and edited by John Pechey, M.D. (London, 1740), 301.

28. John Purcell, preface to *A Treatise of Vapours . . . Containing an Analytical Proof of its Causes, mechanical Explanations of all its symptoms and Accidents, According to the Newest and Most Rational Principles*, 2nd ed. (London, 1707), n.p.; Mandeville, *Treatise*, 292; Peter Shaw, preface to *A New Practice of Physic*, 5th ed. (London, 1738), n.p.

29. Maurice Mandelbaum, *Philosophy, Science, and Sense Perception: Historical and Critical Studies* (Baltimore: Johns Hopkins Press, 1964), 8. For discussions of Locke's and his contemporaries' conceptions of history and empirical methodology, see chap. 1 of Mandelbaum's book. Whereas Mandelbaum's purpose is to show that Locke accepted Boyle's "corpuscular hypothesis," John W. Yolton argues, in *Locke and the Compass of Human Understanding: A Selective Commentary on*

the *"Essay"* (Cambridge: Cambridge University Press, 1970), that Locke's agenda belongs more to the period's program of "compiling natural histories of bodies" than to defenses of the corpuscular hypothesis; thus, "experimental philosophy" was more important to Locke and his contemporaries than was the "mechanical philosophy" (6–7). See also pp. 4–9 and 52–65.

30. Sydenham, *The Practice of Physick*, in *The Whole Works*, vi–vii.
31. Sydenham, *Epistolary Discourse*, vi–vii.
32. Shaw, preface to *A New Practice of Physic*.
33. Sir Richard Manningham, *The Symptoms, Nature, Causes, and Cure of the Febricula, or little Fever: Commonly called the Nervous or Hysteric Fever, the Fever on the Spirits; Vapours, Hypo, or Spleen*, 2nd ed. (London, 1750), 72.
34. Bender, *Imagining the Penitentiary*, 183.
35. Hunter, *Occasional Form*, 205. Similarly, Martin Battestin comments in the Wesleyan edition of Amelia that whereas Fielding "claimed . . . to supply 'the History of the World in general,' recording timeless and universal 'Truth'" in the earlier novels, "he came to repudiate this fundamental tenet of his 'poetics'" in *Journal of a Voyage to Lisbon*, where he contrasts the "true history" of writers such as Herodotus with the "romance" of epics (73n.1).
36. In the preface to *Joseph Andrews*, Fielding is willing to accept the label *romance* for his novel, though he warns that he has "a different Idea of Romance" than "the mere English Reader may have." In other words, the label is not very important to Fielding in 1742, though he is careful to distinguish his "comic Epic-Poem in Prose" from "those voluminous Works commonly called Romances" by claiming that in *Joseph Andrews*, "everything is copied from the Book of Nature," *Joseph Andrews*, ed. Martin C. Battestin (Middletown, Conn.: Wesleyan University Press, 1967), 4–5, 10. By 1749, labels seem to have become more important. In the dedication and first chapter of *Tom Jones*, Fielding drops *romance* in favor of history. At the same time, though, he qualifies the inductive implications of *history* by claiming a right to "hash and ragoo" his subject, "Human Nature," and by warning readers, "I intend to digress, through this whole History, as often as I see Occasion," *The History of Tom Jones, A Foundling*, ed. Fredson Bowers with an introduction and commentary by Martin C. Battestin (Middletown, Conn.: Wesleyan University Press, 1975), 34, 37. By 1752, Fielding has changed not only the label for his narrative, but also, to quote Hunter, the narrator's "attitudes toward [the] action" and "the resultant tones" (*Occasional Form*, 207).
37. Mandeville, *Treatise*, v; Shaw, preface to *New Practice of Physic*.
38. I am drawing on Michel Foucault's influential notions that natural philosophy in the eighteenth century consisted in a set of discourses and that the truth of statements was determined by reference to the dominant discourses legitimated by social and political systems. For a convenient bibliography and an excellent discussion of Foucault's theories in comparison with other theories of the history of science, see the concluding section of Simon Schaffer's historiographical essay, "Natural Philosophy," in *The Ferment of Knowledge*, 55–91.
39. Purcell, *Treatise of Vapours*, 4.
40. Strother, *Essay on Sickness and Health*, 264.

41. Purcell, *Treatise of Vapours*, 4–5.
42. Sydenham, *Epistolary Discourse*, 301, 307.
43. Shaw, preface to *New Practice of Physic*.
44. Sydenham, *Epistolary Discourse*, vii.
45. Ibid., 307–8. The struggle for power between the physicians and other kinds of medical practioners, the "empiricks" as they were known in the period, no doubt accounts at least partially for this distinction between their respective provinces and abilities. See Lester S. King, *The Medical World of the Eighteenth Century* (Chicago: University of Chicago Press, 1958) and Roy Porter, *Disease, Medicine, and Society in England, 1550–1860* (London: Macmillan, 1987).
46. Mandeville, *Treatise*, 208, 132.
47. Manningham, *Symptoms, Nature, Causes, and Cure*, 54, 58.
48. In *A Mechanical Account of the Non-Naturals* (London, 1707), for example, Jeremiah Wainewright claims that a physician must "be a good Philosopher; but all the Philosophy that has yet appear'd in the World, is no better than Trifling Romance, except what hath been writ by the famous Sir Isaac Newton, and some few others" (unpaginated preface). For discussion of this opposition between "history" and "romance" in the period's thought, see McKeon, *Origins of the Novel*, part 1. On the polemical nature of scientific discourse in the period, see Larry Stewart, *The Rise of Public Science: Rhetoric, Technology, and Natural Philosophy in Newtonian Britain* (Cambridge, England: Cambridge University Press, 1992).
49. George Cheyne, for example, stridently rebuts the hypothesis of most of his predecessors and contemporaries when he claims that the nerves are solid and "the Notion of animal Spirits is of the same Leaven with the substantial Forms of Aristotle, and the caelestial System of Ptolemy" (*English Malady*, 58).
50. Many accept the view, expressed by Jeremiah Wainewright in *Mechanical Account*, that the "Humane Body is a curious Machine . . . ; but yet it is subject to the same Laws of Motion, by which the infinitely Wise God governs the Universe," and that Newtonian mathematics will elucidate those laws (unpaginated preface). Others agree with Mandeville that in "the Practice of Physick, . . . there is no Part of the Mathematicks that can be of greater Help, or give more Light in the Mysteries of it, than it can in those of reveal'd Religion," because it is an error to assert that "all the Operations of the Body [are] mechanical" (Mandeville, *Treatise*, 173, 170). In *Observations on the Nature, Causes, and Cure of those Disorders which have been commonly called Nervous, Hypochondriac, or Hysteric*, 2nd ed. (London, 1765), Robert Whytt takes a similar position, claiming that the "sympathy" between "every sensible part" and "the whole," which is central to his conception of the body and his diagnosis of hysteria, "cannot be explained upon mechanical principles" (32).
51. Jacob, *The Newtonians*, 18. I take this Newtonian vision to be one manifestation of what Michel Foucault calls the "Classical *episteme*," the belief in a natural order, the laws of which are accessible to experimental science. See *The Order of Things: An Archaeology of the Human Sciences* (New York: Random House, 1970), especially chapter 5. Needless to say, my juxtaposition of literary and medical discourse as a means of elucidating some of the period's ways of seeing has been

influenced by Foucault's "archaeological" approach and his notion that eighteenth-century natural philosophy is best understood as a set of discourses competing for dominance.

52. Mandeville, *Treatise*, 159.

53. Cheyne, *English Malady*, 3–4.

54. It seems likely that *Amelia* would be informed by a specifically Newtonian belief that providentially ordained, predictable laws animate the machine-like body, because some of the major propagandists for the "new mechanical philosophy" were latitudin arians whom Fielding quotes or alludes to approvingly: Isaac Barrow, Samuel Clarke, and John Tillotson. For the first extended argument, now widely accepted, that latitudinarianism had a profound influence on Fielding's thinking and art, see Martin Battestin, *The Moral Basis of Fielding's Art* (Middletown, Conn.: Wesleyan University Press, 1959). For the connections between Newtonian science and the latitudinarians, see Margaret Jacob, *The Newtonians*. Also important here is Yolton 's recent clarification of the issues of "materialism" and "mechanism" in eighteenthcentury religious and scientific debates. Yolton shows that—contrary to what many recent historians of science have claimed—the belief in "mechanism" or "dynamic corpuscularity" was consistent with the orthodox "immaterialism" of the period, so that the real distinction between "immaterialists" and "materialists" is that the former "defended a passive concept of matter," whereas the latter "made matter active" (*Thinking Matter*, 92). Thus, medical writers on either side of the debates—and orthodox as well as heterodox thinkers—could invoke images of the machine to characterize the human body, though they might postulate different origins for the machine's activating power.

55. Bender, *Imagining the Penitentiary*, 187.

56. Jacob, *Cultural Meaning of the Scientific Revolution*, 116.

57. Peter Brooks, *Reading for the Plot: Design and Intention in Narrative* (Cambridge, Mass.: Harvard University Press, 1992), xi, 326n.8. Brooks cites Roland Barthes and Vladimir Propp for the idea that "if plot appears to turn sequence into consequence, this may often be illusory."

58. See Pierre Macherey, *A Theory of Literary Production*, trans. Geoffrey Wall (Boston: Routledge and Kegan Paul, 1978), for the notion that "gaps" in the seamless coherence which is the classical ideal of a text betray the ideological burden of the text.

59. In Rousseau's words, hysteria is "a unique phenomenon in the entire repertoire of Western medicine because it exposes the traditional binary components of the medical model—mind/body, pathology/normalcy, health/sickness, doctor/patient—as no other condition ever has" ("'A Strange Pathology,'" 92). For a discussion of the moral overtones of treatises on hysteria, see Mullan, *Sentiment and Sociability*, 214–15. See also "Bodies, Details, and the Humanitarian Novel," in which Laqueur draws connections between the "secular mastery of the body" conveyed by scientific scrutiny and the "ameliorative action" represented by humanitarian narratives as "morally imperative" (184, 178).

60. Mandeville, *Treatise*, iii–iv.

61. Ibid., v.

62. Ibid., iv.

63. Roy Porter, "'Expressing Yourself Ill': The Language of Sickness in Georgian England," *Language, Self, and Society*, 281.

64. Mandeville, *Treatise*, 135.

65. Ibid., 159.

66. Ibid., 170–71.

67. Ibid., 246–47.

68. Ibid., v.

69. In a note to this passage in the Wesleyan edition, Battestin summarizes the stoicist origins of the sentiment (16n.2).

70. Whytt, *Observations*, 85.

71. Ibid., 87–88.

72. On the use of analogy by the period's scientists, see Mandelbaum, *Philosophy, Science, and Sense Perception*, 106–7. On its use by Locke, see Yolton, *Locke and the Compass of Human Understanding*, 17–18. Rousseau writes that in Elizabethan medical treatises, "one trope stands out over and over again: analogy. Analogy, common in the medical literature of the time, is everywhere present in th[e] construction of hysteria" ("'A Strange Pathology,'" 197n.100).

73. Sydenham, *Epistolary Discourse*, 308.

74. Ludmilla Jordanova, *Sexual Visions: Images of Gender in Science and Medicine between the Eighteenth and Twentieth Centuries* (Madison: University of Wisconsin Press, 1989), 52.

75. Sontag, *Illness as Metaphor*, 41–43.

76. This is especially true if the disease falls under the purview of psychology, as hysteria does, because as Sontag writes, "Psychological theories of illness are a powerful means of placing the blame on the ill" (*Illness as Metaphor* 57).

77. Manningham, *Symptoms, Nature, Causes, and Cure*, 49.

78. Almost every treatise mentioned in the present essay scoffs at the idea that hysteria is the result of a uterine mobility, and Mandeville explicitly rejects the notion that women's "immortal Substance" is not "the same with" men's (*Treatise*, 246). I take the ostensible enlightenment of medicine in this area to be part of the larger shift, analyzed by Thomas Laqueur, in which "[a]n anatomy and physiology incommensurability replaced a metaphysics of hierarchy in the representation of woman in relation to man," so that biological difference became the touchstone for asserting difference "in every conceivable aspect of body and soul, in every physical and moral aspect," *Making Sex: Body and Gender from the Greeks to Freud* (Cambridge, Mass.: Harvard University Press, 1990), 5–6. Especially important here is Laqueur's argument that advancements in scientific knowledge cannot be invoked to explain change from the "one-sex/flesh model to a two-sex/flesh model" (8–9), and therefore that the "remaking of the body" arose from the new "competition for power" that characterized political and social developments of the eighteenth century (11).

79. Cheyne, *English Malady*, 9.

80. Ibid., 6, 20, 30–31.

81. Ibid., 16–17, 34.

82. Ibid., 39.

83. Ibid., 36. I have profited from John Sekora's account of the complex history of attacks on luxury and his sophisticated discussion of the concept's many meanings in *Luxury: The Concept in Western Thought, Eden to Smollett* (Baltimore: Johns Hopkins University Press, 1977). Though Sekora is not interested in the connections among gender, social class, and luxury in quite the same way I am, I have found the discussion of these associations in chap. 2 extremely suggestive.

84. Purcell, *Treatise of Vapours*, 68–69.

85. Fielding, *Amelia*, 120n.1.

86. Claude Rawson points out in *Henry Fielding and the Augustan Ideal under Stress* that the portrait of Moll evinces a "charged, formulaic interplay between startling incongruity and the order it subverts"; its "uniqueness . . . resides in the intensified emphasis, in the combination of *extreme* grotesquerie with *so many* reminders of order" (80–81, Rawson's italics). I would suggest that the subversion of an external order itself reminds readers of the conceptual order in which the outside mirrors the inside.

87. Smallwood, *Fielding and the Woman Question*, 165.

88. Castle, *Masquerade and Civilization*, 236–41.

89. In his *Epistolary Discourse*, for example, Sydenham claims that "very few Women, which Sex is the half of grown People, are quite free from every Assault of this Disease, excepting those who being accustomed to labour, live hardly; yea, many Men that live sedentary Lives, and are wont to study hard, are afflicted with the same Disease" (302). Sydenham's successors repeat this idea that most upperclass women and many upper-class men are prone to hysteria, whereas the laboring classes of both sexes are free from it, so that hysteria becomes a class marker.

90. Purcell, *Treatise of Vapours*, 166–67.

91. In *Seductive Forms: Women's Amatory Fiction from 1684 to 1740* (New York: Oxford University Press, 1992), Ros Ballaster characterizes Ian Watt as "the equivalent of the eighteenth-century modern," who "appropriated feminine sensibility as the model for a new relation between the masculine subject and social order while refusing women any active shaping role in culture beyond their role as literary objects and consumers" (10).

92. Rousseau, "'A Strange Pathology,'" 92.

93. Cheyne, *English Malady*, 14–15. For excellent discussions of ambivalence in eighteenth-century reactions to hysteria, see Mullan, "Hypochondria and Hysteria," and the last chapter of Mullan's *Sentiment and Sociability*.

94. Ioan Williams, *Novel and Romance, 1700–1800* (New York: Barnes and Noble, 1970), 160, 271.

95. Ibid., 151.

96. Ibid., 240.

97. Ibid., 238.

98. Ibid., 241. This belief was given its most widely known and influential statement, of course, in Johnson's *Rambler* No. 4.

99. Sydenham, *Epistolary Discourse*, 302. In "The Body and the Mind, the Doctor and the Patient: Negotiating Hysteria," *Hysteria Beyond Freud*, 225–85, Roy

Porter writes that in "the clinical encounter between the sensitive patient and the sympathetic physician" during the eighteenth century, "[t]he ambience was elitist, and it was in principle unisex" (244), but of course definitions of hysteria were gender nonspecific *only* "in principle." As Mullan points out, "There is still a separation of male and female, a separation which allows for new forms of concentration on the woman, new ways in which she is constituted as disordered, inconstant, precarious" (*Sentiment and Sociability*, 208).

100. Williams, *Novel and Romance*, 151.

101. Ibid., 238.

102. On the "feminization" of eighteenth-century English culture and literature, see Jane Spencer, *The Rise of the Woman Novelist: From Aphra Behn to Jane Austen* (New York: Blackwell, 1986); Catherine Ingrassia, "Women Writing/Writing Women: Pope, Dulness, and 'Feminization' in the *Dunciad*," *Eighteenth-Century Life* 14 (1990): 40–58; and Linda Zionkowski, "Gray, the Marketplace, and the Masculine Poet," *Criticism* 35 (1993): 589–608.

103. The same may be said of interest in and debates about hysteria. See Helen King, "Once upon a Text: Hysteria from Hippocrates," *Hysteria Beyond Freud*, 910; and Rousseau, "'A Strange Pathology,'" 92–93.

104. Rousseau, "'A Strange Pathology,'" 92. On the "sense of the novel's lack of 'internal' rules, its resistance to the authority of traditional convention, its self-creation through the negation of other forms" as the "apprehensions of the novel's generic incoherence" (11), see McKeon's introduction to *Origins of the English Novel*. As Michelle Brandwein has pointed out in a paper read at the 1993 meeting of the Midwest American Society for Eighteenth Century Studies, "Overlapping Universes: The Novel and Empirical Science on the Rise" (a copy of which she graciously made available to me), twentieth-century critics and theorists have focused on the novel's "quality of 'incompleteness'" and "its evasion of the type of definition that is compatible with generic frameworks."

105. Walter Reed, *An Exemplary History of the Novel: The Quixotic versus the Picaresque* (Chicago: University of Chicago Press, 1981), 7.

106. See McKeon's comparison, in his introduction to *Origins of the English Novel*, of the devolutionary characterization of novels by Northrop Frye and Claude Lévi Strauss with the evolutionary characterization by Erich Auerbach and Ian Watt.

107. On the concept of the "natural" and its influence, see Jordanova, *Sexual Visions*, especially chaps. 2 and 3. In *Making Sex*, Laqueur states that in "pre-Enlightenment texts, ... sex, or the body, must be understood as the epiphenomenon, while *gender*, what we would take to be a cultural category, was primary or 'real'" (8); this historicizing of what is usually considered to be simply "natural" offers a paradigm for stepping outside the enlightenment, scientific perspective in other matters.

Figures of Female Alienation: The Use of Periphrasis in *Lettres d'une Péruvienne*

BARBARA KNAUFF

When Françoise de Graffigny's eighteenth-century "best-seller," *Lettres d'une Péruvienne* (1747), was finally republished in a widely available paperback in 1983, it was as one of the titles included in an anthology classed by its editors as "romans d'amour par lettres."[1] Though Graffigny's novel had thus made the leap from a relatively recent rediscovery known chiefly in academic circles to almost-inclusion in the canon of eighteenth-century fiction, the text's presentation and marketing primarily as a love story, suggest that marginalization continued. For while thwarted love interests are central to the story's plot, the "roman d'amour" is not the literary tradition which Graffigny evokes in her preface to *Lettres d'une Péruvienne*. Rather, the two-page "Avertissement" cites Montesquieu's *Lettres persanes* and Voltaire's *Alzire* and adopts the language not of sensibility, but of Enlightenment ideology: Eurocentric prejudice is evoked and castigated throughout this brief introduction, whereas Incan sagacity, wisdom, and philosophy are redeemed.[2]

Graffigny's preface places *Lettres d'une Péruvienne* within the context of one of the eighteenth century's most popular genres, in which the confrontation between Self and Other is particularly prominent: the imaginary voyage. Here, the traveler's encounter with a foreign culture and ideology leads him, or less frequently her, to reevaluate the home culture and his or her own beliefs, customs, and prejudices. Given the genre's critical and self-reflexive potential, it is not surprising to find the imaginary voyage widely used as an "Enlightenment tool," that is, polemically, with the goal of undermining prejudice and tradition. *Gulliver's Travels* subscribes to this spirit, as do Voltaire's writings in which voyages figure prominently (*Contes philosophiques*), and Montesquieu's *Lettres persanes*, quoted by Graffigny—to name but a few texts among possible hundreds.[3]

In order to create the effect of alienation or defamiliarization which prompts a critical reevaluation of the status quo, the imaginary voyage makes heavy use of one particular stylistic device: periphrasis. A custom or circumstance familiar to the reader is not named, but described and redefined from the point of view of the foreign culture, the Other. This device is found especially often in texts which have been classed as "reverse voyages" or "foreign spy literature," in which a foreign observer visits the culture familiar to the author and readers and reports back on it to his or her fictive compatriots. In these cases, it is commonly the linguistic obstacle faced by the traveler which prompts the use of periphrasis: since the proper noun for an unknown object or custom is not known to the visitor, a definition is supplied in its stead.

Some examples show the considerable critical and demystifying force wielded by this common figure of alienation: in the *Lettres persanes* (1721), a rosary becomes simply "des petits grains de bois,"[4] and, in a much quoted passage, the Persian Rica describes the king, the pope and the central Catholic dogmas of Trinity and transubstantiation thus:

> Le roi de France ... est un grand magicien ... il y a un autre magicien plus fort que lui, qui n'est pas moins maître de son esprit, qu'il l'est lui-même de celui des autres. Ce magicien s'appelle le pape: tantôt il lui fait croire que trois ne sont qu'un; que le pain qu'on mange n'est pas du pain, ou que le vin qu'on boit n'est pas du vin.[5]

Similarly, in Voltaire's *Lettres philosophiques* (1726–30), the Quaker with whom the narrator converses destroys the drum-rolling glory of the royal army by calling it "des meurtriers vêtus de rouge, avec un bonnet haut de deux pieds, [qui] enrôlent des Citoyens en faisant du bruit avec deux petits bâtons sur une peau d'âne bien tendu";[6] and in *L'Ingénu* (1767), the Huron visitor discovers that the Christian institution of the convent, is really "une espèce de prison où l'on tenait les filles renfermées, chose horrible, inconnue chez les Hurons."[7]

It is against this background that I would like to place a reading of the figures of defamiliarization in Graffigny's imaginary voyage, in which French society is seen through the eyes of a Peruvian princess, Zilia, who is abducted to France. Graffigny's preface, while establishing the context and an epistemological framework for her novel, has also been at least partly responsible for the text's dismissal as a mere imitation of the *Lettres persanes*, and an inferior and less philosophical one at that. Recent criticism has done much to question this view and to counter the condescension of a Sainte-Beuve,[8] both by placing Graffigny within a female literary tradition, and by questioning and redefining the very notion of literary imitation.[9]

Yet such analyses stop short of a rigorous rereading of Graffigny's stylistic devices, and Zilia's figures of alienation still suffer from a reputation of facile superficiality. Where the periphrases of Montesquieu's Rica boldly attack religion and the French state, those of Zilia defamiliarize objects of daily life, such as a mirror, a coach, a pair of scissors, or a telescope. They have been called a stock device modeled on the *Lettres persanes*, but lacking the sharp edge of Montesquieu's irony. Henri Coulet, in his study of the French novel before the Revolution, seems to have set the tone for many later critics in this regard by his categorical denial of philosophical interest in Zilia's periphrases:

> La partie "philosophique" de ces lettres, c'est-à-dire tout ce qui devrait proposer au lecteur, par les yeux de Zilia, une vision inhabituelle et critique de la civilisation, est sans grand intérêt. Montesquieu avait fait mieux . . . le fait d'être étrangère, au lieu de lui ouvrir l'esprit, rend Zilia parfois niaise et son langage périphrastique et approximatif (ce langage du bon sauvage . . .) rend impossibles la précision et la profondeur.[10]

Similarly, for Jürgen von Stackelberg, whose overall assessment of *Lettres d'une Péruvienne* is far less condescending than Coulet's, Zilia's periphrases are nevertheless "not much more than a superficiality, a common place taken from the arsenal of 'bon-sauvage' literature";[11] for Clifton Cherpack they are "not particularly original"[12]—and the list could be continued. To my knowledge, there has been only one attempt to decipher the coherence or internal logic in Graffigny's use of periphrasis, and this attempt denies, interestingly, any dimension of cultural criticism. Rather than call into question French institutions and social customs, Zilia's alienated descriptions of boats, coaches, telescopes, and the like become, for Robert Granderoute, "un hommage . . . à l'esprit inventif des Français, des Européens," an hommage which invites the reader to rediscover the ingenuity and marvelousness at the root of French culture.[13]

This view of Graffigny's figures of alienation, either as a bland and somewhat failed imitation of Montesquieu's cultural criticism or of Voltaire's irony, or as an affirmation and celebration of European civilization, deserves to be challenged. A thorough analysis of Zilia's periphrases in *Lettres d'une Péruvienne* reveals them to be central to the novel's key issues, rather than the ancillary elements of style called for by Graffigny's choice of narrative genre. In order to reassess fully the function of this figure of speech in *Lettres d'une Péruvienne*, it will be necessary to take stock of the periphrases used by Zilia, and, more importantly, to examine how they function within the fictional universe of the *Lettres d'une Péruvienne*.

As recent critics have not failed to notice, a catalog of Zilia's defamiliarizing descriptions reveals that most of her periphrases are indeed references to ordinary household or everyday objects, and not to institutions or to symbolically imbued objects such as the religious paraphernalia or uniforms demystified by Montesquieu or Voltaire. Julia Douthwaite finds that "Usbek and Rica deconstruct such highly charged objects as rosaries and the Pope; Zilia's first discoveries are common material objects, symbols of the most elementary kinds of public exchange."[14] Yet Douthwaite does not take this analysis further than to remark somewhat summarily that "Graffigny uses the same technique [periphrasis] to show the Peruvian's extreme ignorance and sexual vulnerability in French society."[15]

A closer reading reveals that Zilia's periphrases of "common objects" tend to fall into three distinct thematic groups. By seeing them in this light we can move beyond the label of banality commonly attached to Zilia's descriptions of needles, scissors, and so forth, and do justice to Graffigny's integration of figures of alienation within the framework of her novel. First, a number of periphrases describe the means of Zilia's forced confinement at the hand of her European captors. There is the "maison flottante" (40) on which she is held captive as a piece of war booty; there is the coach in which she is ferried from her port of landing in France to Paris, and which is described in great detail; and there is the convent or "maison de Vierges" (80) in which she is confined soon after her arrival in Paris, before attaining the freedom afforded by her country estate. The very terms used by Zilia in her definitions of these objects insist on their confining, limiting function. The ship's cabin, for example, becomes "un lieu plus étroit et plus incommode que n'avait jamais été ma première prison" (29); the coach is described as "une petite chambre où l'on ne peut se tenir debout sans incommodité, où il n'y a pas assez d'espace pour marcher" (57); and the only material depiction of French convents is a description of the iron grate separating visitors and residents in the parlor:" des morceaux de fer croisés, assez près l'un de l'autre, pour empêcher de sortir" (81).

A second thematic cluster of periphrases is centered on the objects used by French women both in their domestic occupations and for social functions. Such are the precious stones and jewels offered to Zilia by Déterville and worn on various parts of the body (69); such are also the needles and scissors used by Céline and Zilia in their textile work: "de petits outils d'un métal fort dur, et d'une commodité singulière. Les uns servent à composer des ouvrages que Céline m'apprend à faire; d'autres, d'une forme tranchante, servent à diviser toutes sortes d'étoffes" (70). The production of textiles and the production of text are, of course, closely related in *Lettres d'une Péruvienne*, since Zilia gives permanence to her thoughts and experiences in the first half of her narrative not by committing them to paper, but by using "quipos," or knots executed with multicolored threads. This parallel between text and textiles is reinforced by the fact that the production of both, in France, is described periphrastically by Zilia. In the very letter following her account of needles and scissors, Zilia details her apprenticeship at alphabetic writing under the guidance of a language master hired by Déterville ("un Sauvage de cette contrée"), which involves, in her description, tracing "de petites figures . . . sur une matière blanche et mince" (72).

A final class of objects described periphrastically are those which enhance or sharpen perception, both of the Other and of the Self. Such are, notably, the "espèce de canne percée" (44) which allows Zilia to scan the horizon and to see Europe for the first time, and the mirror, or the "machine qui double les objets" (55) which Zilia encounters in one of the text's key scenes, in which she is confronted, for the first time, with her own reflection.

By grouping Zilia's periphrases thus—objects of confinement, women's occupations, aids in perception—we can easily see that the choice of Zilia's periphrases is neither arbitrary nor motivated by the desire to achieve a quaint exoticism or to conform to the stylistic expectations of a public satiated with travel literature. Rather, these rhetorical devices are perfectly integrated both with Zilia's criticism of French society, and with her own psychological and intellectual evolution. Briefly, it can be said that the three classes of periphrases used by Zilia focus the reader's attention respectively on three issues which are central to the *Lettres d'une Péruvienne* and which are treated at length throughout the novel.

The first of these issues is Zilia's fate as a piece of war booty transferred from one prison or enclosure to the next, whether a ship's cabin, a Parisian apartment, a convent or a salon that she is not free to leave. Images of en/closure dominate throughout the novel and shape and limit Zilia's existence. They culminate in her mental and physical breakdown aboard Déterville's ship, where she sees herself as a being whose liberty has been so far compromised as to undermine her selfhood as an independent being. Zilia's multifaceted imprisonment in various spaces and in various social roles does not find a resolution until she becomes the owner of her country house, whose doors are all open, whose keys are handed over to her, and whose rooms and gardens are, finally, spacious enough.

What is particularly surprising about the series of periphrases used by Zilia to describe her progress from confinement to liberty is that these figures of speech seem to undermine the very notion of a progressive liberation. A casual reading of Zilia's letters gives the impression that the narrator's horizon expands as she passes from one foreign enclosure to the next. While the ships—Spanish and French—on which Zilia passes to Europe provoke only claustrophobia and mental paralysis, she describes the next leg of her journey by coach as an eye opening experience which leads to an expansion of the Self ("Les campagnes immenses . . . emportent mon âme" 58–9), and to a critical reevaluation of the past. Watching the French countryside move past the windows of the coach, Zilia does not reflect on the limitations of her present confinement, but comes to see her Peruvian past as a form of imprisonment: "J'ai goûté pendant ce voyage des plaisirs qui m'étaient inconnus. Renfermée dans le temple dès ma plus tendre enfance, je ne connaissais pas les beautés de l'univers; quel bien j'avais perdu!" (58). Similarly, the stay in a French convent prompts a comparison between convents and the Peruvian temple of the Sun in which Zilia had grown up—a comparison which is decided in favor of the convent, since it does allow its female inmates some measure of liberty: "Enfermées comme les nôtres," Zilia writes, "elles ont un avantage que l'on n'a pas dans les temples du Soleil: ici les murs ouverts en quelques endroits . . . laissent la liberté de voir et d'entretenir les gens du dehors, c'est ce qu'on appelle parloirs" (81). And yet we have seen that these new liberties are tied to spaces which are described, periphrastically, as prison houses, enclosures, or tight spaces in which one is not free to move. Subjective experience and periphrastic description diverge, and in this rift between stylistic expression and apparent content a new level of alienation emerges: Zilia's figures of defamiliarization do not merely transmit the linguistic limitations of a foreigner confronted with an unfamiliar culture, but they capture the narrator's disorientation and vacillation between two cultural worlds by permitting an internal contradiction to emerge in her discourse.

This dialectical tension between periphrastic description and apparent meaning operates even with regard to the novel's most powerful symbol of female liberty, namely Zilia's country estate, to which she retires at the story's end for a life devoted to friendship, literature, and the translation of her own letters. Though her use of periphrasis declines as the novel progresses and as her familiarity with French language and culture increases, Zilia resorts to a figure of alienation when describing the legal transfer of the property to herself: "Je vis entrer un homme vêtu de noir, qui tenait une écritoire et du papier déjà écrit; il me le présenta, et j'y plaçai mon nom où l'on voulut" (147).[16] This is the very act which, as Zilia reports elsewhere, puts her in possession of the estate and assures her "une vie indépendante" (150), yet the periphrasis' language obviously contradicts such a reading of female empowerment: Zilia still does someone else's bidding by accepting others' authority; she continues to be governed by an impersonal "on" that aptly summarizes the societal pressures bearing on her. Again, the meaning of the figure of defamiliarization (i.e., the legal act of transferral of ownership, empowering Zilia) and its manner or style diverge, creating a space in which the narrator's alienation finds expression, even at the very point in the novel where Zilia seemingly finds her place. Taken together, Zilia's periphrases describing the spaces through which she passes on the journey towards her country estate seem to subtly question the notion of progress towards Enlightenment and freedom that Zilia elaborates elsewhere in her letters.

Zilia's lack of physical and social liberty is occasioned not only by her position as a foreign prisoner in France, but even more so by her position as a woman, which brings us to the second issue central to the novel brought out by the use of periphrases. Zilia herself is more than aware of her position and lucidly analyzes the role of women in French society in several of her letters, castigating a legal system that privileges men, moral standards that are not based on equality but place women under greater constraint, and an educational system that denies women intellectual development, nurture, and freedom. The women in the social circles in which Zilia moves in France adorn salons but lack an education and the liberty to pursue their own interests, such as reading and writing, in privacy or a "room of their own." They waste their time on handiwork and other occupations which Zilia terms "puériles, toujour inutiles, et peut-être au-dessus de l'oisivieté" (142); a woman's function in French society is not that of an active participant, but that of "une figure d'ornement [qui] ne participe au tout de ce petit univers que par la représentation" (142). Zilia herself, once the process of cultural assimilation has begun, is forced into the role French society reserves for women. Richly attired by her French keepers, she is repeatedly put on show as a human exoticum in Parisian salons. Instead of knotting her quipos, she learns to do needlework, and instead of being given the liberty to read and write, she is forced to spend most of her waking hours sitting quietly next to Déterville's mother in her reception room, a constraint on her physical and intellectual freedom which she terms "un supplice" (73). From the drawing room, Zilia eventually moves to the convent, an environment in which her occupations change little and in which her intellectual isolation only increases.

It seems, then, that Zilia's admiring periphrases of needles, scissors, and precious jewelry stand in marked contrast to her severe comments on French women as mere objects of representation engaged in worthless pursuits. Rather than constituting, as Granderoute would have it, an admiring homage to such marvelous French inventions as scissors or elaborately carved precious stones, they could equally well be seen as translating Zilia's experience of bewilderment and confusion when faced with the trappings of French womanhood, thus sensitizing the reader, on a stylistic level, to the cultural criticism made explicit elsewhere in *Lettres d'une Péruvienne*. Yet this reading, in its way as simplistic as Granderoute's, fails to account for the curious stylistic parallel in the description of French women's textile work and that of alphabetic writing, which is anything but criticized in the novel. On needlework, Zilia's pronouncements seem clear-cut enough: just as women's role in French society is essentially one of representation, of reference to a signifier which is ultimately not located within themselves—such as husband, father, or even mere rank within a patriarchal society—so their productions are, in Zilia's view, devoid of significance, "childish, useless, and idle." As such, French women's needlework stands in contrast to writing, which throughout the novel is seen as a meaningful occupation unjustly withheld from Zilia in favor of feminine drawing room pursuits. Zilia's quipos, which are a kind of textile production which signifies, occupy an obvious midpoint between alphabetic writing and what Zilia perceives as mindless needlework.

However, the parallel in Zilia's figures of alienation, which are applied to writing and needlework but not to the—familiar—quipos scrambles this hierarchy of signifying systems. Despite her obvious admiration for writing and authorship, her periphrases show Zilia to be as alienated at the writing table as she is when sitting embroidering in Déterville's salon. Writing is an alien and difficult craft, access to which has to be gained through a (male) language master's mediation, or which is denied altogether when Zilia is forced to abandon "cette nouvelle et singulière étude" (72) in order to keep company with the women in the Déterville household. Though Zilia does, in the end, master this medium—the very existence of the narrative is proof of her success as a writer—and though she eventually becomes the owner of an extensive library, she never seems entirely at ease in the world of literary exchange. Periphrases emphasizing imprisonment and lack of access make a reappearance in the midst of the description of her country estate, seemingly a space of freedom and independence: Zilia's periphrasis for her estate's library evokes a plethora of books locked away in a golden cage. Zilia's library is a library of surfaces, an esthetic object, which does not offer up its—signifying—contents:

Le seul endroit où je m'arrêtais fut une assez grande chambre entourée d'un grillage d'or, légèrement travaillé, qui renfermait une infinité de livres de toutes couleurs, de toutes formes, et d'une propreté admirable. (151)

The novel's preface that frames *Lettres d'une Péruvienne* as a cross-cultural voyage contains another troubling reference to Zilia's access to literary discourse. The fictive editor lets the readers know that the collection of letters they are about to read has been translated into French by Zilia herself: this editorial comment invites us to read the novel as a voyage towards biculturalism (the ability to translate between two cultural contexts) and, as Nancy K. Miller cogently suggests, as a novel of "coming-to-writing."[17] Yet the editor continues: "Nous devons cette traduction au loisir de Zilia dans sa retraite. La complaisance qu'elle a eue de les communiquer au chevalier Déterville, et la permission qu'il obtint de les garder les a fait passer jusqu'à nous" (4). Such a reference to female authorship as primarily a leisure-time occupation readies us for the periphrastic parallel between female drawing room pursuits and writing which Zilia will draw later in the text. And finally, Zilia's lasting alienation as a writer is rendered on a stylistic level by the fact that the editor manages to describe her authorship without once putting Zilia in a subject position. In addition to the passage cited, which assigns responsibility for the text to Déterville rather than to Zilia herself, we encounter an unwieldy passive ("les premières lettres de Zilia ont été traduites par elle-même") and a reduction of the writer to a writing hand ("si la même main ne les eût écrites dans notre langue" [4]). Clearly, Zilia never participates as an equal in the literary exchange of ideas which she so admires in France.

In the final analysis, Zilia's figures of alienation underline the lack of *any* medium of meaningful expression open to women in a French cultural context. The quipos, on the contrary, emerge as such a medium not because they present a technical synthesis between writing and textile work, but precisely because they are familiar and accessible to Zilia: they constitute a complex signifying system, not vacuous and empty like French women's needlework, *and* they admit her authorship as a woman.

This overarching question of authorship and women's individual expression is closely related to the third issue brought into focus by Zilia's periphrases, which is none other than the narrator's own psychological evolution and transformation. Through her involuntary voyage, Zilia not only gains a new view of the world and of the relative merits and abuses of French and Incan society, but also of herself, and of her own place within the new world that she is forced to discover. Before her abduction, Zilia knew nothing but the confines of the Incan temple of the Sun, in which she was kept as a temple virgin, and had an absolute faith in her king and lover Aza, representative of God, of the Sun. At the voyage's end she has discovered the notion of relativity and is able to critique both European and Incan societies, just as she is able to speak both French and her native tongue, and to translate her letters from one into the other. The telescope through which Zilia perceives France for the first time is instrumental in provoking one of the first instances in which Zilia recognizes that her heliocentric view of the world is inadequate and needs to be replaced by a more relativistic model. Aboard the French ship carrying her, Zilia notices that the sailors suddenly begin to celebrate, by dancing, singing, and drinking. Believing her own sun-worship to be universal, Zilia interprets this as the sailors' way of worshipping the sun, since the revelers often looked at the sun while rejoicing. Only when using the telescope and seeing their destination, France, does she realize "que sa vue était l'unique objet des réjouissances que j'ai prises pour un sacrifice au Soleil" (44). Though this discovery does not solve all of Zilia's cultural misunderstandings, it is the first serious blow to her absolutist world view. There is perhaps, if we adopt a Freudian reading, some ironic poignancy in the fact that the instrument which undermines one of the patriarchal ideologies present in the novel, is described as "une espèce de canne pércee" (44). Be this as it may, Zilia's alienating periphrasis certainly lends emphasis, stylistically, to this first moment of skepticism and confused doubt.

Zilia's confrontation with "la machine qui double les objets" (55) underscores, above all, the protagonist's psychological evolution and the erosion of the categories of Self and Other in the face of the cross-cultural encounter. She describes her first view of the mirror thus:

> J'ai vu dans l'enfoncement une jeune personne habillée comme une Vierge du Soleil; j'ai couru à elle les bras ouverts. Quelle surprise . . . de ne trouver qu'une résistance impénétrable où je voyais une figure humaine se mouvoir dans un espace fort étendu . . . Déterville m'a fait remarquer sa propre figure à côté de celle qui occupait toute mon attention: je le touchais, je lui parlais, et je le voyais en même temps fort près et fort loin de moi. (49-50)

It is in France that Zilia sees herself for the first time, and the important mirror scene[18] emphasizes that her voyage is, to a large extent, a voyage towards and an encounter with herself. The complex periphrasis allows Graffigny here to develop and to detail the process of self-distancing which is triggered by the encounter with the mirror. Zilia's description, which tries to define the optical effect of the looking glass without naming it, freely mixes both first (je, moi) and third person references (une jeune personne, une figure humaine), thus syntactically mirroring the optical doubling. The Self, seen from this new, alienated vantage point is seen as Other, from the outside, and described as such. Zilia's insistence on surfaces—both the impenetrable surface of the mirror, and the costume of the mirrored Self ("habillée comme une Vierge du Soleil")—further stresses the mirror's alienating effect: her description of herself not as a Virgin of the Sun, but as someone *dressed* as such, marks the first instance where Zilia mentions, with regard to herself, the chasm between "être" and "paraître" so prominent in her criticism of Spanish and French duplicity and deceit elsewhere in the novel.

The mirror destabilizes not only the narrator's view of the Self, but creates spatial confusion and demands a revision of the relationship between Self and Others. Interestingly, Déterville, who in the passages surrounding the mirror scene is consistently referred to with the honorific attribute "le Cacique," is here reduced to his proper name, and to a function as a mere spatial marker whose presence helps Zilia regain control over space. What matters about Déterville is nothing but his (spatial) relationship to the viewing subject, while it is her own reflection that commands Zilia's entire attention. It is consequently not surprising to find, at the end of the passage cited, as conclusion to the entire periphrasis the focal word "moi," which identifies the Self as such and signals the end of alienation both thematically and stylistically. Clearly, in the case of the telescope and especially the looking glass, Zilia's periphrases add to the novel's psychological dimension a degree of depth that far transcends the use of periphrasis for the sake of ironic cultural criticism alone.

A systematic reading of the three thematic clusters of figures of defamiliarization used by Zilia shows that, rather than imitating a stock device to put an exotic yet familiar veneer on *Lettres d'une Péruvienne*, Graffigny integrates periphrases into her text in a unique manner, subverting and reappropriating a device which had become commonplace in Enlightenment travel literature. Unlike, or at least to a far greater degree than, any of her predecessors in the imaginary voyage tradition, Graffigny exploits the device in order to further an in-depth psychological analysis of the narrator-traveler. Zilia's periphrastic descriptions center the reader's attention on some of the novel's most important issues, and thus have a unifying effect; yet they also allow Graffigny to introduce a level of ambiguity in Zilia's discourse and to undercut what is often seen as this imaginary voyage's Enlightenment stance, i.e., Zilia's journey towards freedom, independence, intellectual liberty, and self-expression. Though admittedly less biting when cited as isolated "bon mots," Zilia's figures of alienation, when seen within the context of *Lettres d'une Péruvienne* are no less "original" or polemical than Rica's or the Ingénu's. The main difference remains the fact that they reflect a *woman's* encounter with eighteenth-century France. Their choice is directly determined by *her* experiences of enclosure and confinement, of intellectual deprivation, and of her socialization as a figure of representation in a patriarchal society.

But our reading of periphrases in *Lettres d'une Péruvienne* yields more than an analysis of the functioning of a given figure of speech in a given text. It might also serve as an example elucidating the stylistic compromises struck by eighteenth-century women writers who dared, as did Graffigny, to invoke an almost exclusively male literary tradition, such as the imaginary voyage. We have seen that Graffigny embraces the stylistic repertoire associated with the genre, but that she freely adapts it as well: the role of periphrases in *Lettres d'une Péruvienne* is reminiscent of its occurrence in texts such as *Lettres persanes*, yet its use is qualitatively very different, creating a new level of psychological depth and introducing a measure of disorientation into the novel's philosophical trajectory—a disorientation which ultimately stems from Zilia's position as a woman.

Does the permutation of the stylistic arsenal at her disposal offer Graffigny a way out of the woman writer's dilemma? Zilia's letters on the inequality of women's position in French society, and Graffigny's own correspondence clearly show that Graffigny was more than aware of the gender gap prevailing in mid-eighteenth-century France. As a woman and salon hostess, Graffigny could not without ridicule or the reproach of transgression adopt the authorial position of her male contemporaries; she could not write a philosophical novel. The "roman d'amour par lettres," on the other hand—intimate, conversational, seemingly penned as a leisure-time occupation—was a genre accessible to the woman writer. In this regard, Zilia's enduring alienation from authorship perfectly mirrors the limitations of Graffigny's own authorial role. Stylistically at least, *Lettres d'une Péruvienne* is not easily accommodated by this gendered model of genre, since Zilia's periphrases are not quite those of a philosophical novel, yet they clearly move the novel's focus away from the love interest. Many of the critical reactions to *Lettres d'une Péruvienne* seem so unsatisfactory precisely because they ignore the novel's hybrid nature, pegging it as either a love story, or as an—inferior—philosophical novel. It might be an overstatement to claim that Graffigny's unusual use of periphrases in *Lettres d'une Péruvienne* carves out a novel space for her which allows her to skirt the issue of genre. Yet any reading of the text informed by a stylistic analysis needs to recognize that the novel's uncommon periphrases are shaped by the pressures of a gendered model of genre, and that, figures of alienation in more than one sense, they reflect both Zilia's alienation as a woman traveler, and Graffigny's position as a woman writer in eighteenth-century France.

NOTES

1. Bernard Bray and Isabelle Landy-Houillon, intro. to *Lettres portugaises, Lettres d'une Péruvienne et autres romans d'amour par lettres* (Paris: Garnier Flammarion, 1983).
2. Françoise de Graffigny, *Lettres d'une Péruvienne* (New York: MLA, 1993), 3–5. Future references to *Lettres d'une Péruvienne* pertain to this edition and will be cited parenthetically in the text.
3. See Philip Babcock Gove, *The Imaginary Voyage in Prose Fiction: A History of its Criticism and a Guide for its Study, with an Annotated Check List of 215 Imaginary Voyages from 1700 to 1800* (New York: Columbia University Press, 1941) for an account of the genre's proliferation during the eighteenth century.
4. Montesquieu, *Lettres persanes*, Coll. Folio (Paris: Gallimard, 1973), 103.
5. Ibid., 91–92.
6. Voltaire, *Lettres philosophiques* (Paris: Garnier, 1988), 6–7.
7. Voltaire, "L'Ingénu," in *Romans et Contes* (Paris: Garnier Flammarion, 1966), 341.
8. Sainte-Beuve mentions the novel as *Lettres péruviennes* [sic] in one of his *Causeries*, conferring a judgment of "[un] de ces ouvrages plus ou moins agréables à leur moment, et aujourd'hui tout à fait passés" (*Causeries du lundi*, vol. 2 [Paris: Garnier, 1850], 208).
9. Nancy K. Miller reads the novel as a reflection on female coming-to-writing and sees it as filiated to *La Princesse de Clèves* (*Subject to Change* [New York: Columbia University Press, 1988], 125–61). See Janet Altman, "Making Room for 'Peru': Graffigny's Novel Reconsidered," in *Dilemmes du roman: Essays in Honor of Georges May*, ed. Catherine Lafarge (Saratoga, Calif.: Anma Libri, 1990), 33–46, for a revision of the notion of "imitation" in the context of *Lettres d'une Péruvienne*.
10. Henri Coulet, *Le roman jusqu'à la Révolution*, 2 vols. (Paris: Armand Colin, 1967), 1: 383.
11. "Nicht viel mehr als eine Äußerlichkeit, ein Gemeinplatz aus dem Arsenal der Bon-sauvage-Literatur," Jürgen von Stackelberg, "Die Kritik an der Zivilisationsgesellschaft aus der Sicht einer 'guten Wilden': Mme de Grafigny und ihre *Lettres d'une Péruvienne*," in *Die französische Autorin vom Mittelalter bis zur Gegenwart*, ed. Renate Baader and Dietmar Fricke (Wiesbaden: Akademische Verlagsgesellschaft Athenaion, 1979), 136.
12. Clifton Cherpack, *Logos in Mythos: Ideas and Early French Narrative* (Lexington: French Forum, 1983), 148.
13. Robert Granderoute, "Comment peut-on être péruvienne? Ou *Les lettres d'une Péruvienne* de Madame de Grafigny," in *Regard de/sur l'étranger au XVIIIe siècle*, ed. J. Mondot (Bordeaux: Presses universitaires de Bordeaux, 1985), 41. "Un hommage est ici rendu à l'esprit inventif des Français, des Européens... C'est en même temps inciter le lecteur à redécouvrir ce que l'objet devenu quotidien peut avoir de réellement merveilleux."

14. Julia Douthwaite, *Exotic Women* (Philadelphia: University of Pennsylvania Press, 1992), 115.

15. Ibid.

16. While not commenting on its periphrastic nature, Nancy K. Miller also underlines the ambivalent implications of this passage (*Subject to Change*, 151), in the context of her discussion of female authorship in *Lettres d'une Péruvienne*.

17. Miller, *Subject to Change*, 147 and passim.

18. The mirror scene was perceived as central by eighteenth-century readers. Many illustrations depict Zilia facing her image for the first time; and Goldoni, in his adaptation, assigns a large part to the scene as well. See Janet Altman, "Graffigny's Epistemology and the Emergence of Third-World Ideology," in *Writing the Female Voice: Essays on Epistolary Literature*, ed. Elizabeth Goldsmith (Boston: Northeastern University Press, 1989), 172–202.

Wieland and Wezel: Divergent Trends within the German Enlightenment

FRANZ A. BIRGEL

Like most eighteenth-century satirists, Christoph Martin Wieland and Johann Karl Wezel believed in the pedagogical or formative function of their writings and hoped that by focusing on the discrepancies between the real and the ideal, their works would contribute to the betterment of humanity. In addition to ridiculing human frailties, their political satires attack social inequalities and injustices. Although both Wieland and Wezel expose the aristocracy's capriciousness and preoccupation with luxuries as manifestations of selfishness and extreme egotism, they reject revolutions and retreats into Rousseauistic idylls as answers to social and political problems, hoping instead that reforms will come from above, from absolute rulers who will let themselves be guided by reason and wise advisers. In spite of these similarities, the two authors possessed different temperaments, philosophies, and views of aesthetics that caused them to diverge in their representation of reality and brought their brief friendship to an end. As recorded in their published works and correspondence, the relationship between Wieland and Wezel can be understood as a literary feud which sheds some light on two opposing intellectual movements within eighteenth-century German literature and evokes a sense of the German Enlightenment's essential multidimensionality. With his optimism, faith in human progress, and belief in the sympathetic bond of humanity, Wieland emerges as an idealist, while Wezel, influenced by Locke and La Mettrie, rejects the dominant Leibnizean world view and possesses a more realistic albeit pessimistic outlook. Whereas Wieland's moderate, conciliatory, and playful satires with their gentle irony are in the tradition of Horace and exhibit the golden mean of German Classicism, Wezel made use of aggressive criticism in the tradition of Juvenal, resorting to black humor and caricature because he saw and depicted more flaws and vices in the human race than Wieland did.

Wieland and Wezel are prime examples of how changing historical, intellectual, and political circumstances affect the reception of an author. The popularity of both writers reached a high point during the 1770s and declined around 1800. Having survived the attacks of the *Göttinger Hainbündler* and the *Stürmer und Dränger*, Wieland's reputation was to suffer from the negative image perpetrated by the German Romantics and from the nationalism evident in much of nineteenth-century literary scholarship. Nevertheless, Wieland remained part of the canon, and a Wieland renaissance began after World War II. Wezel, one of the most popular novelists of the late Enlightenment, had been virtually forgotten for almost two hundred years or at best relegated to a few sentences in literary histories. His decline can be ascribed to the fact that he was a Swiftian satirist whose radical skepticism and occasionally grotesque depictions provoked his readers. It must also be noted that satire has only recently received the attention which had been afforded more sublime genres such as the *Bildungsroman*. The renewed interest in Wezel is due in part to the shift in political views after the 1960s, but also to the efforts of scholars in the former German Democratic Republic. Because he was a materialist, harsh social critic, and agnostic, Wezel was often in conflict with the censors. As such, his writings are conducive to Marxist analyses of class struggle, and he is a prime example of a neglected writer who has been rediscovered under the cultural policies of the GDR. In other words, the cultural framework or dominant ideology played a significant role behind the reception of the two authors.

In discussing Wieland's role as mentor of the younger Wezel, earlier and present-day scholars employ the same tactic of playing one author off against the other. Previous literary historians were clearly on the side of Wieland. In 1900 Carl Schüddekopf calls Wieland "ein wahrer Erzieher der jungeren Generation" and praises Wieland's letters to Wezel as "diese ehrenvolle Zeugnisse Wielandischer Gesinnung."[1] The current vindication of Wezel from injustices done to him by his contemporaries and nineteenth-century literary historians has brought about a vilification of Wieland. Wolfgang Jansen writes in 1980 that if one tries to view the relationship from Wezel's perspective, then Wieland's "Wohlwollen [wird] zu einer sublimen, unertraglichen Arroganz und Intoleranz."[2] In 1984 Albert R. Schmitt perceives Wieland as an established author who took out his own frustrations on younger writers who were to feel his wrath and almost incomprehensible injustice.[3] The following summary of the relationship between the two authors will attempt to show that because of their opposing world views, Wieland did indeed lose his patience with Wezel and did not treat the younger writer fairly, but also that Wezel got his revenge on several occasions.

As a young aspiring writer, Wezel wrote his first letter to Wieland on November 6, 1773, apparently after having read the *Vorrede* to the first edition of *Der Teutsche Merkur* (published January 1773) in which Wieland invites established as well as younger writers to contribute to the journal.[4] In his letter, Wezel confesses his earnest need for a mentor, now that his former teachers Giseke and Gellert have died. He encloses a writing sample, presumably one of the short works in his *Satirische Erzählungen*, and mentions that volume one of his *Tobias Knaut* and another work have already been published.[5] In his response of December 18, 1773, Wieland offers Wezel a reading list of writers from whom he could learn how to write: Lucian, Horace, Juvenal, Boileau, and Pope as well as all the newer authors of French and English novels and comedies; yet he warns him to read the latter "cum grano salis und mit Vorsicht . . .; denn die meisten schildem nur Profile und oft bey falschem Lichte."[6] Wieland does not state to what extent a writer of comedies and satires may oversimplify and exaggerate in order to present his case, but he does warn Wezel to beware of one-sided presentations which result in crude simplifications and caricature. He advises Wezel to wait for the proper mood and then write down everything. Later, when the passion has cooled, he is to rewrite everything a hundred times until it is perfect so that he can not only win the loud applause of the world but also the softer but more flattering applause of people of taste. Already this first letter by Wieland gives some indications of why he would later reject *Belphegor*: the problem of caricature and the importance of an elegant style.

The exchange of letters continued until May 25, 1777. In these letters Wieland initially offers the younger writer encouragement, advice, and constructive criticism. Along with the reviews of Wezel's works which appeared in *Der Teutsche Merkur* between 1774 and 1780, these letters document the tension which developed between the two writers. Beginning with the first review of *Tobias Knaut*, Wieland attempted to write balanced, conciliatory reviews. Since Wieland had taken Wezel under his wing, he tried to be gentle with him at the beginning. The first serious disagreement came after the publication of Wezel's tragedy, *Der Graf von Wickham*, in 1774. Wieland writes: "Warum, warum per omnes deos deasque, fragten Sie mich nicht lieber, eh sie es drucken liessen? . . . Alles, was ich einstweilen für Sie thun kan, ist dafür zu sorgen, daß Sie im teutschen Merkur so glimpflich als möglich ist, behandelt werden."[7] The review which appeared states: "Der Verfasser von

Knauts Leben wollte die Zahl unsrer bürgerlichen Trauerspiele vermehren, und hat in der That die Zahl derer vom zweyten Range vermehrt durch sein Stück."[8] The letter and the review had their desired effect: Wezel never wrote another tragedy. A later review by Christian Heinrich Schmidt of performances by the Ackermann Troupe on the Hamburger Schaubühne lists *Clavigo, Götz von Berlichingen* and *Der Graf von Wickham* as the most important new works.[9] For some strange reason, Schmidt's report ends right where a discussion of Wezel's play should begin. According to Albert R. Schmitt, this is the passage "wo Wieland mit 'Unparteylichkeit' die Schere ansetzte."[10] To be fair to Wieland, the apparent deletion was justified because the preceding pages consist of a rather tedious listing of which actors played which roles and how well they performed them.

In the third edition of the *Merkur* (March 1773), Wieland comments that the journal intends to give reasonable and impartial reviews: "vernünftig, unparteyisch und bescheiden zu urteilen,"[11] repeating the guidelines in the introduction to the first edition, according to which literary works will be reviewed: "Nur gute Schriftsteller verdienen eine scharfe Beurtheilung, denn ihnen ist alles, bis auf die Fehler selbst, merkwürdig und unterrichtend. . . . Unser Tadel wird daher ofter den Ton des Zweifels, der sich zu belehren sucht, als den herrischen Ton der Unfehlbarkeit haben, die ihre Richtersprüche wie Orakel von sich giebt."[12] Wieland states further that he and his reviewers prefer to notice the beauty of a work instead of the flaws, yet they will not shy away from commenting on them. Although Wieland himself only reviewed volumes 1 and 2 of *Tobias Knaut* in the *Merkur*, Wezel correctly assumed that the later evaluations of his writings by the journal's other contributors reflected Wieland's personal views. As editor, Wieland influenced the book review sections by determining which works would be included, choosing the critics, editing and revising or even rejecting reviews, adding postscripts or footnotes as disclaimers, and also by instructing the reviewers what they should write.

At the end of 1775, Wieland dismissed Schmidt entirely and, at Goethe's suggestion, placed Johann Heinrich Merck in charge of writing and editing reviews for the *Merkur*. In a letter dated January 5, 1776, he gives Merck a free hand and states that he will not interfere with his critical evaluations. Wieland mentions only Gebler in Vienna and Wezel in Berlin as the two authors whom he owes "lehnherrlichen Schirm und Schutz,"[13] presumably because he needed them as allies in their respective cities. Three weeks later, Wieland asks Merck to review volume four of Wezel's *Tobias Knaut*, the final and only volume in which any real action takes place and in which the protagonist finally begins to speak.[14] In his review, Merck comments that Wezel may have finally realized that the reader of a novel expects a narrative. Merck goes on to criticize the current fashion of imitating Laurence Sterne by rambling on and giving opinions,[15] arguing that the narrator should disappear completely behind the narrative and no digressions should be permitted. He basically gives a thumbnail definition of the novel when he concludes: "Eigentlich soll der Roman nichts anders seyn als Nachbildung des gesellschaftlichen Lebens, und besonders der Sittenmasse der Zeit, worinn der V[erfasser] schreibt."[16] Merck's review must have evoked an ambivalent reaction on the part of Wezel since it appeared in the same issue of the *Merkur* (March 1776) as the third installment of his *Ehestandsgeschichte des Herrn Philip Peter Marks*. In a letter to Merck, Wieland refers to *Peter Marks* as an "erbauliche Matrimonialgeschichte—ein herrlich Fressen für den größeren Haufen unserer Tischgänger."[17] (As an educator, Wieland aspired to elevate the tastes of his readers, but as a publisher, he also knew that he had to meet their demand for lighter and more amusing reading matter if they were to continue subscribing to the journal.)

The final blow came with Merck's review of *Belphegor*, Wezel's most pessimistic work, which has as its motto *bellum omnia contra omnes* and satirizes the Enlightenment's optimistic belief in the perfectibility of man, the power of reason, and the goodness of the Creator. By May 1776, Merck had grown tired of reviewing works for the *Merkur* because he considered few books worth the effort,[18] but Wieland encouraged him to stay on as the journal's chief reviewer.[19] Wieland agrees with a suggestion Merck made in a letter apparently no longer extant that more emphasis be placed on praise in the reviews. However, Wieland advises him that the journal occasionally needs an execution to satisfy the readers: "weil das l[iebe] Publikum von Zeit zu Zeit gerne jemand hängen oder köpfen sieht; secundo, weil wir uns dadurch im Besitz unserer hohen Gerichtsbarkeit halten. Und eben müßen solche Executionen selten, ne in tyrannidem degeneret imperium. aber wenn sie geschehen, desto feyerlicher und exemplarischer seyn."[20] Wezel's *Belphegor* was to be the first work sacrificed in the *Merkur*'s arena. Wieland writes Merck that within sixteen days he wants a review of this "verdammtes Zeug, die dummste Composition der Welt."[21] Wieland assumed the role of judge, and Merck that of willing executioner. Given Merck's dismissive attitude toward satires, he would have written a negative review without Wieland's admonition. In a letter from July 22, 1776, Wieland chastises Wezel for having wasted his talents on writing such a pessimistic and misanthropic novel: "Was zum Henker ist Sie nun wieder angekommen, diesen neuen Frevel an der armen Menschheit zu begehen, diesen verwünschten *Belphegor*, ... es ist beynahe kein wahres Wort an Ihrer ganzen Menschenfeindlichen Theorie; und Sie haben aus der Menschl[ichen] Natur und der Geschichte der Menschheit ein so verzogenes, verschobenes, affentheurliches und

Raupengheurliches Unding gemacht, daß unser Herr Gott gewiß seine Arbeit in Ihren Gemählden nicht erkennen wird." He advises him that the *Merkur* will take him to task for this. Wieland urges him to become "weise," to follow his true vocation to become Germany's Fielding, and to acquire "gute Laune ... statt böser."[22] The letter closes with both expressions of affection and the threat of banishment from the literary scene if he doesn't change: "Adieu, lieber Wezel! behalten Sie mich lieb, und lassen Sichs wohl seyn, und schreiben bald etwas te dignum, oder beym Anubis! ich werde Sie in die Poetische Acht und Aberacht erklären."[23]

Like Wieland, Merck was more inclined to a harmonious view of reality, and he argues in the review that the novel is not only false but also poorly written. If *Belphegor*'s premise that "Neid" and "Vorzugssucht" (envy and egotism) were truly the motivating forces behind all human actions, then better examples and more artistic depictions would have made the argument more convincing. Coming from an optimistic Leibnizean or Wolffean perspective, Merck claims that every negative action in the world evokes a positive counteraction to create a balance. He finds no irony in the novel nor variation in its mechanical structure.[24] After having received the review, Wieland wrote to Merck: "Über den Belphegor haben Sie aus meiner Seele geurteilt. ... junge Sünder sollen sich bessern oder gehangen werden!"[25] Wezel responded to the review with a lost but apparently very angry letter in which he accuses Wieland of having written the review. In response, Wieland denies this and expresses his confidence in the reviewer without mentioning Merck by name.[26] Although the review had caused the final break between Wieland and Wezel, the *Merkur* continued to review Wezel's later works rather positively, and in a letter to Bertuch, Wieland reportedly refers to Wezel 's *Herrmann und Ulrike* (1780) as "den besten deutschen Roman, der ihm jemals vor Augen kam."[27]

It was around this time that Wezel sought to vent some of his anger and gain some public satisfaction by satirizing Wieland in a farce entitled "Fragment eines Schauspiels: Der blinde Apollo. Geschrieben fur das Jahr 1776." This short work attacks the patronage system and contemporary writers, in particular those of the *Geniebewegung*. In the play, Apollo tries to teach these writers some manners, but they beat him up and throw so much sand in his eyes that they blind him, hence the title. The final scene presents a masquerade in which Wezel lampoons Wieland, Johann Georg Jacobi, the Storm and Stress geniuses, and presumably Goethe (the latter in the guise of Horribilicribrifax). Wieland appears as Nugatormagnus, the great fool, whose appearance is described as "eine Maske, von unten auf in eine schwarze devote Kleidung gehüllt, eine Larve mit der verbuhltesten Miene vor dem Gesicht und einem ausgebreiteten Flügel an jeder Seite des Kopfs, schreitet stolz einher, indem zwei kleine, mit einem leichten Gewand bedeckte Mädchen ihm einen Altar vortragen."[28] (The "verbuhlteste Miene" refers to Wieland's *Comische Erzählungen* and the "Flügel" to *Der Teutsche Merkur*.) Nugatormagnus considers himself to be the greatest *Kerl* in Germany, compared to whom all other writers are merely scoundrels: "Ich bin denn nun doch wohl der größte Kerl in Deutschland: die andern Schriftsteller sind nur Schurken gegen mich. Auch da der Horribilicribrifax ist ein Scheißkerl: aber man muß ihn loben; er macht so närrisches Zeug, daß er vermuthlich einen großen Anhang kriegen wird."[29] Wezel's satisfaction, however, was not immediate since the satire did not appear until 1780 in Dyk's *Taschenbuch für Dichter und Dichterfreunde*.

Wezel revenged himself on Wieland for the *Belphegor* review with his article on Wieland's *Oberon* which was published in 1781 in Dyk's *Neue Bibliothek der schönen Wissenschaften und der freyen Künste*, one year after the verse epic had appeared. The smooth verse forms of which Wieland had been so proud are relegated by Wezel to a position of secondary significance. Wezel argues that the more prose writing develops, the more the talent for writing verses declines in importance. He sets up a typological classification in which he contrasts his works with those of the older, more established poet: the realist bases his characters, situations, and plot on the real present-day world or on past events, whereas the idealist raises himself above reality, rejects the course of nature and human events, imparts his characters with virtues and vices which no mortal ever possessed, places his characters in situations which happen nowhere on earth, and lets no event occur through natural causes. The realist uses his perceptions as a model for his imagination, but the idealist ignores the laws of cause and effect and creates implausible characters. Applying laws of physics to poetic creations, he applies an inappropriate standard to judging the *Feenmärchen*. He goes on to focus on his many misgivings about the epic: the use of the fantastic or the machinery of supernatural beings, the double plot, the cause of the catastrophe, trivial motifs, and the depiction of erotic situations. He even goes so far as to promote his own novel by inviting the reader to compare Wieland's depiction of love-making with that in his novel *Herrmann und Ulrike*, in which he describes the inner conflicts before the protagonists unwittingly yield to their desires. Wezel ends the review with a warning to those who may want to imitate Wieland's *Oberon*, stating that it does not deserve to be imitated.[30] Wezel is obviously settling the score here.[31]

There is, however, some evidence which suggests that Wieland and Weimar had already been satirized by Wezel during the summer or fall of 1775, that is, before the disagreement over *Belphegor*. The rococo library in Weimar may have served as the model for "Sylvans Bibliothek oder Die gelehrten

Abenteuer," a short satirical story based on Swift's "The Battle of the Books."[32] More significant, however, are the numerous satiric echoes of Wieland which can be found in *Belphegor*. The novel's idylls parody similar communities in *Der goldene Spiegel* and *Geschichte des weisen Danischmend* (although it should not be forgotten that Wieland also satirizes the attempts to return to a patriarchal Rousseauistic utopia in the "Republik des Diogenes" section of his *Sokrates Mainomenos oder die Dialogen des Diogenes von Sinope*). Wezel's criticism of Alexander the Great as a "Menschenwürger" and blood-thirsty leader of a band of robbers can be understood as a comment on Diogenes' respect for him (in *Sokrates Mainomenos*), and Zaninny, the black woman, can be seen as a counterpart to Democritus' Black Venus in *Die Abderiten*. Medardus, the Lutheran minister in *Belphegor*, strongly resembles not only Wieland, but also his true Christian as he is characterized in the *Sympathien*. This kind-hearted optimist and believer in Divine Providence who repeatedly states "die Vorsicht lebt noch" was obviously based on Voltaire's Dr. Pangloss, but the similarities between Medardus and Wieland cannot be ignored: both were Lutherans with many children, and both enjoyed domestic bliss and their wine.[33] Although Wieland was no longer a naive optimist during the 1770s as he had been in the early 1750s when he wrote the *Sympathien*, Wieland undoubtedly recognized himself in Medardus. He obviously must have felt insulted and betrayed, yet there exists no documented evidence to indicate this. Having repeatedly experienced that he was being misunderstood and misrepresented, Wezel's satire on his former world view came at a time when he had had his fill.

Although the satiric jabs directed at Wieland and his ideals provide ample evidence for speculating that he may have wanted to get even with the younger writer for mocking him in *Belphegor*, the actual cause for the break between Wieland and Wezel transcended personal feelings. It lies in the individual aesthetic and world views of the two authors and was foreshadowed in Wieland's earlier rejection of Swift, Rousseau[34] and Voltaire.[35] When Wieland admonished Wezel to become a German Fielding—something Wezel eventually did with *Herrmann und Ulrike*—he meant that Wezel should work in the tradition of Fielding's "comic Romance"[36] in prose. With *Belphegor*, however, Wezel wrote what Fielding calls a prose "Burlesque," a genre which the English novelist compares to a "*Caricatura*" in painting. According to Fielding, "in the *Caricatura* [and by implication, in the burlesque] we allow all License. Its Aim is to exhibit Monsters, not Men; and all distortions and Exaggerations whatever are within its proper Province."[37] With his use of black humor and the depiction of grotesque situations, Wezel violated the rules of decorum and sinned against what Wieland believed to be the Beautiful, True, and Good. In addition, the negative image of humanity which Wezel presents in *Belphegor* is stripped of all ideal attributes, and being determined mainly by "Neid" and "Vorzugssucht" as well as external forces, humans have no possibility of striving toward perfectibility. From Wieland's point of view, *Belphegor* was a "Frevel an der armen Menschheit" because it ignored the sympathetic bond which he believed united all people. Wieland was unable to recognize that the process of satiric negation as employed by Swift and Wezel, even in the depiction of the most corrupt worlds, also expresses, albeit indirectly, an author's hope that the readers may be reformed.

Unable to maintain the "gute Laune" which Wieland had urged him to acquire and being less timid than his predecessors, Wezel chose an aggressive satiric mode of expression and caricature because he considered them the appropriate literary styles in this imperfect world. Wieland, on the other hand, attempted during much of his life to view everything, as he states in a 1769 letter to Sophie La Roche, "im mildesten Lichte, in einer Art von Helldunkel oder Mondlicht, welches mir viele Fehler verbirgt oder die Schönheiten rührender macht."[38] Wieland's optimistic belief in the progress of the Enlightenment determined the moderate, playful narrative style of his satires, yet this did not prevent him from having the *Merkur* counter bitter satires with equally bitter reviews.

The conflict between Wieland and Wezel reveals that the German Enlightenment was not the stereotypical or monolithic "Age of Reason" and illustrates that the ideals of progress and human perfectibility were not shared by all authors of the period. In this sense, Wezel represents the left wing and Wieland the right wing of the German Enlightenment. With his uncompromisingly harsh social criticism, Wezel is closer to the Storm and Stress movement and can be considered as a forerunner of the tradition running from Büchner to Brecht.

In Act 3 of *Der gestiefelte Kater*, Ludwig Tieck presents an appropriate image for the two authors under consideration. The king and the princess are taking a ride through the countryside and stop the coach. The monarch then climbs a tree to look at the neighboring lands:

> KÖNIG: Ich liebe in der schönen Natur die freien Aussichten.
> PRINZESSIN: Sieht man weit?
> KÖNIG: O ja, und wenn mir die fatalen Berge hier nicht vor der Nase ständen, so würde ich noch weiter sehn. —O weh! der Baum ist voller Raupen. (Er steigt wieder hinunter.)
> PRINZESSIN: Das macht, es ist eine Natur, die noch nicht idealisiert ist, die Phantasie muß sie erst veredeln.
> KÖNIG: Ich wollte, du könntest mir mit der Phantasie die Raupen abnehmen.[39]

While Wezel saw the caterpillars and wrote about them, Wieland removed them with his imagination. Needless to say, both approaches are valid for an author, and depending on the readers' horizons of expectations, they will prefer one over the other.

NOTES

1. Carl Schüddekopf, "Klassische Findlinge," in *Freundesgaben für Carl August Hugo Burkhardt zum siebzigsten Geburtstag*, ed. Paul F. W. Bojanowski (Weimar: H. Böhlaus Nachfolger, 1900), 91, 108.
2. Wolfgang Jansen, *Das Groteske in der deutschen Literatur der Spätaufklärung. Ein Versuch über das Erzählwerk Johann Karl Wezels* (Bonn: Bouvier, 1980), 18.
3. Albert R. Schmitt, "Wieland und Johann Benjamin Michaelis: Die 'Pastor-Amor'-Affäre," *MLN* 99, no. 3 (Apr. 1984): 608.
4. *Der Teutsche Merkur* 1, no. 1 (Jan. 1773): iv–v. The journal will hereafter be abbreviated as *TM*.
5. Christoph Martin Wieland, *Wielands Briefwechsel*, vol. 5, ed. Hans Werner Seiffert (Berlin: Akademie, 1983), 178–79.
6. Ibid., 208.
7. Ibid., 310–11.
8. *TM* 8, no. 2 (Nov. 1774): 190. Most contemporary reviewers of *Der Graf von Wickham* shared Wieland's opinion. Schubart's review, *Deutsche Chronik* 66 (Nov. 14, 1774): 526, constitutes an exception to the prevalent opinions: "Der Stoff ist der schönste tragische Stoff, den man finden kann. . . . Kurz, dieses Trauerspiel verdient eben den Beyfall der Nation, den Miß Sara Samson [sic] erhielt."
9. *TM* 2nd qr. (June) 1775: 271.
10. Albert R. Schmitt, "Wezel und Wieland," in *Christoph Martin Wieland: North American Scholarly Contributions on the Occasion of the 250th Anniversary of His Birth. 1983*, ed. Hansjörg Schelle (Tübingen: Niemeyer, 1984), 257.
11. *TM* 1, no. 3 (Mar. 1773): 285.
12. *TM* 1, no. 1 (Jan. 1773): xii.
13. *Wielands Briefwechsel*, 5: 460.
14. Ibid., 465.
15. *TM* 1st qr. (Mar.) 1776: 272.
16. Ibid. It is ironic that Wezel believed he was doing just that in *Tobias Knaut*. In the "Vorrede" to the longer version of volume two he writes that the novel contains "Gemählde und Begebenheiten des gewöhnlichen menschlichen Lebens." *Lebensgeschichte Tobias Knauts, des Weisen, sonst der Stammler genannt* (1773–1776; facsim. reprint, ed. Victor Lange, Stuttgart: Metzler, 1971), 4: 53*.
17. *Wielands Briefwechsel*, 5: 483.
18. Ibid., 500.

19. Ibid., 505.
20. Ibid., 510.
21. Ibid., 519.
22. Ibid., 529
23. Ibid., 530.
24. *TM* 3rd qr. (July) 1776: 79–81.
25. *Wielands Briefwechsel*, 5: 531.
26. Ibid., 544.
27. Quoted by Schuddekopf, "Klassische Findlinge," 106.
28. Wezel, "Fragment eines Schauspiels: Der blinde Apollo. Geschrieben fur das Jahr 1776," in *Taschenbuch für Dichter und Dichterfreunde* 11 (Leipzig: Dyk,1780): 76. See also "Anmerkungen" in Wezel, *Kritische Schriften*, a collection of facsimile reprints edited by Albert R. Schmitt (Stuttgart: Metzler, 1971), 2: 780–82.
29. Wezel, "Fragment eines Schauspiels," 79.
30. *Neue Bibliothek der schönen Wissenschaften und der freyen Künste* 25, no. 2 (1781): 230–73, a facsimile reprint in Wezel, *Kritische Schriften*, 2: 560–603.
31. In his *Kakerlak oder die Geschichte eines Rosenkreuzers aus dem vorigen Jahrhundert* (1784), Wezel continues the feud by showing that he too can write a *Feenmärchen* which integrates two mutually dependent plot lines. Several scenes in this satirical novel, especially the episode in Constantinople, can be interpreted as travesties of Oberon. See Phillip S. McKnight, *The Novels of Johann Karl Wezel: Satire, Realism and Social Criticism in Late Eighteenth Century Literature* (Bern, Frankfurt am Main, and Las Vegas: Peter Lang, 1981), 78–84.
32. Hans Henning, "Satire, Aufklärung und Philosophie—Johann Karl Wezel," *Goethe Jahrbuch*, 104 (1987): 340–41.
33. Lenz Prütting, "Nachwort" to *Belphegor* (Frankfurt am Main: Zweitausendeins, 1978): 487.
34. In his 1770 essay "Über J. J. Rousseaus ursprünglichen Zustand des Menschen," Wieland dismisses both Swift and Rousseau as "berühmte Misanthropen" who degraded the human race in their writings. (See *Sämmtliche Werke*, a facsimile reprint of the Göschen "Ausgabe letzter Hand," [Nördlingen: Greno, 1984], 5/14: 191). Wieland's criticism is directed specifically at Rousseau's theories on natural or savage man and Swift's subhuman Yahoos. In this essay and in "Über die von J. J. Rousseau vorgeschlagene Versuche den wahren Stand der Natur des Menschen zu entdecken nebst einem Traumgespräch mit Prometheus" (1770), he carries Rousseau's arguments ad absurdam because he believes human striving toward perfectibility must occur in a social environment and is therefore impossible in Rousseau's natural state.
35. Wieland's feelings toward Voltaire vacillated between admiration and rejection for a number of years. Wieland was initially unable to appreciate the humor in *Candide* which he perceived as mocking wit. In a letter to his friend Johann Georg Zimmermann dated June 25 and 26, 1756, he refers to Voltaire as "nicht nur ein mittelmäßiger Philosoph sondern ein recht seichter Pursche" (*Wielands Brief-wechsel*, vol. 1, ed. Hans Werner Seiffert [Berlin: Akademie,

1963], 263). Two years later he expresses his admiration for Voltaire's style but admits he is unable to love him because of his sophistry and disrespect for Shakespeare: "Je suis mortifié de ne pouvoir aimer cet homme que j'admire" (*Wielands Briefwechsel*, 1: 336–37). In the 1770s Wieland no longer criticizes Voltaire's mocking wit, and in a review of a new German translation, he praises *Candide* as "ein Lieblingsbuch aller Leute von Verstand" (*TM* 1st qr. [Mar.] 1778: 297).

    36. Henry Fielding, "Preface to *Joseph Andrews*," in *Joseph Andrews with Shamela and Related Writings*, ed. Homer Goldberg (New York: W. W. Norton, 1987), 4.

    37. Fielding, "Preface to *Joseph Andrews*," 5.

    38. Quoted by Johann Gottfried Gruber in *C. M. Wielands Leben* (1827; facsim. reprint, Nördlingen: Greno, 1984), Pt. 2, Bk. 4: 568.

    39. Ludwig Tieck, *Der gestiefelte Kater*, in *Ludwig Tieck Schriften*, vol. 6, *Phantasus*, ed. Manfred Frank (Frankfurt am Main: Deutscher Klassiker Verlag, 1985), 550–51.

Wilkes and Libertinism

JOHN SAINSBURY

"I believe you to be a very Whig and a very libertine." Thus James Boswell rebuked his friend John Wilkes. Most contemporaries would probably have accepted the accuracy of the judgment, while placing different constructions on what it signified. It would, for example, undoubtedly have won hearty endorsement from Boswell's mentor, Samuel Johnson, for whom Whiggism and libertinism were simply two sides of the same tarnished coin. It was Johnson, after all, who declared that "the first Whig was the Devil," interpreted by Boswell as meaning that "the Devil was impatient of subordination." What is noteworthy, though, about Wilkes's astonishing career is that, despite the force of the moral indictment that relentlessly pursued him, he would succeed in achieving a status that approached political canonization. Horace Walpole caught the paradox in his quip that "despotism will for ever reproach freedom with the profligacy of such a saint."[1]

The paradox begins to dissolve, though, once we recognize that, in many respects, Wilkes's libertinism was an asset not merely a liability in his assault on authoritarian government. After all, *pace* the Tory Johnson, its association with Whiggism implied some kind of legitimacy. This essay's argument is that libertinism—in a context of fluid discourses of politics, religion, and gender—was not only a convenient target for mid-century anxieties about the moral order, but was also an ethical force in its own right, yielding polemical devices to assail the alleged corruption and tyranny of Britain's political and ecclesiastical establishment. Hence Wilkes acquired a simultaneous reputation as moral bandit and moral scourge. The controversy that erupted over his *An Essay on Woman* served to highlight this duality, despite hostile expectations that his exposure as a pornographer would brand him unequivocally as a reprobate.

Behind the controversies of Wilkes's career loomed fundamental debates about the competing claims of orthodox religion and nature, as reified by Enlightenment culture, to mandate the political, social, and sexual order. The libertine, in many respects became a kind of militant for nature's claim, a status which around mid-century recast him in the role of the enemy of sodomy. Such important dimensions of Wilkes's career have been overlooked by many leading commentators, who, while acknowledging his libertinism, have judged it incidental to the real social and political significance of the Wilkite controversy.[2]

Although (remarkably) no systematic study of Wilkes's libertinism has been undertaken hitherto, there is at least a partial recognition that dimensions of it may be of more than narrowly biographical interest. John Brewer has argued that Wilkes's irreverent and rakish style, while repellent to many, was a crucial element in his recruitment of political support.[3] Brewer's insight is addressed implicitly in the essay's conclusion, where an attempt is made to comprehend the complex connections between libertinism and the political radicalism with which Wilkes in twentieth-century historiography is indelibly associated. This exploration will proceed, though, with the recognition that Wilkes's libertinism was of a typically aristocratic cast. He retained a censorious attitude toward plebeian indulgence in those vices to which he was himself attached.[4]

From a different historiographical quarter, Jonathan Clark also implicitly supports the notion that Wilkes's libertinism was at the core of the contentions that swirled around him. In a few acerbic paragraphs, he identifies the Wilkite controversy's central significance in Wilkes's heterodox assault—in which blasphemy was combined with obscenity—on a confessional state whose central pillar, the Anglican church, "was increasingly committed to monarchical and theological orthodoxy."[5] Clark has performed a major service in locating the religious significance of the Wilkite controversy. This essay dissents, however, from his insistence on the intellectual hegemony of Anglican orthodoxy. It will follow a contrary line: that it was precisely because the issue of religious order remained controversial that Wilkes, an unusual religious polemicist to say the least, was provided with his opportunity to assail the political and religious establishment. To put it another way:

Wilkes identified in mid-eighteenth-century polity, a zone of discomfort which he sought to aggravate with the ideological instruments of the libertine Whig tradition to which he saw himself the heir.

I

What kind of libertine was Wilkes? The answer to that question will be refined through the course of the essay, but it needs to be approached at the outset because the term was a nebulous one. The meaning and connotations of libertinism shifted over time without at any point taking on precise definition. In its early modern origins, it denoted both a philosophical detachment from orthodox Christianity (*libertinage erudit*) and the ecstacies of some antinomian Protestant sects, who cast off the doctrinal burden of original sin in favor of a (usually sensual) pursuit of Heaven on Earth. From the late seventeenth century onwards, libertinism was becoming more squarely equated with sexual license of the kind that brought notoriety to the aristocratic Restoration rakes. Thus James Boswell, a sexually promiscuous religious *devot*, on occasion guiltily referred to himself as a libertine. In charging Wilkes with the same offence, though, Boswell undoubtedly had in mind his friend's religious freethinking, as well as the sexual philandering which Wilkes indulged in without the anxiety that periodically afflicted Boswell.[6]

Wilkes, then, exhibited both the spiritual and secular dimensions of libertinism. Although as a leading scholar of the subject, James Turner, correctly points out "there is no necessary connection, much less identity" between the two,[7] it was widely accepted (especially but not exclusively by orthodox religionists) that there was a *causal* connection between freethinking and licentious behavior. Laxity in religion, went the claim, led down a slippery slope to sexual misconduct.[8]

Any libertine who sought legitimacy for his behavior and attitudes confronted this well-rehearsed argument as Wilkes would discover. And in the eighteenth century, the attack on the libertine would come not only from churchmen but also increasingly from reformers (male and female) suffused by the new culture of sensibility, a trend with secular origins, but which in England converged with religious piety. What largely defined it was opposition to the traditional male culture that libertinism supposedly represented. Its proponents embraced the equal humanity of women and sought to curb men's predatory sexual impulses in favor of heterosocial conduct in a domestic setting. The rake was to be converted to the man of feeling. Mothers were accorded a significant role in this process, and Wilkes's doting mother, Sarah Wilkes, did not shrink from the responsibility. Her son's reformation, she wrote, would "cause a mother's heart to sing for joy."[9]

There was certainly, then, an array of forces that was tending to push the libertine to the margins of cultural respectability. Yet the eighteenth century also yielded some countervailing tendencies, associated with the Enlightenment and its antecedent deism, that sharpened the libertine's assault on Christian orthodoxy, while at the same time deflecting the critique of the new sensibility. Wilkes was scarcely an intellectual pioneer of these forces, but he proved to be an effective (if sometimes reluctant) standard-bearer for them. The study of Wilkes's libertinism—in both its religious and sexual aspects—thus becomes, to an extent, an investigation of the presentation of Enlightenment culture in the public arena. What adds spice to the enquiry is that Wilkes was a cosmopolitan figure, who despite contrived displays of Francophobia, was well-acquainted with libertine culture across the English Channel. His libraries were well-stocked with French erotica; he would acquire, for example, an illustrated edition of Laclos's *Les Liaisons Dangereuses*. In late adolescence he spent a couple of years at Leiden University where he established what would prove to be an enduring friendship with Baron d' Holbach, soon to emerge as a leading apostle of philosophical materialism. During Wilkes's exile in France (1764–67), he was in frequent attendance at d'Holbach's celebrated salon in Paris, and his range of acquaintances included Diderot and Voltaire, as well as the celebrated German classicist, Johann Winckelmann.[10]

The neo-pagan character of the continental Enlightenment certainly chimed with Wilkes's own predilections. He shared the movement's delight in sensuality; he also embraced its dedication to the classics, not just as a source of pleasure, but as a critical tool to be deployed against the alleged pretensions of organized religion. Yet it would be wrong to characterize Wilkes's libertinism as simply the import of an alien tradition. In his friendship with d'Holbach, one might catch a glimpse of an emerging "religion of nature" in their youthful and rather contrived rusticity, but their later correspondence is largely devoid of any philosophical content. Insofar as there was an intellectual traffic between them, it moved in both directions, with Wilkes acquainting d'Holbach with the writings of English freethinkers.[11]

Wilkes's continental connections are certainly a subject worthy of closer attention than can be provided here; but the evidence is in any case compelling that Wilkes's intellectual libertinism, though refined by his cosmopolitanism, sprang from native sources. Sometimes vaunted as a post-Restoration "English" or "early" Enlightenment that preceded and conditioned the continental one, this cluster of articulated ideas and attitudes had at its core the phenomenon known as English deism.[12] The movement involved an advocacy of natural religion at the expense of Christian revelation and a fierce attack on Trinitarian orthodoxy, as laid down in the Athanasian creed, as being tantamount to polytheism. By challenging the orthodox conception of Christ's divinity and sacrifice, deists were seeking to clear away any theological obstructions to their assault on "priestcraft," the most derogatory term in the freethinker's lexicon. "Priestcraft," in the deist view, derived its sway from a false distinction between clergy and laity and sought to perpetuate it through the manipulation of superstition and mystery, instruments which were directly contrary to the spirit of true religion. It was over the question of ecclesiology that deism converged with a radical Whiggery that was continually alert to the disruptive challenge of High-Churchmanship. The connections were emphatically drawn in the writings of Thomas Gordon. His "Creed of an Independent Whig (1720)," for example, scoffed at "the mystery of the blessed Trinity" and offered an unflattering depiction of its priestly advocate.[13]

Despite, however, Gordon's anticlericalism and his unqualified support for religious toleration, he accepted the need for "a regimen in the church, and its government by bishops."[14] The national church that he envisaged, though, was to be entirely Erastian in its subordination to the virtuous interests of the secular community and to the authority of the magistracy. Gordon thus recast as Whig doctrine the classical notion of civil religion, whose end was civic virtue not the maintenance of credal orthodoxy.

Wilkes was well-acquainted with the works of Gordon and other deist writers, such as Lord Bolingbroke and the third earl of Shaftesbury. Their books were on his library shelves,[15] and the manner in which his polemic echoed theirs suggests that they had been studied with some care. In Parliament, Wilkes boasted about his depth of reading in religious controversy, and even a hostile modern commentator concedes that he was "theologically well-informed."[16] Despite such credentials, however, the notion of Wilkes as a religious controversialist needs to be qualified. He was not one in the sense of being a direct participant in serious debate with the defenders of conservative Anglicanism, who were more engaged in confronting the formidable intellectual challenge posed by sceptics such as David Hume and unitarians such as Joseph Priestley.[17] Wilkes was dangerous, from the conservative perspective, not as a worthy intellectual opponent, but as the symbol and agent of unruly (even diabolical) passions unleashed by defiance of the established order.

It is true that with the encouragement of his mentor, the Scottish philosopher Andrew Baxter, the young Wilkes had shown a flickering interest in metaphysical enquiry;[18] but it proved to be just a passing phase, as James Boswell would discover. After Wilkes and Boswell had clambered up Mount Vesuvius (an experience calculated to elicit speculation on the religious immensities), Boswell taxed his friend on questions of fate and free will. "Let 'em alone," was Wilkes's prompt advice. He showed a similar indifference to speculation about an afterlife. "It is difficult to get you to think philosophically," Boswell later conceded.[19]

Yet in his very resistance to the larger propositional debates, Wilkes was at one with his deist forbears, whose usual mode of enquiry was critical rather than rational. Among their instruments were satire and mockery, both wielded in full measure by Wilkes, at least in private. In Parliament, Wilkes's tone was measured, but his defence of deism uncompromising. In an unguarded display of cosmopolitanism, he declared that it "is almost become the religion of Europe." He denied that it was tantamount to atheism, retorting with the well-worn argument that the "doctrine of the Trinity . . . is direct *polytheism*."[20]

What made such comments more provocative is that they were made, not by an avowed enemy of the Church, but by someone who claimed to be its friend. The attitude of *écrasez l'infâme*, which Wilkes shared with his *philosophe* friends, extended in his case only to the superstitions and persecutions allegedly associated with "priestcraft," not to the notion of a religious establishment *per se*. While visiting Naples, for example, Wilkes claimed to have exposed as a priestly cheat, the biannual "miracle" of the liquefaction of the blood of St. Januarius.[21] Yet though, like Gordon, Wilkes was severe in his anticlericalism, he was at the same time eager to give merit in the Anglican Church its due. Worthy of applause were individuals such as Robert Lowth, the bishop of London, lauded by Wilkes as "a gentleman . . . of solid piety, . . . the soundest learning, and of exquisite classical taste."[22] As a young man, Wilkes was possibly the author of a sonnet addressed to Thomas Herring, the archbishop of Canterbury, praising him for keeping "the sacred vessel of religion . . . secure from superstition's dangerous tide."[23]

It is tempting, of course, to dismiss Wilkes's professed allegiance to Anglicanism as prompted by cynical ambition. Such an explanation, however, fails to account for the fact that Wilkes's involvement in, and support for, public worship went beyond the occasional conformity required for active participation in political life. Despite the fact that his parents had provided him with dissenting tutors, he seems to have regarded himself as an Anglican as a matter of course, thus following the denomination of his father, not that of his nonconformist mother. He went to church on Sundays (usually twice) and received the sacrament regularly. While a resident in Aylesbury in the 1750s, he was selected by the parish to supervise renovations to the church, and he sought and received permission to enlarge his family pew. In 1759, he served as churchwarden for St. Margaret's, Westminster. During his Parisian exile, according to David Hume, Wilkes was "a most regular, & devout, and edifying, and pious Attendant" at chapel.[24]

Admittedly, there is some credibility in the charge that Wilkes implicitly mocked the religious establishment by an apparent predisposition for renegade priests, exemplified by his close friend, the rake and poet Charles Churchill, who condemned the clergy as "scripture pumping divines . . . mercenary precept-mongers . . . retailers of revelation."[25] But acknowledging some elements of mischief and opportunism in Wilkes's conduct simply points to a larger question. What were the circumstances that provided this libertine and self-confessed heretic with the opportunity to present himself as a faithful son of the church even while assailing its central dogmas? The heritage of Thomas Gordon *et al.*, is part of the answer, though in his public pronouncements Wilkes generally avoided direct association with specific deist forbears. Instead he sought to legitimize his strictures on orthodoxy by linking them to the views of leading latitudinarian churchmen. By so doing, he was appealing to a tradition that was rich in historical associations with mainstream Whiggery and which retained resonance despite, or perhaps because of, the revival of High-Churchmanship in the latter decades of the eighteenth century.[26] In theological terms, Wilkes was engaged in a dubious exercise. Modern scholarship has identified some clear distinctions between deism and latitudinarianism. The latitudinarians' attachment to natural religion, it appears, though central to their definition, was a qualified one. Unlike the deists, they generally continued to uphold that "the hope and promise of salvation through Christ rested upon revelations and mysteries that had no place in the realm of natural knowledge. . . ."[27]

Yet the distinctions between latitudinarianism and deism, real as they were, tended to collapse inside the polarities of religious and political debate. The pressure came from both ends of the religious spectrum. Whereas Wilkes sought to consecrate his libertinism by associating it with a mainstream tradition, religious conservatives sought to defame latitudinarianism by characterizing it as a half-way house on the road to full-blown infidelity.[28] Within Anglicanism, this tendency to doctrinal polarization was connected with the divisions over polity expressed by the terms High Church and Low Church. Wilkes claimed legitimacy for his position within a Low Church tradition that though not defined by heterodoxy, enabled its expression through an emphasis on tolerance over conformity, the unity of the Protestant community over the prerogatives of a church establishment, and the priority of free religious enquiry over the maintenance of an officially prescribed orthodoxy.

Wilkes's own family circumstances personified the important alliance between Low Church Anglicanism and dissent, a cornerstone of Whiggism. His parents attended the religious services of their partner's denomination as well as of their own, a pattern that Wilkes replicated during his own brief marriage to a dissenter. Taking Low Church affiliation to its logical extreme, he maintained in Parliament that allegiance to his "mother church" was consistent with a secular basis for civil society and an all-encompassing religious toleration that embraced, not just Protestant dissenters, but Jews, Muslims, and sun-worshippers as well.[29]

II

Wrapped in the precepts and platitudes of Whiggery, Wilkes's religious libertinism could be deployed to counter an insurgent High Churchmanship in the mid-eighteenth century. By contrast, his sexual libertinism seemed on the face of it to be a point of vulnerability, or at least an improbable instrument in any battle of competing political and religious credos. Indeed, Wilkes seemed to be a living endorsement of the conservative insistence, alluded to earlier, that religious infidelity led ineluctably to sexual depravity. Admittedly, he eschewed the kind of misogynistic displays of sexual exhibitionism, euphemistically described as "frolics," engaged in by the Restoration rakes. Yet what remains striking about his sexual career is its predatory phallicism, a quality scarcely concealed by the arcadian ambience in which it was pursued. The Society of Dilettanti certainly knew its man when they deemed that Wilkes would be a suitable recipient for its luxurious publication on the Isernian priapic cult.[30] For Wilkes and his libertine friends, the pursuit of women was akin to the hunt (with virgins being the most desirable game) in which the penis was the weapon—"a seven inch Toledo," a "long spear." Wilkes, himself, was praised by one of his friends as "a vigorous and mighty Cunter [sic] . . . the Nimrod of Bucks."[31]

Important insights into Wilkes's sexual attitudes can be gleaned from his account of his relationship with the Italian courtesan, Gertrude Corradini, whom he met in Paris in 1764. Writing twenty years or so after the affair, Wilkes took a manly pride in the recollection that he had conducted it in a state of emotional detachment. The only positive qualities that he acknowledged in his mistress were physical ones, which he relished as a connoisseur: "She was a perfect Grecian figure, cast in the mould of the Florentine Venus . . . Her whole form was the most perfect symmetry . . ." He was titillated by her aptitude for feigning the moral qualities that she evidently lacked. "It was impossible to conterfeit virtue and modesty in a more dextrous manner," he wrote. He acknowledged her religious scruples, but derided these as superstitions which merely served to add piquancy to their lovemaking.[32]

Wilkes's erotic hedonism, especially tainted as it was with blasphemy, clearly violated the proscriptions of orthodox religion and was also at odds with the emerging culture of sensibility. It was, however, endorsed by the counterculture of the Enlightenment and its positive reification of nature.

Wilkes's onetime friend, Dr John Armstrong, expressed the mandate in his *Oeconomy of Love:* "What Nature bids / Is good, is wise; and faultless we obey."[33] In this formulation, the latitudinarian concept of natural religion has been clearly transformed into a "religion of nature." Wilkes was speaking the language of this neo-paganism when he referred to "lust" as a "noble passion" and praised Corradini for possessing "the divine gift of lewdness." Armstrong made specific reference to the "religion of nature" in an envious tribute to Wilkes's involvement in that mysterious libertine society, the Medmenham monks.[34]

In its self-representation, the "religion of nature" conceded no moral ground to orthodox religion or to the culture of sensibility. Its adherents insisted that a reified nature was the ultimate guarantor of social order, not a prescription for sexual anarchy. Although the Rabelasian motto of the Medmenham monks was *"fay ce que voudras* [do what you will]," they were reportedly enjoined to observe the proprieties and decencies that nature intended in human conduct.[35] Wilkes himself claimed high standards of responsibility and decorum in his relationships with women. Without a hint of irony, the radical publisher John Almon described him as "perhaps, the best lady's preceptor ever known." Secure in his own rectitude, Wilkes could summon moral outrage to condemn the callousness of the earl of Sandwich, a rake-companion who became his political foe. Sandwich's "conduct, with respect to women," wrote Wilkes, "was not only loose and barefaced, but perfidious mean and tricking. He was restrained by no consideration of private character, nor checked by any regard to public decorum."[36]

Though he showed a studied resistance to the intrusion of sentiment into sensual relationships, Wilkes nonetheless sometimes gave expression to the new sensibility which sought to reform the very rakishness with which he is customarily identified.[37] Yet his resort to such language has a hollow ring in a way that testifies to its increasing pervasiveness rather than, in his case at least, to any effectiveness in transforming actual conduct. For Wilkes's libertine circle, a self-proclaimed defence of womanhood would be expressed, not by any heartfelt capitulation to the culture of sensibility, but in an increasingly shrill crusade against sodomy.

How the libertine came to assume this role is a complex story, intimately tied to the changing constructions of gender and sexual identity that historians such as Randolph Trumbach are beginning to recover. Following the Restoration, sodomy was regarded as an act that defined libertine excess; its practice, though subject to penalty and censure, did not necessarily bring with it aspersions of unmanliness. Even into the eighteenth century, the cult of phallicism was possibly connected with homoerotic tendencies among gentlemen libertines. Conceivably, Wilkes himself, while a student at Leiden, crossed the indistinct line that distinguished homosocial conduct from the homoerotic. Yet, whatever the precise nature of his own erotic impulses, Wilkes after mid-century eagerly joined the escalating attack on the sodomite, who was by now reviled as an effeminate and hence despicable anomaly, a third gender, in nature's benign plan. This campaign, endorsed by the proscriptions of a reified nature, took place within a context of deepening anxieties about definitions of masculinity, now increasingly blurred by sentimental efforts to domesticate the male. The social construction of the effeminate sodomite became a means whereby acceptable margins for masculinity could be reinstated.[38]

Typically, the attack on the sodomite was connected with jeremiads against decadence in Church and State. Wilkes's soulmate Charles Churchill—a Grub Street "outsider" who gazed with jaundiced eye on the vices of the establishment—produced an egregious example of this genre. His poem *The Times* painted a lurid picture of metropolitan society in which the advance of sodomy was leading to the abandonment of "Woman, the pride and happiness of Man." "The smug PULPITEER / Loud 'gainst all other crimes, is silent here," he lamented.[39]

III

As an expression of the both the religious and sexual components of libertinism (including the attack on sodomy), the poem *An Essay on Woman* is a key text. Together with some ancillary parodies, it was composed by Wilkes sometime in the 1750s, probably in collaboration with Thomas Potter, a well-connected libertine friend.[40] Its sensational exposure in 1763 would become a means of ejecting Wilkes from polite society. Yet, ironically, it was probably written in the first place as one way for the middle-class Wilkes to ingratiate himself with the highborn circle of Lord Temple, a faction that included William Pitt. The stakes were high for Wilkes, in terms both of possibilities for political advancement and the opportunity to immerse himself in the refined libertine culture of Stowe, Temple's neoclassical palace.[41]

Dedicated to Fanny Murray, the famous courtesan, the poem is a parody of Alexander Pope's *An Essay on Man* in which Pope's subtle theodicy is transformed into a scabrous celebration of a reified nature's erotic imperatives. In it, Wilkes's phallicism is given unbridled expression. As Paul-Gabriel Boucé has pointed out, the parody is replete with metaphorical images of sexual intercourse as a hunting zone.[42]

The poem assailed a range of targets. Wilkes obviously amended it after Potter's death in 1759 in order to direct some satirical shafts at Lord Bute, the *bête-noire* of Wilkes's political friends. The title page, on which Wilkes lavished considerable care, contained stinging allusions to an alleged homosexual affair between George Stone, Anglican Primate of Ireland, and Lord George Sackville. Wilkes referred to Sackville as "an intrepid hero," a sarcastic reference to the unmanliness he allegedly displayed at the Battle of Minden in 1759.[43]

Neither Bute, Stone, nor Sackville were the principal targets of the satire, however, nor was Alexander Pope, whom Wilkes admired. The opprobrium of Wilkes and Potter was directed principally at William Warburton, a disputatious clergyman who, in the 1740s, had appointed himself the scourge of the "pestilent Herd of libertine Scriblers [sic] with which the Island is overrun." Warburton had once regarded Pope himself as one of them; but in a curious *volte-face*, he befriended the poet before his death, wrote a vindication of *An Essay on Man*, and published a posthumous edition of his works in 1751.[44]

The detestation that Wilkes and Potter felt towards Warburton was heartfelt, though in some respects a little puzzling. He would, after all, be elevated to the bishopric of Gloucester in 1759 on the recommendation of William Pitt. And he was far from being a dogmatic High Churchman; some of his defences of orthodoxy were so eccentric that they were criticized for conceding too much ground to infidelity. Yet though his voluminous writings breathed the language of the Enlightenment (he admired Pierre Bayle!), they were insistent in their defence of the prerogatives of the Anglican Church, in which, as his enemies never tired of pointing out, he entertained great hopes of advancement.[45] His treatise *The Alliance of Church and State*, for example, used Lockean social contract theory to justify the Test Acts. From the perspective of Wilkes and his circle, Warburton's cardinal sin was his heavy-handed attempt to represent Pope, an icon of neoclassicism and arguably a deist himself, as a pillar of religious orthodoxy. "Mr. Pope's *Essay on Man* is a real vindication of Providence against *Libertines* and *Atheists*," wrote Warburton,[46] a case that he tried to reinforce in his annotations to the poem. What lent irony and additional controversy to Warburton's assault on libertinism was the fact that the *Essay on Man* had originally been dedicated by Pope to Lord Bolingbroke, whose collected works (published posthumously in 1753) Warburton savagely criticized.

Wilkes and Potter followed these paper wars with great attention,[47] and *An Essay on Woman* should be understood as their idiosyncratic contribution to them. Certainly, Warburton had made himself a broad target for ridicule through the long-windedness and pedantry of his notes to *An Essay on Man*, which Wilkes mercilessly parodied, implying that his victim was both gluttonous and sexually impotent.[48]

Though such calumny would become the stuff of a revived anticlericalism, it was meant for the titillation of a select circle of gentlemen libertines, not for popular consumption. It would, moreover, have been inappropriate for an aspiring Whig statesman, such as Wilkes, to be suspected of entering the polemical lists on behalf of an infamous Tory-Jacobite like Lord Bolingbroke. Knowledge of the existence of the *Essay*, let alone rumors of its content, would have been withheld from the public had not the government decided to prosecute Wilkes as its printer and publisher.

That prosecution is an uproarious story and one that has been retold with varying degrees of accuracy.[49] It is not necessary to repeat the details here. What requires some emphasis, though, is the centrality of the episode to the heated political and religious conflicts of the 1760s. There are admittedly some grounds for seeing the affair as merely a colorful sideshow to the legal and constitutional issues aroused by Wilkes's vehement attacks on the government and its policies, most famously in *North Briton*, No. 45. Wilkes might well have been correct in his conjecture "that if the North Briton had never appeared, the Essay on Woman would never have been called into question."[50] Certainly the convenient "discovery" of the *Essay* provided the government with an irresistible chance to hobble a dangerous opponent.

Yet this opportunity was clearly framed and conditioned by the tenor of the times. Though assertions of a "new Toryism" in the 1760s have been repeatedly refuted with respect to Westminster politics, a number of accounts now point to a resurgence of High-Churchmanship associated with an authoritarian and anti-Enlightenment agenda.[51] The tendency found endorsement at the center of national life in George III's desire to "attack the irreligious."[52] Whatever public support there might have been for such a crusade, however, its expression as credal orthodoxy was bound to encounter difficulties. Reflecting the diffusion of Enlightenment thought, reservations about trinitarianism were expressed even in the progovernment periodical, the *Critical Review*; and Bute's fall from office was attributed by one supporter to the political nation's contempt for his displays of sacramentalism.[53] The pursuit of a notorious libertine like Wilkes thus became one means for the government to reassert its Christian credentials. Even before the exposure of the *Essay*, progovernment scribes had tried to impugn Wilkes's criticisms of the ministry by reference to his libertinism. "Canst thou persuade oneself that an Enemy to a *Saviour*, can be a Friend to Mankind?" asked one squib.[54]

In some ways, the official mood paralleled the kind of anxiety that had brought forth the Blasphemy Act at the end of the previous century.[55] When the *Essay* did fall into government hands, thought could well have been given to prosecuting Wilkes under the provisions of that legislation, which was directed specifically against apostates who denied the truth of Christianity and the doctrine of the Trinity. In the event, though, the crown chose to prosecute Wilkes for obscene and impious libel, a felony under common law, and one that was relatively easier to prove. In the Solicitor-General's Information, Wilkes was charged with endeavoring, through the "publication" of his blasphemy, "to introduce and diffuse ... a general debauchery and depravity of manners and a total contempt of Religion Modesty and virtue."[56]

Wilkes was convicted of libel *in absentia* and sentenced shortly after his return from exile in 1768. In the meantime, his defence was keyed not to the courts, but to the forum of public opinion. Wilkes and his friends at least had the advantage that knowledge of the offensive material was largely confined to a prurient exposé by the Reverend John Kidgell,[57] a disreputable priest who had played an active though shadowy role in Wilkes's prosecution. The defence included an (unconvincing) display of classical pedantry to rebut Kidgell's charge that Wilkes had defamed the Blessed Savior.[58] Wilkes readily admitted, though, to strictures on the Trinity, but with typical audacity compared them to reservations about the Athanasian Creed, expressed by none other than Archbishop John Tillotson, a leading light of late- seventeenth-century latitudinarianism. Wilkes omitted to mention that he had expressed his own anti-Trinitarian scruples in an obscene parody that the saintly Tillotson would hardly have approved: "Immortal Honour, endless Fame,/ Almighty Pego! to thy Name;/ And equal Adoration be/ Paid to the neighbouring Pair with thee,/ Thrice blessed Glorious Trinity."[59]

Wilkes deployed the rhetoric of the "religion of nature" to counter charges (couched in the language of sensibility) that the *Essay* was "calculated to depreciate" women, that it ridiculed and abused them. On the contrary, Wilkes argued, it was "the *apotheosis* of the fair sex." Its "luscious" descriptions were something that "Nature and woman might pardon."[60]

Wilkes's apologia was not confined to defending the *Essay's* contents. He sought to expose, as a demonstration of corrupt Church-State power, the unsavory means employed by the minstry's agents (from bribing his employees to downright theft) in bringing them to light. His victimization, he argued, was comparable to that of the seventeenth-century Whig martyr, Algemon Sidney. Without ever adequately explaining why he arranged for a dozen or so copies of the Essay to be printed, he insisted that the work was intended for private amusement only. It was the government itself that committed the very offence for which he was prosecuted by "THEIR PUBLISHING to the world" the offending material. Stressing his own acute sense of decorum, he claimed to have been "put to the blush" by this exposure, which, in the specific context of his widely reported denunciation in the House of Lords, constituted "a public insult on order and decency."[61]

Whereas the *cause-célèbre* of the *North Briton*, No. 45, raised questions of the liberty of public expression, Wilkes glossed the imbroglio of the *Essay* as an attack on the liberty of private conscience, casting himself as its staunch defender. It was an artful strategy because, by the 1760s, only a few diehard

Tories, such as John Shebbeare, were prepared to challenge publicly this irreducible Whig principle. It needs to be underscored just how precisely and effectively Wilkes's defence of libertinism ultimately rested on the secular orthodoxies of Whiggism, notwithstanding the fact that his emerging political support drew on a legacy of anti-oligarchical Toryism.[62] The usual representation of Wilkes in the aftermath of the *Essay on Woman* affair is that of a loose cannon on a ship of state which had slipped its moorings; his *self-representation*, by contrast, was that of the stern protector of a Whig tradition, threatened by a sinister array of forces.[63] The evident erosion of party distinctions at Westminster did not diminish this rhetorical insistence on a critical challenge to Whiggism; on the contrary, it fueled it. (From the other side, Samuel Johnson's Toryism was sharpened by his mordant recognition of what historians seem perpetually doomed to rediscover: that the notion of a parliamentary Tory party was losing meaning by the 1760s.)[64]

In the *North Briton*, Wilkes had identified the chief menace as an insidious Toryism, determined to ravage the Whig fold and instill its hateful notions of prerogative and passive obedience. His own persecutions were then adduced as evidence to support the contention. After his humiliation over the *Essay*, the polemical focus of Wilkes and his supporters shifted to the apostacy of false Whig friends.[65] Most venom was reserved for William Pitt, who had denounced Wilkes in the House of Commons as a "blasphemer and libeller of his king" and, newly ennobled, would return to head the ministry in 1766. Pitt's condemnation of Wilkes was represented by the latter, not simply as an act of personal betrayal, but as evidence of the power of the corrupt Church-State alliance to subvert Whig patriotism by encouraging false allegiances. Wilkes charged Pitt with abandoning philosophical libertinism, claiming that Pitt had once been "charmed" by his parodies (including quite possibly the *Essay* itself) and that "the whole ridicule of those ... pieces was confined to certain mysteries which formerly the *unplaced and unpensioned* Mr. P[itt] did not think himself obliged even to affect to believe."[66]

IV

The mutual disenchantment between Wilkes and the Whig grandees carried connotations of class, as well as of ideological, conflict. The group to which he had assiduously sought entry was now disparaged by him as the "damn'd aristocracy."[67] The corollary of this reversal was his celebrated emergence as a "man of the people," a process that left him, fleetingly anyway, as the symbol and agent of those forces that modern historians place under the general rubric of political radicalism. What, then, was the significance of Wilkes's libertinism to the popular, as distinct from aristocratic, politics in which he now found himself embroiled?

The answer is far from straightforward. Connections between libertinism, with its aristocratic resonances, and the various manifestations of popular radicalism were complex and ambivalent. At one level, the two stood in stark opposition, and the public exposure of upper-class vice became an instrument to be wielded against oligarchy. With the perversity that was the hallmark of his career, Wilkes played a pioneer role in such activity, distancing himself from the aristocratic libertinism which he emulated by exposing some of its dark secrets to an inquisitive public. His task was made considerably easier by the fact that, in the 1760s, government left so many hostages to fortune when it embarked on the risky business of invoking piety in support of power and privilege. "A WHIG" warned in June of 1763 that he would "take care to convince the World, that the principal Men of the reigning Party are no greater *Saints* than Mr. Wilkes."[68] Subsequently, the vices and foibles of those who had launched the attack on Wilkes over *An Essay on Woman*—including Lord Sandwich, Warburton, and Kidgell—were systematically exposed in pamphlets, poetry, and the press.[69]

Wilkes's own contribution to this campaign of counter-defamation included some tantalizing revelations about the Medmenham monks, whose fellowship had been sundered by the decision of Sir Francis Dashwood, their founder, to join the Bute administration in 1762. Initially fairly anodyne (alluding only to "the *English Eleusinian* Mysteries of that renown'd Convent"),[70] the disclosures became more lurid in step with the escalating level of Wilkes's problems and persecutions. He hinted darkly at the strange vices of the older members (including presumably Dashwood and Lord Sandwich) in his comment that "the younger monks . . . seemed at least to have sinned *naturally*."[71]

Few, of course, could have been convinced by the pose of outraged virtue that Wilkes adopted as his revelatory style. And as he set out to recover his political fortunes by seeking election to Parliament in 1768, ministry scribes continued to brand him as a demonic as well as a demotic agent. Indeed, the discourse on libertinism suffused those famous electoral contests in ways that have been inadequately acknowledged. During the first Middlesex election, a group of his opponents carried a banner with the inscription, "No Blasphemer."[72] The charge of blasphemy had, in fact, already become the common stuff of a press campaign against him, accompanied by assertions that his candidacy threatened sexual anarchy. If elected, one scribe claimed (with tongue only partly in cheek), Wilkes would "labour for a repeal of the laws against rapes and adulteries" and prepare "a bill for the general toleration of those seminaries which are dedicated to the votaries of Venus." For their part, the Wilkites trotted out the language of the libertine Whig tradition by charging that their champion was the continuing object of persecution "by the votaries of despotism, and superstition." In a novel twist, a *North Briton Extraordinary* argued that the government's alleged acts of tyranny constituted "blasphemy against god and king."[73]

Privately, Wilkes took a mischievous pleasure in being identified as a lord of misrule. In May 1768, he wrote to a confidant: "England is now a demono-cracy [*sic*]—Who is the demon?—Wilkes." Yet his public posture remained that of the patrician tribune of the people, protecting them from the violations of a corrupt government and senate, not that of an avowed agent of social, let alone sexual, revolution. It was government action, he insisted, that precipitated public disorder; his own served to quell it.[74]

It was not only critics, though, who glimpsed a very different image behind the guise of the austere Whig patriot. There are hints that his reputation as a rake, firmly established in the wake of the *Essay* affair, contributed as much to his popularity as it did to his defamation. His machismo found approval from among the denizens of the all-male clubs and associations that threw him their support. He was "free from cock to wig," commented a drayman.[75] With its complex dynamic of deference and dissent, the "bi-polar field of force" of eighteenth-century class politics, identified by Edward Thompson,[76] seems to have provided an appropriate setting for a dissolute aristocrat-manqué, such as Wilkes, to preside over the exuberant rituals of plebeian dissidence.

This particular dimension of the Wilkes phenomenon was an ephemeral one, essentially over by 1774, but with respect to longer term trends, Wilkes can be plausibly represented as a bridge between the religious heterodoxy of early Whiggism and its later instantiation in the Jacobinism of the 1790s." Under Wilkes's influence, the poor apprentice "openly ridicules the religion of his country at the *Robinhood* . . . ," according to one pamphleteer. In December 1776, the members of another London debating club, the Society of Free Debate, discussed the following question: "Whether the Athanasian Creed can be defended on the Principles of Reason and Revelation?" The question was determined in the negative, before the society moved on to discuss the urgent problem of how best to resolve Wilkes's chronic financial indebtedness.[78]

Heterodoxy was not, of course, synonymous with religious nonconformity, that vital strand of emergent radicalism, and one whose concerns, as James Bradley has reminded us, had more to do with polity than with doctrine. Yet here, too, there was a connection with libertinism, though a much more complex one. Throughout his adult life, Wilkes himself remained constant to his family heritage by his support for dissenters' demands for relief from legal constraints. Indeed, such activity represented the most consistent theme in an otherwise mercurial career, continuing long after he is usually represented as having lapsed into political senescence.[79]

The unqualified support that Wilkes offered to nonconformists was, however, reciprocated unevenly and in ways that reflect the heterogeneity of radicalism itself. Many dissenters, it is true, were prepared to acknowledge that Wilkes's cause was their own. Like him, they felt that they were being thrust to the political margins by what they perceived as the rise of an authoritarian, High Church polity in the 1760s. The effect was that, from being loyal pillars of the Hanoverian state, the dissenters would become some of its harshest critics. The intensity of nonconformist anticlericalism, which envisaged the Church as "a bloated and arrogant instrument of state control," matched that of the most fervent Wilkite.[80] Wilkes's absolute defence of freedom of religious enquiry also struck a positive chord among a group for whom dissent now carried its own rationale. "Freedom of thought" had shed the connotation of moral determinism that had made "freethinking" repugnant to many religious liberals at the beginning of the century and had become the assumed basis of free moral agency.[81] For all these reasons, many dissenters, including Joseph Priestley, gave enthusiastic backing to Wilkes during the Middlesex election controversy, lending some credence to Samuel Johnson's scurrilous judgment that he was "supported by the sectaries, the natural fomenters of sedition, and confederates of the rabble, of whose religion little now remains but hatred of establishments. . . ."[82]

Yet support for a sexual libertine such as Wilkes also stuck in the craw of many influential dissenters whose agenda included moral regeneration as well as religious and political reform. The rational dissenter James Burgh, for example, urged marital fidelity and condemned illicit sex in any form. Not surprisingly then, he balked at supporting such a dissolute character as Wilkes, though he felt obliged to uphold the cause of electors' rights that Wilkes's expulsion by Parliament raised.[83]

Richard Price, Burgh's Arian friend, who had a "puritanical abhorrence of all forms of dissipation," was left in a similarly uncomfortable position. Like Wilkes, Price espoused freedom of conscience, enquiry, and worship. But there the resemblance ended. Price believed that "every man's will, if perfectly free from restraint, would carry him invariably to rectitude and virtue." It was an optimistic view, directly contrary to the conservative defence of a priestly establishment as the essential instrument to restrain an inevitable tendency to human depravity. Its key was the operation of reason which served to prevent an individual's moral capacity from being overpowered by instinctive desires. Wilkes's libertinism, justified as a response to the "reasonable" imperatives of nature, clearly undermined Price's case.

Hence, though supporting Wilkes's political cause, Price resorted to some untypically strong language in condemning him. "He [Wilkes] was a man he could trample under his foot," he said.[84]

Price's concerns were echoed, though more sympathetically, by Wilkes's own mother. In 1771, Wilkes caused a minor riot when he visited a courtesan in Sarah Wilkes's neighborhood. She was swift to reprove him, imploring him in a manner that Richard Price would have fully endorsed, to control his passions through the exercise of his reason: "O! my dear son," she wrote, "do not sacrifice temporal and eternal felicity to any criminal indulgences; but let that . . . gift reason regulate and subdue inordinate passions, which will be the noblest triumph and reward you with inexpressible satisfaction and tranquility. . . ."[85]

Wilkes remained unchastened. But his mother's comments prophesied a potent challenge to the libertinism that he embodied. Libertinism had withstood, even undermined, the coercive instruments of Church and State; in the radical appeal to the interior religious conscience, it faced a much more tenacious adversary.[86]

NOTES

1. [James Boswell], *Boswell on the Grand Tour: Italy, Corsica, and France, 1765–1766*, ed. Frank Brady and Frederick Pottle (New York: McGraw Hill, 1955), 69; James Boswell, *Life of Johnson*, ed. R. W. Chapman, 3rd ed. (Oxford: Oxford University Press,1970),973; Horace Walpole, *Memoirs of the Reign of King George the Third*, ed. G. F. Russell Barker, 4 vols. (London, 1894), 1: 142.

2. Such is the tack, for example, of George Rudé, *Wilkes and Liberty:A Social Study of 1763 to 1774* (Oxford: Clarendon Press, 1962).

3. John Brewer, *Party Ideology and Popular Politics at the Accession of George III* (Cambridge: Cambridge University Press, 1976), 163–200.

4. On John Wilkes's negative attitude to plebeian debauchery, see [Boswell], *Boswell on the Grand Tour*, 56. As a London magistrate, Wilkes sought to curb prostitution in his jurisdiction: *Bingley's Journal*, 29 December 1770, and *Gazetteer*, 18 April 1776.

5. J. C. D. Clark, *English Society 1688–1832: Ideology, Social Structure and Political Practice during theAncien Regime* (Cambridge: Cambridge University Press, 1985), esp. 309–11; the quotation is from 315.

6. This discussion of the varieties of libertinism borrows from the following: Christopher Hill, *The World Turned Upside Down: Radical Ideas during the English Revolution* (New York: Viking Press, 1972), 148–85, 204–5, 334–35; George Huntston Williams, *The Radical Reformation* (Philadelphia: Westminster Press, 1962), passim; Peter N. Miller, "'Freethinking' and 'Freedom of Thought' in Eigh-

teenth-Century Britain," *Historical Journal* 36 (1993): 599–617; and James G. Turner, "The Properties of Libertinism," in *'Tis Nature's Fault: Unauthorized Sexuality during the Enlightenment*, ed. Robert Purks Maccubbin (Cambridge: Cambridge University Press, 1987), 75 87. Boswell's libertinism is examined in detail in Lawrence Stone, *The Family, Sex and Marriage in England 1500–1800* (New York: Harper and Row, 1977), 572–99, and in Bruce Redford, *The Converse of the Pen: Acts of Intimacy in the Eighteenth-Century Familiar Letter* (Chicago: University of Chicago Press,1986),179–205. Other studies from the growing literature on libertinism will be referred to during the course of the essay.

7. Turner, "Properties of Libertinism," 79.

8. J. H[utchinson], *The Religion of Satan: or Antichrist delineated* (London, 1736), 68; John Leland, quoted in Clark, English Society, 284; William Warburton, *A View of Lord Bolingbroke's Philosophy; in Four Letters to a Friend*, 3 vols. (1754–55), 2: xxxiv.

9. G. J. Barker-Benfield, *The Culture of Sensibility: Sex and Society in Eighteenth-Century Britain* (Chicago and London: University of Chicago Press, 1992), esp.37–103, 215–86; Sarah Wilkes to John Wilkes, 23 October 1771, Wilkes MSS, 2: Letter 95, William L. Clements Library, University of Michigan, Ann Arbor.

10. *Sale Catalogues of Libraries of Eminent Persons*, general editor A. N. L. Munby, vol. 8, *Politicians*, ed. Seamus Deane (London: Mansell with Sotheby Parke Publications, 1973), 119; Alan Charles Kors, *D'Holbach's Coterie: An Enlightenment in Paris* (Princeton: Princeton University Press, 1976), 25–26, 101–2, 109, 113, 150, 302; John Wilkes to Heaton Wilkes, Geneva, 17 August 1765, Wilkes MSS, 1: Letter 87, Clements Library; Karl Schudekopf, "Winckelmann und John Wilkes," *Zeitschrift fur Bildende Kunst* (Leipzig, 1888), 138–42.

11. D'Holbach to Wilkes, Leiden, 3 December 1746, British Library Add. MSS 30867, fol. 18; *The Correspondence of the Late John Wilkes with his Friends*, ed. John Almon, 5 vols. (London, 1805), 1: 41 (hereafter cited as *Wilkes Correspondence*); Margaret C. Jacob, *The Radical Enlightenment: Pantheists, Freemasons and Republicans* (London: George Allen and Unwin, 1981), 175, 263. D'Holbach translated Thomas Gordon's *The Independent Whig* into French in 1767: J. A. 1. Champion, *The Pillars of Priestcraft Shaken: The Church of England and its Enemies* (Cambridge: Cambridge University Press, 1992), 175n.14. See also, Mark Goldie, "Civil Religion and the English Enlightenment," in *Proceedings of the Folger Institute Center for the History of British Political Thought*, No. 5 (1993), ed. Gordon J. Schochet, 34, 45.

12. The following account draws from an important recent study of English deism: Champion, *Pillars of Priestcraft Shaken*.

13. Thomas Gordon, *A Cordial for Low Spirits: Being a Collection of Curious Tracts*, ed. Richard Baron, 3rd ed., 3 vols. (London, 1763), 2: 49–50.

14. Gordon, "Priestianity: Or, a View of the Disparity between the Apostles and the Modern Inferior Clergy (1720),"*A Cordial*, 2: 237.

15. *Sale Catalogues of Libraries of Eminent Persons*, 8, ed. Deane, 102–4.

16. *The Speeches of Mr. Wilkes in the House of Commons* (1786), 318 (hereafter cited as Wilkes Speeches); Clark, *English Society*, 337.

17. Nigel Aston, "Horne and Heterodoxy: The Defence of Anglican Beliefs in the Late Enlightenment," *English Historical Review* 108 (1993): 895–919.

18. On the Wilkes/Baxter friendship, see G. S. Rousseau, "'In the House of Madam Vander Tasse, on the Long Bridge': A Homosocial University Club in Early Modern Europe," in *The Pursuit of Sodomy: Male Homosexuality in Renaissance and Enlightenment Europe*, ed. Kent Gerard and Gert Hekma (New York and London: Harrington Park Press, 1989), 312–14, 319, 322–24.

19. [Boswell], *Boswell on the Grand Tour*, 55, 110.

20. John Redwood, *Reason, Ridicule and Religion: The Age of the Enlightenment in England, 1660–1750* (London: Thames and Hudson, 1976); John Wilkes to Jean-Baptiste Suard, 29 June 1769, Wilkes MSS, 3: Letter 23, Clements Library; *Wilkes Speeches*, 318–19, 332.

21. [John Wilkes], *Patriot: An Unfinished Autobiography* (Harrow: William F. Taylor, 1888), 43–47.

22. *Wilkes Speeches*, 144 45, 331. John Wilkes's enthusiasm for Lowth was possibly inspired by the fact that Lowth had quarelled with William Warburton, Wilkes's bitter enemy.

23. Wilkes MSS, 4: fol. 29, Clements Library. On the document, there is a penciled note attributing the sonnet to Wilkes, but the poem is not in his hand.

24. *Wilkes Correspondence*, 1: 20; Horace Bleackley, *Life of John Wilkes* (London: John Lane, 1917), 3–11; Robert Gibbs, *A History of Aylesbury* (Aylesbury, 1884), 23–24; Parish Records, PR. 11/5/1.Q. and Faculty Book, 1723–1785, D/A/X/9 Buckinghamshire Record Office, Aylesbury; *The Diaries of Thomas Wilson D.D. 1731–37 and 1750*, ed. C. S. L. Linnell (London: S. P. C. K., 1964), 15; J. Y. T. Greig, ed., *The Letters of David Hume*, 2 vols. (Oxford: Clarendon Press, 1932), 1: 444.

25. Churchill to Wilkes, 13 July 1762, *The Correspondence of John Wilkes and Charles Churchill*, ed. Edward H. Weatherly (New York: Columbia University Press, 1954), 5.

26. *Wilkes Speeches*, 332. On the continuities of latitudinarianism, and the political implications of that, see John Gascoigne, "Anglican Latitudinarianism and Political Radicalism in the Late Eighteenth Century," *History* 71 (1986): 23–38.

27. Roger L. Emerson, "Latitudinarianism and the English Deists," in *Deism, Masonry, and the Enlightenment: Essays honoring Alfred Owen Aldridge*, ed. J. A. Leo Lemay (Newark: University of Delaware Press, 1987), 30.

28. Clark, *English Society*, 282–84; Redwood, *Reason, Ridicule and Religion*, 163.

29. Sarah Wilkes to ?, 22 April 1750, Wilkes MSS, 1: Letter 25, Clements Library; *Wilkes Correspondence*, 1: 20; Wilkes Speeches, 329, 331. On the importance of the Whig/Low Church alliance, see James E. Bradley, *Religion, Revolution and English Radicalism: Nonconformity in Eighteenth-Century Politics and Society* (Cambridge: Cambridge University Press, 1990), 413.

30. *History of the Society of Dilettanti*, compiled by Leonard Cust, ed. Sidney Colvin (London: Macmillan, 1898), 122–23.

31. BL Add. MSS 30880B, fols. 5, 7, 8, 15.

32. [John Wilkes], *Patriot*, 15–17, 28–29.

33. Quoted in Geoffrey Ashe, *Do What You Will: A History of Anti-Morality* (London and New York: W. H. Allen, 1974), 75.

34. [Boswell], *Boswell on the Grand Tour*, 56; [John Wilkes], *Patriot*, 15; Armstrong to Wilkes, 20 December 1760, BL Add. MSS 30867, fol. 165. See also Roy Porter, "Mixed Feelings: The Enlightenment and Sexuality in Eighteenth-Century Britain," in *Sexuality in Eighteenth-Century Britain*, ed. Paul-Gabriel Boucé (Manchester: Manchester University Press, 1982), 1–46. Randolph Trumbach boldly refers to a priapic "religion of libertinism" which stood "in contradistinction to orthodox Christianity": "Erotic Fantasy and Male Libertinism in Enlightenment England," in *The Invention of Pornography: Obscenity and the Origins of Modernity, 1500–1800*, ed. Lynn Hunt (New York: Zone Books, 1993), 254.

35. Introduction to *Nocturnal Revels: or the History of King's Place, and Other Modern Nunneries*, 2 vols. (London, 1779), 1.

36. *Wilkes Correspondence*, 5: 286, and 1: 230n.

37. Ibid., 4: 97–98; [John Wilkes], *Some Bath Love Letters of John Wilkes, Esq.*, ed. Emmanuel Green (Bath, 1918), 22.

38. In this discussion, I use the term sodomy (in preference to the anachronism "homosexuality"), not in its precise sense of anal penetration of either sex, but in its usual eighteenth-century meaning as a general reference to sexual acts, active and passive, between males. On the shift of "enlightened" aristocratic libertinism to a position opposed to sodomy, see Randolph Trumbach, "Sodomy Transformed: Aristocratic Libertinage, Public Reputation and the Gender Revolution of the 18th Century," *Journal of Homosexuality* 19 (1990): 105–24; Randolph Trumbach, "Sex, Gender, and Sexual Identity in Modern Culture: Male Sodomy and Female Prostitution in Enlightenment London," *Journal of the History of Sexuality* 2 (1991): 186–203; and Porter, "Mixed Feelings," 17–18. Phallicism is linked to homosocial bonding in Shearer West, "Libertinism and the Ideology of Male Friendship in the Portraits of the Society of the Dilettanti," *Eighteenth-Century Life* 16 (1992): 76–104, and to homoeroticism in G. S. Rousseau, "The Sorrows of Priapus; anticlericalism, homosocial desire, and Richard Payne Knight," in *Sexual Underworlds of the Enlightenment*, ed. G. S. Rousseau and Roy Porter (Chapel Hill: University of North Carolina Press, 1988), 101–53. On fears of effeminacy and their connection to the "sentimental" revolution, see Barker-Benfield, *Culture of Sensibility*, esp. 104–53. Rousseau speculates, on the basis of scanty evidence, about John Wilkes's adolescent sexuality in " 'In the House of Madam Vander Tasse,'" 311–47. For the antisodomy stance of Wilkes and his circle, see [Wilkes], *Patriot*, 34–35; Ashe, *Do What You Will*, 76–77; Trumbach, "Sodomy Transformed," 121–22; and the references to Charles Churchill and to *An Essay on Woman* below.

39. Charles Churchill, "The Times," in *The Poetical Works of Charles Churchill*, ed. Douglas Grant (Oxford: Clarendon Press, 1956), 399, 408.

40. The question of principal authorship has long been debated. A strong case in favor of John Wilkes was made eighty years ago in Eric Watson, "John Wilkes and 'The Essay on Woman,'" *Notes and Queries*, 11th set, 9 (1914): 121–23, 143–45, 162–64, 183–85, 203–205, 222, 241–42. Watson's argument has been generally

neglected by Wilkes's biographers, who tend to plump for Potter, but it finds support in Calhoun Winton, "John Wilkes and 'An Essay on Woman,'" in *A Provision of Human Nature: Essays on Fielding and Others in Honor of Miriam Austin Locke*, ed. Donald Kay (Montgomery: University of Alabama Press,1977), 123–25. Wilkes almost certainly wrote the inflammatory notes to the main text, attributed to Dr Warburton, as well as the ancillary parodies.

41. On the erotic imagery at Stowe, see James G. Turner, "The Sexual Politics of Landscape: Images of Venus in Eighteenth-Century English Poetry and Landscape Gardening," *Studies in Eighteenth-Century Culture* 11 (1982): 345–47.

42. Paul-Gabriel Boucé, "Chthonic and Pelagic Metaphorization in Eighteenth-Century English Erotica," in *'Tis Nature's Fault*, 213. My references to the *Essay* are to the facsimile edition in Adrian Hamilton, *The Infamous Essay on Woman: or John Wilkes seated between Vice and Virtue* (London: André Deutsch, 1972), 195-246.

43. [John Wilkes], *Essay on Woman*, in Hamilton, *Infamous Essay*, 223, 195.

44. William Warburton, *Remarks on Several Occasional Reflections*, part 2, in *The Works of the Right Reverend William Warburton, Lord Bishop of Gloucester*, 7 vols. (London, 1788–94), 6: 536.

45. *Dictionary of National Biography*, s.v. "Warburton, William."

46. Warburton, *View of Bolingbroke's Philosophy*, 1: 80.

47. Potter to Wilkes, 10 October 1754, BL Add. MS 30867, fol. 101.

48. [John Wilkes], *Essay on Woman*, in Hamilton, *Infamous Essay*, 206–11,213–17, 224–25, 228–29.

49. Hamilton, *Infamous Essay*, 91–246, contains a useful and well-documented gulde.

50. John Wilkes quoted in *The History of the Minority; during the Years 1762, 1763, 1764, and 1765* (London, 1766),208. See also, "Epigram on a late affair," *St. James's Chronicle*, 8–10 December 1763.

51. James J. Sack, *From Jacobite to Conservative: Reaction and Orthodoxy in Britain, c. 1760–1832* (Cambridge: Cambridge University Press, 1993), 75–79; Clark, *English Society*, 275–76; J. A. W. Gunn, *Beyond Liberty and Property: The Process of Self-Recognition in Eighteenth-Century Political Thought* (Kingston and Montreal: McGill-Queen's University Press, 1987), 168.

52. Romney Sedgwick, ed., *Letters from George III to Lord Bute, 1756–1766* (London: Macmillan, 1939), 166.

53. Sack, *From Jacobite to Conservative*, 63, 75.

54. ISRAEL LOYAL, *St. James's Chronicle*, 12–14 May 1763.

55. Then, according to William Blackstone, "civil liberties . . . being used as a cloke of maliciousness, and the most horrid doctrines subversive of all religion being publicly avowed . . . it was found necessary . . . for the civil power to interpose, by not admitting those miscreants to the privileges of society, who maintained such principles as destroyed all moral obligation," *Commentaries on the Laws of England*, 4 vols. (1764–69), 4: 44.

56. MS 214/2: fols. 165–66, Guildhall, London; BL Add. MSS 57733, fols. 2–3.

57. John Kidgell, *A Genuine and Succinct Narrative of a scandalous, obscence, and exceedingly profane Libel, entitled An Essay on Woman* (London, 1763).

58. *A Letter to J. Kidgell, containing a full Answer to his Narrative* (London, 1763), 20–21.

59. "A Letter to the Worthy Electors of the Borough of Aylesbury (1767)," in *Wilkes Correspondence*, 3: 113; "Veni Creator; or the Maid's Prayer," in Hamilton, *Infamous Essay*, 245.

60. Kidgell, *Genuine and Succinct Narrative*, 9; *Political Register* 2 (1768): 414; "Letter to Electors of Aylesbury," *Wilkes Correspondence*, 3: 116.

61. "Letter to Electors of Aylesbury," *Wilkes Correspondence* 3: 113–14; *Letters between the Duke of Grafton . . . and John Wilkes* (London, 1769), 112.

62. "Letter to Electors of Aylesbury," *Wilkes Correspondence*, 3: 113; [John Shebbeare], *The History of the Excellence and Decline of the Constitution, Religion, Manners and Genius of the Sumatrans. And of the Restoration thereof in the Reign of Amurath the Third*, 2 vols. (London, c. 1763), 1: 254. On Tory antecedents of the Wilkite movement, see Linda Colley, "Eighteenth-Century English Radicalism before Wilkes," *Transactions of the Royal Historical Society*, 5th ser., 31 (1981): 1–19.

63. John Wilkes's defence of Revolution principles was clearly delineated in the introduction (the only completed portion) of his *The History of England from the Revolution to the Accession of the Brunswick Line* (London, 1768).

64. *Samuel Johnson: Political Writings*, ed. Donald J. Greene (New Haven: Yale University Press, 1977), 344.

65. See, for example, [John Hall-Stevenson], *A Pastoral Puke:A Second Sermon preached before the People called Whigs* (London, 1764).

66. John Wilkes, *A Letter to his Grace the Duke of Grafton, First Commissioner of His Majesty's Treasury*, 8th ed. (London, 1767), 1–15.

67. John Wilkes to Jean-Baptiste Suard, 2 March 1770, Wilkes MSS, 3: Letter 30, Clements Library.

68. *Public Advertiser*, 16 June 1763.

69. The popular literature on the subject is vast. For a poetic squib that neatly defames all three men, see *St. James's Chronicle*, 17–20 December 1763.

70. *Public Advertiser*, 2 June 1763.

71. *Letters between the Duke of Grafton and Wilkes*,37. See also *The New Found ling Hospital for Wit*, 2nd ed . (London, 1768), 42–6; *Humours of the Times* (London, 1771), 47–53; and Shearer, "Libertinism and the Ideology of Male Frier~ship," 98.

72. *St. James's Chronicle*, 26–29 March 1769.

73. *The Battle of the Quills: or, Wilkes Attacked and Defended* (1768), 31, 60; North Briton Extraordinary, 13 November 1770.

74. John Wilkes to Jean-Baptiste Suard, 3 May 1763, Wilkes MSS, 3: Letter 18, Clements Library; *Wilkes Correspondence*, 1: 261–71.

75. Quoted in Richard Sennett,*The Fall of Public Man* (NewYork: W.W. Norton, 1992), 103. See also Shearer, "Libertinism and the Ideology of Male Friendship,"

88–89. Connections between Wilkite radicalism and sexual libertinism are explored in Kathleen Wilson, *The Sense of the People: Politics, Culture and Imperialism in England, 1715–1785* (Cambridge: Cambridge University Press, 1995), esp. 219–25. This important work was published after my essay was already completed.

76. Edward Thompson, *Customs in Common* (New York: New Press, 1993), 16–96.

77. For some suggestive comments concerning the connections between Tom Paine *et al* and Whigs of the early Enlightenment, see Roy Porter, "The Enlightenment in England," in *The Enlightenment in National Context* (Cambridge: Cambridge University Press, 1981), 16.

78. [Joseph Cradock], *The Life of John Wilkes, Esq,; in the Manner of Plutarch* (London, 1773), 26; *Gazetteer*, 27 December 1776. For a rich account of the diffusion of the sexual and religious components of libertinism, see Iain McCalman, *Radical Underworld: Prophets, Revolutionaries, and Pornographers in London, 1795–1840* (Oxford: Clarendon Press, 1993), passim.

79. Bradley, *Religion, Revolution, and English Radicalism*, 137–2; *Wilkes Correspondence*, 1: 20; *Wilkes Speeches*, 326–43; G. M. Ditchfield, "The Subscription Issue in British Parliamentary Politics, 1772–79," *Parliamentary History* 7, pt. 1 (1988), 79n.148.

80. Bradley, *Religion, Revolution and English Radicalism*, 418.

81. Russell E. Richey, "The Origins of British Radicalism: The Changing Rationale for Dissent," *Eighteenth-Century Studies* 7 (1974): 179–92; Miller, "'Freethinking' and 'Freedom of Thought,'" 599–617.

82. Joseph Priestley, *A View of the Principles and Conduct of the Protestant Dissenters with Respect to the Civil and Ecclesiastical Constitution of England* (1769); Priestley to Wilkes, *Wilkes Correspondence*, 5: 251; *Johnson: Political Writings*, ed. Greene, 344.

83. Carla H. Hay, *James Burgh: Spokesman for Reform in Hanoverian England* (Washington, D.C: University Press of America, 1979), 36, 73–74.

84. D. O. Thomas, *The Honest Mind: The Thought and Work of Richard Price* (Oxford: Clarendon Press, 1977), 7, 170, 172; Thomas Somerville, *My Own Life and Times* (Edinburgh, 1861), 146.

85. Sarah Wilkes to John Wilkes, 23 October 1771, Wilkes MSS, 2: Letter 95, Clements Library.

86. For the continuing story, see in particular Leonore Davidoff and Catherine Hall, *Family Fortunes: Men and Women of the English Middle Class, 1780–1850* (Chicago: University of Chicago Press, 1987), 13–192.

Gender Bending and Corporeal Limitations: The Modern Body in *Tristram Shandy*

MIRIAM L. WALLACE

Bodies in History/Bodies of Feminism

Eighteenth-century England has emerged as a particularly contested site for competing sociocultural understandings of the relation between sex and gender.[1] Thomas Laqueur, for example, identifies the eighteenth century as the historic location of a paradigm shift from the one-sex body of ancient and Renaissance medicine to the modern two-sex body.[2] This historical shift marks the emergence of the modern presumption that sex/gender relations are naturally and intrinsically connected; one's sex defines one's gender in a one-to-one correspondence. In contrast to Michel Foucault, Laqueur argues that the one-sex paradigm was never comprehensively replaced by the two-sex paradigm, but still exerts influence today as evidenced in modern philosophic, juridical, and medical discourse which take feminine gendered bodies and subjects as special cases of the human (i.e., masculine).[3] As Laqueur puts it, "Political judgements, the claims of gender, are already contained in judgements about sex because politics is already contained in the biology of generation."[4] Sociohistorical understanding of biology and anatomy is always politically implicated. Thus, even as biological anatomy is used to establish the base for the social implications of gender, that anatomy already incorporates the meaning of those differences which it is invoked to explain. Biology and anatomy themselves are invested with social and political meanings and so can never be objective referees in the debate, although they have often been invoked in this capacity. Indeed, that very invocation is part of a specific historical and social moment when the anatomical body, conceived as two distinct and irreducibly different sexes, becomes the root rationale for a binary conception of gender. Laqueur's work points to an important instability in the cultural understanding of the body in Western Europe. Specifically, in eighteenth-century England two systems for understanding the body, both with the aim of maintaining strategic gender differences, are in uneasy coexistence. As European culture changed, different rationales were needed to maintain patriarchal social order.

Laurence Sterne's *The Life and Opinions of Tristram Shandy, Gentleman* (1759–67) is situated at this historical site of cultural and psychic fracture. *Tristram Shandy's* obsession with the status of the (male) body demands reinterpretation in light of its historical location. In turn, attention to the complex and, I will argue, resistantly anti-phallic construction of masculinity in *Tristram Shandy* raises implications for modern feminist and "queer" theorists' attempts to interrogate gender/sex/sexuality as historically and culturally inflected.

Randolph Trumbach offers a correlating but different account from Laqueur's, interpolating the axis of sexuality into the historical account of gender and sex. Under the shift to modernity, which Trumbach also dates about the mid-eighteenth century, "the modern gender role for men presumed that most men desired women exclusively and that all masculine behavior flowed from such desire.[5] Previously considered *more* masculine by having adolescent male lovers, men in the eighteenth century forfeited their gender right to power and authority by such behavior. After this shift, men who included other men among their lovers were understood as *outside* the masculine gender, belonging instead to a third gender, the sodomite, regardless of whether they took a predominantly passive or active role.[6]

Despite a difference in terminology, Laqueur and Trumbach both suggest that shifts in sexual morphology and gender identity have consistently been in the interest of maintaining male/masculine social authority and material power. Any sex or gender position which overtly undermined that prerogative (such as the passive sodomite) was socially and culturally negated. Laqueur and Trumbach emphasize the historic shifts in popular, medical, and juridical understandings of the body, thereby destabilizing the modern assumption that the body has always been of two distinct sexes and two parallel genders. Accounts which incorporate a psychoanalytic elaboration of embodiment like Luce Irigaray's and (particularly) Judith Butler's destabilize the rigidly sexed body even further.[7]

Gender Bending and Corporeal Limitations / 177

Butler and Irigaray both emphasize that the body is neither some *a priori* material stuff which is then overlayered with the social significance of gender, sex, race, and sexuality, nor a purely discursive formation. Rather, corporeality is theorized as a complex interrelation of materiality, anatomy, the fantasmatic (or the Lacanian imaginary), and discursivity (or the Lacanian symbolic). Butler, for example, locates the body in the tension between the psychic and the material:

> psychic projection confers boundaries and, hence, unity on the body, so that the very contours of the body are sites which vacillate between the psychic and the material. Bodily contours and morphology are not merely implicated in an irreducible tension between the psychic and the material but are that tension. Hence, the psyche is not a grid through which a pre-given body appears. That formulation would figure the body as an ontological in-itself which only becomes available through a psyche which establishes its mode of appearance as an epistemological object
>
> ... the materiality of the body ought not to be conceptualized as a unilateral or causal *effect* of the psyche in any sense that would reduce that materiality to the psyche or make of the psyche the monistic stuff out of which that materiality is produced and/or derived.[8]

Butler specifically rejects the notion that the body has a material *a priori* existence which is then filtered through the psyche to become the culturally marked body we know. Nor does she want to reduce the body's materiality to purely psychical matter. Rather than privileging internal psychic embodiment or an external, material and natural body, Butler gestures toward a body which exceeds both psychic and material locations. In this she is in unexpected conjunction with Irigaray, whose emphasis on female morphology implies a sexual difference neither purely anatomical nor purely psychic, but excessive of both. It is this sense of body as both a *material*, and thus socially important, locus of accreted cultural meanings, and as a *psychically* experienced and inflected locus beyond pure materiality, which informs the following examination of morphology in *Tristram Shandy*.

The other well-documented historic change of the eighteenth century is the gendered division of labor, which becomes particularly rigid as the middle classes begin to dominate the social scene.[9] Thus, modern gender is decisively invented in the eighteenth century at the same time as fundamental changes take place in the material means of production and reproduction. Gendered bodies have different meanings and different materialities in different historical and cultural locations. These lost or forgotten differences proffer a possibility of resistance to the seeming inevitability of modern gendered identity, and therefore to dominant systems of knowledge and social relations since these systems are crucially pegged to gender. If, as Laqueur and Trumbach suggest, gender and sexuality are historically constructed to maintain the dominance of one social class and one gender over another, then marking the instability of gender and sexuality in those key historical moments raises the possibility of resistance to or even transformation of current gender/sex relations.

According to Irigaray both the imaginary and the symbolic are sexuate, the prevailing forms being masculine or "phallomorphic." Irigaray links her complex understanding of the interrelation of the imaginary and the symbolic with the morphology of femininity and masculinity. As Margaret Whitford notes:

> She [Irigaray] goes further than previous phenomenologists in that she conceptualizes the imaginary in terms of sex, either male or female: the imaginary either bears the morphological marks of the male body, whose cultural products are characterized by unity, teleology, linearity, self-identity, and so on or it bears the morphological marks of the female body, characterized by plurality, non-linearity, fluid identity and so on.[10]

Irigaray does not claim that the male body is essentially unified, linear and self-identified, or that the female body is essentially fluid, plural and nonlinear. Rather she claims that there is a masculine-encoded morphology, and an oppositionally constituted morphology which is encoded feminine. Subjects take their places in the symbolic economy in part by psychically accepting these morphologies which are simultaneously socioculturally imposed. These morphologies undergird the very construction of knowledge, informing not only the symbolic but the imaginary. Morphology, then, is experienced as a social or material identity (symbolic) and also as a psychic and projective identity (imaginary). "The imaginary has a projective dimension.... Imaginary identity cannot be limited to the unconscious phantasy of an individual. These phantasies are themselves structured by the symbolic, so that identity is also collective and social."[11] Combined sexual, gender, and racial identity is therefore complexly experienced as the internal and social "truth" of one's ontology.

The subject's role in accepting as true his or her own morphology even as it is imposed offers an important site of resistance. If identity is collective and social as well as individual, then contradictions, excesses, and failures of identity to maintain a coherent outline in the imaginary will also have an effect in the social realm. Thus, contradictory social demands placed upon individual morphology, as well as psychic conflicts between one's socially imposed morphology and one's internalized accepted morphology, disrupt the smooth conjunction of the dominant symbolic and the gendered imaginary. This disjunction is promising and likely to be available to all subjects.

Aligned with Louis Althusser's notion of interpellation and operating as a corrective to Foucault's tendency to theorize dominant structures as monolithically powerful, Irigaray's analysis of morphology and symbolic location suggests that the dominant symbolic is never completely successful. The subject always risks exceeding or failing to fulfill the demands of the dominant symbolic. Irigaray theorizes "mimicry" as a resistant strategy of feminine excess.[12] Restricted to the negative position of femininity within the dominant symbolic, the feminine subject may overplay her part, effectively parodying femininity and making her restrictive position self-consciously present in its inability to correspond to her sense of complete self. While Irigaray focuses most explicitly on the excessive nature of sexual difference itself—insisting on feminine sexual specificity in order to disrupt a symbolic order based on a *singular* (and masculine-phallic) sexuality—she also hints that there are excesses to be explored within *masculine* subjectivity. Irigaray returns again and again to the body and to feminine corporeality as being particularly problematic for the dominant symbolic. She implies that male corporeality, if investigated in its material specificity, would also exceed the phallic order.

Butler also identifies corporeality as an important site for theorizing resistance to the dominant binary system of sex/gender. In *Gender Trouble* she argues that gender is performative rather than natural, advocating parodic gender performance as a strategy for resisting the dominant symbolic system. *Bodies That Matter*, especially her essay "The Lesbian Phallus and the Morphological Imagination," pursues this point further, arguing that the phallus in particular is available for resistant appropriation. Asserting the phallus's idealized nature, Butler detaches the phallus from its location as the "transcendental signifier" with a privileged relation to the penis. As an idealized symbolic structure the phallus is fluid and avoids any easy assimilation to anatomical markers such as the penis. But because the phallus traditionally bears a privileged relation to the penis, it undergirds male privilege. Because it functions both as an idealized anatomical referent and as a signifier which floats above all referents, the phallus is in conflict with its own claims. Thus, she is able to argue for "an aggressive reterritorialization" of the phallus as ultimately transferable, and therefore available for resistant lesbian morphology.[13]

The dominant symbolic as a phallomorphic structure is particularly vulnerable in both Irigaray's and Butler's estimation. Irigaray insists upon the specificity of feminine corporeal difference, making overt the covert gendering of the seemingly neutral concepts of "human," "subject," "imaginary," and "symbolic." She serves as an important reminder of the potential cooptation of Butler's argument that gender and sex are performative rather than natural. While Butler enables a reading of Shandean masculinity and corporeality as subversively fluid, Irigaray reasserts the ultimate exclusivity of that vision which depends upon male homosociality. Finally, I suggest that Sterne's narrative experiment with subversive subjectivity clarifies the stakes of Butler's argument for fluid performative gendering and Irigaray's argument for feminine specificity. The novel helps to focus the ways in which each theorist's work is itself limited or susceptible to cooptation. Butler's strategy of performative resistance in *Gender Trouble* is particularly available for appropriation, while Irigaray's strategy of transformation floats between immaterial style and essentialism.

Tristram Shandy *and Male Corporeality*

Tristram Shandy represents the underside of an emerging structure of gender and sexuality in eighteenth-century England. Rather than merely appropriating or excluding femininity as some feminist readings have argued, *Tristram Shandy* reveals the anxiety at the heart of modern, western, phallic masculinity at its moment of inception.[14] In particular, the male body emerges as a potent site for theorizing a history of resistant male subjectivity. Obsessively and emphatically present, the (male) body in *Tristram Shandy* is central to imagining an "other masculine" subject. The Shandean subject is embodied as at once male/masculine, and other than the dominant disembodied, specular male body of Enlightenment thought. *Tristram Shandy* reveals the embodied male subject caught between two systems of gendered corporeality. The novel places the Shandean men firmly within the context of Laqueur's modern two-sex system, yet it represents their bodies as of the older Renaissance variety, liable to change and insistently threatening to betray their gender privilege. The Shandean body is aligned with Trumbach's third gender through its tendency to rupture, its lack of stable boundaries, its inconsistent and undependable behavior, and its penetrability. Without overtly questioning the system of two distinct genders anymore than they question the class divisions of their world, Shandean subjects reveal an instability at the heart of those social institutions, and hence of dominant masculinity itself, signaling both social and psychic resistance from within the privileged symbolic order.

As Shandean subjects exceed cultural delineations of the individual through sentimental bonding, so do they exceed the corporeal delineations which mark

Gender Bending and Corporeal Limitations / 181

the white western male subject as the neutral body of human subjectivity.[15] A male body which insists upon its own corporeality disrupts the hierarchic binary between transcendent male and immanently embodied female.[16] Furthermore, a male body which experiences itself as permeable, penetrable, incoherent, and polymorphous threatens to undo the grounding modern definition of anatomy as a complementary structure of male and female. Laqueur's argument that, in the eighteenth century, anatomy had become the naturalized ground on which gender as a complementary two-sex system rested, reveals how deeply troubling the Shandean male body with its ruptures, openings, and shifting erogenous zones could be for Sterne's contemporaries, as well as for his successors.

Bodily anatomy is an unreliable source of truth and knowledge in the Shandean world. Illustrating the imaginative slippage of anatomy, Uncle Toby supplies a missing rationale for Mrs. Shandy's preference for the old midwife: "——My sister, I dare say, added he, does not care to let a man come so near her . . .," to which Walter replies "——To think, said my father, of a man living to your age, brother, and knowing so little about women! . . .—Me thinks, brother, . . . you might, at least, know so much as the right end of a woman from the wrong."[17] Walter mocks Toby's confusion of Mrs. Shandy's "arse" with her vagina, inducing the knowing (male) reader to laugh with him. Surely there can be no confusion about the location of a woman's genitalia, the synecdochal site of her identity? Yet the confusion the passage marks is an important and pervasive one, despite Walter's assumption that there can be no confusion for a man who "knows" women. Toby's naive remark, proof of his own modest ignorance of "the sex" and his moral innocence, implies the opposite and implicates the reader in that immodest knowledge. The passage marks a slippage between the "recto" and "verso" entrances to the body. Like the "nose-penis" conflation, once the suggestion of anal intercourse is raised in *Tristram*, it proliferates throughout the text. A favorite in eighteenth-century erotica, portrayal of rear-entry sex between men and women implies that the port of ingress is the vagina. However, the erotic titillation of such representations arises from the possibility that the point of entry might equally well be the anus, or that the woman might not be one. Once the question of the "right" and "wrong" end of a woman is raised, right and wrong ends of all bodies become difficult to distinguish absolutely.

Walter himself establishes this slippage in volume 8, when he refers to the bodily passions as Toby's "ass." The situation is further complicated when Walter inquires how Toby's "asse" is today, which Toby mistakes for a solicitous inquiry about his blistered "arse."[18] Walter's insistence that the "right" end of a woman is a thing easily known is undermined by his obfuscation of the right and wrong ends of a man. The recto becomes confused with the verso, the male with the female, the right side with the wrong side, the front with the back, and the anus with the vagina.[19] The confusion between the mind and body, the anus and the vagina, and even between the interior and exterior of the body marks a particularly subversive construction of masculinity.[20] This confusion, proliferating through the text's bawdy jokes and double entendres, suggests both an excessive male imaginary resistant to the dominant "anal imaginary" (which Irigaray identifies in *This Sex*) and a conservative masculine anxiety about the instability of sex and gender identifications.

If, as Eve Sedgwick argues, eighteenth-century male homosociality is predicated upon a denial of homosexuality, then homoerotic desire constitutes an excess of the masculine imaginary structurally repressed by the symbolic.[21] Characterized by Irigaray as an "hom(m)osexual economy of the same," the dominant symbolic rests upon an "anal imaginary."[22] Irigaray theorizes this as an appropriative monosexual gesture, containing the possible excesses of feminine morphology. I argue that the monosexual anal imaginary also contains and excludes the excesses of *male* morphology, and that this is an important extension of Irigaray's work. Irigaray's emphasis on the body as mediated through the imaginary (and thus the symbolic) suggests that the body serves as an effective site for interrogating the "hom(m)osexual economy of the same." If the corporeality of the male body disrupts the smooth operation of phallicism, it may also be presumed to disrupt phallicism's other side, the anal imaginary. Attention to the corporeality of the penis and the anus is therefore a subversive move, returning the phallus and the anus to their unidealized morphological components. It is important then, to theorize the morphological meaning of the anus as opposed to the anal imaginary.

The "anus" itself may be understood as a threshold in its subversion of the anal imaginary. The "threshold," an important term in Irigaray's work, marks feminine morphological supplementarity through resisting categorization as internal or external to the body proper. The threshold marks a privileged site of non-logical, non-rational excess.[23] Understood as a threshold, the anus no longer functions merely as an appropriation of the vagina, but as another site of morphological excess. This is a different symbolic use of the anus than the dominant one of the anal imaginary or Sigmund Freud's "anal phase." The economy of the anal imaginary depends upon a radical separation and disjunction of other from self and inside from outside. That Freudian economy depends also upon a metaphoric chain of substitution among baby-feces-gold-penis-gift.[24] This type of anal operates in only one sense, the phallic one, synecdochally standing for a unified subject instead of figuring the subject's undecidability or multiplicity. I suggest we differentiate between two senses of anal: the Irigarian anal imaginary as an articulation of phallicism in which radical separation and categorization predominate, and an alternative sense as a morphological metonym for threshold, where thresholds serve as place-holders to disrupt the function of the phallomorphic symbolic. Close attention to the proliferating and confused references to buggery, asses and backsides throughout *Tristram Shandy* enables the differentiation of anus-as-threshold from anal imaginary which I have teased out between the lines of Irigaray's arguments, and reveals the other masculine within the textual representation of dominant phallic masculinity.

Shandean corporeality highlights the instability of binary gender, insistently conflating recto with verso and mind with body. Uncle Toby confuses his own anatomical and psychic corporeality in particularly suggestive ways, for example when he first suffers the pangs of love for the Widow Wadman:

> In truth, he had mistook it at first; for having taken a ride with my father, that very morning, to save if possible a beautiful wood, which the dean and chapter were hewing down to give the poor; ... by trotting on too hastily to save it—upon an uneasy saddle—worse horse, &c. &c ... it had so happened, that the serous part of the blood had got betwixt the two skins, in the nethermost part of my uncle Toby—the first shootings of which (as my uncle *Toby* had no experience of love) he had taken for a part of the passion—till the blister breaking in the one case—and the other remaining—my uncle *Toby* was presently convinced, that his wound was not a skin-deep-wound—but that it had gone to his heart.[25]

This passage conflates a blister near the anus with the emotional pain of love. Spiritual love and physical desire are also conflated. Following the slippage of front-to-back, Uncle Toby's swollen backside also suggests the swelling frontside of an erection. The rupture of the blister, the flowing of fluid, and the relief which accompanies it convinces Uncle Toby that he is in love. Anatomy is already morphology; that is, anatomy is implicated in cultural meanings which suggest that Shandean morphology bears a problematic relation to a binary understanding of male morphology. As the nose becomes a penis, so the posterior and the anterior are confounded and genital sensations and sentimental feelings (the heart wound Toby finally recognizes) are conflated. The body is not distinct from nor in opposition to the spirit, but each is implicated in the other. The body is shiftingly charged with erotic significance in defiance of compulsory heterosexuality which would restrict erotic significance to specific anatomical sites.

The Shandean (male) body with its multiple and shifting erotics and its conflation of soul and body is in direct contrast to the dominant specular and contained body of patriarchal social organization. As Elizabeth Grosz explains:

> ... the pre-existence of patriarchal social relations relies on the *production* of a specific form of male sexuality through internalisation of images representations and signifying practices. In other words, men do not form discourse in their own image(s); rather, phallocentric discourses form male sexuality in their image(s).[26]

Grosz emphasizes that male bodies are not *essentially* phallic, but, in a complementary fashion, specific forms of sexuality and gendering are required by both social discursive structures and individual psychic structures for intelligible male subjectivity under patriarchy. The Shandy men both are and are not successful in this formation; they interpellate masculinity, but in a problematic form. Phallic bodily organization is neither successful nor coherent in the Shandean world. Shandean homosociality depends upon the dissolution, or at least the permeability, of individually bounded bodies through male-male sentimental bonding.

Bodily functions and mental functions impinge upon each other throughout the text. For example, the author's preface mocks the assumption that judgement and wit are inherently separate functions, never to be found in the same works:

> Now, *Agelastes* (speaking dispraisingly) sayeth, That there may be some wit in it for aught he knows,——but no judgement at all. And *Triptolemus* and *Phutatorius* agreeing thereto, ask How is it possible there should? for that wit and judgement in this world never go together; inasmuch as they are two operations differing from each other as wide as east is from west. —So, says *Locke*,—so are farting and hickuping, say I.[27]

The narrator, in arguing for the coexistence of wit and judgement, suggests that philosophically abstract arguments may be effectively argued from the body. His assertion is a disrespectful and mocking attack, humorous precisely because of its insistence on bodily functions within the abstract, disembodied context of philosophy. However, the linking of wit and judgement with farting and hiccuping contains implications for the body which interrogate male privilege.

Arguing that wit and judgement do in fact occur together and occur at their best together, invites speculation about the appropriate relation of the bodily locations of the aforementioned fart and hiccup. There is a masked reference to the mouth and the anus here which suggests a relation between these two which is generally overlooked. While east and west mark the farthest parameters of difference here, if both are explosions of air and gas from the body's interior then not only are different bodily openings aligned, but the very boundaries of the body are put into question. Both farting and hiccuping are rude reminders of the body's material functions. The hiccup and the fart reveal an even deeper anxiety than the recognition of the material body's pressure upon abstract rationality; the bodily boundaries defining what is interior and therefore proper to the body and what is exterior and therefore other are put into question. The specularizing function is destabilized as the body reveals its fragmentation and permeability to other less privileged senses. Hearing and smell reveal what sight works to hide; the (male) body and thus the (male) subject is not solid, contained, or in complete control of itself. "Specularity," a central term in Lacanian psychoanalytic subject formation, implies a psychic splitting of the "I" that sees (the symbolic or subject) from the "me" that is seen (the imaginary or ego).[28] The specularity of the subject is central to a psychoanalytic account of the subject's splitting as part of the cost of accession to the symbolic realm.

Subject formation is one point where psychoanalytic and materialist theories intersect, despite the different terminologies and histories of each. While psychoanalytic and poststructuralist accounts have been critiqued for their inattention to material effects, materialist analyses also theorize a divided subject in their attention to the body/labor split located in John Locke's founding claim that "every man has a property in himself."[29] Mary Poovey draws out the implications of Locke's seemingly self-evident statement:

> This amounted to every individual male being constituted as a divided subject. This internal division was the basis for the "free" exchange of labour and therefore the production of surplus value, but it was also the basis for the alienation every man experienced in the market economy.[30]

The psychoanalytic account locates the subject-object split in an internal psychic division which is projected outward onto other subjects. These others are then positioned as objects in relation to which the subject gains an imaginary coherence. The materialist account locates the source of the market economy in an internalized division between ontology and labor. Both accounts converge in a self-alienation created in the interests of hegemonic cultural ideology, and both demand an "other" to bear the burden of the self's loss. This convergence is an important corrective to the easy dismissal of psychoanalytic accounts of subjectivity as abstract and ahistorical, or of materialist theorizing as uncritical of latent essentialism. Both forms of theorizing at their best posit a complex relation between social forces and the body as constitutive of the "self."

Tristram Shandy effectively reveals alienation as intrinsic to male middle-class subjectivity, but stops short of recognizing the part which class, property relations, and race play in this loss. Walter Shandy is a retired Turkey merchant, a popular and lucrative trade requiring ready capital and profiting from the exotic appeal of Eastern goods for British and Western European bourgeois and aristocrats. Toby Shandy is a veteran of the War of the Spanish Succession. The history of this war is rife with British political and economic interests, and it is an important foundation for emerging national identity. While excluded from the text of the novel directly, British colonialism and domination of trade within and outside of Europe subtextually support the construction of the Shandean subject, even at its most resistant.

Shandean permeability and wounds obliquely reiterate the anxieties which trade and colonialism open in the national body and the denial which protects that body's integrity. The unidirectional cultural influence which Walter's trade, Toby's soldiering, and Tristram's tour of France proclaim is parallel to the unidirectional subject-merging of the sentimental episodes with the ass and Maria. The possibilities opened by the insistence on male corporeality as permeable are thus delimited by the exclusive and restrictive nature of the European male homosocial world in which such exchanges are figured. In a heterosocial or heterocultural context, permeability is delimited. *Tristram Shandy* fails to extend the logic of the Shandean male beyond a western male/masculine context, while class is problematically subsumed into homosociality through the figure of Trim as the ideal servant/partner. This blind spot in *Tristram Shandy's* revisioning of masculinity mirrors the limitations of psychoanalytic accounts which fail to take historical and cultural specificity into account.

The text, however, insists that the impotent Shandean body is nevertheless a *male* body, not merely subsumable into a feminized "third gender." If the Shandean subject were located as a feminized body, then the hegemonic system of masculine/feminine genders parallel to and based upon male/female sex would be upheld. Language itself works to reestablish this structure, tempting the reader to identify the Shandean subject as "feminine" or "feminized." In other words, we are invited to read Shandy men as "not-masculine" and "abject," thereby reinscribing the phallic masculine as the human from which they are humorously and pathetically excluded. The anomalous falls into an oppositional "feminine" category which contains that which threatens dominant phallic masculinity. The symbolic realm of language returns us to the binary sex/gender system. The Shandean body, however, is consistently and insistently male and masculine, although its parameters conflict with more traditional understandings of that designation. It is a body open to sentimental homosociality and corporeal penetration, as the persistent references to bodily openings and buggery suggest. Thus the Shandean body is permeable in ways the modern representation of the heterosexual male body denies.

The Shandean body also bears a complex relation to corporeal effects most often attributed to the *female* body. The eighteenth-century physician William Harvey proposed the biological function of conception as the male idea initiating conception in the woman's womb.[31] The slippage here between the metaphoric implications of the term "conception" and its material consequences marks a longer trajectory of the gender politics of biology. Aristotle suggested that sperm was frothy, consisting largely of animal heat and so of a higher order than the "matter" of blood which was woman's contribution to conception.[32] The female in accordance with her social status contributed the lesser element, "matter," while the male in accordance with his higher nature contributed the "necessary cause" for shaping matter and endowing it with spirit. Following in this trajectory, the Anglican and the Roman Catholic churches emphasize baptism as a second birth. Institutionalized Christianity embodies the division of labor in conception and birth, allocating the birth of the flesh to woman and the birth of the spirit to the sacrament of baptism, performed by a priest of the church. The birth of the flesh belongs to women, that of the spirit to men.

Tristram's discussion of the homunculi conflates the birth of the flesh with the birth of the spirit, writing male bodies as pregnant and permeable. His satirical anti-Catholic commentary works to mask the broader implications of his proposition. Tristram's address to the learned doctors humorously links their tedious discussion with the labor of childbirth itself: "Mr. Tristram Shandy's compliments to Messrs. *Le Moyne, DeRomigny*, and *De Marcilly*, hopes they all rested well the night after so tiresome a consultation."[33] Their discussion is "tiresome" or boring as specious and excessive argument, and it is "tiresome" or tiring, like the work of birth itself Tristram goes on with a proposition of his own:

> —He begs to know, whether, after the ceremony of marriage, and before that of consummation, the baptizing all the HOMUNCULI at once, slapdash, by *injection*, would not be a shorter and safer cut still; on condition, as above, That if the HOMUNCULI do well and come safe into the world after this, that each and every of them shall be baptized again (*sous condition*)——And provided, in the second place, That the thing can be done, which Mr. *Shandy* apprehends it may, *par le moyen d'une* petite canulle, and *sans faire aucun tort au père* (italics in the original).[34]

While Tristram's solution, baptizing all the homunculi after the sacrament of marriage and before consummation, is meant to mock Catholic theological hair-splitting, it also makes a more serious suggestion. As the locus of the homunculi, the male body becomes a childbearing body. The male body takes on the very attributes which are newly used to define woman as an irreducibly different body. But this is neither simply a feminization of the masculine/male body, nor an appropriation of the female capacity for bodily reproduction. What is invoked but left unsaid is that this baptism would involve penetrating the penis. Tristram's final claim, that this could be done, if at all "without any harm to the father," mirrors the earlier remark about not harming the mother in the process, but also reconstructs the male body as a penetrable body. His remark, while overtly mocking the absurdity of the learned doctors, also reminds us that the male body, defined under phallicism by its unity and impenetrability, is in fact penetrable. The very organ of penetration, the penis, which is aligned most directly with the all-powerful phallus, is itself penetrable. Even as Tristram's joke depends upon the unquestioned assumption of absolute and natural differences between the male and female body which make the idea of baptizing homunculi ridiculous, it reveals the instability of those presumably fixed differences. If the male body generally and the penis specifically are penetrable, then the different construction of feminine bodies as penetrable and male bodies as impermeable, of feminine as vulnerable and masculine as dominant, become unstable. Working within a two-sex model, this passage evokes the destabilizing remainder of the one sex system.

One of the most interesting and underdeveloped aspects of Irigaray's work is her suggestion that attention to the specifics of male corporeality would be anti-phallic in its effects, and might even lead to an "other" (male) imaginary. Irigaray's own project is to release the feminine imaginary from its position as the repressed "other of the same." This evades the oppositional framework which contains the female imaginary as the supportive "other" to the dominant male imaginary so that a truly feminine imaginary, or "other of the other" may be realized. This "other of the other" is an utopic, specifically feminine location, imagined as truly "other" rather than as merely *oppositional* to male imaginaries, and is thus a new female imaginary. If an oppositional *male* imaginary were articulated within Irigaray's framework, this might free the feminine imaginary to create itself as the "other of the other." In fact, taking her suggestion seriously, an "other male imaginary" might mean the beginning of an entirely different order of discourse and sexual relations, exploding the binary sex/gender system and rearticulating what "sexual specificity" could mean.

Gender Bending and Corporeal Limitations / 189

A mark of the phallocratic agency of language is the difficulty scholars find in attempting to describe alternate subjectivities and sexualities without returning to the binary language of masculinity and femininity. If to be penetrable is a mark of women's social, historical and psychic construction as the complement to masculine subjectivity, what language is available to discuss the male/masculine as penetrable? To avoid collapsing penetrable and penetrated male/masculine subject positions into feminine subjectivity, I suggest an "other masculine." It is here that I locate the Shandean subject as an exploration of male corporeality which is antithetical to phallocentrism.[35] Phallocentrism *depends* upon the substitution of the phallus for the specificity of the male body. It is the phallus which gives the male-gaze its specular properties and allows for what Donna Haraway terms "the god trick."[36] As Grosz explains:

> [Irigaray's] claim is that the masculine can speak of and for the feminine largely because it has emptied itself of any relation to the male body, its specificity, and socio-political existence. This process of evacuating the male body from (an oedipalized) masculinity is the precondition for the establishment of the "disinterested" neutered space of male spe-cul(ariz)ation. Within this (virtual or imaginary) space, the space of the ego, and its mirror-double, the male can look at itself from outside, take itself as an object while retaining its position as a subject.[37]

Irigaray implies that where the male subject *refuses* to take that external, specular, objective, unified and disembodied position, where it insists upon its own corporeality, it works against the phallocentric and patriarchal project. *Tristram Shandy* is a suggestive example of such resistance given its location in the history of the novel.

Tristram Shandy clarifies some of the possibilities and limitations of a dynamic insistence on male corporeality. Such an emphasis invokes broader possibilities of the experience of male corporeality, and suggests that the attendant imaginary differs from Irigaray's "hom(m)osexual" imaginary. *Tristram Shandy*'s corporeality operates as radically as it does, however, only within the homosocial and homocultural Shandean world of men. The Shandean body maintains its male/masculine identity at the cost of overt misogyny. Within a heterosexual context the Shandean males insist on their male privilege despite their apparent impotence. Walter speaks for Mrs. Shandy, Toby escapes from the predatory Widow Wadman, and Tristram sends Madame back to reread an entire chapter. While the masculine/male is reimagined as exceeding traditional boundaries, the female/feminine is restricted to overdetermined locations and is unavailable for reimagining. The male body is reconstituted phallically in the context of female bodies. The Shandean permeable body is finally an exclusionary model.

Conclusion

Ultimately, Sterne's is a vision of limited potential because it fails fundamentally to question the divisions of class, race, culture, and gender, portraying a possible alternate world only by excluding racialized, classed, and gendered others. *Tristram Shandy* is able to explore corporeal and masculine excess by excluding women from the central subversive vision. Relations among men are multiple, complex, and various, while relations with women and other subalterns are sentimental or antagonistic. The very strategies by which gendered individuation may be resisted are themselves specifically sexed and gendered. Nevertheless, such early and insistent resistance to the privileged construction of dominant male subjectivity is suggestive. Despite its limitations, Sterne's text is able to use (male) corporeality in conjunction with experimental narrative form effectively to disrupt rational individualism and phallic masculinity. *Tristram Shandy* marks the cost to the western middle-class male subject of its own dominance, and recognizes at least that that cost is significant.

Male subversions of masculinity—ones especially historically and culturally located—are important for current feminist work as well as for queer theory and cultural studies. The problem of exclusionary constructions which *Tristram Shandy* exemplifies has returned as a particularly pressing concern for feminism, as critiques of Irigaray's essentialism show and which Butler's turn to performance only partially solves. Feminist theory needs to investigate the construction of masculinity from a *feminist* standpoint rather than abdicating that articulation to other theoretical approaches. Masculinity is a crucial and viable subject of study for feminists in part because femininity has historically been closely appended to and delimited by the needs of masculinity. That relation can only be shifted and undermined by destabilizing both masculinity and femininity at the same time. Western representational and hegemonic material structures depend upon a certain formulation of masculinity. Thus *Tristram Shandy*'s successes in reimagining masculinity and its limitations in imagining femininity are intrinsic to the project of feminism. Feminism, to avoid exclusionary definitions of "women," needs both to continue Butler's work toward fluid gender bending and to honor Irigaray's demand for feminine specificity, while maintaining a clear awareness of the limitations and liabilities of each strategy in isolation.

Finally, the specificities of the various projects of queer theorists, gender studies more broadly, and feminism need to be recognized and delineated. As some theorists have pointed out, feminism and lesbian and gay studies share theoretical and political concerns, but are attuned to different, if parallel, histories of oppression and resistance.[38] The loss of those specificities under a broad umbrella such as gender studies may effectively depoliticize and mainstream the subversive resistance inherent in each of those approaches.

NOTES

I would like to thank George Haggerty, John O. Jordan, Helene Moglen, Sally O'Driscoll, Stephen Shapiro, Ron Silver, and Richard Terdiman for critical responses to this essay at various stages of its development. I would also like to extend my gratitude to the three outside readers for *SECC* 26 for their substantive and specific suggestions.

1. For varying accounts of the relation between sexuality, gender, and eighteenth century culture, see Randolph Trumbach, "Sex, Gender, and Sexual Identity in Modern Culture: Male Sodomy and Female Prostitution in Enlightenment London," *Journal of the History of Sexuality* 2.2 (1991): 186–203; Thomas Laqueur, *Making Sex: Body and Gender from the Greeks to Freud* (New York: Routledge, 1990); Nancy Armstrong, *Desire and Domestic Fiction: A Political History of the Novel* (New York: Oxford University Press, 1987); and Michel Foucault, *A History of Sexuality: Volume 1: An Introduction*, trans. Robert Hurley (New York: Vintage/Random House, 1980).

2. Laqueur, *Making Sex*. Laqueur notes that even the physical facts of anatomy, the body's very materiality, were seen and understood differently by authorities and common people, physicians and midwives, under the rubric of the "one-sex body." The one-sex body understood female and male as different locations on a gradient of more or less perfect bodies with God as the ultimate perfection, man as the closest approximation, and woman as an imperfectly formed man (*Making Sex*, Chap. 1, and the introduction to *The Making of the Modern Body: Sexuality and Society in the Nineteenth Century*, ed. Catherine Gallagher and Thomas Laqueur [Berkeley: University of California Press, 1987]).

3. An example of this is the language and diagrams used in medical and biology texts which present the human as the male body, and the female as an anomalous type of the larger human form. See *Gray's Anatomy*, 38th ed., edited by Lawrence H. Bannister et al. (Edinburgh and New York: Churchill Livingstone, 1995), originally published in London in 1858 by Henry Gray (1825–1861) under the title *Anatomy, Descriptive and Surgical*. The notion of the "citizen" prevalent in political science and legal studies often still as-

sumes a male subject, the differences of gender and race defining an anomalous case, or more perniciously, assumed to be unimportant or non-existent.

4. Laqueur, *Making Sex*, 141.
5. Trumbach, "Sex, Gender, and Sexual Identity," 187.
6. Ibid., 192–93.
7. See Luce Irigaray, *Speculum of the Other Woman*, trans. Gillian C. Gill (Ithaca: Cornell University Press,1985); *This Sex Which Is Not One*, trans. Catherine Porter with Carolyn Burke (Ithaca: Cornell University Press, 1985); *An Ethics of Sexual Difference*, trans. Caroline Burke and Gillian C. Gill (Ithaca: Cornell University Press, 1993); and *Sexes and Genealogies*, trans. Gillian C. Gill (New York: Columhia University Press, 1993); Judith Butler, *Gender Trouble: Feminism and the Subversion of Identity* (New York: Routledge, 1990); *Bodies That Matter: On the Discursive Limits of "Sex"* (New York: Routledge, 1993).
8. Butler, *Bodies*, 66.
9. See Ian Watt, *The Rise of the Novel* (Berkeley: University of California Press, 1957); Terry Lovell, *Consuming Fiction* (New York: Verso, 1987); Armstrong, *Desire and Domestic Fiction;* Lawrence Stone, *The Family, Sex and Marriage in England, 1500–1800* (New York: Harper and Row, 1977).
10. Margaret Whitford, *Luce Irigaray: Philosophy in the Feminine* (New York: Routledge, 1991), 54.
11. Whitford, *Luce Irigaray*, 90.
12. Irigaray, *This Sex*, 152, 76.
13. Butler, *Bodies*, 86.
14. Ruth Perry's essay, "Words for Sex: The Verbal/Sexual Continuum in *Tristram Shandy*," is one of very few feminist readings of *Tristram Shandy*. Perry argues that Sterne appropriates the place of women (for example in Toby and Trim's affectionate coupling or "marriage"), and that the book then denies and excludes its female characters and women generally (*Studies in the Novel* 20.1 [Spring 1988]: 27–42).
15. Miriam L. Wallace, "Male-male Sentiment and the Subversion of Masculinity: The Case of *Tristram Shandy*" (Paper delivered at "Early Modern Culture 1450–1850 Conference," University of Rochester, Rochester, New York, 4 November, 1994).
16. See Genevieve Lloyd's *The Man of Reason: "Male" and "Female" in Western Philosophy* (Minneapolis: University of Minnesota Press,1984); Irigaray's *This Sex* and *Speculum*; and Earl Jackson's "Scandalous Subjects: Robert Gluck's Embodied Narratives," *Differences* 3.2 (1991): 112–34.
17. Laurence Sterne, *The Life and Opinions of Tristram Shandy, Gentleman*, ed. Ian Watt (Boston: Houghton Mifflin, 1965), 76–77. All further references will be to this edition.
18. Sterne, *Tristram Shandy*, 450.
19. Lee Edelman, "Seeing Things: Representation, the Scene of Surveillance, and the Spectacle of Gay Male Sex," in *Inside/Out: Lesbian Theories, Gay Theories*, ed. Diana Fuss (New York: Routledge Chapman Hall, 1991), 93–116.

20. The only essay I have found which addresses the under-analyzed proliferation of buggery in the novel is Frank Brady, "*Tristram Shandy*: Sexuality, Morality, and Sensibility," in *New Casebooks: The Life and Opinions of Tristram Shandy, Gentleman*, ed. Melvyn New (New York: St. Martin's Press, 1989), 79.

21. Eve Sedgwick, *Between Men: Male Homosocial Desire in English Literature* (New York: Columbia University Press, 1985).

22. See Irigaray, *This Sex*, particularly "Power of Discourse," "Cosi Fan Tutti," and "Women on the Market."

23. I am indebted to Margaret Whitford's explanation of the "threshold" in Irigaray's work, although I have a slightly different understanding (*Luce Irigaray*, 159–65). I understand Irigaray's figure of the "angel" shuttling between heaven and earth, the human and the divine in *Sexes and Genealogies*, and the "two lips" from *This Sex* which are neither open nor closed, but *entre ouvert*, or parted, neither definitively mouth nor labia but both, as threshold figures.

24. Irigaray, *Speculum*, 74–75.

25. Sterne, *Tristram Shandy*, 446–47.

26. Elizabeth Grosz, *Sexual Subversions: Three French Feminists* (Boston: Allen and Unwin, 1989), 112.

27. Sterne, *Tristram Shandy*, 143.

28. See Kaja Silverman, introduction to *Male Subjectivity at the Margins* (New York: Routledge, 1992).

29. As cited in Mary Poovey, "Covered But Not Bound: Caroline Norton and the 1857 Matrimonial Causes Act," *Feminist Studies* 14.3 (Fall 1988): 276; John Locke, *The Second Treatise of Government* (Indianapolis: Bobbs-Merrill, 1952), 17.

30. Poovey, "Covered," 476.

31. Laqueur, *Making Sex*, 142–48. Laqueur refers to Harvey as " . . . the man who thought that conception was the having of an idea, sparked by sperm, in the womb" (*Making Sex*, 42).

32. See Giulia Sissa, "Bodies," in *Zone Magazine: Fragments for a History of the Human Body*, ed. Michael Feher et al. (Cambridge: MIT Press, 1989), 3: 13356; and Thomas Laqueur, "Amor Veneris vel Dulcedo Appelatur," in Feher, *Zone*, 91–132.

33. Sterne, *Tristram Shandy*, 47.

34. Ibid., 47–48.

35. I do not call this a male-homosexual subject for several reasons. First, that naming would misrepresent modern male-homosexual diversity and historical specificity. Second, I want to suggest that while the Shandean subject is homosocial, it is also more polymorphously sexual than the term "homosexual" is commonly understood to imply.

36. See Donna Haraway, "Situated Knowledges: The Science Question in Feminism as a Site of Discourse on the Privilege of Partial Perspective," *Feminist Studies* 14.3 (1988): 575–99.

37. Elizabeth Grosz, *Jacques Lacan: A Feminist Introduction* (New York: Routledge, 1990), 173.

38. One of the bravest and most detailed discussions of this volatile topic is Eve Sedgwick's second axiom in "Introduction: Axiomatic," in *Epistemology of the Closet* (Berkeley: University of California Press,1990). Axiom 2 begins thus: "The study of sexuality is not coextensive with the study of gender; correspondingly, antihomophobic inquiry is not coextensive with feminist inquiry. But we can't know in advance how they will be different" (27).

Ut Pictura Poesis Non Erit: Diderot's Quest for the Limits of Expression in the *Salons*

HUGUETTE COHEN

Denis Diderot's attempt to defy the finite nature of the writer's craft in his *Salons* yielded some remarkable "paintings with a pen," with an expressive climax reached in the "Promenade Vernet" of the *Salon* of 1767.[1] However, this same *Salon* discloses a crucial turning point: at the end of the "Promenade" and from then on, the paintings on display in the Louvre are no longer a genuine source of inspiration for Diderot's *musée imaginaire*, and I will argue that this new direction in his art criticism reflected an awareness that he had reached limits of expression not to be transgressed: his dream of reproductive powers superior to the paintings' potential to arouse emotions was shattered by his admission that language could turn into a self-activated wellspring of images and meanings divorced from critical discourse on the paintings on view in the Louvre.

When Friedrich Grimm asked Diderot in 1759 to report on the biennial Salons for an exclusive circle of foreign subscribers who would, perhaps, never see the paintings, the invitation was extended with a full knowledge of Diderot's involvement with the act of seeing and translating images into language. His challenging assignment would be to forge the kind of hieroglyphic language he had envisioned in the *Lettre sur les sourds et muets* (1751) "qui fait que les choses sont dites et représentées tout à la fois,"[2] but representation thrice removed, with the painter's work transmitted into words to an audience who would create its own mental images. In spite of the optimism expressed in the *Lettre*, Diderot often lamented in the *Salons* on the obstacle of distance between the paintings and the final message: "Mais que signifient mes expressions exsangues et froides, mes lignes sans chaleur et sans vie? ... Rien, mais rien du tout. Il faut voir la chose"(7: 174). On the positive side, the ancient rivalry between the pen and the brush, poetry and painting, and the strict demarcation of fields of endeavor was rapidly eliminated by a new alliance between the "Sister Arts."[3] This blurring of differences figured prominently in Diderot's "Prospectus" for the *Encyclopédie*, in which he used the all-inclusive heading of poetry for the arts, "car il n'est pas moins vrai de dire du Peintre qu'il est un Poète, que du Poète qu'il est un Peintre" (2: 311). After several years devoted to learning the technical intricacies of painting for his three first *Salons* of 1759, 1761 and 1763, he rated himself with much pride as the painter's peer: "Chardin, Lagrenée, Greuze et d'autres m'ont assuré, et les anistes ne flattent point les littérateurs, que j'étais presque le seul d'entre ceux-ci dont les images pouvaient passer sur la toile, presque comme elles étaient ordonnées dans ma tête" (7:104). He conceded that he could neither paint nor draw, but was confident that his mental imaging could produce a message clear enough to be communicated to his audience.

Translating an alien discourse into his own was Diderot's dominant mental bent. Jean Starobinski has pointed out in a seminal article this intimate relationship with "la parole des autres,"[4] which enabled Diderot to penetrate the language of Otherness, verbal or figurative, his free adaptation of Anthony Ashley Cooper, third Earl of Shaftesbury's *Essai sur le mérite et la vertu* (1745) being the best early example in his work of this process of translating to mimic and eventually appropriate. This inexhaustible appetite for mimesis would serve Diderot well—up to a point—in the *Salons* in which he assimilated his favorite artists' styles to reinvent them into his own versions. He described the pitfalls of this activity to Grimm, perhaps as a form of apology for his straying from the straight path of mimesis:

> Pour décrire un Salon à mon gré et au vôtre, savez-vous, mon ami, ce qu'il faudrait avoir? Toutes les sortes de goût, un coeur sensible à tous les charmes, une âme susceptible d'une infinité d'enthousiasmes différents, une variété de style qui répondît à la variété des pinceaux; pouvoir être grand ou voluptueux avec Deshays, simple et vrai avec Chardin, délicat avec Vien, pathétique avec Greuze, produire toutes les illusions possibles avec Vernet, et dites-moi où est ce Vertumne-là?" (5: 394).

Two avenues were open to Diderot: the conventional descriptive method, linked to the act of reading, that would offer an inventory of visible reality, and a "poetic" method, based on the power of the paintings to transcend the visible and carry readers beyond the narrowly rational, with the obvious entrapment of losing sight of the paintings.[5] The descriptive method will prevail in the first four *Salons*, where Diderot is still thinking in terms of the *Encyclopédie*, with a stress on maximum readability: "Ma description sera telle qu'avec un peu d'imagination et de goût, on les réalisera dans l'espace, et qu'on y posera les objets à peu près comme nous les avons vus sur la toile" (6:19). He would attempt to revive the ancient concept of *enargeia*, and Horace's injunction of *ut pictura poesis*, words reproducing the vivid perception of the natural objects.[6]

This initial project of verbal pictorialism faced a considerable hurdle: the gap between the point of time imposed on the artist and the consecutive images produced by language, an eighteenth-century commonplace.[7] Following the Abbé Jean-Baptiste DuBos' lead, Diderot thought to have found the link between the verbal and the visual in drama, with actors as the pictured characters in a painting. His own dramatic theory, with its emphasis on the *tableau*, "une disposition de ces personnages sur la scène, si naturelle et si vraie, que rendue fidèlement par un peintre, elle me plairait sur la toile" (3: 127–28), had a profound impact on his first *Salons*, and the *tableau* would be his measure of value for the artist's selection of the right *moment*. The artist most likely to fulfill the demands of Diderot's "dramatic conception"[8] would have to be Greuze, whose supremacy was undisputed in the *Salons* of 1761, 1763 and, 1765; However, when positioned in front of Jean-Baptiste Greuze's narrative paintings, Diderot was no longer the art critic or creator of verbal *tableaux*. He applied to Greuze criteria associated with literary criticism, and praised him for his ability to "enchaîner des événements d'après lesquels il serait facile de faire un roman" (6:131). He treated the acclaimed "Accordée de village" (1761) as an embryonic play, deconstructing it into separate scenes. The best illustration of the itinerary that led him back into literature is his report on "La Jeune Fille qui pleure son oiseau mort" (1765) with its first lines praising the primacy of poetry: "La jolie élégie! Le joli poème! La belle idylle que Gessner en ferait! C'est la vignette d'un morceau de ce poète" (132). The painting is lost in Diderot's lengthy address to the grieving *jeune fille*, the literary idyll that he had longed for in his opening remarks.[9]

Michael Fried is accurate in his view that Diderot's "dramatic conception" fitted in better with history painting, one of the chief tendencies of French art of the late 1750s and early 1760s, with its grand representation of action and passion, calling for the fiction of the beholder's absence in front of a closed system.[10] But even in his first *Salons*, Diderot's insistent persona shatters the myth of the nonexistent beholder, displaying early examples of transgression of the limits assigned to the spectator. The chief reason for the great deal of attention he devoted to the *grandes machines* of Joseph-Marie Vien, Jean-Baptiste Deshays and Gabriel-François Doyen, Charles-

Michel-Ange Challe and Noël Hallé, beside their preeminence in the hierarchy of genres, may well have been a subject matter with a storyline that he could reinvent, repaint, with his own choice of *moment* and place, a first level of appropriation of the paintings by the observing *je*, that will ultimately lead to the transgression of all limits assigned to the art critic in the "Promenade Vernet."

Diderot's tireless search for the pregnant *moment* was facilitated by his vast knowledge of mythology and history. His early article on the elder Lagrenée's "Vénus aux forges de Lemnos" (1759) is a good early example of his practice of substituting his own dazzling painterly version, followed by a bare outline of the painting under consideration, described in an utterly negative mode:

> Si j'avais dû peindre la descente de Vénus dans les forges de Lemnos, on aurait vu les forges en feu sous des masses de roches; Vulcain debout, devant son enclume, les mains appuyées sur son marteau; la déesse toute nue lui passant la main sous le menton; ici le travail des cyclopes suspendu; quelques-uns regardant leur maître que sa femme séduit, et souriant ironiquement; d'autres cependant auraient fait étinceler le fer embrasé. . . . Au lieu de cela, c'est une grande toile nue où quelques figures oisives et muettes se perdent. On ne regarde ni Vulcain ni la déesse. Je ne sais s'il y a des cyclopes. La seule figure qu'on remarque, c'est un homme placé sur le devant qui soulève une poutre ferrée par le bout (3: 565–66).

Another instance of Diderot's early take-over of the space of painting is his account of Jean-Baptiste-Marie Pierre's "Jugement de Pâris" (1761). The painter's version is briefly disposed of with a surcharge of negatives: "Le moment est mal choisi. Pâris a jugé. Déjà une des déesses, perdue dans les nues, est hors de la scène; l'autre, retirée dans un coin, est de mauvaise humeur. Vénus, tout entière à son triomphe, oublie ce qui se passe à côté d'elle, et Pâris n'y pense pas davantage. Voilà trois groupes que rien ne lie" (5: 60). Diderot is eager to fill up the ample space with his own brilliantly lit scene: "Que Pâris . . . soit dans l'ombre, que la lumière qui vient d'en haut arrive sur les déesses diversement rompue par les arbres pénétrés par les rayons du soleil; qu'elle se partage sur elles et les éclaire diversement; que le peintre s'en serve pour faire sortir tout l'éclat de Vénus" (62). He points out that he has not even touched upon the expressions of Pâris and the goddesses, opening up the space even further to the imagination of his readers invited to cooperate in this re-creation: "Mais qui est-ce qui imaginera le caractère et la tête de Paris? Qui est-ce qui donnera aux déesses leurs vraies physionomies? Qui est-ce qui me montrera leurs perplexités et celle du juge?"(62).

The escape into the sublime, the "horriblement beau" that will completely undermine the description in the *Salon de 1767* is already at work in Diderot's treatment of mythological and historical subjects. Pierre's rendering of John the Baptist's beheading, "La Décollation de Saint Jean" (1761), a particularly grisly theme, stirs up Diderot's verve. He objects to the lack of blood in Pierre's scene, and offers his own version: "Le peintre n'a pas senti l'effet du sang qui eût coulé le long du bras de l'éxécuteur, et arrosé le cadavre même. ... J'aime bien les tableaux de ce genre dont on détourne la vue, pourvu que ce soit d'horreur, et non de dégoût" (60).

The highest form of transgression is the dream situation, present for the first time in the re-creation of Jean-Honoré Fragonard's "Corésus et Callirhoé"(1765; 6: 188–201). The vehicle of the dream produces a series of word-*tableaux*[11] leading to the climactic *moment* which happens to coincide with Fragonard's own choice of the time when the high priest Corésus kills himself to spare the virgin Callirhoé whom he had been urged to sacrifice to Bacchus. The shift from the dream zone back to the description of the artist's canvas goes unnoticed until pointed out by a fictional Grimm who emphatically claims perfect equivalence in expressive quality between the verbal *tableaux* and Fragonard's work: "C'est le même temple, la même ordonnance, les mêmes personnages, la même action, les mêmes caractères, le même intérêt général, les mêmes qualités, les mêmes défauts. ... C'est un beau rêve que vous avez fait, c'est un beau rêve qu'il a peint" (6: 197). The artist-beholder relationship is deftly reversed, with the artist turned into mere painter of the spectator's dream. This is Diderot's first extended venture in the *Salons* into a state transcending reason, and a forerunner of the transgressive process of an inverted pyramid of value in the "Promenade Vernet," ascending to the apex of the critic's verbal creations.[12]

An intriguing change occurred in 1767 in Diderot's response to history paintings. He complained, for instance, about Doyen's much talked about "Miracle des ardents": "Tout cela n'a pas assez d'air et de champ" (7: 212), but commented approvingly on "Saint-Grégoire pape": "Il règne dans cette composition un calme qui me plaît" (74). He had become weary of mythology: "Les peintres se jettent dans cette mythologie, ils perdent le goût des événements naturels de la vie" (86). There is, in all these remarks, a longing for space, airiness, *repos*, an alternate world outside the confines of the Louvre. The paintings most likely to fulfill this wish—landscapes, seascapes, ruins—belonged to the lesser *peinture de genre* group, along with still lifes. A close association with the work of landscape painters such as Jean-Baptiste Leprince, Jacques-Philippe Loutherbourg, Claude-Joseph Vernet and Hubert Robert led Diderot to adopt a new "pastoral conception"[13] in the mid-1760s.

An impressionistic, mood-producing state required new reporting techniques, with the attendant risk of losing sight of the paintings. Diderot's response to two Jean-Baptiste-Siméon Chardin still lifes of musical instruments is a striking example of this drive to escape inwardly. The critic fails to provide the expected description, choosing instead to evoke the landscape of restful calm that Chardin's work brings to his mind: "On s'arrête devant un Chardin, comme d'instinct, comme un voyageur fatigué de sa route va s'asseoir, sans presque s'en apercevoir, dans l'endroit qui lui offre un siège de verdure, du silence, des eaux, de l'ombre et du frais" (131).

With this new way of reporting which elicited distant mental metaphors, Diderot was following in the footsteps of Longinus whose concept of the "image" is amazingly close to his: "The word is predominantly used in cases where, carried away by enthusiasm and passion, you think you see what you describe, and you place it before the eyes of your hearers."[14] Intense emotional response to the object to be represented carries with it a primacy of the affective over the mimetic.[15] Edmund Burke's privileging of language over the visual confirmed Diderot's critical intuitions. No enemy of paradox, Burke argued that precisely because language is vague, it has unlimited suggestiveness:

> If I make a drawing of a palace or a temple, or a landscape, I present a very clear idea of these objects; but then . . . my picture can at most affect only as the palace, temple or landscape would have affected in the reality. On the other hand, the most lively and spirited verbal description I can give raises a very obscure and imperfect idea of such objects; but then it is in my power to raise a stronger *emotion* by the description than I could do by the best painting. . . . The proper manner of conveying the *affections* of the mind from one to another is by words.[16]

Murray Krieger points out Burke's impact on the language arts in the 1760s: "Painting, so long guaranteed its place as the model art by the *ut pictura poesis* assumptions of the pictorialist tradition, yields up this place as the spectrum gradually reverses itself."[17]

The highest form of fusion with the paintings, through the fiction of the spectator physically entering them,[18] occurs in the *Salons* from 1763 on, and signifies unmitigated approval: "Un tableau . . . qui vous met en scène . . . n'est jamais un mauvais tableau" (6: 168), a statement later on confirmed with Diderot's rejection of the connoisseur's approach: "Il reste toujours hors de la scène; il n'y entre jamais" (7: 277). This appetite for intrusion and appropriation expresses itself in an embryonic form in front of a Chardin still life: "C'est qu'il n'y a qu'à prendre ces biscuits et les manger" (1763; 5: 432). Farther on, in the same *Salon*, the *je*-spectator steps into a glowing account of a Loutherbourg pastoral scene with a fictional Grimm. The painting recedes to mere pre-text for a word-*tableau* with sound and lighting effects and the couple Diderot-Grimm as a centerpiece (5: 435–46):

> Ah! Mon ami, que la nature est belle dans ce petit canton! Arrêtons-nous y; la chaleur du jour commence à se faire sentir, couchons-nous le long de ces animaux . . . la conversation de ce pâtre et de cette paysanne nous amusera; nos oreilles ne dédaigneront pas les sons rustiques de ce bouvier qui charme le silence de cette solitude et trompe les ennuis de sa condition en jouant de la flûte. Reposons-nous; vous serez à côté de moi, je serai à vos pieds tranquille et en sûreté, comme ce chien, compagnon assidu de la vie de son maître et garde fidèle de son troupeau; et lorsque le poids du jour sera tombé nous continuerons notre route. . . . (436)

We are no longer dealing with the correctives of the earlier "dramatic conception," but with a genuine creation by an effusive Diderot developing a painterly style of his own, and eager for pleasurable physical contact and identification with the contents of the painting, both real and imaginary.

The same eagerness to share enjoyable experiences and achieve physical contact is evident in the article on Leprince's "Pastorale russe" (1765; 6:168–69). After a favorable review of a peaceful pastoral scene with three characters, two of them playing musical instruments, the *je*-spectator abruptly enters the painting: "Je me trouve bien là. Je resterai appuyé contre cet arbre, entre ce vieillard et sa jeune fille tant que le jeune garcon jouera." This first scene keeping the artist's choice of *moment* gives way to an imaginary scene introducing movement and physical closeness with one of the characters: "Quand il aura cessé de jouer et que le vieillard remettra ses doigts sur sa balalaye, j'irai m'asseoir à côté du jeune garçon." A third and final word-*tableau* dwells on the insistent presence of the *je* within the group originally depicted by the artist: "Lorsque la nuit s'approchera, nous reconduirons tous les trois ensemble le bon vieillard dans sa cabane." Stimulated by the proper ingredients in Leprince's rendition, "un sombre, un repos, une paix, un silence, une innocence qui m'enchantent," Diderot has achieved cinematic imagery of his own, brought to an end with this fitting conclusion: "La peinture est l'art d'aller à l'âme par l'entremise des yeux. Si l'effet s'arrête aux yeux, le peintre n'a fait que la moindre partie du chemin."

A striking process of chiastic interpenetration between the artist's work and Diderot's creations, with the removal of the dividing line between reality and fiction was achieved in the Loutherbourg and Leprince articles, both harbingers of the 1767 Vernet article which gave rise to Diderot's most spectacular acts of fusion and vicarious participation. He had entered a Vernet shipwreck scene in the *Salon* of 1765, getting deeply involved in the characters' actions (6: 79). This kind of self-involvement will reach extraordinary proportions in the "Promenade Vernet," leading to a hallucinatory state and total estrangement from Vernet's work at the end of the article. In a puzzling oscillation between art and nature, Vernet's and Diderot's imagery, the *je*-spectator and the *je*-creator, description and digression, reality and dream, the reader is tossing about without moorings, until a final plunge into phantasmatic shipwreck scenes. At midstream in the article, the *je* turned creator expresses feelings evidently shared by the reader: "Je demeurais absorbé dans diverses spéculations entre lesquelles mon esprit était balancé, sans trouver d'ancre qui me fixât" (7:157).[19]

To achieve this act of fusion and unlimited sympathy, distance from the paintings must evidently be abolished. Through the channels of imagination and enthusiasm, both praised in the Sixth Site as required components of creation (165), the art critic will expand his mission far beyond the limits required by *jugement* and *esprit philosophique*, displaying the level of intensity expected from the artist. To compete with Vernet, "le génie [qui] crée les beautés" (167), the critic turned creator will retrace the artist's steps, penetrate the artist's creations from within, and share his emotions during the process of creation. He will achieve what Diderot referred to in his *Lettre sur les sourds* as "l'intelligence de l'emblème poétique: il faut être presque en état de le créer pour le sentir fortement (2: 549).[20]

The *je*-spectator enters the paintings with accounts of his own gesturing and attitudes: "J'étais immobile: mes regards erraient sans s'arrêter sur aucun objet; mes bras tombaient à mes côtés. J'avais la bouche entr'ouverte.... Quelquefois mes yeux et mes bras s'élevaient vers le ciel, quelquefois ils retombaient à mes côtés comme entraînés de lassitude. Je crois que je versai quelques larmes" (7: 139, 163). In this trance-like state, experienced for the first time within the Second Site, the critic-creator describes the paintings as nature, with the added twist of terms borrowed from the artist's vocabulary. Nature is the supreme outcome of art at its best:

> Mille beautés éparses dans l'univers ont été rassemblées sur cette toile, sans confusion, sans effort, et liées par un goût exquis. C'est une vue romanesque dont on suppose la réalité quelque part.... Qu'il est doux de goûter la fraîcheur de ces eaux, après avoir éprouvé la chaleur qui brûle ce lointain! Que ces roches sont majestueuses! Que ces eaux sont belles et vraies! Comment l'artiste en a-t-il obscurci la transparence! (140)

God, nature's Creator, is the artist taking his cues from Vernet: "C'est qu'il dit: Que la lumière se fasse, et la lumière est faite.... C'est qu'en effet ses compositions prêchent plus fortement la grandeur, la puissance, la majesté de nature que la nature même" (175). There is an increasing build-up in the

"Promenade," with an inverted pyramid of value that will lead up from God to Vernet to the critic's creations at the apex of the pyramid.

The first lines of the "Promenade" make it clear that the *je* who takes his reader along for a walk plans to do away with Vernet and the walls of the Salon: "J'avais écrit le nom de cet artiste au haut de ma page, et j'allais vous entretenir de ses ouvrages, lorsque je suis parti pour une campagne voisine de la mer et renommée pour la beauté de ses sites" (131). The proliferation of the *je* made evident by the semantic overload, and reasserted by the projection of his presence into the various sites, confirms an intent to use discretionary powers to seize the artist's role, and become one with his work. The act of verbal painting occurring in the "Promenade" originates in a scanning of the artist's canvas by the imagination of a *je* who will, in a supreme display of narcissism, rate his own compositions as superior to God's and Vernet's creations.[21]

The *délire* aroused by his verbal creations leads him to identify with God: "Nos artistes n'y entendent rien, puisque le spectacle de leurs plus belles productions ne m'a jamais fait éprouver le délire que j'éprouve.... S'il est un Dieu, c'est ainsi qu'il est. Il jouit de lui-même" (146). There is a dual sensation of vacuum and plenitude: "Où suis-je dans ce moment? Qu'est-ce qui m'environne? Je ne le sais, je l'ignore. Que me manque-t-il? Rien. Que désiré-je? Rien" (146).[22] The vacuum is soon to be replenished with the "Quatrième Site," offered to Vernet as a model, with explicit directions on how to hold his brush:

> Que ce bouquet d'arbres vigoureux et touffus fait bien à droite! Cette langue de terre ménagée en pointe au devant de ces arbres et descendant par une pente facile vers la surface de ces eaux est tout à fait pittoresque. Que ces eaux qui rafraichissent cette péninsule en baignant sa rive sont belles!... Ami, Vernet, prends tes crayons et dépêche-toi d'enrichir ton portefeuille.... Si... tu places dans une de tes compositions... des montagnes vaporeuses dont je n'apercoive que le sommet, l'horizon de ta toile en sera renvoyé aussi loin que tu le voudras. (146–47)

The critic's display of artistic intensity will gradually lead to exhaustion after the "Quatrième Site." His most obvious token of power, an unrestrained license to depart from discourse on the paintings, turns out to be a sign of weakness, with the textual space being submerged in an ever-increasing flow of digressions on wide-ranging topics such as determinism (136) and the problem of language (154–57, 168–70). The *je* turned autocratic refers with pride to his ability to wield the threat of an endless discourse: "Je vous raconte simplement la chose. Dans un moment plus poétique, j'aurais déchaîné les vents, soulevé les flots" (144–45), offering this sweeping excuse for his shedding of restraints: "Il n'y a ... point de signes si disparates qui ne confinent, point d'idées si bizarres qui ne se touchent" (169). A brief return to conventional art criticism in the "Septième Tableau"—Vernet's "Clair de lune," allegedly his most beautiful work—is cut short by the critic's rejection of straight descriptive activity: "Mais que signifient mes expressions exsangues et froides.... Rien, mais rien du tout" (174).[23]

There were forewarnings of the climactic ending of the "Promenade" in the text on Fragonard's "Corésus" which assumed equal status for the artist's work and the dream sequence of word-*tableaux* that preceded it. At the conclusion of the "Promenade" through the various sites, Diderot claims to have dreamed the most horrifying shipwreck scenes.[24] These dream scenes demonstrate once again the *je*-creator's impulse to tear down the walls of the Salon and give precedence to his own *tableaux*, in the terminal act of a quest for the limits of expression. The remarks prefacing the account of these shipwrecks may be seen as a clue to the "Promenade": "Rêvé-je quand je crois veiller? ... Les eaux, les arbres, les forêts que j'ai vus en nature, m'ont certainement fait une impression moins forte que les mêmes objets en rêve" (178–79). The reader may infer that Vernet's landscapes, previously rated as the equivalent of nature, are inferior in expressive quality to the critic's dreams, and creative excellence is passed on to the *je*-dreamer.

The shipwreck dreams lead the reader into the ambiguous zone of the sublime, with the *je*-dreamer witnessing scenes of unparalleled cruelty:

> J'étais éperdu sur le rivage, à l'aspect d'un navire enflammé. J'ai vu la chaloupe s'approcher du navire, se remplir d'hommes et s'éloigner.... J'ai vu la chaloupe prête à être submergée, et elle l'aurait été, si ceux qui l'occupaient, ô loi terrible de la nécessité, n'eussent coupé les mains, fendu la tête, enfoncé le glaive dans la gorge et dans la poitrine, tué, massacré impitoyablement leurs semblables, les compagnons de leur voyage, qui leur tendaient en vain du milieu des flots, des bords de la chaloupe, des mains suppliantes. (179)

The real-life quality is emphasized by an anaphoric *j'ai vu* producing a "self-accentuating rhythm,"[25] and reinforced by a revealing remark: "Ce spectacle terrible avait attiré sur le rivage et sur les rochers les habitants de la contrée qui en détournaient leurs regards" (179), confirming Diderot's Burkean suggestion in the "Promenade" that a distinction must be made between "l'objet dans la nature, et le même objet dans l'art ou l'imitation. Ce terrible incendie ... vous plonge dans la consternation.... Qu'on vous [le] montre sur la toile ... et vos yeux s'y arrêteront avec joie" (150).[26] The status of genuine scenes of nature is thereby conferred to the phantasms of the dreaming *je*.

The orgasmic dream which follows these scenes of terror brings the article to a fitting closure with an apology of the sublime directly inspired by Burke's *Enquiry*. Diderot's association of the sublime with terror followed by sensual delight confirms a yearning to escape beyond the beautiful (offered in Vernet's scenery) into a world of darkness and delirium: "L'obscurité ajoute à la terreur.... La clarté est bonne pour convaincre, elle ne vaut rien pour émouvoir.... Poètes ... soyez ténébreux" (183).[27] The eventuality lurking at the end of this quest for the ultimate conditions of creativity is madness, mentioned in the course of the "Promenade," in remarks setting the stage for its conclusion: "Celui-ci est un imitateur sublime de nature, voyez ce qu'il sait exécuter soit avec l'ébauchoir, soit avec le crayon, soit avec le pinceau.... Eh bien, il n'a pas sitôt déposé l'instrument de son métier qu'il est fou" (159). The itinerary that led from the first *Salons* to the "Promenade" may now be read as a quest which brings the critic-creator on the brink of the unthinkable. After the "Promenade," in the same *Salon*, a subdued Diderot describes the perilous situation reached by the *inspiré*: "[Il] est lui-même incertain, quelquefois, si la chose qu'il annonce est une réalité ou une chimère, si elle exista jamais hors de lui; il est alors *sur la dernière limite* de l'énergie de la nature de l'homme et à l'extrémité des ressources de l'art.... Malgré l'impulsion qui me presse, je n'ose me suivre plus loin, de peur de m'enivrer et de tomber dans des choses tout à fait inintelligibles" (246; my emphasis).[28]

NOTES

1. Diderot referred to the Vernet article in this *Salon* as "Promenade Vernet" in an undated letter to Friedrich Melchior Grimm (*Correspondance*, ed. G. Roth, 16 vols. [Paris: Minuit, 1955–70], 8:199). Jacques Chouillet's extensive study of this article is entitled "La Promenade Vernet," *Recherches sur Diderot et sur l'Encyclopedie*, 2 (1987): 123–63; hereafter *RDE*.

2. Diderot, *Oeuvres complètes*, ed. R. Lewinter, 15 vols. (Paris: Club français du livre, 1969–73), 2: 549; references will be given in the text.

3. For accounts of this rivalry, see Jean H. Hagstrum, *The Sister Arts* (Chicago: University of Chicago Press, 1958), 3–92; and Rémy G. Saisselin, "Ut Pictura Poesis: Du Bos to Diderot," *Journal of Aesthetics and Art Criticism* 20 (1961): 145–52.

4. "Diderot et la parole des autres," *Critique* 296 (1972): 3–22.

5. Else Marie Bukdahl refers to Diderot's two methods of description as *méthodes scientifiques* and *méthodes poétiques*, in *Diderot critique d'art*, 2 vols. (Copenhagen: Rosenkilde and Bagger, 1980), 1: 302–20. Similarly, Marian Hobson defines Diderot's two attitudes to art as *adequatio*, where the techniques of illusion

strive to bring about an exact replica, and *aletheia* where truth to nature is mediated by an elevated state of consciousness, in *The Object of Art* (Cambridge: Cambridge University Press, 1982), 43, 79–80.

6. About the Greek rhetorical trope of *enargeia* and Horace's phrase, see Murray Krieger, *Ekphrasis: The Illusion of the Natural Sign* (Baltimore: Johns Hopkins University Press, 1992), 66–90.

7. DuBos made this point clear: "Comme le tableau qui représente une action, ne nous fait voir qu'un instant de la durée, le Peintre ne saurait atteindre au sublime, que les choses qui ont précédé la situation présente jettent quelquefois dans un sentiment ordinaire. Au contraire la Poésie nous décrit tous les incidens remarquables de l'action qu'elle traite." *Réflexions critiques sur la poésie et sur la peinture*, 7th ed. (1770; reprint, Geneva: Slatkine, 1967),1: 87. The first edition appeared in 1719.

8. Michael Fried uses this terminology for the group of paintings examined by Diderot as a spectator in a theater, in *Absorption and Theatricality: Painting and Beholder in the Age of Diderot* (Berkeley: University of California Press, 1980), 75–77.

9. The role of literature in Diderot's art criticism has been examined by Huguette Cohen in "Diderot et les limites de la litterature dans les *Salons*," *Diderot Studies* 24 (1991): 25–45. The present essay discusses *ekphrasis*, i.e., "painting" with words.

10. Fried, *Absorption and Theatricality*, 71–105.

11. I am borrowing this term from Norman Bryson who uses it to refer to Diderot's imagery in *Word and Image* (Cambridge: Cambridge University Press, 1981),183.

12. Bernadette Fort argues against literary critics that Diderot's review is not "mere 'pretext' for the deployment of the writer's literary genius," but "a hybrid type of art criticism, best called perhaps 'critical ekphrasis'"; see "Ekphrasis as Art Criticism: Diderot and Fragonard's *Corésus and Callirhoé*," in *Icons-Texts-Iconotexts: Essays on Ekphrasis and Intermediality*, ed. P. Wagner (Berlin: W. De Gruyter, 1995), 3. My own interpretation argues for a kind of "creative ekphrasis."

13. Fried's terminology for this group of paintings (*Absorption and Theatricality*, 132).

14. Quoted in Krieger, *Ekphrasis*, 93, from the translation of *On the Sublime* by W. Rhys Roberts (1899).

15. See Krieger, *Ekphrasis*, 92–112, on "Representation as *Enargeia* II."

16. *A Philosophical Enquiry into the Origin of our Ideas of the Sublime and Beautiful*, 2nd ed. (1759; reprint, Menston: Scolar Press, 1970), 101–2. A French translation was published in 1765; see Gita May, "Diderot and Burke: A Study in Aesthetic Affinity," *PMLA* 75 (1960): 527–39.

17. Krieger, *Ekphrasis*, 104.

18. See Fried, *Absorption*, 118–32. J. Chouillet's linguistic interpretation confirms Fried's views: "L'énergie du langage est liée à la présence physique du locuteur," *Diderot, poète de l'énergie* (Paris: Presses universitaires de France, 1984), 27–28.

19. The Vernet article covers fifty-three pages in the Lewinter edition (7: 131–84). A leisurely walk through six majestic scenes of nature in the company of an abbé and his pupils is revealed to be a pseudo-mystification. The article reverts to the reality of Vernet's canvas in a seventh painting.

20. See James Doolittle, "Criticism as Creation in the Work of Diderot," *Yale French Studies* 2.1 (1949): 14–23; and Margaret Gilrnan, "Imagination and Creation in Diderot," *Diderot Studies* 2 (1952): 200–220.

21. A parallel can be drawn between this process of interiorization and Marie-Hélène Huet's description of the romantics' link between art and procreation: "The artist shows himself to be the source of art, putting on the canvas what he carries within himself, as a woman bears a child modeled after an image"; see *Monstrous Imagination* (Cambridge: Harvard University Press, 1993), 187.

22. J. Starobinski points out identical limits reached by Diderot in the *Rêve de d'Alembert* (1769): "Dans cet *état limite* où plus rien ne transcende ou n'est transcendé, l'individu englobé se sent l'égal de l'immensité englobante" ("Le Philosophe, le géomètre, l'hybride," *Poétique* 21 [1975]: 22; my emphasis).

23. This paradox of hypercreativity leading to exhaustion recalls the nephew's collapse in *Le Neveu de Rameau*. James Creech has noted the association of "death" and intensified experience throughout Diderot's writings; see "Diderot and the Pleasure of the Other," *Eighteenth-Century Studies* 11 (1978): 448–56.

24. Vernet had shown shipwreck scenes in previous Salons (1763, 1765); see Michel Delon, "Joseph Vernet et Diderot dans la tempête," *RDE* 15 (1993): 31–39.

25. I am borrowing Leo Spitzer's way of referring to this rhythmic pattern "suggesting that the speaker is swept away by a wave of passion *which tends to flood all limits*"; see "The Style of Diderot," in *Linguistics and Literary History* (Princeton: Princeton University Press, 1948), 135; my emphasis.

26. A free translation of Burke: "It is a common observation, that objects which in the reality would shock, are in tragical, and such like representations, the source of a very high species of pleasure" (*Enquiry*, 71).

27. Another borrowing from Burke: "In reality a great clearness helps but little towards affecting the passions, as it is in some sort an enemy to all enthusiasms whatsoever.... The images raised by poetry are always of this obscure kind" (*Enquiry*, 102, 106).

28. The part of the *Salon* of 1767 that follows the Vernet article, as well as the last *Salons*, display Diderot's open rejection of enthusiasm as a component of artistic expression. About this reversal after the "Promenade," see Cohen, "Diderot et les limites," 38–45.

Isabelle de Charrière's *Sainte Anne*, or A Woman's Wayward Quest for Knowledge

JACQUELINE LETZTER

Throughout the eighteenth century, novelists, philosophers, teachers, and intellectuals of salon society debated the woman question. Although the Enlightenment held promise for the equality and education of women (since it challenged the dogma of Original Sin which used to explain the subordination of women in the past), its conclusions proved almost as repressive for women as the theological prejudice. Using scientific observation, most philosophes concluded that women were "naturally" feebler than men, unfit for autonomy, and incapable of performing duties in the public domain. Relegated to home and family, women's education was neglected, which perpetuated their illiteracy and their subjugation to men. Even women intellectuals suffered the consequences of poor education: the novelist Françoise de Graffigny never received any formal instruction, and the political activist Olympe de Gouges was said to dictate her works to a secretary because she had never learned how to write.[1]

During the French Revolution the question of women's education reached the political arena, as it touched upon crucial issues for the Republic, including the meaning of equality, the role of the family, and the weight to be given to moral and civic instruction in the family. Although in principle the Revolution encouraged women's emancipation, it fostered simultaneously an increased fear of women's access to the public sphere. Male politicians opposed such access, declaring that women were far more useful to the nation when they remained at home, performing their "natural" tasks.[2] As Jean Jacques Rousseau had done thirty years earlier, they argued that a strict separation between the sexes was necessary for the Republic's welfare. Depite a few voices of opposition against this discriminatory gender ideology, it prevailed and was encoded in the Napoleonic Civil Code (1804). The Code held that women were unfit for legal autonomy and were to remain under the tutelage of men (their fathers or husbands). In doing so, it deprived women of most of the rights they had acquired during the Revolution (including the right to divorce, plead in court in their own name, sign contracts, or inherit property).[3] Legal discrimination, exclusion from politics, and minimal access to education were not all French women had to suffer in the post-revolutionary period. The early Empire saw a proliferation of misogynous tracts intent on silencing women in every area of societal life.[4]

It is during this backlash against women that Isabelle de Charrière (1740–1805), a Dutch aristocrat and intellectual writing in Neuchâtel, expressed some of her most provocative ideas about women's relationship to knowledge and education. Charrière had gained her reputation as a novelist before the French Revolution with the publication of four short epistolary novels. Set in Switzerland and England, they described various aspects of the condition of women in a traditional patriarchal society.[5] During the French Revolution, Charrière's interest shifted to more general political questions. Hopeful that the Revolution would fulfill its promises to all disfavored groups—including women—she struggled to influence political events principally through pamphlets and revolutionary plays. Until the Revolution she consistently advocated a better education for women. She was convinced that, if women were given the chance to develop their intellect, they would understand the means of their oppression and be able to elude the limitations patriarchal society imposed on them. Consequently, her heroines of that period were generally well-educated, resourceful, and capable of taking charge of their own lives. The Revolution disillusioned her, however. Its abuses and extremisms and virulent misogyny showed her the limits of intellect and knowledge and made her less confident that intellectual instruction alone could provide a solution for women.

Charrière's most important post-revolutionary literary achievement is a series of philosophical novels and short stories published under the collective title *L'abbé de la Tour ou Recueil de nouvelles et autres écrits divers* (1798–99).[6] These works are linked not only by a shared narrative frame, but also a common *problématique*, an inquiry inspired by Rousseau into the value and consequences of knowledge for various individuals and groups in society. Rather than stick with one strong thesis as Rousseau had done, Charrière engages in a number of "thought experiments" in which she evaluates the appropriateness of Rousseau's position for each given scenario. *Sainte Anne* (1799), the fourth of the works in *L'abbé de la Tour*, is one of the most provocative in the series, for it gives an incongruous turn to Charrière's assessment of women's relationship to knowledge and education.

Sainte Anne is odd in that it seems to belie everything Charrière had advocated for women in her previous novels.[7] She sets out to outdo Rousseau by presenting a heroine who has never learned to read. The novel opens with the provocative exclamation: "Elle ne sait pas lire! Figurez-vous qu'elle ne sait pas lire!" (257) [She cannot read! Imagine that: she cannot read!]. Indeed, the rest of the novel serves to demonstrate that illiteracy is an advantage for the heroine rather than an affliction. However, the novel's intriguing title immediately alerts us to the fact that this assumption must be checked. Why does a novel whose main heroine is Babet d'Estival carry the title *Sainte Anne*, the surname of Babet's admirer, who is only a secondary character in the novel and a mere sounding board for Babet and the two other heroines? (Significantly the German translation of 1800 did away with this confusion by entitling the novel *Babet von Etibal*.)[6] Arguably the French title makes more sense if we explain it by its religious and regional symbolism. Ste. Anne is the patron saint of Bretagne, where the novel takes place. She represents matrimonial bliss and harmony, one of the novel's central themes. Even if we accept this hagiographic interpretation, however, the title is still puzzling. For Ste. Anne is not only the patroness of marriage, but also of women's intellectual instruction. Iconographically she is almost always represented as teaching her daughter, the Virgin Mary, how to read.[9] A novel ostensibly about the value of female ignorance, which uses as its title the name of the patroness of women's intellectual instruction, invites us to read the messages between the lines.

This essay demonstrates that, contrary to first appearances, Charrière's reflection about women's education follows a disconcerting, zigzag course between two contradictory models of women's education: Babet's "natural" education and the two other heroines's "intellectual" instruction. It is not my purpose to elaborate on these various models.[10] Rather I intend to show that Charrière's zigzag course was an ingenious textual tactic. It reflected both her realistic sense of the limitations each of these educations presented for women (which made it difficult to choose between them), and it allowed her to question their exclusivity and universalism. This in turn gave her room to insinuate herself in the interstices between these models and create a space for exploring alternative possibilities for the education of women. Interestingly, Charrière herself articulated this tactic in her novel *Trois femmes* [Three Women] (1795), the first work she included in *L'abbé de la Tour*. In *Trois femmes*, she used the term *louvoyer*—literally to tack back and forth when sailing against a head wind—to characterize one of her strongest and most appealing characters, Constance de Vaucourt, who adopts "tacking" as a way of life and recommends it as a tactic of reform to her idealistic friend Théobald:

> N'excitez pas de grands mouvements dans les esprits; n'essayez d'arriver au mieux possible que par degrés; *il faut se contenter de louvoyer*.
>
> [Do not stir up the minds too much; try to get to the best possible results gradually; *one must be satisfied to tack*.][11]

Constance deems it best to "tack" to reach her goals because she realizes that the resistance against which she is pitted is stronger than herself.[12]

The nautical term *louvoyer* was still fairly new in French in the mid-eighteenth century and was used predominantly in its literal, technical meaning.[13] The *Encyclopédie* defines it as follows:

> LOUVOYER, verbe neutre, (Marine) c'est voguer quelque temps d'un côté, puis virer de cap, & aller autant de l'autre, afin de se conserver toujours une même hauteur, & dériver de sa route le moins qu'il est possible. On *louvoie* quand le vent est contraire.
>
> [To tack, neutral verb (Nautical), to sail some time in one direction, then change tack and sail in the other direction, in order to stay on course and deviate as little as possible. One tacks when there is a head wind.][14]

Tacking against a head wind is considered one of the most difficult manoeuvres in sailing because it requires a series of carefully calculated turns, making use of sudden wind shifts. Since the wind gusts are never constant, it is risky to stray too far from the line joining the starting point to the set goal. At the same time, if the boat is pointed too close into the wind, she will be halted, as the sails will pick up no wind, and start to shake or luff[15] In sum, the main objective of tacking is to avoid being caught in this immobile position and keep the boat's momentum, all the while remaining as close as possible to one's intended route. When we keep this technical definition of "tacking" in mind, Charrière's "tacking" in both *Trois femmes* (through Constance) and *Sainte Anne* makes even more sense. Confronted by societal values which were overwhelmingly misogynous and a great resistance to any idea of emancipation for women, Charrière had to take a zigzag course in order to advance her own views in favor of women. She had to calculate her "tacks" carefully, however, for if she went too forcefully against the dominant opinions she risked being silenced. On the other hand, if she strayed too far from her "feminist" ideas, she would loose her momentum and be misunderstood by her faithful (female) readership. Charrière's positioning as an intellectual, therefore, required great skill and inventiveness, as well as the energy to move constantly forward despite the resistance exerted by a patriarchal society.

Before examining more closely how Charrière positions herself vis-à-vis the dominant models of women's education represented in her novel, a brief review of the plot is in order. Sainte Anne is a young and learned nobleman who returns from exile to his native Bretagne after the French Revolution. At his mother's manor, he meets Babet d'Estival, a distant relative. She is the daughter of an illiterate peasant woman and a nobleman who married Babet's mother before his death in order to legitimize their daughter. As in a fairy tale, Sainte Anne immediately falls in love with Babet. What attracts him is her unspoiled simplicity, her love of nature, and her innate common sense. She has lived in poverty and has never received any formal education. She has remained illiterate like her mother and is superstitious like many Breton peasants. Being quick and alert, however, she has taught herself many practical skills, such as healing with plants, weaving cloth, and caring for the animals on the farm. Sainte Anne does not hold it against her that she cannot read. On the contrary, he thinks that her knowledge is more authentic because of it:

> J'ai aimé Mademoiselle d'Estival avant de savoir qu'on ne lui avoit pas montré à lire. Mais quand je l'ai su, je me suis étonné de ne l'avoir pas deviné, et j'en ai été bien aise. Il m'a semblé qu'elle en voyoit et en entendoit mieux, qu'elle en avoit l'esprit plus net et la mémoire plus fidelle; il m'a semblé qu'ignorant totalement beaucoup de choses, elle en savoit plus parfaitement celles qu'il lui avoit été utile de savoir. (278)

> [I fell in love with Mlle d'Estival well before I knew that she had not been taught how to read. But when I found out, I was surprised that I had not guessed it, and I was very pleased. It seemed to me that she saw and understood everything much better, that her intelligence was unencumbered, and her memory trustworthy. It was as if, because she ignored so much, she knew more perfectly the few things that had been useful for her to know.]

Expecting to find in her a loving, devoted, and most of all dependent wife, Sainte Anne defies his mother by breaking his engagement with Mademoiselle de Rhédon—the fiancée she preferred—and marries Babet.

At a first glance, the novel unequivocally favors Babet's Rousseauvian "natural" education above the more sophisticated, intellectual education received by the novel's other female characters, Mesdemoiselles de Rhédon and de Kerber. Sainte Anne prefers Babet to Mademoiselle de Rhédon because she was not exposed to any "superfluous" instruction which would only have distracted her from "les choses qu'il lui avoit été utile de savoir" (278) [the things that had been useful for her to know]. In Sainte Anne's preference for Babet's selective ignorance we recognize Rousseau's prescription for Sophie, whom he advises to concentrate on "ces choses qu'il [lui] convient de savoir" [these things that are suitable for her to know].[16] Sainte Anne has a heated argument with his cousin, Mademoiselle de Kerber, who is characterized as a free-thinking woman, during which he denounces not only books and a book-fed education, but the government's plans to institute a national education system. An intellectual himself, he believes that instruction should be reserved for an elite of the mind:

> Ma Cousine, je ne suis point fâché de voir s'anéantir les anciennes écoles et les nouvelles ne s'établir point. Que la science soit de difficile accès. Que le talent la viole pour ainsi dire.... Je voudrois que le talent seul, qui devine en partie la science, voulût désormais apprendre ce qu'on ne peut deviner. Il l'apprendra sans écoles primaires, sans institut national, sans universités, sans académies. (277)

> [My cousin, I am hardly upset to see the old schools destroyed and the new ones not coming off the ground. Science should be hard to reach. It should be violated by talent, so to speak.... I wish that from now on only talented people, who acquire science intuitively, would be encouraged to study what they cannot guess. They would do so without elementary schools, a national institute, universities, or academies.]

More vehement than Rousseau in his belief that books and instruction are useless for the general public, Sainte Anne takes Rousseau's argument in the *Letter to d'Alembert* one step further and condemns not only the theater, but reading as well:

> Ce que dit Rousseau relativement aux spectacles, dans son admirable lettre à d'Alembert, me parait devoir s'étendre à la lecture de toute pièce de théâtre, et en général à presque toutes les lectures des femmes et des jeunes gens.... (276–7)

> [What Rousseau says about the theater in his wonderful letter to d'Alembert, seems to me to hold equally for the reading of plays, and generally for most all reading done by women and young men.]

Even scientific books fall under his condemnation, for in his eyes they can be useful only to the professionals to whom they are addressed:

Quant aux livres de science, je ne les trouve guere plus utiles que les romans, pour quiconque n'en fait qu'une étude superficielle ou qui ne se borne pas à étudier des sciences analogues à sa profession. (277)

[As for scientific works, I do not find them much more useful than novels, especially for those who study them only superficially and not in connection with their profession.]

Although Sainte Anne's comments are directed to both men and women, they affect women more, for in Sainte Anne's world women are excluded from professions and rarely have the chance to pursue their talents. Consequently, he considers any instruction lavished on them useless. On the contrary, he approves Babet's lack of structured education which he believes to be the source of her innate intelligence and useful practical know-how, which he admires as "un mélange de science et de simplicité fort extraordinaire" (268) [a quite extraordinary mixture of knowledge and simplicity].

Charrière shows, however, that despite Sainte Anne's protestations about the superiority of Babet's unstructured education and innate intelligence, he is attracted to her simplicity mainly because it brings out his own intellectual strength and her need of his counsel. Significantly, he proposes marriage to Babet in the village cemetery, where he has been able to still her superstitious fear of ghosts. In addition, he relishes his authority to shape her according to his own ideals. On the eve of their marriage, when Babet asks him once again when he will teach her how to read,[17] he reiterates that he does not care if she reads and writes:

Il m'est assez égal, dit-il à sa future, que vous sachiez lire et écrire ou que vous ne le sachiez pas; ce qui ne m'est point égal, c'est que vous vous défassiez de toute crainte chimérique. (310)

[It is the same to me, he said to his future wife, whether or not you learn to read and write; what is important to me, though, is that you get rid of your superstitious fears.]

What adds to Babet's appeal in Sainte Anne's eyes is her precarious financial and social position, which gives him yet another opportunity to enact his ideals. Babet and her mother are at the mercy of Sainte Anne's vindictive mother, who holds a grudge against them and has the power to evict them from their home. Sainte Anne, who sees Babet and her mother as "deux femmes sans appui, sans conseil et isolées" (284) [two isolated women without support or advice], makes it his mission in life to offer shelter and protection to Babet. To this end he plans to restore the castle of his ancestors—a project deeply significant to him because of his attachment to his past:

> C'est là qu'ont vécu mes ayeux, c'est là que vivra Mademoiselle d'Estival, se disoit-il. Le passé et l'avenir se joignant, se pressant dans son ame, y éttouffoient le sentiment du présent. (284)

> [It is there that my ancestors lived, it is there that Mademoiselle d'Estival will live. The past and the future thus joining and pressing themselves in his soul, he suppressed his feeling about the present.]

This plan not only ensures Babet's continued dependence on him, but also appeases his fears about the present and gives him a much-needed sense of purpose. Indeed, after his exile and the disappointments of the Revolution, Sainte Anne—like his exiled friend Tonquedec—feels alienated and hesitates to participate in public life, satisfied to care for his own and his friend's interests:

> Tous deux étoient bien résolus à ne se mêler jamais [de querelles politiques], et à laisser leur pays s'arranger au gré du grand nombre. . . . Tonquedec et Ste. Anne disoient l'un et l'autre: je n'attaquerai ni les hommes nouveaux ni les opinions nouvelles. Si l'on m'attaque ou si l'on t'attaque, je défendrai et toi et moi. (301–2)

> [Both were resolved not to get involved in political disputes and to let their country sort itself out according to the will of the majority. . . . Tonquedec and Sainte Anne said to each other: I will attack neither the new men nor their new ideas. But if you or I are attacked, I will defend both you and me.]

By showing that Babet's attractiveness resides even more in the voids she can fill for Sainte Anne than in her personality, Charrière casts doubts about Sainte Anne's motives for preferring Babet's ignorance over the intellectual sophistication of the two other heroines.

Charrière further complicates the novel's message by making Mesdemoiselles de Rhédon and de Kerber as appealing as Babet. This requires considerable skill on Charrière's part, for although these heroines seem innocuous to our twentieth-century eyes they would certainly have been considered subversive by Charrière's conservative readers. Not only have they received instruction, but they are also free-thinkers, and do not heed the conventional interdictions imposed on women in their society. For example, they avidly read the novels Sainte Anne so vehemently condemns. In fact, their reading habit is what sparks the argument with Sainte Anne. To defend her heroines, Charrière immediately demonstrates that their intelligence and lively critical minds immunize them against the dangers of reading novels. Moreover, she shows Mademoiselle de Kerber to be an excellent tactician. Kerber coyly concedes defeat to Sainte Anne in their argument about the advantages of reading. She agrees with him that the lessons of novels carry little weight with readers, including herself:

> Nous admirons tel ou tel caractere dans un livre, puis ensuite nous faisons ce qui nous convient. . . . Bref, il se pourroit bien que vous eussiez raison, et qu'il valut autant pour nous ne savoir pas lire. (275)
>
> [We admire such or such character in a novel, but then we do exactly what suits us. . . . In short, it is quite possible that you are right and that we might as well not have learned how to read.]

However, she continues to read and clearly benefits from it. Not only is she able to engage in a serious intellectual argument with Sainte Anne, but she also finds a creative outlet in writing to him: "Mon humeur ne s'est remise que lorsque j'ai pensé à vous et au récit que je vous ferois" (275). [My mood only improved when I started thinking about you and the story I would be able to write you.] Mademoiselle de Kerber's intelligence and common sense are not lost on Sainte Anne. In fact, his epistolary interactions with her make him wonder whether reading might not be beneficial to some women after all:

> Où avez-vous pris ma très aimable cousine, votre candeur et votre très aimable esprit? Si vous en devez la moindre partie à vos livres, je me réconcilie avec eux, et même je leur rends très-humblement hommage. (276)
>
> [Where, my sweet cousin, did you learn to be so candid and intelligent? If it is in your books, let me at once make peace with them and give them the honor they deserve.]

Sainte Anne is equally touched by Mademoiselle de Rhédon's thoughtful remarks about reading, even though they disagree about books. For her, there is no question that the advice of books is invaluable. She considers it similar to the advice of good friends, even though she understands the limitations of books:

> Je ne crois pas . . . que de petits accidens me fissent oublier les conseils que viendroit de me donner un livre: ils sont comme ceux d'un ami; mais il y a des peines qui rendroient inutiles pour moi tout ce que j'aurois pu lire ou entendre de plus raisonnable. (275)
>
> [I do not think that little accidents would make me forget the advice a book would just have given me: it is like the advice of friends; however, sometimes I have sorrows that make useless everything I read or hear, even the most sensible things.]

Charrière further undermines the stereotypes attached to free-thinking women by showing their outspokenness and strength of opinion to be motivated by their generosity. Mademoiselle de Rhédon firmly withstands the pressures Sainte Anne's mother exerts on her, even though she has much to gain from cooperating with her, since Madame de Sainte Anne wants her son to marry Mademoiselle de Rhédon and not Babet. Mademoiselle de Rhédon wants no part in the malicious schemes Madame de Sainte Anne plots against Babet, however, because she feels loyal to Babet, who depends entirely on her while Sainte Anne is away. Sainte Anne himself confidently relies on Mademoiselle de Rhédon's loyalty to Babet, as well as on Mademoiselle de Kerber's power to persuade his mother to let him marry Babet. Although Mademoiselle de Kerber's first loyalty is to her friend Mademoiselle de Rhédon (and not to Babet), she does what Sainte Anne asks her. Indeed, she realizes that it would be useless for her to try to steer her cousin's affections to her friend. Moreover, Mademoiselle de Rhédon would not be happy with a man who has to be convinced to appreciate her. By showing her two intellectual heroines to be strong and independent, yet at the same time generous, humane, and even selfless, Charrière paves the way for her most radical argument—that they are capable of taking charge of their lives when needed because of their intellectual instruction.

Toward the end of the novel, when Mademoiselle de Rhédon's plans of marriage with Sainte Anne fall through because he prefers Babet, Mademoiselle de Kerber, "qui *lisoit* dans le coeur de son amie" (307) [who *read* in the heart of her friend], immediately proposes a plan of action to relieve her rejected friend's sorrow. She will write to one of Mademoiselle de Rhédon's former admirers to tell him that she is now free, for "rien n'est ennuyeux comme d'assister à un mariage, à moins de se marier aussi" (307) [nothing is as annoying as attending a wedding, unless one is getting married too]. What Mademoiselle de Kerber hopes for does not happen, but by the end of the novel the two young women have plans to get married. Mademoiselle de Rhédon invites a marriage proposal from Tonquedec, who gallantly switches his affections from Babet to her. (Initially Tonquedec intended to marry Babet, and not Mademoiselle de Rhédon, whom he believed engaged to Sainte Anne.) "S'il ne faut pour avoir des droits sur Mademoiselle de Rhédon que sentir bien tout ce qu'elle vaut, la trouver infiniment aimable, bonne et généreuse, admirer sa figure, ses graces et ses talens, je ne le cède à personne" (307–8). [If, to have the right to propose to Mademoiselle de Rhédon, one must realize what she is worth and find her infinitely lovable, good, and generous, admire her figure, graces, and talents, I should be counted among the first.] As for Mademoiselle de Kerber, she attracts the attentions of Villedieu who, having always appreciated her wit and intelligence, now also recognizes her warmth and generosity: "Villedieu aimoit dans Mademoiselle de Kerber une vivacité d'esprit qui n'empêchoit pas qu'elle n'eût le coeur fort bon; elle venoit de donner des preuves de cette bonté hardie et zèlée, qui furent racontées à Villedieu par Tonquedec, Ste. Anne, et Mademoiselle de Rhédon elle-même. Là-dessus il a pris son parti, s'est offert et a été franchement accepté" (308). [Villedieu admired Mademoiselle de Kerber's quick wit, which did not take away from her very good heart; lately she had given new evidence of her easy and forthcoming generosity, which was reported to him by Tonquedec, Sainte Anne, and Mademoiselle de Rhédon herself. Thereupon he decided to propose to her and was frankly accepted.] These women's unions may not compare to Babet's fairy tale-like marriage with Sainte Anne; still, they have found husbands who appreciate their qualities of heart and intellect.

In a parenthesis to this happy *dénouement* (at least three weddings!), the narrator expresses his relief that the young women have not been too influenced by the novels they have read. He especially compliments those people who, like Mademoiselle de Rhédon, are able to adapt to changed circumstances and do not pine exaggeratedly for lost love. He compares their realistic attitude in matters of love and marriage to the sentimental idealism promoted in novels:

> C'est bien assez que les lectures soient inutiles; elles seroient très nuisibles, si d'après de romanesques folies qui n'ont rien coûté à l'auteur, on sacrifioit des sentimens plus vrais, plus naturels, et qui sont parfaitement honnêtes. Laissons quelques admirateurs de Werther se tuer, et quelques folles pleurer toute leur vie ce qu'elles n'ont peut-être jamais eu sujet d'aimer. 11 ne faut pas dans la vie véritable imiter un invraisemblable roman. (308)
>
> [It is bad enough that reading is useless; it would be truly harmful if, based on idealistic follies that cost the author nothing, readers sacrificed less romantic, but truer, more natural, and perfectly honest feelings. Let us leave suicide to the admirers of Werther, and life-long sorrow to silly women who have no reason to love the heroes they regret all their lives. It is much better not to try to imitate unrealistic novels in real life.]

This is a disconcerting parenthesis in a novel that so centrally features the sentimental love story between Sainte Anne and Babet. By deriding sentimental plots, Charrière subtly devalues the importance of her own novel's main plot and gives relatively more weight to the actions of the characters at the margins. By doing so, she also invites her readers to be receptive to more unconventional ideas about love, marriage, and women.

Despite the considerable attention Charrière pays to her intellectual heroines, it would be wrong to conclude that she portrays Babet negatively or one-dimensionally. On the contrary, she takes pains to explain that, despite Babet's limitations and dependency, she is almost as perceptive and outspoken as the "femme d'esprit," Mademoiselle de Kerber. Babet knows what she wants and clearly lets her desires be known. When Sainte Anne offers to marry her and take care of her, she does not automatically accept, even though it would solve her problems. Because in her experience marriage is a hypocritical institution, not the seal of love it should represent, she wants to make sure that their love is genuine and springs from a pure and mutual attraction:

> Je suis bien aise de ne devoir (vos complaisances) pas uniquement à la pitié, mais aussi à un certaine . . . comment dirai-je? sympathie, je crois est le mot, que je sentis d'abord pour vous en vous voyant, et qui pour être vraîment de la sympathie doit, je crois, être réciproque. (269)

> [I am very happy that your attentions for me are due not only to pity, but also a . . . how shall I say it . . . an instinctive attraction I believe is the word for what I first felt for you. I am also convinced that to be true this feeling must be reciprocal.]

In addition, Babet does not simply submit to her illiteracy. She is self-conscious about it and realizes that Sainte Anne is attracted to her because of it: "je suis persuadée qu'on a augmenté votre amitié pour moi, en vous disant qu'on ne m'avoit rien appris; pas même à lire" (269). [I am sure that your interest for me increased when you were told that I had not learned anything, not even how to read.]

Despite first appearances then, Charrière does not pit her two types of heroines against each other, nor one's ignorance and dependency against the others' intellectual sophistication and autonomy. Rather, she lays bare the constraints attached to each of these characterizations. She points out how—ironically—Babet's relative ignorance of social conventions allows her to express her desires much more clearly and directly than Mademoiselle de Rhédon, who seems overly selfless as a result of her too successful socialization as a woman. At the same time, she underlines how Babet's ignorance puts her at the mercy of those on whom she must depend for her every interaction with the outside world. In the same way, Charrière demonstrates that Mademoiselle de Rhédon's intellectual and social sophistication both hurt and benefit her. On the one hand they cause her to be rejected by Sainte Anne, and to be overly sensitive to the needs of others at the expense of her own. On the other hand they help her overcome her rejection, stand on her own feet in difficult times, and find a compatible suitor instead of simply letting herself be chosen. By highlighting the respective qualities of her two types of heroines and giving an ironic dimension to what she perceives as the shortcomings attached to their respective educations, Charrière suggests that women would benefit from a more flexible education which would circumvent the drawbacks of these traditional models. She "tacks" between classifications (of women and their education), thereby demonstrating that these classifications are neither monolithic nor universal. "Tacking" thus allows her to give a new, oblique *sens*—direction or meaning—to the concept of women's education.

These constant shifts in position were tricky for both Charrière and her readers. Her correspondence reveals that many of her readers missed the point she had wanted to make by going back and forth between Babet and her two other heroines, and between these heroines and Sainte Anne's comments on them. They tended either to read the novel as a straight apology of Babet and Sainte Anne's views on women or, if they did not like Babet, to ignore her altogether, to read Sainte Anne's comments ironically, and to prefer the other female characters. In other words, they did not understand Charrière's efforts to "tack" between these polarized positions and find a new direction, different but derived from these positions. Instead, they were frustrated by what they perceived as her surprising insertion in the novel of incongruous statements that could not possibly reflect her real thoughts on women's role and education. Especially among Charrière's female readers, many were bitterly disappointed by Babet, who was so different from the independent, well-educated heroines they had admired in Charrière's previous novels.[18]

Charrière was annoyed that she could not make her point more clearly, and that her readers did not take Babet or Sainte Anne's comments more seriously:

> On lit Assés l'abbé de la Tour à Neuchâtel mais quoiqu'il me revienne de très jolis petits éloges il m'est avis qu'on ne l'entend pas trop. Par exemple Mad^elle de Rhédon est trouvée fort aimable, on la préfèrerait à Mad^elle d'Estival & la pensée que j'ai eue en les imaginant toutes deux, et en faisant parler St Anne échappe totalement.[19]

> [L'abbé de la Tour is read widely in Neuchâtel but, although I am receiving quite a few pretty compliments about the work, I am convinced my readers misunderstand it. For example, they love Mademoiselle de Rhédon; they even prefer her to Mlle d'Estival. What escapes them completely is the idea I wanted to convey by imagining them both and having Sainte Anne comment on them.]

The same readers were probably equally confused by the mixture of genres that characterizes the novel. A realistic novel on the surface, it has elements of a fairy tale punctuated by theoretical digressions about education, knowledge, and love, all of which made it difficult to determine when the novel was to be taken seriously. Most disconcerting is the novel's ending with its proliferation of the adjective "heureux" [happy]—"La ferme vit ce soir-là l'heureuse Babet, accompagnée de son heureux époux, qui . . . la mena à Auray pour la présenter aux deux amis, et hâter les réparations du vieux manoir de ses pères" (310). [That evening the farm saw the happy Babet, accompanied by her happy husband, who . . . took her to Auray a few days later in order to introduce her to his two friends and start with the repair of his ancestral manor.] Since in the past Charrière had written more realistic plots with open endings, where heroines had to consider possibilities other than marriage and "a happy life ever after," this fairy tale-like ending seemed odd to her readers.[20] Indeed, they complained about the novel's exaggerated idealism, as can be inferred from one of Charrière's most defensive letters about Sainte Anne:

> Je conviens que Melle d'Estival est ideale mais pourvu que mes personnages soient possibles je ne leur en demande pas davantage. . . . Je n'aime pas les aventures romanesques mais bien les gens un peu merveilleux.[21]

> [I admit that Mlle d'Estival is idealized, but as long as my characters are possible I am satisfied. . . . I do not like extraordinary adventures, but I have nothing against slightly fantastic characters.]

Although there was nothing unusual about Charrière's experimentation with genre in an age when traditional genre requirements were being abandoned in favor of freer and more personal expression, Charrière's experimentation shocked her regular readers, because it seemed to rehabilitate the very images of women Charrière had previously rejected for their stereotypical sentimentality.

Charrière's closest readers were further puzzled by the character of Babet and Sainte Anne's comments about her because they contradicted everything Charrière appreciated in real-life women. At the very same time Charrière was creating the "natural" and illiterate Babet, she was coaching Isabelle de Gélieu, one of her most talented and intelligent *protégées*, to become an accomplished writer and scholar. To Benjamin Constant she wrote that Gélieu was one of the most promising scholars she knew and that this did not in the least detract from her feminine charms, quite the contrary. In Charrière's words, Gélieu had nothing of a ridiculous *femme savante* and all the intellectual rigor of a scholar:

> Il seroit bien singulier que de tout ce que j'ai eu le bonheur de connoitre jeune avant qu'il ne fut flétri & trop mur une tres jolie fille devint seule savant & eut consistance d'homrne. Je ne dis pas une savante car elle

n'aura aucun des ridicules que présente ce mot. . . . Je n'ai jamais vu tant de memoire, d'application de persévérance. Elle a avec cela beaucoup d'esprit.[22]

[It is remarkable that of all the young people I was fortunate to meet before they were too old and too ripe, only a young woman became a scholar and had the fortitude of a man. I am not saying that she became *savante* because she has none of the ridiculous defects associated with that term. . . . I have never seen such memory, industry, and perseverance. Moreover she is very witty.]

No wonder readers who knew of Charrière's personal interest in Gélieu and read *Sainte Anne* as a straightforward indictment of intellectualism were puzzled by Charrière's motives in creating the character of the illiterate Babet.

It is significant that Charrière herself admitted feeling insecure during the composition of her novel, to the point that she hesitated to release it. To her friend and translator, Ludwig Ferdinand Huber, she wrote:

Je ne sai pourquoi j'ai pour *s^{te} Anne* une poltronerie que je n'ai jamais eue. Cela est au point que je pense à faire venir un copiste de Neuchâtel ne me souciant pas que *s^{te} Anne* sorte du tout de dessous de mon toict. Cela me passera à ce que j'espère & quand je n'irai plus le corrigeant sans cesse j'en agirai plus courageusement.[23]

[I do not know why I feel such cowardice with regard to *Sainte Anne*. I have never experienced this before. It has reached the point that I am sending for a copyist from Neuchâtel since I would prefer that the novel not leave the house at all. I hope this feeling will pass, and I shall act more bravely once I stop constantly correcting my novel.]

I believe that Charrière's cowardice, *poltronerie*, and her admission that she was constantly "correcting" her novel indicate that she feared that her readers would misunderstand what she wanted to get across. In addition, she sensed that she was operating on tricky ideological terrain. Considering the extreme hostility toward women's learning that characterized the late 1790s, she was understandably concerned about how she could effectively convey her message that women should be able to choose the paths of their lives and careers and tailor their educations to their own needs. To her nephew Willem-René she explained the idea she had wanted to convey in *Sainte Anne*, as follows:

Dans le dernier petit roman, l'héroïne ne sait pas lire & mes idées sur la liberté qu'on a de choisir entre une connoissance profonde des sciences relatives à la profession de chacun, & l'absence totale de toute science, de toute etude, mes idées, dis je, sur ce point y sont developpées hardiment et tout de leur long. *Un peu de tout* est la devise de bien des gens & n'est pas la mienne. Avec ce un peu, on est assez agreable pendant la jeunesse mais voila tout. Melle de Gelieu vient de lire Salluste & lit Ciceron en latin, qu'une autre fille ne lise pas seulement la fontaine en françois j'y consens. L'une fera des livres, l'autre des patés, des tourtelettes, sans compter les chemises qu'elle poura filer & coudre mais qu'on lise un peu & tripotte & tricotte un peu c'est ce que j'aime le moins.[24]

[In my new novel the heroine cannot read, and I boldly develop my ideas about each individual's freedom to choose between knowledge of one's field of expertise and the total absence of any science or scholarship. A *little of everything* is many people's motto, but not mine. With a *little of everything*, one is pleasant when one is young, but that is all. Mlle de Gélieu just finished reading Sallust, and is now reading Cicero in Latin; let another girl read nothing at all if she wants, not even La Fontaine in French. The first will write books; the second bake breads, pastries, and tarts; and I do not even mention all the shirts she will weave and sew. What I dislike most of all is when one does a little of everything and nothing very seriously: reading a little; puttering a little; or knitting a little.]

This quote makes clear that far from proposing a "golden medium" for the education of women—which would only further immobilize women in dilettantism—Charrière advocated for their admittance to professions and their access to a rigorous intellectual education. Although she presented the *problématique* of her novel in terms of women's freedom to choose the career and education that suited them best, the real issue was evidently women's access to serious intellectual instruction, since the (lack of) education Babet had received was commonly the lot of women in her time. By showing that Babet remains illiterate against her will and despite the fact that she repeatedly asks for the opportunity to learn to read and write, Charrière makes clear that the real difficulty for women was to get instruction, not to decide to forego it for a more "natural" education.

The misogynous climate of the late 1790s explains why Charrière could not more openly advocate women's right to education. Writing in a society which condemned both her own intellectual activity and women's knowledge in general, she had to use indirect ways to question the dominant gender ideology that limited women's access to education. In *L'invention du quotidien*, Michel de Certeau examines the various *tactics* individuals use when they must operate in hostile environments.[25] To give concrete examples of these tactics, he refers to the work of the classicists Marcel Detienne and Jean-Pierre Vernant who, on the basis of ancient Greek mythology and literature, have documented the role of *mètis*, the god-given quality of cunning intelligence, in the ancient Greek world.[26] Among the individuals and animals who were said to rely on *mètis* were hunters, sailors, and sophists, as well as seacrows, cuttlefish, and foxes. What these holders of *mètis* have in common is that they use ruse, flexibility, and deceit, and take roundabout ways to their destination. In a way similar to the ancient holders of *mètis*, Charrière used tactics of diversion and circumvention and created ambiguity, in order to express thoughts that went counter to the dominant ideology. When she wanted to put Mesdemoiselles de Rhédon and de Kerber on equal footing with Babet, she used a tactic of diversion similar to that of the hunter who diverts his prey's attention with a decoy.[27] Babet is Charrière's "safe" heroine, her decoy at the center of the novel, who can divert the readers' attention away from the two more subversive intellectual heroines in the novel's margins. Charrière used the nautical tactic of "tacking" in order to destabilize the dominant models of female education and suggest new alternatives for women.[28] Finally, to be able to express herself more freely on controversial topics, she used the tactic of the cuttlefish who generates a darkness in which it can hide.[29] By mixing genres and zigzagging between theories and points of view, she created a climate of ambiguity and uncertainty which made it difficult for her critics to determine where exactly she situated herself.

To that end irony was particularly useful to Charrière, for it makes meaning and authority less determinable. Moreover, because it only destabilizes meaning without completely erasing it, it allows for the creation of new meaning derived from the original meaning. An example of irony occurs toward the end of the novel, when Babet asks her future husband once again to teach her how to read and write. Her mother intervenes to warn Sainte Anne against it: Thereupon the mother pleads with Sainte Anne to adopt in his own marriage a principle that served her perfectly as a married woman:

> Je me souviens encore des seuls vers que j'aye jamais sus. Mon oncle le maître d'école me les a assez répétés pour que je m'en souvienne tout ma vie. Il ne voulut pas seulement m'apprendre l'ABC, quelque prière que je lui en fisse. Une femme disoit-il qui connoîtroit les lettres, voudroit apprendre à lire: en sachant lire, elle pourroit apprendre toute seule à écrire; or, et je tiens ceci d'un sage:
>
> > "Dans ses meubles, dût-elle en avoir de l'ennui
> > Il ne faut écritoire, encre, papier ni plumes.
> > Le mari doit dans les bonnes coutumes
> > Ecrire tout ce qui s'écrit chez lui."   (309–10)

[I still remember the only verses I ever knew, for my uncle the schoolteacher repeated them so often to me that I will never forget them. Even though I begged him to teach me the alphabet, he refused. His reason was that a woman who knew the alphabet would want to learn to read; and if she could read, she could teach herself how to write. And a wise man had once told him the following truth:

"Make sure that a woman's room
Has neither desk, ink or paper
For fair custom dictates:
A man should write all
That is written in his home."]

Readers who recognize these maxims as those of the ultra-conservative Arnolphe in Molière's *L'école des femmes* might detect mockery on the part of Charrière. Others might take these lines at face value, as reinforcing Sainte Anne's ideas about women's education. A similar ambiguity exists with regard to the character of Sainte Anne himself. Although at first glance he seems a serious character with valid (albeit conservative) ideas, in the course of the novel his credibility falls prey to Charrière's irony. Indeed, a large part of the novel revolves around his romantic attachment to his past and the manor of his forefathers, which he wants to rebuild as a shelter for Babet.

However, there can be little doubt that Charrière viewed Sainte Anne's fascination with his ancestry with great skepticism. Since her youth, she had been contemptuous of the nobility's exaggerated attention to lineage and name. Her first published work, *Le noble* (1763), specifically satirized the prejudice of birth and the sanctity of the ancestral manor. When she wrote *Sainte Anne*, the Revolution had abolished the privileges of name and birth—one of its greatest accomplishments in Charrière's eyes. The fact that she applauds Sainte Anne's liberalism in choosing for a wife the illegitimate daughter of a houseservant shows that she was still very much in favor of social equalization. In this light Sainte Anne's romantic attachment to his ancestry can be read ironically, as evidence of his misguided attachment to outmoded prejudices, including his prejudice in favor of birth and—even more pointedly for this novel—his prejudice against women's learning.

Even though Charrière succeeded in inserting subversive messages between the lines of her "anti-intellectual" novel, they are hardly meant to serve as a feminist call to arms. Her rather uncommitted stance with regard to women's education in *Sainte Anne* cannot be blamed solely on her fear of reprisal. It reflects her deep ambivalence about how to resolve the question of women's education in the post-revolutionary period. Aware of the unfortunate fate of the women who had dared challenge openly the intellectual limitations imposed on them,[30] and having grown distrustful of intellect after having witnessed its uncontrollable forces during the Revolution, she was no longer sure that women should try to attain autonomy and self-fulfillment through knowledge and education. Still, when she tried to envision a more traditional destiny for women (as in her portrayal of Babet), she found the ignorance and subordination it implied equally undesirable. Unable to conceive of a livable alternative for women, she limited herself in *Sainte Anne* to exploring the problems and limitations the dominant models of education presented for women, stopping short of proposing a clear solution to the dilemmas and contradictions she uncovered.

Using the psychoanalytical concept of ambivalence, the feminist psychoanalyst and philosopher Jane Flax explains that, especially in periods of sharp transition and change (of which the post-revolutionary period is a prime example), contradictions and indeterminacy are a healthy sign that an individual does not repress her ambivalence about the conflictual situation in which she finds herself. "Ambivalence is an appropriate response to an inherently conflictual situation. The problem lies not in the ambivalence, but in the premature attempts to resolve or deny conflicts."[31] Flax would therefore applaud Charrière's unwillingness to achieve premature closure with regard to the question of women's education. In light of Flax's argument, the concept of "tacking" assumes an added and useful significance. By "tacking" between various theories of women's education, Charrière not only suggested a possible new direction for women's instruction. By allowing the dialogues between theories to persist, she left open the possibility of continuous change and bravely confronted the impossibility of resolving the question once and for all. Her tacking therefore gives us a key for reading her, for in order to fully appreciate her writing we should not seek to reconcile her contradictions and achieve syntheses, but rather accept the vacillations of her text, learn to be as supple as she is herself, and read her message between the lines.

NOTES

1. Samia Spencer, "Women and Education in Eighteenth-Century France," in *Proceedings of the Tenth Annual Meeting of the Western Society of French History*, ed. John F. Sweets (Lawrence: University of Kansas Press, 1984), 274.

2. See among other speeches, "Discours de Chaumette à la Commune de Paris," 27 brumaire an II (17 Novembre 1793), cited in *Paroles d'hommes*, ed. Elisabeth Badinter (Paris: P. O. L, 1989), 181–82.

3. Joan B. Landes, *Women and the Public Sphere in the Age of the French Revolution* (Ithaca: Cornell University Press, 1988), 145–46.

4. To give an idea of the extremism of some of these tracts Geneviève Fraisse examines Sylvain Maréchal's "Projet d'une loi portant défense d'apprendre à lire aux femmes," in *Muse de la raison: la démocratie exclusive et la différence des sexes* (Alinéa: Aix-en-Provence, 1989), 13–45.

5. *Lettres neuchâteloises* (1784), *Lettres de Mistriss Henley, publiées par son amie* (1784), *Lettres écrites de Lausanne* (1785), followed by its sequel, *Caliste* (1787).

6. *L'abbé de la Tour* includes the following works: *Trois femmes, Honorine d'Userche, De l'esprit et des rois, Sainte Anne,* and *Les ruines de Yedburg.* For information on the genesis and publication of *L'abbé de la Tour,* see Isabelle de Charrière, *œuvres complètes,* 10 vols. (Amsterdam: Van Oorschot, 1979–81), 9: 7–11. All subsequent references to Charrière's works are to this edition.

7. Charrière, *œuvres,* 9: 265–310. Hereafter quotations from *Sainte Anne* will simply be followed in the text by a page number in parentheses. I have kept the original spelling and punctuation, which is not modernized in the complete works.

8. For bibliographical information, see Charrière, *œuvres,* 9: 805–6.

9. Otto Wimmer, *Handbuch der Namen der Heiligen* (Innsbruck: Tyrolio, 1959).

10. For more information on the instructional options available to women at the end of the eighteenth century, see Jean H. Bloch, *Rousseauism and Education in Eighteenth-Century France* (Oxford: Voltaire Foundation, 1995), 215–22 and "Knowledge as a Source of Virtue: Changes and Contrasts in Ideas Concerning the Education of Boys and Girls in Eighteenth-Century France," *British Journal for Eighteenth-Century Studies* 8.1 (1985): 83–92; Dominique Julia, "Les lumières sont-elles féministes?" in *Les trois couleurs du tableau noir de la Révolution* (Paris: Belin, 1981), 310–31; and Samia Spencer, "Women and Education in Eighteenth Century France," 274–84.

11. Charrière, *œuvres,* 9: 110 (emphasis added).

12. It is worth noting that Charrière gives her heroine Constance a proper name (constancy) that "says" the opposite of "tacking." In a similar way Charrière uses rhetorical tactics in *Sainte Anne,* thanks to which she can present opinions diametrically opposed to the dominant opinions voiced by the title character.

13. *Larousse Lexis* indicates that it was only after 1762 that the verb started to be used figuratively to mean proceeding by indirect methods (Paris; Librairie Larousse, 1988).

14. Denis Diderot and Jean le Rond d'Alembert, eds., *Encyclopédie, ou dictionnaire raisonné des sciences, des arts et des métiers* (1751–1772; reprint, New York and Paris: Pergamon, 1969).

15. The English verb "to luff" derives from the same Middle-Dutch stem *loef* as does the French verb *louvoyer*. The *American Heritage Dictionary* defines it as follows: 1. To steer a sailing vessel nearer into the wind especially with the sails flapping. 2. To flap while loosing wind. Used of a sail.

16. "S'ensuit-il que [Sophie] doive être élevée dans l'ignorance de toute chose, et bornée aux seuls fonctions du ménage? . . . Non, sans doute; ainsi ne l'a pas dit la nature, qui donne aux femmes un esprit si agréable et si délié; au contraire; elle veut qu'elles pensent; qu'elles jugent; qu'elles aiment; qu'elles connaissent; qu'elles cultivent leur esprit comme leur figure; ce sont les armes qu'elle leur donne pour

suppléer à la force qui leur manque et pour diriger la nôtre. Elles doivent apprendre beaucoup de choses, mais seulement *celles qu'il leur convient de savoir*." [Does it follow that Sophie must be brought up in general ignorance and be limited to household tasks? No, indeed; this is not how nature wanted it, why else would it give women such a ready and quick mind; on the contrary, nature wants women to think, judge for themselves, love, acquire knowledge, and beautify their mind as they do their figure; these are the weapons nature gives them to make up for their lacking strength and direct ours. Women must learn many things, but only those *things that are suitable for them to know*] (emphasis added). Jean-Jacques Rousseau, *Emile ou de l'éducation* (Paris: Garnier-Flammarion, 1966), 474.

17. In the course of the novel, Babet repeatedly asks Sainte Anne to teach her how to read and write: "Voulez-vous l'hiver prochain m'enseigner à lire?" (269) [Would you teach me how to read next winter?]; and "A l'avenir pourtant il me seroit plus agréable de savoir lire, et vous m'apprendrez, vous me l'avez promis; j'espère que vous m'apprendrez aussi à ecrire" (309) [In the future, I would prefer to know how to read, and you will teach me, will you not? You promised. I hope you will also teach me how to write.]

18. Education and autonomy are essential to the heroines of *Henriette et Richard* (1792), *Lettres trouvées dans des porte-feuilles d'émigrés* (1794), *Trois femmes* (1795), and even *Honorine d'Userche* (1796).

19. Charrière to Ludwig Ferdinand Huber, 3–6 October 1799, Charrière, *œuvres*, 5: 628.

20. In *Lettres de Mistriss Henley* and, to some degree, in *Trois Femmes*, the trouble starts with the heroine's wedding; in *Lettres de Lausanne* and *Caliste* the heroines have difficulties in landing the right husband; in *Henriette et Richard* and *Lettres trouvées dans des porte-feuilles d'émigrés* the French Revolution separates the lovers and forces the heroines to lead independent lives; finally in *Honorine d'Userche* incest excludes any possibility of marriage between the lovers, forcing the heroine again to contemplate a different destiny than marriage. Moreover, except for *Caliste*, where the heroine dies, none of Charrière's novels have a neat and definite ending, emphasizing Charrière's tendency to give more open-endedness to her plots. In an interesting article comparing the endings of *Lettres de Lausanne* and *Caliste*, Elizabeth MacArthur suggests that Charrière's refusal of traditional endings must be interpreted as a feminist and subversive gesture. "Devious Narratives: Refusal of Closure in Two Eighteenth-Century Epistolary Novels," *Eighteenth-Century Studies* 21.1 (1987): 1–20.

21. Charrière to Caroline de Sandoz-Rollin, 18 October 1797, Charrière, *œuvres*, 5: 359. The letter containing the objections formulated by Caroline de Sandoz-Rollin is lost. We have only Charrière's response.

22. Charrière to Benjamin Constant, 13 June 1797, Charrière, *œuvres*, 5: 318.

23. Charrière to Ludwig Ferdinand Huber, 22 August 1797, Charrière, *œuvres*, 5: 341.

24. Charrière to Willem-René van Tuyll van Serooskerken, 2 November 1797, Charrière, *œuvres*, 5: 368 (original emphasis).

25. Michel de Certeau, *L'invention du quotidien*, 2 vols. (Paris: Gallimard, Coll. Folio, 1990), 1: 35.

26. Marcel Detienne and Jean-Pierre Vernant, *Les ruses de l'intelligence: la mètis des Grecs* (Paris: Flammarion, 1974).

27. Détienne and Vernant, *Les ruses*, 35–37.

28. Ibid., 19.

29. Ibid., 163.

30. In a letter of 11 November 1793, Benjamin Constant informed her of the execution of the feminist Olympe de Gouges: "Mais comment voulez-vous qu'on écrive parmi les têtes qui roulent? La pauvre Olympes de Gouges m'a fait un moment de peine. Je dis un moment parce qu'on n'a pas le temps de plaindre longtemps des victimes qui se succèdent si rapidement" (Charrière, *œuvres*, 4: 266). [How do you want us to write among the heads that roll? Poor Olympe saddened me for a moment. But only a moment because we do not have time to grieve when the victims succeed each other so rapidly.]

31. Jane Flax, *Thinking Fragments: Psychoanalysis, Feminism, and Postmodernism in the Contemporary West* (Berkeley: University of California Press, 1990), 11.

The Unaverted Eye: Dangerous Charity in Burney's *Evelina* and *The Wanderer*

SHARON LONG DAMOFF

Recent scholarship on Frances Burney has been largely silent on charity, focusing instead on two general, and often overlapping, issues: the "darkness" of Burney's fictions—the violence, suicide, and madness; and questions of female identity and female authorship. Such are the subjects, for example, of the major book-length studies in recent years: Kristina Straub's *Divided Fictions,* Julia Epstein's *The Iron Pen,* and Joanne Cutting-Gray's *Woman as "Nobody."*[1] Similarly, Margaret Anne Doody's exploration of the relationship between Burney's personal life and her fiction, by giving particular emphasis to the domineering role of her father, was instrumental in directing Burney criticism toward issues of female identity and female authorship.[2] The special *Evelina* issue of *Eighteenth-Century Fiction* strikingly reveals this direction of recent scholarship; all four major articles deal with issues of identity and naming raised by the frame story of *Evelina,* a homogeneity noted in a concluding essay by Doody,[3] who calls for a new direction in Burney criticism, one that locates her in a broader context of history and literature.[4]

In none of these works is sufficient attention paid to Christianity as an important context—to me, an essential one—for understanding Burney's works. Thus, while many modern studies contain a statement that the author wants to examine the cultural, social, legal, political, economic, medical, and other contexts (most of them ending in *-al,* as Tristram Shandy might note) of her work, often as they related to women (Epstein, for example, mentions the "structure of social, political, economic, and cultural relations" [*Iron Pen,* 11])—the striking omission, to me, in these lists of contextual interests is "religious," still the dominant ethical context in the eighteenth century and the one into which I want to resituate Burney. In *Superintending the Poor,* Beth Fowkes Tobin claims, "Contextualizing . . . novels by surrounding them with contemporary economic, political, and social texts highlights ideological implications in fiction that otherwise might remain obscure to modern readers,"[5] a statement with which I agree; but I would like additionally to suggest that the religious context of eighteenth- and nineteenth-century novels is increasingly more likely to be "obscure to modern readers" than are the "ideological implications" that concern Tobin and others, implications that construct in many ways the "religion" of a secular age. Hence, though it might seem to some that I am offering special privileges to Christianity in this essay, establishing it outside the realm of the social and cultural, that is not at all the case. What I am trying to do is to restore the dominant religious ideology precisely to where it belongs and from where it has been significantly and effectively displaced: in the very center of any social or cultural discourse concerning the eighteenth century.

All of Burney's novels explore the issue of charity, the complexities involved in loving one's neighbor, the central doctrine of Christian ethics, and still very much the central subject of eighteenth-century Anglican moral teaching. From her first novel, *Evelina* (1778), to her last, *The Wanderer* (1814), thirty-six years later, Burney not only sustains her statement that charity is the essential measure of ethical worth, she repeats it with increasing intensity.[6] In *Evelina,* charity is central to the plot, which chronicles the growth of a young woman from moral dependence to moral independence. In *The Wanderer,* charity offered—or, more commonly, not offered—to the destitute and isolated heroine is the absolute measure of character, Burney's most direct statement that morality and charity amount to the same thing.

Evelina's kindness and generosity to the poor Macartney are far more than perfunctory instances of charitableness to provide evidence that she is a good, compassionate person or even a good Christian. Evelina's charitable efforts come at a great price. She resolves to behave charitably to the impoverished and suffering Macartney even if it costs her the good opinion of Lord Orville, the man she loves. That is, she willingly risks her entire future happiness on earth by behaving charitably. Her relationship with Macartney is the one encounter that causes Orville seriously to question her behavior. Appearances have been against her repeatedly in the past, as when Orville sees her in the company of the two prostitutes, but with Macartney, she seems to Orville willfully to be ignoring his advice and displeasing him.

Ultimately, Orville too adopts the charitable course of action by giving her seemingly indecorous behavior a charitable interpretation. In fact, he extends charity toward Macartney, a man he initially viewed as a potential, although unequal, rival; he assists Evelina in meeting privately with Macartney, first initiating the acquaintance and then discreetly leaving them alone together. Evelina's charity toward Macartney, including Orville's struggle over how to respond to it, is arguably the most crucial action of the novel. On the one hand, it reveals Evelina's moral worthiness and strength—her ability to judge and to act for herself; and on the other, it reveals Orville's willingness to repose faith in her judgment. The ability to judge and act for herself, always a crucial requirement for a Burney heroine, is the moral lesson Villars most urges her to learn.[7] Similarly, it is a major point of growth for the almost, but not quite, perfect Orville to trust, without jealousy, the motives of this inexperienced young woman. Evelina's firmness in her charitable course of action and Orville's voluntary and equally charitable subordination of his judgment to hers mark the point at which these two people become equals. Charity—that is, compassion and concern for a suffering human being and consistent and determined efforts to help that person despite all dangers and appearances—comprises the centerpiece of the plot.

In this regard, it might be noted, Captain Mirvan, the Branghtons, and Madame Duval do far more than provide comic interludes in Burney's moral fable. They serve, in addition, to round out Burney's emphasis on charity by revealing various deviations from the required standard. The captain is an extreme example of an uncharitable person; his worst flaw is his underlying meanness, not his rough manners. He is vicious to Madame Duval, with an excess that seems sadistic, particularly during the fake robbery and its aftermath. His treatment of the fop Lovel at the end of the novel is also excessively cruel.[8] As is often the case in her novels, Burney tests our own charity (and lack of it) through her extended portrayals of annoying characters and the very harsh punishments they receive. Our desire to see pests and fops and other undesirables punished (a desire Tobias Smollett relishes satisfying) is itself always punished in Burney by the reminder, underlying the episode in some fashion or another, that our pleasure in the event is tainted with uncharitableness and cruelty.[9]

With Madame Duval and the Branghtons, Burney again addresses the issue of how one is to deal with others who are themselves uncharitable—vulgar, selfish, and manipulative—but this time from the viewpoint of the sufferer rather than the avenger. Madame Duval is particularly a thorn in

Evelina's side because of the authority she has over her. Her domineering and embarrassing ways are a thorough test of Evelina's charitableness, but Evelina consistently treats her with respect, politeness, and charity—more than any reader is able to muster. The Branghtons are simultaneously uncharitable and a test of the charitableness of others. They seek to use people rather than assist them, a fault that had become, according to Burney and others, all too common among members of their class—as shopkeepers, tradesmen, and others sought to achieve the status and trappings of those above them without any recognition of the ethical responsibilities that traditionally, through the influence of religion, had accrued to wealth (although sometimes, of course, those responsibilities had been neglected even by those who were aware of them).

The Branghtons, as representative of the whole rising merchant class, endeavor to associate themselves as much as possible with the gentry and nobility and simultaneously to distance themselves from any acquaintance they perceive to be beneath them. Hence, not only do they insult and mistreat Macartney, being willing to turn him out and let him starve, they also seek to profit from Evelina's acquaintance with Orville. In their eagerness to associate themselves with those above them, however, they revert to their habits of trade, thus revealing—despite their pride—not only their shopkeeping roots but, much worse, their view of people as commodities. When, for example, they want to commandeer Orville's carriage to carry them home from Kensington-gardens, Mr. Branghton declares, "that would be making some use of a Lord's acquaintance, for it would save us coach-hire." When Evelina protests, he demands, "where's the good of your knowing a Lord, if you're never the better for him?" (244). Even after they break the window of Orville's carriage, Tom intrudes, by an unauthorized use of Evelina's name, to solicit a silver order from Orville. Throughout, they are alert to ways they can profit from others, and they, like Madame Duval, greatly test Evelina's powers of politeness and restraint. Again, it is important to note that Evelina's charity toward them exceeds the reader's, whose own judgmental readiness to condemn others must be called to account. We should understand, for example, that Burney's comedy is, finally, directed not so much toward shopkeepers and their necessary attention to money and trade, but toward the unabashed *use* of other people, toward the attitude that all others—people as well as objects—are valuable only for what they might profit oneself, an attitude that reveals the greed and pride running much deeper through the Branghtons than the accidents of birth and livelihood. Burney's attention is consistently more ethical than social, despite much criticism to the contrary.

What I particularly want to address in this essay, however, is Burney's exploration of the difficulties encountered by women in their practice of charity. In the eighteenth century, virtue for women was always linked with chastity; the virtuous woman was "pure," and the distinction between spiritually pure and sexually pure was easily blurred. Especially for unmarried women, virtue was frequently reduced to modesty—not speaking in company, not expressing opinions, keeping the face hidden, averting the eyes, and not conferring "favors" (such as smiles).[10] Above all, a modest woman should not reveal a preference for any particular man before she had a firm commitment to marriage—one of Burney's most consistent themes. Revealing such a preference had the status of conferring the "last favor"; all would be lost. In Burney's third novel, *Camilla* (1796), for example, Mr. Tyrold writes a famous letter of advice on this matter to his daughter, a letter that was often extracted and printed as conduct literature for young ladies.[11] Mr. Tyrold cautions Camilla in strong terms to overcome her feelings of partiality: "Struggle then against yourself as you would struggle against an enemy" (358). Above all, he cautions her to guard her secret: "Carefully, then, beyond all other care, shut up every avenue by which a secret which should die untold can further escape you" (360). Keeping the face hidden and the eyes averted (or shut) become crucial to the maintenance of virtue because these are the avenues through which the fact of one's preference shines forth.

For women, then, virtue meant withholding oneself—socially, emotionally, and, of course, sexually. For unmarried women such as Evelina, it meant a mode of life in which one's slightest outward gesture was replete with danger. Charity, to the contrary, requires the giving of oneself. It requires giving generously to others—of one's time, one's money, and, above all, one's attention. Loving others, in other words, requires a willingness to share thoughts and offer ourselves, a willingness to act (and not merely to feel) that makes us vulnerable. It is precisely an understanding of this vulnerability that constructs the eighteenth-century prohibition against a woman's revealing any preference for a particular man. This inherent tension between giving and withholding, between charity and "virtue," is what Burney explores. Evelina must be somewhat forward and aggressive in her efforts to help Macartney, neither of which is a desirable quality for a modest, unmarried young woman. She must show an interest in him, a particular interest that is open to damaging and uncharitable interpretations.

The issue of charity and women is further complicated because much of the language surrounding sexual relations between men and women employs the metaphor of gifts and giving ("she gave herself to him," "she gave up her honor"). Traditionally, the man entreats the woman to give the gift of her body, and charity thus becomes diametrically opposed to chastity, although both are upheld as virtues. In English, we also use one word—"love"—to express both charitable love and love of a sexual mate, and the two meanings of the word are blurred in that (in)famous line: "If you loved me, you would."

Charity is elevated in 1 Cor. 13:13 and by numerous eighteenth-century sermon writers as the highest virtue, but because of the conflicting requirements for giving and withholding, women—even women of means—are hindered from practicing it. Evelina's actions surrounding Macartney illustrate this tension. She should be socially withdrawn from him according to the rules of decorum, but charity urges her to give to him, to hear his story and be his friend and benefactor. Evelina's behavior toward Macartney, although ultimately vindicated, is not without peril. She violates the strict rules of propriety when she establishes a relationship with him and especially when she agrees to meet him on her morning walk (as Orville makes obvious). In the end, Burney is careful to distance Evelina from any wrongdoing. That Macartney proves to be Evelina's brother is a rich twist on the scriptural rewarding of kindnesses to "the least of my brethren," but it is also a way of further desexualizing the relationship between Evelina and Macartney.

Throughout the pistol scene, in which Evelina rushes into Macartney's room to prevent him, as she thinks, from shooting himself on the spot, Evelina alternates between bold action—grabbing his arms, seizing the pistols—and frozen inaction—collapsing on the floor "breathless and senseless" (182), leaning on the table, and finally "totter[ing] down stairs" (183). This scene (over)dramatizes the conflicting behaviors required of women. They are to be moral actors, but they are also to be passive and subdued. Villars recognizes this tension between the bold action required during the pistol scene and the demure action usually required of women: "the courage with which you pursued this desperate man, at once delighted and terrified me" (216)—that is, Evelina's charitable interest in a suffering human being pleases him, but he is aware of the danger to her as a person and as a woman in *"pursu[ing]"* a "desperate *man.*" Nevertheless, he urges her, "Be ever thus . . . dauntless in the cause of distress!" (217). He concludes: "Though gentleness and modesty are the peculiar attributes of your sex, yet fortitude and firmness, when occasion demands them, are virtues as noble and as becoming in women as in men: the right line of conduct is the same for both sexes, though the manner in which it is pursued, may somewhat vary . . ." (217). This last demur is frustratingly vague. He does not say that right conduct is the same for both sexes; he says the *line* of conduct is the same. Nor does he specify what would be the varying right manner of following that line for men and for women. His vagueness underscores the danger for women in a world in which right conduct differs for men and women, but in which women are nevertheless exhorted to be "dauntless in the cause of distress." Women must decide for themselves when "occasion demands" the "unwomanly" virtues of boldness and "firmness," but the stakes are high, and an error in boldness would be far more costly for them than for a man. Even though Villars praises Evelina for her boldness, his vagueness serves as a warning that such bold action is always dangerous for women—and particularly so for women in a world governed not by charity but by uncharitable judgments.

Burney's emphasis on charity is rooted in the fundamental scriptural injunction to love one's neighbor as oneself (Lev. 19:18, Matt. 22:39), and her narrative reflects scriptural narratives: Evelina is a Good Samaritan—albeit a tottering one—stooping to lift and assist a suffering stranger when she rushes into Macartney's room. In this case, she saves the sufferer from committing robbery, and, like the biblical Good Samaritan, gives him money that enables him to survive until his friends learn of his plight and assist him. Macartney perceives her intervention as from God: "I beheld you as an angel!—I thought you dropt from the clouds." His reaction is partly caused by her beauty ("a form so celestial!" "too beautiful to be human" [230]), and a cynical reader might be tempted to emphasize these comments and consider his reaction simply that of a young man's physical attraction for a pretty young woman. It should be remembered, however, that Macartney never treats Evelina in a forward manner (unlike just about every other single male she encounters); he always treats her reverently. The very act of giving charity seems to protect her; she appears to him to have more than earthly beauty precisely because she is demonstrating love—and grace—towards him. Her charity gives her both heavenly beauty and heavenly protection—grace given is grace received, as one might put it scripturally. Macartney thus sees her as a divine agent saving him from eternal ruin: "the hand of Providence seemed to intervene between me and eternity" (230). He recognizes her genuine, inspired, feelings of benevolence for him through her repeated politeness, her graciousness, we might say, toward him. She deliberately avoids humiliating him as she gives her purse to him, and she consistently treats him as a person with dignity who deserves to be respected even though he is penniless. Good manners and a charitable suspension of the critical faculty become important signs of divine intervention in the human scene.

Evelina's charitable intervention is also directly opposed to wealth's indifference in the parable of Lazarus and the rich man (Luke 16:19–31), another scriptural narrative behind Burney's narrative and a parable that seems to have particularly captured the interest of eighteenth-century Anglicans. John Tillotson (1630–94), the influential latitudinarian Archbishop of Canterbury, whose sermons were widely read and borrowed from throughout the eighteenth century, preached a series of three sermons on this parable, emphasizing that the lack of charity is the particular sin attributed to the rich man, who is punished, not for the possession or enjoyment of wealth, both of which are legitimated, but for not sharing it in an appropriate manner.[12] Tillotson stresses that merely refraining from doing wrong is not enough for Christians—they must also practice positive charity. The rich man is punished for failing to notice the poor man in his path, for averting or shutting his eyes. And it is precisely that failure that Burney explores in revealing the special difficulties for women in the injunction to charity. In that watchful and highly critical society in which she finds herself, Evelina is open to censure for "noticing" Macartney as she passes through the Branghtons' shop and again, subsequently, for taking an active interest in him and caring about him. Similarly, the priest and the Levite who pass by the wounded man in the parable of the Good Samaritan are clearly faulted for looking the other way instead of noticing distress and suffering. The averted eye is a virtue for women, but a vice for those commanded to love their neighbors as themselves. On this single dilemma hinges much of Burney's fiction, novels that uniformly deal with the complex search for a female virtue acceptable both to human beings and to the Christian God.

The demure posture suggested for women, their eyes downcast or turned aside, was required in the eighteenth century as an infallible indicator of innocence. Chaste, innocent women are not to see or understand too much of the male world. But by scriptural standards—and Burney's—one can be tainted by failing to see as well as by seeing; averted eyes can be an indicator of indifference, arrogance, selfishness, and hard-heartedness as well as innocence. The woman who averts her eyes, who fails to notice a fellow human being in distress, is not innocent but guilty of a sin. In the words of Proverbs, "He that giveth unto the poor shall not lack: but he that hideth his eyes shall have many a curse" (Prov. 28:27). With the conflicting choices of seeing or not seeing, averting the eyes or looking boldly into the face of another, Burney reveals the double bind of the female situation. However, there can be little doubt about Burney's final position in *Evelina:* women, as well as men, are to follow the scriptural injunction; they are to behave charitably despite the danger, despite the difficulties, and despite the personal costs. To do so is the only Christian way to act, and when one acts charitably, the world comes under the governance of Providence; the happy ending of *Evelina* is a direct result of her ethical choices throughout the work.

Burney places an even more obvious emphasis on charity in her final novel, *The Wanderer.* Here, the heroine, Juliet, is far more vulnerable than Evelina, and her vulnerability centers on the need for charity. The primary measure of character in the novel is the way in which people—male and female—react to Juliet in her distress, their willingness or unwillingness to help her. For reasons that are unknown to the reader through much of the book, Juliet must keep her identity—including her name—a secret and must find some way to survive in England after she flees there from France during the French Revolution. She is completely alone, has no money, and is unable to contact the friend she had expected to meet at Brighthelmstone. The entire novel—and it is a very long novel—chronicles the efforts of this woman alone trying to support herself, and the responses—from generously helpful to cruel and predatory—of the people she encounters.

The Wanderer is, among other things, Burney's re-presentation of the parable of the Good Samaritan and is a much more fully developed exploration of this central parable than the brief but significant scene in *Evelina*. Most important, in Burney's retelling, the person in need is a woman, a final instance of her exploration of the difficulties facing women in a society that considered itself highly charitable but that was also profoundly judgmental.[13] The telling of the biblical parable is prompted when an expert in the Law, who wants to justify himself, asks Jesus, "And who is my neighbor?" (Luke 10:29). The question is critical because the most important scriptural commandment concerning human relationships is to love one's neighbor as oneself. In Jesus's response, the parable of the Good Samaritan, it is significant that the person in need of help is a stranger, even an ethnic foe, who has been the victim of crime (robbery and beating). In a reading of *The Wanderer* as a version of this parable, Juliet fits this profile exactly. She is a stranger to everyone; she is initially thought to be French (and the French, of course, were the long-standing foes of the English); and she is without money because her purse has been stolen (although for a long time she thinks it simply lost). She is also emotionally battered and later threatened with physical abuse.

The important question "And who is my neighbor?" resonates richly throughout *The Wanderer*. Most of the characters are obsessed with finding out Juliet's true identity.[14] For Mrs. Maple, the question "Who is my neighbor?" means "Of what family is she? What connections does she have? What makes her worthy of my attention?" Mrs. Maple and others want to know who she is in order to determine whether they are obligated to help her; they do not acknowledge that everyone they meet, regardless of social standing, is a neighbor who deserves help if in need. Mrs. Maple thus uses the query to exclude rather than include, to lessen the number of people she is obligated to help rather than to increase it as the parable teaches.

This twisting of a well-known biblical precept is a technique Burney had previously employed. In *Evelina,* for example, Miss Polly Branghton suggests that Evelina should lie to break a previous engagement so that she could go with them to the opera. For Polly, breaking an engagement is a matter of course: "I dare say; it's only doing as one would be done by, you know" (84). She (im)piously quotes the Golden Rule with no awareness that she is grossly misusing it. "Doing as one would be done by" means to her doing what others would do if they had the opportunity, not doing as one would *like* to be done by. She is, of course, revealing her own standards of behavior; she would feel no guilt in lying to break an engagement with Evelina if she received a better offer. By twisting well-known precepts in this way, Burney reveals the deeply rooted hypocrisy of unthinking human beings in a Christian society and the ease with which they justify their misdeeds in the language of their religion.

The parable of Lazarus and the rich man is also, again, an important background for Burney's narrative. Although Juliet's story does not have as many parallels to this story as to that of the Good Samaritan, several points are apt. For example, while Juliet is not nearly as pitiful as Lazarus (she is not covered with sores which the dogs lick), when she initially appears, pleading to be allowed in the boat leaving France, she is covered with bandages as part of her disguise. Furthermore, for much of the novel, she is homeless and alone, often hungry. While some characters, such as Mrs. Ireton, are positively mean to her, most simply fail to help her, as the rich man failed to help Lazarus. Of course actual abuse causes suffering, but Burney also dramatizes the real suffering that results from a lack of charity, from simply ignoring those in need of help. Burney is presenting a life made hard, sorrowful, and dangerous through the uncharitableness of other people. This failure of charity is crucial; a willingness to offer shelter or hospitality to strangers is an essential component of Christian charity, one that is always ultimately rewarded: "Come, ye blessed of my Father, inherit the kingdom. . . . For I was an hungred, and ye gave me meat: I was thirsty, and ye gave me drink: I was a stranger, and ye took me in" (Matt. 25:34–35). Juliet's lengthy wanderings through the New Forest afford many characters the chance to shelter her, feed her, and offer her a cup of cold water—that is, they afford many Christians the opportunity to perform the precise instances of charity considered at the final Judgment, at the separation of the sheep from the goats.

In his sermon "Upon Self-Deceit," Joseph Butler (1692–1752), another influential Anglican divine, also makes the point that neglect of charity is an instance of sin: "[A]s there are express determinate Acts of Wickedness, such as Murder, Adultery, Theft: So on the other Hand, there are numberless Cases in which the Vice and Wickedness cannot be exactly defined; but consists in a certain general Temper and Course of Action, or in the Neglect of some Duty, suppose Charity or any other, whose Bounds and Degrees are not fixed."[15] Those people in *The Wanderer* who fail to help Juliet do not think of themselves as committing any "Vice and Wickedness"; on the contrary, Mrs. Maple and Mrs. Howel see themselves as prudent, upstanding, even righteous people because they make it clear that their standards of association are impeccably high. Even when they turn Juliet away from their doors, they see themselves as acting properly because they are protecting the young ladies in their charge. The conflicting demands upon a woman's virtue are thus dramatically highlighted—the need to "protect" young women from their "neighbors" (often, to be sure, with sufficient reason considering characters such as Sir Lyell Sycamore) becomes the very reason to reject giving alms and comfort to a "neighbor" in need. Because the bounds of charity are not clearly fixed, it is easy for people to rationalize their lack of compassion, as Burney demonstrates.

Hence, in *The Wanderer,* Burney continues her exploration of benevolence as it relates to women—their willingness or failure to give it, and, most especially in this work, their failure to help one another and their vulnerability in accepting aid from men. Mrs. Maple, Mrs. Ireton, and Mrs. Howel are women who shamefully fail to help another woman. Not only do they fail to shelter and assist her when they easily could, they contribute to her troubles—by spreading accusations against her or by treating her cruelly and contemptuously. Most of the characters are reluctant to shelter or assist Juliet because they do not know who or what she is. A woman without a declared and certified social station (someone's daughter, someone's wife, someone's widow) is perceived as threatening, in large part because to associate with her could damage one's own reputation if she turns out to be not of a good family or, much worse, to be a "fallen" woman. Burney—usually conservative and always concerned about preserving her reputation as a decorous and proper lady—here criticizes a code of behavior by which turning a woman out into the world friendless, penniless, and homeless is a safer way of preserving a good name than is sheltering or assisting a stranger.

Juliet's situation also makes clear the difficulty of a woman's receiving even good-intentioned benevolence from a man. If a woman—especially a young, single, beautiful woman—accepts money from a man, the world concludes she must be his mistress. Although Harleigh quickly becomes romantically interested in Juliet, it should be remembered that he first extends kindness to her by pleading to allow her in the boat escaping from France when he knows only that she is a woman in distress and when her beauty is hidden by bandages (11). Even when he thinks she is a woman of low social station, he shows her politeness and seeks to assist her discreetly without expecting any sort of obligation in return. Throughout the novel, Harleigh seeks for opportunities to assist Juliet in acceptable ways—but the problem is precisely that almost nothing is acceptable, especially after she is revealed in all her beauty and seeming eligibility.

What Harleigh can do—and he does it consistently—is to treat Juliet with politeness. Although Burney stresses the need for financial assistance in *The Wanderer*, she also refers repeatedly to the little acts of kindness and politeness that smooth Juliet's way when offered and wound her deeply when withheld. Such acts of good manners are deeply significant; they are what mark Juliet as a gentlewoman and thus procure for her a certain level of courteous treatment. In a society obsessed with social station, people take their cue of how to treat their "neighbors" from the way they are treated by others. If a few prominent people show Juliet attention and respect when she enters a room, the rest of the company do so as well; similarly, if the prominent people snub her, everyone snubs her. That is, the women snub her and the men become a threat; they perceive Juliet as easy sexual prey. Consequently, small acts of politeness are enormously significant, her fragile protection and security. When Juliet is treated politely, she feels secure and protected; when basic civilities are withheld from her, she knows she is vulnerable to violence both physical and emotional.

Sir Jaspar illustrates another way in which it is difficult for a woman to accept help from a man. Although Sir Jaspar is so old as to be tottering and initially does not press any advantage with her or make any sexual advances, she can never be entirely sure of his motives or what will be the consequences if she does accept money from him. As it turns out, Sir Jaspar does have more in mind than being a financially generous grandfather, although he is not solely a sexual predator as is Sir Lyell Sycamore. Sir Jaspar at least seems to have a genuine concern for Juliet's well-being in addition to—perhaps even before—his other interests. Because relations between men and women are complicated, a vulnerable woman such as Juliet can never be certain of the motives behind assistance offered from a man and can never be certain of the world's reaction even when she is fairly confident that his motives are not harmful to her. And the world's reaction is important, despite claims to the contrary; maintaining a good reputation is Juliet's only fragile protection from violence. If her reputation suffers, the women will snub her, and the men will prey upon her. The failure of the women in the novel to harbor Juliet becomes all the more culpable precisely because she is alone.

Mrs. Maple, in particular, is obsessed with reputation; she values reputation more than reality—both in herself and others. Burney, however, is exploring the way in which reputation becomes reality in her society, and the consequences of confusing one with the other. If Juliet did turn out to be a "frenchified swindler" (57), as she is more than once accused of being, or a "fallen woman," Mrs. Maple and Mrs. Howel would be guilty of Lady Aurora's *real* ruin by allowing her reputation to be severely tarnished for associating with such a person. The situation is one of Burney's many instances in which the world is fraught with real danger for women if they do not maintain a pristine reputation. One misstep ruins a woman's good name and with it her chances for a good marriage. Because women of a certain social rank but no fortune had virtually no options other than marriage for a decent course in life, a ruined reputation doomed one to a miserable life on earth. A sense of fear lurks in all Burney's novels,[16] and much of that fear is centered on preserving a reputation; frequently, there is very little distance between her heroines and disaster. Uncharitable interpretations make innocent behavior as potentially damaging to reputation as immoral behavior.

Joseph Butler says that part of charity is being willing to think well of others: "It is still true, even in the present State of Things, bad as it is, that a real good Man had rather be deceived, than be suspicious; had rather forego his known Right, than run the Venture of doing even a hard Thing."[17] Mrs. Maple and Mrs. Howel, on the other hand, would rather be suspicious than be deceived, would rather forego doing a good thing than run the venture of being duped. Mrs. Howel rejects even the possibility that Juliet might be innocent: "'Innocent?' repeated Mrs. Howel, . . . 'without a name, without a home, without a friend?'" (133). That is, she considers the fact of Juliet's absolute neediness a reason not to help her. Of course, if Juliet did have a name, a home, and friends, Mrs. Howel would then feel entirely justified in not helping her in that case either; in the context of the novel, Burney censures Mrs. Howel and the others for their pervasive lack of compassion. Part of their problem, however, might be that Butler's statement—and the standard behind it—is in regard to a good *man*. As women, Mrs. Maple and Mrs. Howel cannot risk being deceived because they have less hope of recovering afterwards. A man risks losing whatever cash he might have given to an imposter; a woman risks losing her good reputation—her tenuous link to a respectable life.

Thus, *The Wanderer* shows, just as *Evelina* does, that practicing charity is fundamentally and paradoxically difficult for women in her society; furthermore, *The Wanderer* explores in painful detail the fact that receiving charity is also dangerously problematic for women. In addition to the practical matters Juliet continually faces, her essential problem is that giving or receiving aid of any sort carries with it the taint or threat of immodesty or, even worse, unchasteness—and therefore aid is withheld to preserve the modesty of both giver and receiver. The result, however, is that Juliet is forced to pursue increasingly "forward" and public methods of supporting herself and thus becomes increasingly vulnerable. Receiving charity, as in Juliet's case, requires being open to another person, exposing oneself, revealing oneself—which again runs counter to all eighteenth- and nineteenth-century prescriptions for female modesty. Receiving the advances of a loving (charitable) person is perceived as not much different from receiving the advances of a lover. A woman "without a name, without a home, without a friend" has little hope of receiving aid, much less love, from her neighbors in a world characterized not by charity and mercy but by uncharitable interpretations and judgment. And in such a world, giving charity falls under equal suspicion, certainly so if the giver is a man, but also when a woman seems sufficiently careless of her own (or her charges') reputation as to form a bond—even a bond of charity—with an "unknown" neighbor.

As even this brief discussion of charity and women suggests, Burney, from the beginning of her career to the end, was concerned about the ways in which the women of her age were expected to conform their behavior to quite contradictory standards regarding charity. A woman must be simultaneously charitable and modest—that is, simultaneously open and reserved. Furthermore, she must be simultaneously charitable and prudent—that is, simultaneously trusting and suspicious. And, finally, she must be simultaneously charitable and chaste—simultaneously giving and ungiving, generous and penurious of her time, her attention, her eyes, and her self. Juliet, in a momentary indulgence of bitterness at her situation, describes her judgmental and uncharitable society, a society all too ready to condemn women, especially women forced to judge and act for themselves:

> Deeply hurt and strongly affected, how insufficient, she exclaimed, is a female to herself! How utterly dependent upon situation—connexions—circumstance! how nameless, how for ever fresh-springing are her difficulties, when she would owe her existence to her own exertions! Her conduct is criticised, not scrutinized; her character is censured, not examined; her labours are unhonoured, and her qualifications are but lures to ill will! Calumny hovers over her head, and slander follows her footsteps! (275)

NOTES

I am grateful to Melvyn New for his thoughtful comments on this essay.

1. Kristina Straub, *Divided Fictions: Fanny Burney and Feminine Strategy* (Lexington: University Press of Kentucky, 1987); Julia Epstein, *The Iron Pen: Frances Burney and the Politics of Women's Writing* (Madison: University of Wisconsin

Press, 1989); Joanne Cutting-Gray, *Woman as "Nobody" and the Novels of Fanny Burney* (Gainesville: University Press of Florida, 1992). Straub briefly discusses charity in *Cecilia* (123–25), but only in the context of whether it empowers Cecilia.

2. Margaret Anne Doody, *Frances Burney: The Life in the Works* (New Brunswick: Rutgers University Press, 1988).

3. Doody, "Beyond *Evelina:* The Individual Novel and the Community of Literature," *Eighteenth-Century Fiction* 3 (1991): 359–71.

4. One notable exception to the silence on charity is Katharine M. Rogers, *Frances Burney: The World of "Female Difficulties"* (New York: Simon & Schuster, 1990), who includes a discussion—albeit a relatively brief one—of benevolence in *The Wanderer* (132–33, 160) and also discusses the good-heartedness of Camilla, Sir Hugh, and Mrs. Arlbery in *Camilla* (109–12), among other passing references to charity.

5. Beth Fowkes Tobin, *Superintending the Poor: Charitable Ladies and Paternal Landlords in British Fiction, 1770–1860* (New Haven: Yale University Press, 1993), 3–4; Tobin does not discuss any of Burney's novels.

6. Clearly in *Cecilia* and *Camilla* Burney elaborates on the exploration of charity begun in *Evelina* and concluded with *The Wanderer.* In limiting my discussion, I do not mean to slight the two middle novels but rather to highlight my point that from the beginning to the end of Burney's long career, the role of charity was a consistent concern. To produce a complete study of that concern would include, of course, not only the two middle novels, but Burney's *Journals* and dramatic writings as well.

7. Fanny Burney, *Evelina, or The History of a Young Lady's Entrance into the World,* ed. Edward A. Bloom and Lillian D. Bloom (1778; reprint, Oxford: Oxford University Press, 1982), 164. Subsequent references will be from this edition and will be cited parenthetically in the text.

8. John Hart, "Frances Burney's *Evelina:* Mirvan and Mezzotint," *Eighteenth-Century Fiction* 7 (1994): 51–70, places Mirvan in the tradition of comic mezzotints of the 1770s, which frequently depict an English tar getting the better of the French and of fops. In my reading, Burney is revealing the fundamental uncharitableness behind this popular image.

9. Emma Woodhouse's treatment of Miss Bates, as the centerpiece of her own moral education, is Jane Austen's tribute to Burney's constant reiteration of this structure.

10. For a thorough discussion of women and modesty, including chapters on "The Language of Modesty," "Modest Blushing," and "Evelina's Self-Effacing," see Ruth Bernard Yeazell, *Fictions of Modesty: Women and Courtship in the English Novel* (Chicago: University of Chicago Press, 1991).

11. Fanny Burney, *Camilla, or A Picture of Youth,* ed. Edward A. Bloom and Lillian D. Bloom (1796; reprint, Oxford: Oxford University Press, 1983), 355–62. For a brief description of the importance and history of this section, see note on p. 941. Subsequent references to *Camilla* will be from this edition and will be cited parenthetically in the text.

12. John Tillotson, *Sermons on Several Subjects and Occasions,* vol. 7 (London, 1757), 355.

13. Hannah More, for example, characterizes the age as very charitable, but she goes on to warn her readers not to allow the general climate of charity to take the place of personal charitable actions; see, for example, *Christian Morals*, vol. 9 of *The Works of Hannah More* (London, 1830), 144.

14. Fanny Burney, *The Wanderer; or, Female Difficulties,* ed. Margaret Anne Doody, Robert L. Mack, and Peter Sabor (1814; reprint, Oxford: Oxford University Press, 1991), 29, 43, 58, 75, 100 contain versions of this question. Subsequent references to *The Wanderer* will be from this edition and will be cited parenthetically in the text.

15. Joseph Butler, *Fifteen Sermons Preached at the Rolls Chapel . . . to Which Are Added, Six Sermons Preached on Publick Occasions*, 5th ed. (London, 1765), 189–90.

16. Doody, *Frances Burney*, 3, and Epstein, *Iron Pen,* 5, 87, have particularly commented on the anxiety that results from the underlying violence in her novels.

17. Butler, *Fifteen Sermons*, 249.

Pre-Romantic Elements in the Aesthetic and Moral Theories of François Hemsterhuis (1721–1790)

A. P. DIERICK

The Dutch philosopher François (Frans) Hemsterhuis is generally not well known in North America, although he was famous in his own time. Scholars have repeatedly insisted on his influence on the German pre-Romantic movement of *Sturm und Drang*, and on Johann Gottfried Herder and Johann Wolfgang von Goethe, and his personal links with many of the well-known personalities of his day are well documented. While Hemsterhuis did not have a noticeable influence on Dutch philosophy—a fact which the most prominent Dutch biographer of Hemsterhuis, L. Brummel, explains by the backwardness of contemporary Dutch cultural life—his links with French philosophy are somewhat stronger; on the one hand because of his obvious borrowings from sensualists like Bonnot de Condillac, on the other because of Denis Diderot's extensive commentaries on one of Hemsterhuis's publications, the *Lettre sur l'homme et ses rapports*. Instrumental in the spreading of Hemsterhuis's fame in Germany was above all the Princess Gallitzin, wife of Prince Dimitri Gallitzin, the Russian ambassador to the Netherlands at the Hague. Gallitzin himself was a friend of Voltaire [François Marie Arouet], Diderot and Jean le Rond d'Alembert, and the protector of Claude Adrien Helvetius. Hemsterhuis over many years maintained a close relationship with the Princess Gallitzin, who not only inspired three of his philosophical dialogues, the *Sophylus* (1778), *Aristée* (1779), and *Simon* (1780), but who was clearly a worthy partner in the discussions of which these dialogues are the end result.

Apart from this crucial relationship with the Princess Gallitzin, platonic yet passionate, Hemsterhuis's own life was rather uneventful. He was born on December 27, 1721 in the small Frisian town of Franeker, which at the time boasted a university. Educated at first by his father, the philologist Tiberius Hemsterhuis, who inspired François' lifelong admiration and fascination with Greek civilization, and especially Greek art, Hemsterhuis matriculated from the University of Leiden in 1747. He became a clerk in the State Council of the Netherlands at the Hague in 1755, and in 1769 was promoted to First Secretary. He met the Princess Gallitzin for the first time in 1773, and in 1779 traveled twice with her to Munster, where she ultimately stayed to live. During a further sojourn in Germany he met Friedrich Heinrich Jacobi, whose enthusiastic reception led to the translation of several of Hemsterhuis's works in the following year. Further tours through Germany in 1785 included meetings with Goethe, Herder, and Christoph Martin Wieland in Weimar. Hemsterhuis visited the Princess for the last time in 1788; a year later a German translation of his *Lettre de Diocles à Diotime sur l'athéisme* appeared in German translation in Jacobi's second edition of his *Über die Lehre des Spinoza*. Hemsterhuis died on July 7, 1790 in the Hague.

Hemsterhuis was a thinker who touched on many topics. His earliest work was on aesthetics, the *Lettre sur une pierre antique* written for Théodore de Smeth, who had the stone in his collection, in 1762, but only published after his death.[1] This short work was followed by the far more important *Lettre sur la sculpture*, published in 1769, but written in 1765. It contains the famous definition of the beautiful, so admired by Herder, Goethe, and other German pre-Romantics. It is also of considerable interest when compared with the better known work of Johann Joachim Winckelmann, published one year earlier, his *Geschichte der Kunst des Altertums*. Hemsterhuis's next work, the *Lettre sur les désirs*, which could be categorized as a mixture of aesthetic and moral considerations, grew out of a point raised in the *Lettre sur la sculpture*. The philosophy of morals was more clearly the subject of his *Lettre sur l'homme et ses rapports*, as well as the dialogue *Simon, ou les facultés de l'âme*. In *Aristée, ou la divinité*, an attempt is made to provide a theodicy, while in *Alexis ou de l'âge d'or*, finally, the myth of the Golden Age is reworked.[2] Hemsterhuis also wrote extensively on optics and geometry.

In this paper I would like to concentrate on Hemsterhuis's aesthetic and moral writings and on the connections which exist between the two. I propose to highlight only those notions which have made history, and which have been proposed to suggest links between the "Dutch Socrates," as he has been called, and the German pre-Romantics. In choosing texts primarily of his earlier phase, before 1775, I am guided by the fact that it is these texts that figure most prominently in the reception history of Hemsterhuis in Germany. At the same time, these are the texts most frequently quoted as proof of an "elective affinity" between Hemsterhuis and the precursors of German Romanticism. If such claims are to have some validity, however, and if the aptness of the term "pre-Romantic" is not merely to be assumed mechanically, it is clear that an examination of Hemsterhuis's philosophical questioning of necessity also raises issues of definition, classification, and periodization in cultural history in general. This fundamental issue is hidden in the title of this paper itself, for it seems to assume that a) there is such a thing as a pre-Romantic movement, and b) that Hemsterhuis's work contains "pre-Romantic" elements.

As far as the first assumption is concerned, it may be useful to remind oneself that as far back as 1963 René Wellek wrote in his *Concepts of Criticism* that the terms "Romanticism" and "Romantic" had already been under attack for a long time;[3] he for one felt, however, that some broad definition of both terms was useful and could be defended. The debate, of course, has continued, not only as to whether it is a European movement or a series of movements, but especially what "catalogue" of elements would have to be established to describe adequately such a movement or movements. The same may of course be said for the even more contested term "pre-Romantic," quite apart from the subtle question as to the exact relationship between *Sturm und Drang* and Romanticism—a question with which many critics have struggled and continue to struggle.

One source of confusion about so-called pre-Romantics should in any case be laid to rest immediately. "Nobody," Wellek writes, "has ever suggested that the precursors of Romanticism were conscious of being precursors." But, he continues, "their anticipations of Romantic views and devices are important." Arguing for or against Romantic and pre-Romantic movements in the eighteenth century is, Wellek points out, often tied to problems of methodology. "The argument against the very existence of Romanticism in the eighteenth century is based on the prejudice that only the totality of a writer's work is the criterion of judgment"; yet on the other hand he must admit that "the hunt for 'Romantic' elements in the eighteenth century has become a rather tiresome game,"[4] while the "atomistic" approach which sets out to provide instances of individual Romantic ideas and motifs dating from the seventeenth century or beyond ignores the question of emphasis, place in a system, and frequency of occurrence. Despite such hesitations, however, Wellek makes an observation, in this case specifically on English literature, which I take to give some validity to my title: "If there were no preparations, anticipations, and undercurrents in the eighteenth century which could be described as pre-Romantic, we would have to make the assumption that Wordsworth and Coleridge fell from heaven...."[5]

Indeed, indicators of a general shift in paradigms towards a new *Gefühlskultur*, a new sensibility, are evident from as early as the 1730s on. In his letters written from Turin (1739), Thomas Gray marvels at the wild beauty of the Alps, thus echoing the famous poem by Albrecht von Haller, "Die Alpen" (1729), with its paean to the Furka and the St. Gothard. Haller also celebrates the simple, uncorrupted life of the *montagnards*, as did Salomon Gessner, whose nature descriptions, in their new sensibility, anticipate those of Jean Jacques Rousseau. A very personal, lyrical, funereal and metaphysical sensibility is expressed in the works of such poets as James Thomson; his poems on the four seasons (published from 1726 to 1730) already contain many of the pre-Romantic elements which culminate in the tender, sad and melancholy scenes in Goethe's *Werther*, and François René de Chateaubriand's *Atala et René*, while Thomas Gray's "Elegy Written in a Country Churchyard" (1750) brought the poet instant and European-wide fame. Charles Dédéyan writes of Gray's verses: "C'est un chef d'oeuvre dans la mesure où ils orchestrent les sentiments d'une Europe déjà préromantique: malgré leur rhétorique et les lieux communs, leur incantation simple et monotone suggère la paix pastorale, l'innocence édénique à laquelle aspirent les coeurs las, dans la sérénité d'un paysage tranquille."[6] James Hervey, in his "Meditations among the Tombs" (1745–47) carried this type of pre-Romantic sensibility to its apogee, whereas the crucial motif of the night is cast in its definitive form in Edward Young's "The Complaint, or Night Thoughts on Life, Death and Immortality" (1742–45), whose title programmatically announces those poetic preoccupations which will lead without interruption into pre-Romanticism, and to Rousseau as its most famous proponent.

Such indicators of a new sensibility are not to be seen as restricted to the poets themselves, moreover. There is, especially after the middle of the century, a paradigmatic shift in the writings on aesthetics which reflects the cult of sensibility introduced in poetry, and which works in parallel with poetic production itself, creating new definitions of the beautiful, stressing sentiment and genius. In particular, a new attitude towards wild, untamed nature is introduced into both poetic production and aesthetic reflections. Nature is no longer a source of moral precepts, but rather a source of disturbing and at the same time fascinating sentiments: wild nature inspires fear *and* a sense of the sublime. Carsten Zelle, in his discussion of the importance of "delightful horror" and "terreur agréable" in England and France, not only unearths substantial evidence for the centrality of untamed rather than cultivated nature in European poetry; he also draws from the material the conclusion that "die Entstehung der positiven Neubewertung der ungestalteten, ja bedrohlichen Naturerscheinungen" are related to the rhetorical concept of the sublime.[7] "Der Betrachter der gewaltigen Naturerscheinungen wird 'in ein angenehmes Erstaunen'—'pleasing astonishment'—und in 'ein ergötz-endes Schrecken und Entsetzen'—'delightful Stillness and Amazement' gesturzt."[8] Crucial in Zelle's discussion is his insistence on the fact that nature thus depicted in art has an emotional rather than an intellectual or moral impact on the reader, just as nature itself has such an impact on the observer. This shift from the thing depicted to, first, the depiction itself, but beyond this, to the *effect* on the observer or reader, in other words, a shift from work (*Werk*) to effect (*Wirkung*) is the most important aesthetic development in the eighteenth century. Evidence of this shift can be observed in the writings of Anthony Ashley Cooper, third earl of Shaftesbury, Francis Hutcheson, Joseph Addison, David Hume, Diderot, Jean-Jacques Rousseau, and especially Johann Jakob Bodmer and Johann Jakob Breitinger—all heralds of pre-Romanticism. In looking at the aesthetic and moral writings of Hemsterhuis, therefore, it will be of crucial importance to note to what extent these writings provide evidence particularly of the cult of sensibility as outlined above, and of an orientation towards *Wirkungsaesthetik*—both essential ingredients of pre-Romanticism.

For most scholars writing on Hemsterhuis the view that there are precursors of Romanticism in the eighteenth century—both creative writers and writers on aesthetics—is a tacit as well as a stated assumption. Hemsterhuis is seen by these critics precisely as a figure mediating between Enlightenment and Romanticism. Indeed, in this view Hemsterhuis is not so much of intrinsic interest than as a figure representative of a particular moment in cultural history. L. Brummel, for example, explains that "in the treatment of Hemsterhuis's ideas we have taken as our starting point the fact that their value is primarily determined by the time in which they were announced."[9]

Here, however, one has to sound a warning about the linking of Hemsterhuis with pre-Romanticism, namely that such linkages might simply by inspired by external evidence, notably the list of illustrious personages generally associated with *Sturm und Drang*, pre-Romanticism, and Romanticism who enthusiastically endorsed Hemsterhuis's work. A more convincing method of establishing a relationship between Hemsterhuis and pre-Romanticism would of course be to provide evidence of true anticipations and preparations, and this is indeed suggested by a number of German critics beginning to write around 1900. In contrast to earlier scholarship, in their "teleological" approach Hemsterhuis is seen in light of things to come, as showing impulses which soon afterwards are more fully developed. Brummel, for example, in stating that Hemsterhuis's philosophy "distinguishes itself not so much by its being so deeply thought, but, rather, subtly felt"[10]—advances a criterion which he understands as pointing to Romanticism. Not surprisingly, however, reading Hemsterhuis "teleologically" in this way has also come under attack, most recently by Paul Pelckmans, who warns us that such readings tend to distort by quoting out of context and by misreading the thrust of the totality of Hemsterhuis's philosophy.[11] We easily recognize elements of the debate to which Wellek referred already in 1963. Given the problems raised here, it is in any case clear that in looking at Hemsterhuis's work we will do well to try to keep the distinction between echoes and correspondences, endorsements and interpretations in mind.

It is not surprising that Hemsterhuis would write on the topic of aesthetics; many eighteenth-century philosophers did. Especially towards the middle of the century aesthetics, first and foremost in England, became one of the central areas of philosophy. Rolf Grimminger has argued that this was the direct result of a feeling that man's "natural," irrational and subjective wishes and desires had been left out of the rational system of Enlightenment philosophy: "Subjektivität, die sich den Regeln der Vernunft nicht restlos beugt, weil sie auf den irregulären Möglichkeiten eines von Affekten geleiteten Daseins beharrt, wird zu einem fundamentalen Problem im System der aufgeklärten Pflichten, dessen Lösung nahezu ausschließlich der Kunst, dem Geschmack, der ästhetisch verfeinerten Sinnlichkeit übertragen wird."[12] It is the question of the legitimacy of pleasure which triggers, as a subdivision, the many inquiries into the place of beauty. A longing for a synthesis of pleasure and reason can, according to Grimminger, be seen in such overarching ideas as unity in multiplicity, reason and nature, art and nature, etc.[13] Moreover, as Brummel has argued, because of a perceived conflict between objective reason and subjective pleasure, aesthetics is also the domain in which one is apt to find the most likely evidence of a tendency towards forms of irrationalism which may herald a transcendence of Enlightenment positions. This idea seems to be borne out by the speculations on aesthetics first in England (Edward Young, Shaftesbury, Hutcheson, Edmund Burke) and then in Germany (Jacobi, Herder, Johann Georg Hamann, later Friedrich Schlegel, Novalis [Friedrich von Hardenberg]). The very fact that Hemsterhuis wrote treatises on aesthetics would therefore suggest a certain irrational tradition, and, perhaps, a pre-Romantic anticipation.

Hemsterhuis's first effort in this vein, however, the *Lettre sur une pierre antique* (1762), is still completely in the tradition of Enlightenment. The essay consists of a mixture of praise for the beauty of the object and a dose of erudition, learning, and "science" inspired by the premise that only the connoisseur is able to appreciate "la belle pièce." Though it anticipates

Winckelmann's efforts to link Greek sculpture with Greek history and culture, the essay carries nothing of the illustrious contemporary's weight, nor of Hemsterhuis's own second text on aesthetics, the far more substantial *Lettre sur la sculpture* (1769).

This second *Lettre* is a two-part essay, consisting of a concise history of sculpture prefaced with a series of general remarks concerning art. The short history of sculpture is the less interesting of the two parts. In this section the author is still firmly in the tradition of contemporary notions. Sculpture is "de toutes les espèces d'imitation des choses visible la première"(33);[14] its invention precedes painting, which requires a greater degree of abstraction (two- rather than three-dimensional representation; focusing on sight rather than the more primitive touch). Of one opinion with Winckelmann in his praise for Greek sculpture, Hemsterhuis rejects the idea that the Greeks learned from the Egyptians, since the latter's art is inspired by a taste for "immensité" and an "esprit de symbole et du merveilleux" (37), qualities alien to the Greeks. Hemsterhuis does make a point which also occurs in Edmund Burke's *Enquiry into the Origins of Our Ideas of the Sublime and Beautiful* of 1757, namely that Greek art is the reflection of a fully developed, healthy personality.[15]

One statement stands out from the conventional discussion: the Greeks had, according to Hemsterhuis, exhausted "les beautés de la nature," and had arrived at "ce beau idéal, suivant lequel ils ont produit tant de chef d'oeuvres inimitables" (38). This remark sends us back to the general discussion on art with which Hemsterhuis begins his treatise, and to the statement that the first goal of art is the imitation of nature, but the *second* its enrichment, "en produisant des effets qu'elle [la nature] ne produit pas aisément ou qu'elle ne sauroit produire" (14). The mimetic function of art, stated as an axiom, does not surprise: it is valid for all Enlightenment aesthetics, though for Hemsterhuis as for other transitional figures the nature of this function is somewhat different from at least early Enlightenment thinking by people like Nicolas Boileau-Despréaux in France or Johann Christoph Gottsched in Germany in that it allows for an improvement on nature. Of course it would be wrong to expect Hemsterhuis to achieve the position reached by a true Romantic like Samuel Taylor Coleridge, who accepted imitation of nature in the form only of "creative imitation," in harmony with a formative drive active in creation; or by William Wordsworth, for whom there is a basic *in*compatibility between the precepts of mimesis and the inspirations of genuine art.[16] But the standard definition of art as a narrowly defined imitation of nature also does not suffice for Hemsterhuis; he is in search, as Albert Funder puts it, of "ein allgemeines Gesetz der ästhetischen Wirkung, eine allgemeine Struktur des ästhetischen Verhaltens."[17] Hemsterhuis finds this law in looking at sculpture itself.

Sculpture relies entirely on contours. Having observed, in a typically practical fashion, how a child draws an object placed in front of him, Hemsterhuis arrives at the claim that such contours are grasped in a process of connecting individual points. "L'ame fait la liaison de tous ces points elementaires et acquiert à la fin l'idée de tout le contour" (17). Such a procedure involves not only the element of time: since different objects affect the observer in different ways, a second element seems to be involved, namely intensity. But even when the intensity can be proven to be the same, the effect of an object may vary; a third element is therefore involved: the *velocity* with which the points are composed into contour. From these observations Hemsterhuis now arrives at the first part of his famous definition of art: "L'ame juge le plus beau ce dont elle peut se faire une idée dans le plus petit espace de temps" (18). This statement is not complete, however, since it would suggest the absurd conclusion that a black dot on a white ground would be the most beautiful. Hemsterhuis in fact argues the contrary: the soul would choose a group rather than a single point, "parce qu'il lui donne un plus grand nombre d'idées à la fois" (19).[18] The final version of the definition of the beautiful therefore involves a maximum of ideas in a minimum of time, and hence "ce que nous appelons grand, sublime et de bon goût, sont de grands touts, dont les parties sont si artistément composées que l'ame en peut faire la liaison dans le moment et sans peine" (21).[19]

Hemsterhuis's definition, often repeated by contemporaries and successive generations, is not entirely new, as Funder has amply demonstrated. There are antecedents as far back as Xenophon, Aristotle, and Boileau for the principle of order underlying Hemsterhuis's definition (an ordered object is more quickly grasped than an un-ordered one), and speculations on the relationship of the parts to the whole can be found in Shaftesbury, Hutcheson, Diderot and Michel de Montaigne. Similarly, for the principle of what Funder calls "Fülle," which we might translate as "abundance"—in Hemsterhuis's case of ideas—antecedents and parallels can be found, according to Funder, in Samuel Richardson, William Hogarth, and Johann Joachim Winckelmann. The principle of unity in multiplicity, finally, is a platonic idea which reoccurs in Gottfried Wilhelm von Leibniz, Jean-Pierre de Crousaz and Hutcheson, as well as in Montesquieu, as Brummel also points out.[20] More original is how Hemsterhuis develops his definition, since this poses for the first time the problem of the relationship between our senses and the objects of our perceptions. Because of the time involved, there is a loss both in the process of creating *and* appreciating a work of art. "L'ame a besoin du temps et de succession de parties lorsqu'elle veut, par la main ou par la parole, rendre, exécuter, ou réaliser une belle idée qu'elle a conçue," Hemsterhuis writes; this long maneuver "doit bien diminuer la splendeur de l'idée." On the other hand, "l'ame [qui] a la faculté de reproduire l'idée de l'objet" (20) works in a *contrary* sense: the observer must divide the object into its constituent components, before re-constituting it. The reception of the idea is further subject to the individual situation of the observer, his or her "situation morale," by which Hemsterhuis means the observer's predisposition to discern "le plus grand nombre d'idées" (29).[21]

In view of this complicated process Hemsterhuis claims: "La première idée distincte et bien conçue d'un homme de génie, qui est rempli du sujet qu'il veut traîter, est non seulement bonne, mais déjà bien au-dessus de l'expression" (26). For the same reasons, sketches convey an idea better than the deliberately "finished" work of art: for the *producer* "parce qu'elles tiennent beaucoup plus de cette divine vivacité de la première idée conçue" (26), for the recipient "parce qu'elles mettent en mouvement la faculté poétique et réproductive de l'ame" (27)—what one might call the imagination. It is an idea which in Romanticism surfaces as the unfinished and unfinishable work of art—Novalis's *Heinrich von Ofterdingen* being the standard example of this idea.

A consideration of the art *medium*, along similar lines, suggests to Hemsterhuis that poetry is superior to the visual arts because it can trigger a greater number of ideas in the recipient than sculpture.[22] Finally, as already indicated, the idea of the limits of art imposed by the senses—a motif which will play an extremely important role not only in Hemsterhuis's writings on aesthetics but also on ethics—surfaces here for the first time; the point will be taken up in greater detail in the *Lettre sur l'homme et ses rapports* and in the dialogue *Sophyle out de la philosophie*. The insufficiency of the senses could be argued to anticipate the tragic notion in Romantic thinking that the work of art will never achieve its perfect expression, nor find its perfect recipient.

Hemsterhuis's definition of beauty can be seen to rely heavily on the relationships between subject and object: it locates in each certain preconditions for production and reception. The optimum desired is not located in things in themselves, but is "l'effet du rapport qu'il y a entre les choses et la construction de mes organes" so that, in Hemsterhuis's pithy formulation, "le beau n'a aucune réalité dans soi-même" (31). This statement introduces a relativism in art criticism which breaks with early Enlightenment: by having the ability of the recipient to react to the work of art made dependent on a number of external conditions—education, training, taste and discernment, personal experiences, applicability of the aesthetic subject to the personal situation, etc., Hemsterhuis seems ready to abandon the idea of absolute standards of beauty in art criticism.

Two crucial notions stand out from this discussion. First, the work of art is the product of a divine spark of genius; it can be conveyed even, and in fact even better than in the finished product, in an original sketch. Because it is the product of genius, it cannot be bound solely by rules, nor can it be judged in terms of a narrow and normative definition of art as imitation of nature. Secondly, the work of art solicits a response in the observer/reader, and hence must be formed with this process in mind. Both nature and the work of art itself produce certain feelings and emotions in the subject; the subjectivization of art goes hand in hand with a search for the most effective form and style to create the desired emotions. We are, with these two notions, entering into two crucial debates in eighteenth-century aesthetics: that surrounding genius, and that surrounding the formulation of an aesthetics of effect (*Wirkungsaesthetik*).

Some critics have made the claim that in his *Lettre sur la sculpture* Hemsterhuis introduces a completely original and new way of looking at art, but such claims cannot be sustained. Hemsterhuis's position is, as noted above, by and large in line with developments in the theory of aesthetics which in fact antedate the writing of the *Lettre* by a relatively large margin. Certainly a substantial body of theory had moved beyond early Enlightenment poetics and had, particularly in England and Germany, formulated aesthetics which broke with the dominance of rules, of didactics and a narrow definition of the concept of imitation of nature, in favor of an emphasis on such key concepts as genius, production, process, and sentiment.

This shift can, for example, be observed in an exemplary fashion in the writings of the Swiss critics Jakob Bodmer and Jakob Breitinger. Their rejection of the rigorous insistence on rules, and on the image of the poet as determined primarily by reason and morality—ideas notably propagated by Johann Christoph Gottsched in his *Critische Dichtkunst* of 1730, is inspired not primarily by their personal aversion to the ambitions of this Leipzig "Literaturpapst," as has sometimes been suggested, but rather by a sea-change in the interpretation of art and the artist. For Gottsched, the disciple of Christian Wolff and the admirer of French classicism, *reason* permeates all and provides the basis for morality, taste, and wit, the latter being defined as the ability to see the similarity between things and to combine them in a striking way. In this scheme of things, imagination ("Einbildungskraft") is understood by Gottsched essentially to reproduce concepts which we have already experienced. His definition of the artist consequently is by and large a rational one: "ein Poet muß dergestalt, sowohl als ein Maler, Bildschnitzer u.s.w.

eine starke Einbildungskraft, viel Scharfsinnigkeit und einen großen Witz schon von Natur besitzen, wenn er den Namen eines Dichters mit Recht führen will."[23] By contrast, in Bodmer and Breitinger, who are influenced by the theories above all of Jean Baptiste Dubos (especially his *Réflexions critiques sur la poésie et sur la peinture* of 1719), the concept of wit is played down in favor of the centrality of genius. No longer is art made dependent on the formulation of certain rules, but it is seen as the product of an artist who derives from his own talent and imagination the rules without which no art can exist. In the model proposed by Leibniz (in *De arte combinatoria* of 1666), wit had been given the role of recreating cosmic unity; Gottsched, as we saw, interpreted wit in terms of rationality as such, as the "Zusammenhang des vernünftigen Verfahrens."[24] In the writings of Bodmer and Breitinger, by contrast, the synthesizing role of art as envisaged by Leibniz is assigned not to wit, but to genius. The difference between wit and genius, according to Jochen Schmidt, is "daß der Witz eine rationale *Methode*, das Genie ein irrationales *Vermögen* darstellt; ferner ... daß der Witz unterhalb des viel umfassenden Ganzheitshorizonts des Geniedenkens bleibt, da er nur *mehr* oder *weniger* kombinieren kann, nicht selbst schon die Ganzheit als subjektive innere Form in sich trägt."[25]

Like Bodmer and Breitinger, like Hume before, and Herder after him, Hemsterhuis, too, comes to the conclusion that a static principle of "taste" cannot determine our judgment of a work of art,[26] that it is the product of an intuition of the whole, characterized by a "divine vivacité" (the example provided is that of Leonardo da Vinci). Shaftesbury had of course already compared the creative act of the genius with that of Prometheus; for Lavater (in his *Physiognomische Fragmente. Zur Beförderung der Menschenkenntnis und Menschenliebe*, 1775–78) the genius is the "proprior deus," whereas Herder's use of the word genius, inspired in turn by Shaftesbury's "original genius" as well as Young's *Conjectures on Original Cormposition* of 1759, shows a connection with his own vitalistic philosophy.[27] Hemsterhuis, in the view of Klaus Hammacher, H. Moenkemeyer, and Brummel, provides a link here between Shaftesbury and these later writers. Moreover, he also provides a connection between the English Enlightenment and German pre-Romanticism (even Romanticism, according to some) by the suggestion that the unfinished work of art is superior to the well executed one because in the recipient it sets the reproductive (in reality productive) imagination free to a higher degree.[28] This notion is reminiscent of the contrast drawn by Addison between the somewhat wild English and the manicured French garden. A further and crucial development of this contrast can be found in the writings of Shaftesbury, where it has much wider aesthetic implications. As Carsten Zelle writes, Shaftesbury "geht ... über die von England ausgehende

Auseinandersetzung zwischen dem geometrischen Stil des französischen Gartens ... und dem offeneren Stil des englischen Landschaftsgartens ... hinaus."[29] Shaftesbury sees the contrast between the different gardens as a paradigm for the contrast between the more unbridled and extravagant character of the work of genius and the elegance and refined character of what the French call the "bel esprit," with Shaftesbury's preference (also because of political reasons!) going to the first. Moreover, and even more significant for the present discussion, "mit der 'Antithetik von unberührter und verfälschter Natur' zielt Shaftesbury auf eine Entgegensetzung von Natürlichkeit und Künstlichkeit" in the direction of a new appreciation of nature in its unbridled state. "Savage" nature cannot be grasped in traditional categories of beauty: to apprehend it, Shaftesbury operates with the notion of the sublime: "Das Schönheitsideal Shaftesburys ist, was später das Schrecklich-Erhabene genannt wird."[30]

Seen against the ongoing debates outlined here, Hemsterhuis's emphasis on genius, his rejection of a static notion of beauty, and his introduction of the notion of the unfinished as a positive aesthetic category, suggest an anticipation of pre-Romantic ideas; again, his acceptance of the primacy of an original idea (the "esquisse" showing the divine spark) over its execution suggests, in line with Addison and Shaftesbury, an anticipation of aesthetic calegories going beyond the traditional ones associated with the concept of beauty.

Hemsterhuis's speculations about the relationship between the producer and the receiver of the work of art permit a further excursion into contemporary aesthetics, whose theme is the progression from a work-oriented aesthetic to an aesthetic of effect. In this excursion, too, it will become clear that Hemsterhuis is very much in line with the major aesthetic currents; and once again also, the work of Bodmer and Breitinger may be cited as seminal in this development.

This is the result of a major shift in Bodmer's and Breitinger's view of the precept of art as an imitation of nature. Although this rule of the imitation of nature still has force for them, nature is less a logically structured order than a source of psychologically determined experiences. The work of art should create similar effects as can be found in nature, and aim to stimulate emotional responses which correspond to those which nature inspires in us. "Einbildungskraft" in their view therefore plays a much more crucial, and different, role in the poetic process than in Gottsched, and it has a much stronger subjective nuance: "Das wirkungsästhetische Ideal Bodmers und Breitingers, von dem her sich die produktionsästhetische Theorie verändert, drückt sich in der Kategorie der 'hertzrührenden Schreibart' aus. Es kommt als nicht mehr so sehr wie bei Gottsched auf die rationale also auf die emotionale Wirkung der Poesie an."[31]

Bodmer found his great model for this kind of writing in John Milton's *Paradise Lost*, a work he had translated in 1724, and for which he wrote his apology in 1740, the *Critische Abhandlung von dem Wunderbaren*. It is in fact in the discussions surrounding Milton's epic that the great aesthetic debates of the eighteenth century are formulated in Germany. These discussions are crucial in two ways. First, they enlarge the range of "acceptable art" in breaking with a *narrow* interpretation of the rule of "imitation of nature." In its depiction of supra-natural dimensions, of God, the Devil, heaven and hell, Milton's work makes claims on the imagination and fantasy which explode the framework in which Gottsched's rule-driven, probability-oriented aesthetics operate. What is miraculous from the start, obviates the rule of probability, Bodmer argues; but his more important point is that the work of art cannot be held up to the mirror of the probable and possible in rationalist terms. Although Gottsched himself had allowed the category of the "possible," he interpreted it narrowly; "Die Einbildungkraft enthält auch in der Poetik Gottscheds die Lizenz, über die bestehende Wirklichkeit hinaus Welten zu erfinden, wenn diese nur den Begriffsbestimmungen der Dinge nicht widersprechen;"[32] Bodmer and Breitinger showed a much greater generosity, in allowing the possible to encompass the wondrous (*das Wunderbare*).[33]

The wondrous, above all, however, makes us "wonder" and be astonished, which is what Bodmer and Breitinger wish the poet to achieve. Jill Kowalik writes that Breitinger desires of the poet that he not merely employ selection and combination as mimetic techniques, but that he follow the principle of analogic transfer of the known to the unknown by straining analogies to their apparent limit: "At that point the image is wondrous, that is, it appears to stand in actual contradiction to the presently known," and thereby astounds.[34] And here we have the second reason why Milton's epic was able to play so crucial a role in eighteenth-century aesthetic discussions. Under the influence of their reading of Milton, Bodmer, and Breitinger begin to propagate fantasy and imagination as central poetic and artistic qualities. Imagination and fantasy are the qualities of the genius who creates autonomously and generates the rules out of himself. As in the case of the breakdown of a normative, essentially rationalistic view of art, Milton's text provides for the Swiss critics a model for the powerful effect art can have on the reader or observer. Subjectivization of poetic production (the stress on genius rather than rules) at the same time therefore entails an emotionalization of writing: the work of art must stir the heart. In fact, Kowalik points out,

Breitinger makes an even bolder claim than his source, Dubos, when he writes: "Die Copie ziehet uns stärcker an sich als das Original."[35] The "hertzrührende Schreibart," as a revolt against Gottsched's rationalism, thus marks a true caesura, and indicates the beginning of a great poetic *Gefühlskultur* around the middle of the eighteenth century.

Hemsterhuis, too, certainly appears to be more concerned with the *effect* of the work of art than with its origin, though his definition has consequences for both. His insistence on the power of genius to provide the divine spark which kindles the process of recognition and identification in the reader or observer, are part of a crucial shift from a work-oriented view of art to a fullblown *Wirkungsästhetik*. In addition, the role of the artist is also brought more clearly into focus, in that the latter must create in such a way that the process of "recognition" and "identification" in the recipient is facilitated. Hemsterhuis believes that he can indicate both process and goal in artistic creation in terms of a central and universal definition from which form flows in a logically inevitable way. This means in his case at least the beginning of a shift from an aesthetics of reproduction to an aesthetics of production and effect,[36] and a shift from an objective type of art based on the precepts of imitation of nature to a subjective perspective which recognizes the realm of artistic freedom.[37] Hemsterhuis is of course still far removed from someone like Herder, for whom the "unconscious" is the real starting point for creative genius. Nevertheless, he is in line here with the whole development of eighteenth-century philosophy of art, in that it moves from a didactic and generally utilitarian view of art, through a phase in which the criteria of taste and the definition of beauty are examined, up to the autonomy of art as stated in the writings of Goethe, Immanuel Kant, and the Romantics,[38] from which many a critic and thinker still derives his or her categories.[39]

Hemsterhuis had concluded his general remarks on art with the statement that the beautiful is not located in the object itself, but in its correspondence with our organs. Both the *Lettre sur les désirs* (1770) and the *Lettre sur l'homme et ses rapports* (1772) develop and elaborate this theme. But whereas the first stresses the limitations of our senses, the second opens up into a vision of a future in which such limitations are transcended.

The *Lettre sur les désirs* begins with a repetition of the definition of the beautiful. But this time Hemsterhuis adds: "Si l'ame pouvoit être affectée par un objet sans le moyen des organes, le temps qu'il lui faudroit pour s'en faire l'idée, seroit réduit exactement à rien" (53). On the other hand, "Si l'objet étoit tel, que l'ame put être affectée par toute la totalité de l'essence de l'objet, le nombre des idées deviendront absolument infinie" (53). In both cases, therefore, the imperfection of our senses is considered a barrier in the way of our grasping the beautiful perfectly, just as the imperfection of our faculties, in causing slowness in execution, stands in the way of the production of perfect art. From these facts derived from *aesthetics* Hemsterhuis now proceeds to establish the same argument for *ethics*.

Both in art and in human relations there is a universal law of nature at work which makes the soul search for unity and homogeneity with objects surrounding it: "Ce qui est l'ouvrage de l'art, n'est que le résultat des rapports désirés dans l'assemblage de choses avec nos organes, ou avec notre façon d'apercevoir ou de sentir" (67). The basic definition of art as a relationship is thus deepened by the understanding that this relationship is founded on desire.[40] At the same time, this view of art articulates a distinction between it and nature which was glossed over without comment in the beginning of the *Lettre sur la sculpture*. Hemsterhuis now writes: "ce qui est l'ouvrage de la nature, est le résultat . . . de sa suffisance à exister, et par conséquent un total déterminé et parfait" (67). Nature's self-sufficiency is contrasted with man's tragic situation expressed in his art: "le tout visible ou sensible se trouve actuellement dans un état forcé, puisque, tendant éternellement à l'union, et restant toujours composé d'individus isolés, la nature du tout se trouve éternellement dans une contradiction manifeste avec elle-même" (68). It is not difficult to see why some critics claim to recognize similarities between Hemsterhuis and the speculations about mankind's divorce from nature as expressed in writings like Friedrich von Schiller's *Uber naive und sentimentalische Dichtung*, or even links with the Romantic "Sehnsucht nach dem Unendlichen."[41] At the same time, Hemsterhuis's insistence on the tendency of all art to strive for cosmic unity is reminiscent of similar claims made by Bodmer and Breitinger. Hemsterhuis's attempts to make the (ultimately tragic) desire for unity a part of the creative process is once again in line with contemporary thinking.

Moving from aesthetics to ethics, Hemsterhuis now claims that in human relationships a similar longing for union prevails: "le but absolu de l'ame, lorsqu' elle desire, est l'union la plus intime et la plus parfaite de son essence avec celle de l'objet désiré" (54). Such union can be sought by two means: physical and intellectual. For the first, Hemsterhuis gives a series of examples showing that perfect *sexual* union is impossible. For the second he provides proof that immediate and intuitive "elective affinities" and spiritual assimilation between friends and lovers is never achieved: "tout est composé d'individus absolument isolés" (67). In the end, a basic dualism remains. And while the *intensity* of desire is measured by the degree of homogeneity sought with the thing desired (one loves a statue less than a friend, the friend less than a lover, and the lover less than the supreme being), the *impossibility* of complete and perfect union brings a disillusionment (*dégoût*) with that object which is proportional with the intensity of desire towards it.

In assuming that not only in art but also in the relations among individuals there exists an all-pervasive desire for union and unity, Hemsterhuis formulates a principle which is not only an integral part of his own general world view, but which also is seminal for pre-Romantics and Romantics, both in their holistic approach to art[42] and in the importance they attach to love and friendship. At this stage of his writing, however, Hemsterhuis does not appear to have found a way to make such a longing productive in the moral sphere. Even in the aesthetic sphere, desire is not given its ultimate satisfaction; this would have to wait, according to Hammacher, until Hemsterhuis would, under the influence of the Princess Gallitzin, embrace more radical forms of irrationalism.[43]

In the *Lettre sur les désirs* Hemsterhuis establishes a close link between the earlier writings on aesthetics and the later writings on ethics. This connection is a familiar one in Enlightenment: the idea that our notions of the good and the beautiful have a common source can be found in Shaftesbury and Hutcheson, for example. Rolf Grimminger has also pointed out that social activity had an aesthetic dimension in the idea of "polite society," or "schöne Gesellschaft," composed of "beautiful souls" ("schöne Seelen") brought together in the name of taste, grace, sympathy.[44] Finally, beauty, according to Grimminger, holds out the promise of happiness: once again a meshing of the good with the beautiful is indicated. But Hemsterhuis takes a different tack. For him the interrelationship between aesthetics and ethics is informed by the common psychological and anthropological point of departure in the theory of the senses.

It is in the *Lettre sur l'homme et ses rapports* (1772) that Hemsterhuis provides the most elaborate account of this theory. Unfortunately, the essay is rather convoluted, in parts pronouncedly uninspired, and at times annoyingly vague. Hemsterhuis was clearly a self-made "philosophe" rather than a systematic philosopher. Two topics have immediate relevance for the present discussion, however: the notion of a moral sense, and the theory of perception.

Hemsterhuis begins his essay with a renewed examination of the role of the senses in the process of perception. While attempting to define this role he proposes the idea that, just as the senses transmit between object and recipient, so there must be an "organe moral" which transmits between "velléités," i.e., members of society. In suggesting such an organ Hemsterhuis appears to take up an idea which was introduced by a number of Enlightenment thinkers, namely the existence of a sixth sense. The notion was not uniform in nature or application, however, and seldom developed systematically. Dubos, for example, conceives of a sixth sense as being concerned with aesthetics, whereas in Rousseau's case the sixth sense is active in the domain of morals. In both Shaftesbury and Hutcheson we find the idea that there is a moral sense in man that finds unique satisfaction in actions directed towards the common good. This sense turns us from the pursuit of pleasure to the performance of duties towards others. We call things good for the same reason we call things beautiful: because we find them agreeable. In this type of ethics there is a large role to be played by feeling and taste; it operates from a strong psychological basis and assumes that exclusively rational knowledge is not sufficient in the domain of ethics. For Shaftesbury, too, the "moral sense" makes man accessible to the good *and* the beautiful; while according to Hutcheson, such a "moral sense" is complemented in both domains by judgment. The main difference between thinkers such as Shaftesbury or Hutcheson and Hemsterhuis is that the latter, pursuing a primarily sensualist line of argument, seems to have conceived of his "organe moral" as a true organ, defined in the same sense in which he had defined eye and ear: "Comme l'oeil sans qu'il y eût de la lumière ou de choses visible, seroit totalement inutile; l'organe que j'appelle le coeur est parfaitement inutile à l'homme, s'il n'y a ni velléités agissantes, ni société avec de telles velléités par les signes communicatifs" (118). Note that Hemsterhuis first uses the word "coeur," clearly in an allegorized sense, and then later the word "organe moral." The "organe moral" is an instrument which establishes "rapports."[45]

The idea of an "organe moral" seems to have appealed to men like Herder, Jacobi, Friedrich Schlegel, and Novalis,[46] not least because of the fact that differently constituted "organes morals" have different duties to fulfill, which suggests to Moenkemeyer Hemsterhuis's greater emphasis on the value of individual life. By contrast, the idea was severely criticized by Diderot, who, being a materialist, insisted on being shown where this "organ" was anatomically located. Hemsterhuis obviously used the parallel between sense organs and the "organe moral" in order to establish the idea that, just as the senses give us immediate and clear ideas about objects, so the "organe moral" gives us immediate ideas about such things as justice, love, hate, and esteem. In this fashion, Hemsterhuis could, in the words of Moenkemeyer, "maintain the independence, irreducibility, even superiority of the moral side of the world against Neo-Spinozism, radical sensualism, materialism."[47] Such a line of defense was necessary in Hemsterhuis's day because in an era of an "esprit géométrique" the moral sense had atrophied and society had instituted organized religion and civil laws to replace it. Hemsterhuis deplored the decline of the "organe moral," and attacked the prevalent materialism of the age in his dialogue *Sophyle ou de la philosophie* (1778).[48] In his critique and criticism of contemporary conditions, Moenkemeyer argues, Hemsterhuis resembles Rousseau: like him, and unlike most *philosophes*, he seems to be calling for a new *Lebensgefühl* going well beyond Enlightenment sensibilities. This is suggested not only in the *Sophyle*, but especially in the conclusion of the present essay, where Hemsterhuis indulges, in Moenkemeyer's words, in "quasi-mystical speculation, indebted to the heritage of Neoplatonism."[49] In these passages the author seems to have broken away completely from his original sensualist position.[50] And indeed, in claiming that mankind may in future acquire a multitude of senses which would allow it to establish innumerable *rapports* hitherto unknown, Hemsterhuis does wax quasi-mystical. But the very *necessity* of such a multitude of senses is but the logical consequence of the limitations he had previously imposed on our perceptions *because* of the senses.

This is not to say that Hemsterhuis embraced a materialism à la Diderot.[51] But the claim that Hemsterhuis, at least in this particular instance, anticipates or approaches an idealist philosophy which would dramatically reduce dependence on the senses appears unfounded. Hemsterhuis's undoubted originality in this case mitigates unequivocally against his being classified a "Pre-Romantic," regardless of the fact that several contemporaries interpreted the notion of an "organe moral" to suit their Romantic speculations. Moreover, by limiting the "organe moral" to activity in the social realm only, the notion does not have the fascination it would have had, had it been capable of transposition into the realm of aesthetics. There is little evidence that Hemsterhuis himself saw in the "organe moral" a link between morality and aesthetics, though commentators repeatedly tried to establish such links.[52] And while the idea of such an "organe" transcends conventional Enlightenment thinking about social relationships, and was capable of inspiring pre-Romantics and Romantics alike, and whereas the possibility of a proliferation of senses is a highly original thought, unique to Hemsterhuis, the sensualist basis which Hemsterhuis provides, and his clinging to the notion of a quasi-physical organ prevents us from calling this idea seminal for post-Enlightenment thought. The argument concerning the "organe moral" is but one more example of how Hemsterhuis is a transitional figure in eighteenth-century philosophy.

The same cannot be claimed so categorically, however, for Hemsterhuis's theory of perception, and particularly his introduction of intuition and immediacy into the philosophical debate. It is with a short discussion of this theory, as it appears also in the *Lettre sur l'homme*, that I would like to conclude.

Hemsterhuis conceives of perception as passive: as a state of being open to the world outside. Since absence of an object causes it to disappear from our mind we use symbols (*signes*) to allow us to think them. Rational beings go beyond primary signs (which animals also have) in that they can conjure up concepts at will. Hemsterhuis writes:

> L'Etre qui a la faculté de sentir, et par conséquent celle d'acquérir des idées, ou, ce qui est la même chose, la faculté contemplative ou intuitive, a donc des sensations vraies, ou des objets qui sont actuellement hors de lui, ou de la modification présente de ses organes, et rien de plus; mais l'Etre qui joint à cette faculté intuitive, celle de pouvoir se rappeler ses idées par le moyen des signes, peut faire agir cette faculté sur autant d'objets à-la-fois qu'il pourra faire coëxister en quelque façon en apparence par le moyen des idées. C'est cette faculté intuitive qu'on appelle Raison, et son application aux idées, Raisonnement. (83)

This passage gives a good example of the vagueness of Hemsterhuis's terminology. But this very vagueness provides ammunition both for those who see Hemsterhuis as continuing the idea of the primacy of reason over emotion, and those who maintain that Hemsterhuis ultimately emphasizes feeling over thought.

It is clearly the slippery nature of the word "sentir" which is responsible for these divergent interpretations. Brummel, for example, claims that the word "sentir" is used here in connection with the acquisition of ideas, with the precondition of reason, in humans as well as in animals; humans combine "sentir" with memory to produce reason. The latter part of the quote suggests to Brummel that Hemsterhuis reinstates Reason as the faculty par excellence.[53] For Hammacher, on the other hand, "sentir" and its synonyms "faculté contemplative ou intuitive" are a clear indication that Hemsterhuis departs from Enlightenment positions, and moves in the direction of a "gefühlsbetonte Betrachtung der philosophischen Frage"—an emotionally oriented consideration of philosophical questions, which, he claims, developed gradually after Hemsterhuis's meeting with the Princess Gallitzin.[54] According to Hammacher, Hemsterhuis breaks with the Cartesian tradition of accepting only one kind of knowledge, namely knowledge rationally arrived at. For Hemsterhuis, *Unmittelbarkeit* is the road to a second, in actual fact the primary kind of knowledge. Hammacher writes: "Bei allen anderen Denkern der Aufklärung wurde das Gefühl bestimmt von der Gewißheit der Erkenntnis her und auf diese bezogen gesehen"; in the case of Hemsterhuis, one may speak of an "Emanzipation des Gefühls als gleichberechtigter Erfahrung des Geistes."[55] Hence Hemsterhuis's dictum, in *Sur la réalité des apparances*: "Je sens, par conséquent je suis."[56] Hemsterhuis needs this claim, according to Hammacher, because the immediacy of feeling is the basis of the sense of self, as well as the basis of the enthusiasm which plays so crucially a role in the discovery and presentation of the true, the beautiful and the sublime. In addition, this "immediacy" points the way to an answer to the question how love is possible, given what was said about it in the *Lettre sur les désirs*. In the "immediacy" of intuition lies a possibility of contact with other human beings. Hammacher concludes, therefore, that Hemsterhuis is far removed from the furthering of Enlightenment thought based exclusively on the analytical method.[57]

It is no doubt to a large extent a function of the perspective from which one approaches Hemsterhuis whether one stresses the "intuitive" over the "reasoned" in such difficult passages. For Hammacher, the fact that Hemsterhuis in his later works indeed turned more irrational, but above all the fact that he, as many other critics, *wished* to see Hemsterhuis in the light of pre-Romanticism, determined his particular reading.[58] It is probably safe to assume, however, that Hemsterhuis shared Herder's hesitation to embrace the kind of excessive emphasis on emotion manifested by the *Stürmer* and *Dränger*. Like Herder, Hemsterhuis continued to see taste as well as reason as regulative mechanisms. On balance, the rational element in both thinkers does seem to remain strong, and particularly in the case of aesthetics, both appear to stress the harmony of *Erkennen* and *Empfinden* as intrinsic to the work of art.[59]

Regardless of the question of ultimate preponderance of reason or emotion, it appears, there was enough material here at least for some of Hemsterhuis's successors on which to build a new aesthetic theory. A similar comment may be made regarding his idea of the limitations imposed on art by the senses, and the ultimate insufficiency of man to find absolute union with creation. Here Hemsterhuis introduced notions about art as well as about human relations, even the human condition, that sound decidedly post-Enlightenment, even modern. It would seem that Brummel was right after all in seeing in Hemsterhuis a representative figure: a figure profoundly ambivalent in an important way, as a (probably mostly unconscious) harbinger of the new, paradoxically arriving at his insights primarily with the tools of at best a contemporary, in some cases in fact an outdated *épistémé*.

NOTES

1. Hemsterhuis himself, in the course of his life, became an avid and eminent collector of Greek precious stones.
2. It was this work which inspired much of Novalis's utopian thinking. Compare August K. Wiedmann, *Romantic Art Theories* (Henley-on-Thames: Gresham, 1986), 84.
3. René Wellek, *Concepts of Criticism*, ed. Stephen G. Nichols, Jr. (New Haven and London: Yale University Press, 1963), 128.

4. Wellek, *Concepts*, 158.
5. Ibid., 159.
6. Charles Dédéyan, *Jean-Jacques Rousseau et la sensibilité littéraire à la fin du XVIIIe siècle* (Paris: Société d'édition d'enseignement supérieur, 1966), 17.
7. Carsten Zelle, "Angenehmes Grauen," in *Literaturhistorische Beiträge zur Ästhetik des Schrecklichen im achtzehnten Jahrhundert* (Hamburg: Felix Meiner, 1987), 107.
8. Zelle, "Angenehmes Grauen," 106.
9. L. Brummel, *Frans Hemsterhuis. Een philosofenleven* (Haarlem: 1925), 258. All translations from the Dutch are my own. There is a sizeable body of Dutch scholarship on Hemsterhuis which tends to pursue arguments favoring a reading of Hemsterhuis along these lines. Compare the relevant sections in P. J. Buijnsters, *Nederlandse Literatuur van de achttiende eeuw* (Utrecht: HES, 1984); G. W. Huygens, *de Nederlandse Auteur en zijn publiek* (Amsterdam: Van Oorschot, 1956); G. Kalff, *Geschiedenis der Nederlandse Letterkunde* (Gröningen: Wolters, 1910), vol. 6; Gerard Knuvelder, *Inleiding to the Nederlandse Letterkunde: Bloemlezing* (1955; reprint, 's Hertogenbosch: Malmberg, 1960); Gerard Knuvelder, *Handboek tot de geschiedenis der Nederlandse letterkunde* ('s Hertogenbosch: Malmberg, 1967), vol. 3; *Frans Hemsterhuis: Waarneming en Werkelijkheid*, ed. M. J. Petry (Baarn: Ambo, 1990); Jan and Annie Romein, "Frans Hemsterhuis: Philosoof van de ziel," in *Erflaters van onze beschaving* (Amsterdam: Querido, 1939). Other general treatments can be found in Reinder P. Meijer, *Literature of the Low Countries. A Short History of Dutch Literature in the Netherlands and Belgium* (The Hague/Boston: Nijhoff, 1978); Michiel Wielema, "Frans Hemsterhuis: A Philosopher's View of the History of the Dutch Republic," *Canadian Journal of Netherlandic Studies* 14.1 (1993): 109–17; Michiel Wielema, "Philosophy in the Netherlands in the Seventeenth and Eighteenth Centuries," *Rivista di Storia della filosofia* 44 (1989): 353–63.
10. Brummel, *Frans Hemsterhuis*, 258.
11. Paul Pelckmans, *Hemsterhuis dans ses rapports: contributions à une lecture distante des Lumières* (Amsterdam: Rodopi, 1987).
12. Rolf Grimminger, "Die Utopie der vernünftigen Lust. Sozialphilosophische Skizze zur Ästhetik des 18. Jahrhunderts bis zü Kant," in *Aufklärung und literarische Öffentlichkeit*, ed. Christa Bürger, Peter Burger and Jochen Schulte-Sasse (Frankfurt am Main: Suhrkamp, 1980), 118.
13. Grimminger, "Utopie," 121.
14. Frans Hemsterhuis, *Oeuvres philosophiques*, ed. L. S. P. Meyboom, 3 vols. (1848–50; reprint, Hildesheim/New York: Georg Olms, 1972). All references in the text are to this edition.
15. Victor Lange, *Das klassische Zeitalter der deutschen Literatur*, 1740–1815 (Darmstadt: Wissenschaftliche Buchgesellschaft, 1984), 151.
16. Viktor Lange, *Das klassische Zeitalter*, argues that it is only with Goethe that the axiom is replaced by a radically different theory of art, in which the artist is seen as taking his objects *out* of the realm of nature. Lange quotes Goethe: "Indem der Kunstler irgendeinen Gegenstand der Natur ergreift, so gehört dieser schon nicht mehr der Natur an, ja man kann sagen, daß der Künstler ihn in diesem Augenblicke

erschaffe, indem er ihm das Bedeutende, Charakteristische, Interessante abgewinnt, oder vielmehr erst den höhern Wert hineinlegt" (207).

17. Albert Funder, *Frans Hemsterhuis und die Ästhetik der Engländer und Franzosen im 18. Jahrhundert* (Bonn: P. Hanstein, 1912), 14.

18. In a footnote on p.20 of vol.1 of Hemsterhuis's *Oeuvres*, his editor Meyboom makes an important remark concerning the relationship between the beautiful and the sublime which hinges on this notion of a maximum of ideas which is not fully present in Hemsterhuis's text itself: "Ce principe explique aussi le rapport qu'il y a entre le simple et le sublime. Ce sont les deux faces principales du beau. Un maximum d'idées dans un mimimum de temps, voilà le beau. On le nomme *simple*, quant à la forme, ou la facilité du contour, *sublime* quant à la richesse et à la grandeur des idées" (see note on page 20). It is interesting to compare this version with the difference between the beautiful and the sublime proposed by Edmund Burke.

19. There are two ways in which the artist can achieve his goal of presenting his idea of beauty, again especially in sculpture: by presenting his figures at rest, or in movement. Adding action and movement to his work will not only inspire the observer's admiration, but will also involve his emotions. A prime example of a sculpture giving the maximum of ideas at the same time is for Hemsterhuis Michelangelo's group of *Hercules and Anteus* (29). There is a trade-off in such an approach, however: opting for a maximum of ideas goes at the expense of the minimum of time required.

20. Brummel, *Frans Hemsterhuis*, 105/6.

21. Hemsterhuis's aesthetics only seemingly echo the concern about style and "clothing" in art expressed by Gotthold Ephraim Lessing (for example in his treatise on the fable) that such "decorative" elements must not endanger an understanding of the "message," but must rather facilitate it. In reality Hemsterhuis does *not* think normatively here, but is simply making an observation of the way the process of transmission works in real life.

22. This line of argument concurs with Lessing's idea about visual arts and poetry. Jochen Schmidt writes: "Da Lessing der Einbildungskraft als produktivem Vermögen—und auch der Rezipient ist produktiv, indem sich seine Vorstellungen entfalten—offensichtlich einen besonders hohen Stellenwert zuerkennt, steht die Dichtung für ihn besonders hoch" (Jochen Schmidt, *Von der Aufklärung bis zum Idealismus*, vol. 1 of *Die Geschichte des Genie-Gedankens: 1750–1945* [Darmstadt: Wissenschaftliche Buchgesellschaft, 1985], 77). The idea can also be found in Breitinger's *Critische Dichtkunst*. In the chapter entitled "Vergleichung der Mahler-Kunst und der Dicht-Kunst" (chap. 40), Breitinger agrees with his source, Dubos, that painting has a more immediate effect than poetry, but, as Jill Kowalik paraphrases Breitinger, "poetry is superior to painting precisely because it works more 'slowly' than painting, and therefore produces images that are infinitely more complex" (Jill Anne Kowalik, *The Poetics of Historical Perspectivism: Breitinger's Critische Dichtkunst and the Neoclassic Tradition* [Chapel Hill: University of North Carolina Press, 1992], 79).

23. Quoted in Schmidt, *Von der Aufklärung*, 33.

24. Ibid., 35.

25. Ibid., 35.

26. "Herder behauptet, die Kraft des Kunstwerks sei es, die mit einer entsprechenden Wahrnehmungsfähigkeit im Betrachter oder Hörer in Wechselbeziehung trete, um damit eine Wirkung auf die Sensibilität auszuüben. Die Beurteilung eines Kunstwerks könne infolgedessen nicht, wie frühere ästhetische Theorien angenommen hatten, von einem statischen Prinzip des 'Geschmacks' abhängen, sondern von einer verwickelten Vielzahl historischer, örtlicher, gesellschaftlicher und persönlicher Voraussetzungen." This view of art also allowed Herder to shift away from Winckelmann and to begin emphasizing the work of art as an expression of different cultures and nations and their "Volkscharakter" (Lange, *Das klassische Zeitalter*, 85, 87).

27. Lange, *Das klassische Zeitalter*, 87–88.

28. Schmidt, *Von der Aufklärung*, 75.

29. Zelle,"Angenehmes Grauen," 100.

30. Ibid., 99.

31. Schmidt, *Von der Aufklärung*, 48.

32. Silvio Vietta, *Literarische Phantasie: Theorie und Geschichte. Barock und Aufklärung* (Stuttgart: J. B. Metzler, 1986), 125.

33. Kowalik, *Poetics*, 37 61.

34. Ibid., 59.

35. Idid., 84.

36. Compare Schmidt, *Von der Aufklärung*: " . . . indem die Kritik [am Prinzip 'ut pictura poesis'] die Bedeutung der Darstellungsmedien und der ihnen zugeordneten spezifischen Wahrnehmungsweisen reflektierte, trug sie zu einer Umstellung der Perspektive bei. Denn dadurch ergab sich eine Umorientierung vom einseitigen Überwiegen des Objektiven und von der objektivistischen Anpassung der künstlerischen Aussage an den Gegenstand . . . zum Subjektiven und zur Anerkennung des schöpferischen Freiraums," 77. Compare also Hans-Friedrich Wessels, ed., *Aufklärung. Ein literaturwissenschaftliches Studienbuch* (Königstein/Ts.: Athenäum, 1984): "Das künstlerische Werk soll Ausdruck der besonderen Individualität des Subjekts sein" (23).

37. Schmidt, *Von der Aufklärung*, 99.

38. "Die Literatur wandelte sich vom Instrument höfischer Representation und religiöser Erbauung zu einem Medium der Moralisierung des Publikums, wobei ihre ästhetischen Eigengesetzlichkeiten immer mehr in den Vordergrund treten" (Wessels, *Aufklärung*, 17).

39. Compare for example E. F. Carritt, *The Theory of Beauty* (London: Methuen, 1928), 87: "What the artist must always imitate, or, as we prefer to say, express, is . . . his own passions and volitions. It is solely for the sake of this expressiveness . . . that we value works of art; and when it is attained it will be a harmoniously organised, individual whole and universally communicable."

40. Emmanuel Baillon writes: "l'esthétique de Hemsterhuis s'articule avant tout à une psychologie, conçue comme l'histoire de la constitution du sujet à partir d'une

base jusque-là rejetée comme règne de la confusion: la sensation, le sentiment, le désir" (foreword to *Lettre sur la Sculpture*, by François Hemsterhuis [Paris: Ecole nationale supérieure des Beaux-Arts, 1991], 10).

41. Brummel, *Frans Hemsterhuis*, 97.

42. A holistic conception of art is seen by Wiedmann, *Romantic Art*, as one of the major tenets of Romantic art: "A quest for the Whole was at the root of the Romantic movement. It determined its hostility to science, mind, mechanism, materialism and its embrace of feeling, mystery and mysticism" (18), and again: "this holistic conception cuts deep into the theory and practice of Romantic art" (19). Wiedmann cites especially Schelling, "the most Romantic of the German Idealists," who strove to reconcile Spinoza's pious pantheism with Fichte's pure Idealism, "by showing that mind and matter, spirit and nature, ego and non-ego had their common origin in an Absolute which was a pure identity of subject and object" (69).

43. Klaus Hammacher, *Unmittelbarkeit und Kritik bei Hemsterhuis* (Munich: Wilhelm Finck, 1971), 19.

44. Grimminger,"Utopie," 122.

45. The process causes man not only to multiply his ego, so that he becomes a social being, but he himself also becomes an object of contemplation; finally, the activity of the "organe moral" leads to a concept of the divinity.

46. H. Moenkemeyer, *François Hemsterhuis* (Boston: Twayne, 1975), 72.

47. Moenkemeyer, *Hemsterhuis*, 74.

48. In *Sophyle*, in *Oeuvres*, Hemsterhuis sets out to prove that immaterial things exist. Hemsterhuis concurs with Kant that we cannot know the "Ding an sich," but that there are correspondences between things and our perceptions of them: "nos idées simples acquises ne nous trompent pas, mais représentent réellement des qualités qui sont essentiellement dans les choses dont elles sont les idées" (1: 177). As Hemsterhuis reminds us, "l'essence n'est visible que par la lumière, et pour ceux qui ont des yeux" (1: 180), just as they are audible because of air and ears. But an essence may have "cent milles côtés, qui tiennent également à sa nature, et parmi lesquels trois ou quatre seulement sont analogue à nos organes actuels" (1: 180). Thousands of aspects of being remain inaccessible to us, since they do not address our senses. The idea of an object depends on the number and nature of my senses: it is the reason why Hemsterhuis speaks of the "pauvreté de l'idée qu nous attachons au mot matière" (1: 183). One way to overcome the limitations of our senses lies in the hope of future acquisition of other senses.

49. Moenkemeyer, *Hemsterhuis*, 82.

50. Ibid., 84.

51. As indicated, his dialogue *Sophyle* specifically sets itself the task of proving that there are immaterial things in creation.

52. The theory of the senses *does* provide a common basis for aesthetics and ethics, but only as a method of explaining the way we receive our ideas and perceptions (of the beautiful as well as of our social impulses). The "organe moral" itself, however, does not link up with the reception *and* production of the moral *and* the beautiful, as we find it in Shaftesbury.

53. On the other hand it must be remembered that Hemsterhuis, *Oeuvres*, rejects the value of what he calls artificial logic: "Notez, je vous prie, que cette Logique artificielle est postérieur à la faculté intuitive, qui est la seule Logique véritable" (1: 88). This does appear in line with Hemsterhuis's caution not to pay too great a compliment to much of what passes for philosophy, which often is "la lie, qui demeure après l'effervessence de l'imagination" (1: 84) and to apply a strict form of argumentation, even resorting to mathematics.

54. Hammacher, *Unmittelbarkeit*, 19.

55. Ibid., 23, points to the later dialogue *Aristée ou de la divinité* (1779), in which the idea that "feeling" or "emotion" is the superior form of knowledge comes through in the statement "Dans l'homme bien constitué, un seul soupir de l'ame . . . est une démonstration plus que géométrique de la nature de la Divinité" (Hemsterhuis, 2: 64).

56. Ibid., 23.

57. Ibid., 47.

58. At the same time it can be said in Hammacher's favour that, despite Brummel's argument against an "intuitive" Hemsterhuis one should not forget what Brummel himself had said earlier about the predominance of writings on aesthetics and morals in eighteenth-century philosophy, namely that these are the two domains in which the rising tide of irrationalism made itself felt the most.

59. Schmidt, *Von der Aufklärung*, 144.

The Road to Wisdom in Mozart's *Magic Flute*

JULIE D. PRANDI

That the music far outshines the libretto, that mythic or fairy tale notions of the triumph of light (good) over darkness (evil) hold sway, and that the chief inspiration for the story and symbols is Enlightenment philosophical ideals seen through Masonic literature and traditions—this much everyone is willing to acknowledge when discussing Mozart's last opera. A historian of Austrian Freemasons has remarked that the accounts of initiations to Masonry in Vienna in the late eighteenth century read in places like stage directions to *The Magic Flute*.[1] Although some aspects of the story have other origins,[2] evidence has consistently pointed to the commanding influence of Abbé Jean Terrasson's novel *Sethos* (1731) on the libretto.[3] The book features an Egyptian prince who is educated by a tutor and initiated, after many harrowing trials, into the mysteries of Isis (the parallels to Tamino strike one immediately). Widely read in Masonic circles, the novel contains lines which are echoed in two prayers in Mozart's opera, in addition to many plot similarities.

Although there is broad agreement on the Enlightenment and Masonic background for the opera, the consensus of the critics starts to crumble when it is a question of a coherent interpretation. There have been many creative stabs at explaining what the opera is fundamentally about and which character is the focal point. Such explanations may supplement one another, but not always. If we find it reasonable that "the central theme of the opera is love for humanity,"[4] we may be dumbfounded by a contrasting assertion that the "deepest meaning is its teaching about death."[5] The reader who is easily persuaded by the argument that the opera is "really about themes of knowledge" and recognition,[6] might well ask if it could at the same time have as its subject "the conflict between the sexes," which has "a harmonious outcome in the Couple."[7] Besides, people do not agree on which character is the hero of *The Magic Flute*. Whereas many focus on Tamino,[8] though he has only one solo aria to his name in the entire opera, the influential musicologist Edward Dent saw Sarastro as the pivotal figure (242). One critic has advanced Pamina as the central character of the opera,[9] whereas there is at least one interpretation which, as a key to deconstructing the text, concentrates on that character who has the lion's share of spoken dialogue and is on stage more than anyone else: the *buffo* figure Papageno.[10]

One reason for the difficulty of pinpointing the hero, I would like to propose, is that this opera is a drama about education, a sort of *Bildungsdrama*.[11] Not just one person is being educated, as we find in some plays around the same time such as Schiller's *Don Carlos* (1787) but at least three: Tamino, Pamina, and Papageno (there is even an attempt to educate the villain Monostatos). In this respect the education drama most likely to have influenced *The Magic Flute* is perhaps Lessing's *Nathan the Wise* (1779). While Nathan, often seen as one model for Sarastro, acts as a teacher, the two young people, the Templar and Recha, go through a learning process. In fact, many of the supporting characters in Mozart's opera, such as the Three Boys, the Three Ladies, Sarastro, and the Priests, intersect with the three heroes Tamino, Pamina, and Papageno mainly as teachers. Concern for how best to educate was of course a major preoccupation in eighteenth-century Europe. Rousseau's *Emile* (1762) and Lessing's *Erziehung des Menschengeschlechts* (1780), in addition to numerous other tracts on education, testify to this. The Johannite lodges, the type Mozart belonged to, like the Freemasons generally, illustrate this vogue for education in their organization and system of advancement through degrees.

Initiates were provided with mentors and progressed from apprentice, to journeyman, and finally to master.[12] On the title-page illustration for the first published text of the opera (1791), the symbols of each degree—compass and trowel, five-pointed star, and hourglass—are prominent.[13] Mozart, who became a Mason in 1784, reached the third degree; Schikaneder the librettist, also a Mason, had reached the second degree.

We can relate the *Bildungsdrama* model in a number of ways to *The Magic Flute*. All three characters, Tamino, Pamina, and Papageno "misinterpret reality"[14] and must change their ideas as to what their calling in life is.[15] This involves a painful process of confusion and self-doubt leading to a crisis that can include suicidal thoughts, as in the case of Pamina and Papageno. When Tamino exclaims, "O ewige Nacht, wann wirst du schwinden? / Wann wird das Licht mein Auge finden?"[16] in his interview with a Priest, he exemplifies such a crisis. All three characters have their moments of insight,[17] and the audience sees the results of their learning in changed behavior.

Just as in the libretto, there are several elements in the music that express the education theme. The overture has a development section which, with its frequent modulations, anticipates the trials and journeys of the prince, the princess, and the bird catcher.[18] The characteristic harmonic pattern of sonata form is excellently suited to convey an educational process. Mozart used it in the overture and in the main part of the opera also.[19] As Dent has noted, in no opera previous to his *Magic Flute* did Mozart "make a single character show a gradual maturing of personality such as we see in Tamino and Pamina" (262).[20] Another example of how the music helps convey the educational progress of a character is Tamino's interview with the Priest at the Three Temples, which features a "symbolic progression of the tonalities."[21] In this dialogue, the key of Tamino's responses gradually approaches that of the interlocutor,[22] who is engaged in teaching him.

If *The Magic Flute* is at its heart a drama of education, what are Tamino, Pamina, and Papageno actually learning over the course of the opera? To answer this question, we must turn to the Three Temples scene (1.15), which has often been singled out as a crucial one, not only for the plot,[23] but also musically, for it involves a through-composed large unit without precedent in opera.[24] Here Tamino is directly engaged in a learning dialogue which is entirely sung, not spoken. One element here deserves more attention than it has hitherto received in literature on the opera: the configuration and labeling of the Three Temples.[25] The stage directions read that the center one, the Temple of Wisdom, is flanked on the right by the Temple of Reason (*Vernunft*) and on the left by the Temple of Nature. A row of pillars connects each of the side temples to the center one. This tripartite symbol steers us away from the easy dichotomies of light-dark, good-evil, male-female that have dominated so much discussion of the opera. Neither of the poles of Reason and Nature is necessarily "evil"; instead, the arrangement of the Three Temples seems to imply that a synthesis of Nature and Reason in human culture would lead to Wisdom.[26]

The motif of the Three Temples with Wisdom in the middle has received little attention in discussions of *The Magic Flute*, perhaps because it is absent from Masonic lore[27] as well as from literary sources for the opera. The prominence of the concept of Wisdom in the libretto is, however, unmistakable. The words for *wise* and *wisdom*, which recur in the libretto a number of times, relate to the placement of the Temples in this scene: Wisdom is the outcome when human beings achieve the proper balance of Reason and Nature. We are introduced to Sarastro as "the wise man" whose words are "full of wisdom."[28] When Tamino declares "Weisheitslehre sey mein Sieg,"[29] he claims the teachings of Wisdom as his goal. In that same scene, the Priest asks Papageno if he too wants to strive for "love of wisdom." The word *Weisheit* (Wisdom) is also invoked in the last line of the opera.

The Temple of Wisdom is mentioned several times; it is where Sarastro's brotherhood dwells and it is the Temple into which Tamino and Pamina are admitted at the end of the opera. Very telling is also the insertion of the word *Weisheit* into a passage otherwise closely patterned on a prayer in Terrasson's *Sethos* novel. Whereas in Matthias Claudius's translation Isis is asked "gieb deinen Geist dem neuen Diener," the Chorus in *The Magic Flute* prays: "schenket der Weisheit Geist dem neuen Paar!"[30]

For Wisdom to become a reality, Reason and Nature must be integrated into the same personality—it is mistaken to believe that the defeat of Nature is the order of the day in the opera.[31] This is why Tamino, the ostensibly reasoning man, is paired with Papageno, the ostensibly natural man. While in the Queen's realm, Tamino gets a lesson from Papageno: he is introduced to the feeling and sensibility that unites all people regardless of class. Despite Tamino's doubt that Papageno is human, Papageno insists he is, just like the prince: "Wer bin ich? [*für sich*] Dumme Frage! [*laut*] Ein Mensch, wie du!"[32] Because Tamino is deficient in feeling, he can be expected to deny that a natural person like Papageno could have anything in common with himself. Papageno however has a measure of Reason to begin with, as he shows when he tells Tamino that if the Three Ladies were really beautiful, as Tamino assumes, they would not always cover their faces with thick veils (1.3). When the pair moves through Sarastro's realm, Tamino models reasoned behavior as opposed to momentary gratification for Papageno, whose ability to compare himself to the Prince helps him integrate more Reason into his personality.

The other pair in the opera who reflects the same dialectic of Reason and Nature is Sarastro and Monostatos. Indeed, Monostatos is "Sarastro's Papageno;"[33] he complements Sarastro's sexual chastity and perfect calm of emotion by personifying sexual drives that incite a person to seduction or murder.[34] Although some observers of the opera have objected that the wise Sarastro tolerates a servant like Monostatos in his realm, there is a logic in this. Sarastro does not think it inappropriate for the holder of the Sevenfold Seal to have a servant of this type. How can tolerance and forgiveness be lived and illustrated if Sarastro does not try to live with Monostatos? Since the wise man must acknowledge the sensual and natural in humans, Sarastro, by including even Monostatos in his kingdom, proves that sexuality is not foreign to him, that he does not ban it from his world.[35] Perhaps his willingness to hand over his realm to the new ruler-pair signals that Sarastro knows that Reason and Nature are not as well integrated in his person as they will be in Tamino and Pamina once their education is complete.

The Queen, who represents the discord of Nature and Reason, tries to infect Tamino and Pamina with this discord, which spawns superstition and prejudice. Although Pamina has inherited the conflict between Nature and Reason, she at the same time embodies the possibility of solving it. Symbolically and thematically Pamina is at the heart of the opera because she is at the center of the Reason-Nature axis. Her affinity with Nature is expressed in her harmony with Papageno (their duet on love, 1.14); whereas her Reason emerges clearly in her sympathy with Sarastro. Because she represents the synthesis of Reason and Nature arguably better by the end of the opera than Tamino, it makes perfect sense that it is she who leads Tamino through the final trials of Fire and Water.

Tamino's development is different from Pamina's, for he has great need of integrating Nature into his personality, whereas Pamina seeks to overcome the discord between Nature and Reason. For Tamino, the Queen of Night's realm has great educative value for exposing him to sensual Nature. His deficiencies are apparent when he, lacking arrows to fight off the serpent, faints helplessly in fear. This contrasts with the parallel scene in *Sethos*, where the hero bravely captures the serpent alive. Instead of a test of valor, Tamino's meeting with the serpent becomes a confrontation with his own sensuality: he's afraid of it. Getting acquainted with Papageno and falling in love with Pamina's portrait (awakening Eros) are the first steps in his development of sensibility, although in his contact with the Queen he falls into error that will need to be corrected when he arrives in Sarastro's realm.

There are nevertheless many parallels in the education of Tamino and Pamina.[36] Just as Tamino is a foreigner in the Queen of Night's kingdom, Pamina begins her education in a place foreign to her: Sarastro's territory. As Tamino faints before the serpent, Pamina also faints from physical threat: that of Monostatos to rape her. Whereas Tamino needs to open up to Nature and sensuality, Pamina needs to practice resistance to these drives. Therefore she can learn more from confrontation with Monostatos than with Papageno. With the challenge from Monostatos and Sarastro's instruction, Pamina is able finally to reject the claim of feeling her mother has on her. Meanwhile Nature and Reason are integrated in her love for Tamino, the man originally sanctioned by both her mother and Sarastro as her future mate.

Papageno too receives an education in this opera, although a concentration on the *Sethos* novel and the Masonic symbolism has led many critics either to ignore his case almost entirely[37] or simply to deny that he develops at all in the opera.[38] If fixed as an allegory of Nature, as Papageno often is, he emerges at a subhuman level as unchanging, outside of real time, nature without culture.[39] However the fact that he is able to teach Tamino about what a man is, to play the silver bells and chase Monostatos and his crew away, and to progress from his solitary subaltern position in the Queen's kingdom to joyfully anticipated fatherhood shows an acculturation process and testifies to his humanity. His failure to pass some of the trials has unfairly been interpreted as a total failure to be educated at all.[40] Papageno "has learned something from the Ladies," who gave him the bells and instructed him not to tell lies;[41] and although he didn't make the cut as an initiate, he has perhaps begun, through his relation to Papagena and Tamino, "to perceive the higher things in life."[42]

Indeed, Papageno is not simply a comic relief figure, an unchanging *commedia dell'arte* fool. He has made some moral progress because of the impact of Tamino's example and the teachings of the Priests. In his final scene, Papageno for the first time expresses regret, almost remorse for his inability to remain silent when bid to do so: "Ich plauderte,—und das war schlecht, / Darum geschieht es mir schon recht."[43] Interestingly, he achieves this insight without threat of corporal punishment.

In the Viennese popular plays of the time, with which Schikaneder was intimately familiar, the betterment of the hero was a frequent result of the action.[44] One of Schikaneder's own *Singspiele* anticipates Papageno. In *Der Dumme Gärtner*, the fool Anton falls prey to love and feels a despair that moves him to contemplate suicide.[45] Similarly, when Papageno believes he has lost his beloved forever, his suicide attempt shows his willingness to end his life for the sake of a principle, his love. This indicates a moral victory for Reason, for he comes to consider the past and future, not just the present moment and creature comforts, which were his sole concern at the beginning of the opera.

If education in Reason and Nature and their integration leading to Wisdom is the course of the plot,[46] then how does the opera solve that age-old problem of how to motivate the pupils to learn their lessons? For recalcitrant Nature, the most primitive way is corporal punishment, which seems a class-angled punishment since it comes into question in the opera only for the servants Papageno and Monostatos. In the Queen's territory, Papageno, whose mouth is padlocked in the first act for lying, actually is punished this way; whereas in Sarastro's realm, Monostatos and Papageno are only threatened with such penalties.[47] Sarastro shows his moral superiority to the Queen by avoiding corporal punishment. In the Masonic eulogy on Mozart's death, the speaker mentioned a cardinal principle of that brotherhood: gentle instruction or correction for the weaknesses of one's brothers.[48] The most important lessons in the opera are learned outside of the formal initiation rites, and the main vehicle is heterosexual love. Love can be both a motive for perfecting Reason as well as a model of integration of Reason and Nature. But unlike fairy tales, where sex within marriage to a desirable partner is the reward, love in the opera has a pedagogical function. The trials of Tamino, Pamina, and Papageno are not the price they pay to get the sexual reward but rather their course of education towards Wisdom. The strategy is to stimulate erotic desire, as when Tamino is shown Pamina's portrait or when the two briefly embrace, but to delay its gratification. Pamina and Papageno, so often forced to separate physically from their loves, likewise experience this somewhat painful delay of sensual gratification. The separations seem manipulated by Sarastro's priests for the sake of developing the reasoning powers of the characters.

Papageno shows insight into the pedagogical function of love when he tells Pamina that this great love for her was a kind of lash of the whip to get him and Tamino moving: "diese große Liebe zu dir war der Peitschenstreich, um unsre Füße in schnellen Gang zu bringen" (1.14). Sarastro's priests likewise lure Papageno on an educative path by promising him a Papagena if he makes appropriate progress in Reason. At first Papageno refuses to go through the trials with Tamino. When a priest tempts him with a bride like himself: "Wenn nun aber Sarastro dir ein Mädchen aufbewahrt hätte, das an Farbe und Kleidung dir ganz gleich wäre?,"[49] he is gradually convinced to go along.

Does Nature then get the short end of the stick in the dialectic with Reason that leads to Wisdom? To judge from Sarastro and Tamino, to whom highest honors are paid officially, the answer is certainly yes. However there is an undercurrent in the opera that ensures Nature will not be lost on the path into the Temple of Wisdom. The importance of Nature is implicit in the symbolism of the flute and bells.

These instruments, both presents from the Queen of Night, fit just as well in Sarastro's realm. In fact some commentators have been puzzled as to why Tamino and Papageno receive their bells and flute from the Queen, since she is supposed to be an evil power.[50] But the flute and bells in Mozart's opera are a meeting place of Nature and Reason, passion and intellect. Although the fairy tale which gave the opera its name grants the flute power either to calm or to stimulate the passions,[51] the role of the instruments is more developed in the opera. Created from a tree under the sign of the four elements earth (ground of oak), fire (lightning), water (rain shower), air (storm wind), the flute is anchored in Nature, therefore in sensuality and emotion.[52] In addition, by virtue of being crafted by Pamina's father, the former owner of the Sevenfold Circle of the Sun, it also partakes of Reason:

Es schnitt in einer Zauberstunde
Mein Vater sie aus tiefstem Grunde
Der tausendjähr'gen Eiche aus
Bey Blitz und Donner, Sturm und Braus.[53]

  The music of the flute is the messenger of love between Tamino and Pamina, arousing Eros, opening them to Nature; but also their protector in the Fire and Water trials, bringing the strength of Reason to calm natural fears. Besides driving away Monostatos, Papageno's bells also bring him his beloved Papagena in the end. In allusion to the Orpheus myth, Tamino's flute playing pacifies the wild animals, thus bringing Reason to Nature. In playing the flute, he exercises the integration of Reason and feeling: this is why it both comforts and protects him. Papageno's ability to play his bells, a more sophisticated instrument than his original pan pipes, shows his educational progress. He is able to turn the attack of Monostatos and the slaves into art: Monostatos and the slaves start singing "und gehen unter dem Gesang marschmäßig ab."[54] The bells, the singing, the march combine sensuality and form, Nature and Reason. As in the Enlightenment aesthetic theory of Friedrich Schiller[55] and others, art is a bridge between Nature and Reason, which makes it in turn an ideal educational tool for the Enlightenment.

  The interaction of the characters, the symbolism of the flute, as well as the course of education followed by Tamino, Papageno, and Pamina all reflect the structural dialectic of Reason and Nature in the play, which is synthesized as Wisdom. Yet the opera does in fact privilege Reason to a certain extent over Nature. Papageno cannot be initiated, and the rhetoric denigrating women is pervasive in the libretto. As so often in Enlightenment aesthetics, an excess of Nature, which means the emotions and sensuality, is presented as a weakness (Papageno), a moral flaw (Monostatos, the Queen), or a danger to the self or others (Pamina, Papageno, Monostatos, the Queen). Not the abstract intellectuality of Sarastro, but the excess of feeling or sensuality of the Queen of the Night or Monostatos is deemed to be the threat to civilization.

  But Papageno as well as Pamina get their innings. He is able to teach Tamino in the Queen's realm about humanity and to rescue Pamina when Tamino and Sarastro are nowhere in sight. As for Pamina, in a world where the teachings of Wisdom in Sarastro's realm boil down to the admonition "Sey ein Mann, / Dann Jüngling wirst du männlich siegen,"[56] it is significant that the direst trials of courage and love seem to be hers rather than Tamino's. Running contrary to the misogynist rhetoric of the libretto, Pamina is the first woman to be initiated into Sarastro's all-male club, and not just because she is Tamino's wife, which would have been the case in *Sethos*, but also because of her bravery: "Ein Weib, das Nacht und Tod nicht scheut, / Ist würdig, und wird eingeweiht."[57]

The lesser eligibility of Papageno and Pamina in Sarastro's ideal community reflects the bias of the time against the lower classes and women, as it does their consignment to Nature. Interestingly, an early interpretation of *The Magic Flute* by a Freemason claimed that Pamina, not Sarastro, represented Enlightenment in the opera.[58] This is a fine perception, for she is indeed being educated towards Enlightenment, and hers and Papageno's education are perhaps more important for the Enlightenment project than Prince Tamino's. At the very least, the opera shows a more humane and complete acceptance of women and the lower classes into the body politic than was previously customary and holds out the hope for education as a force that will marry their Nature to Reason. Tamino and Papageno model the integration of Reason and Nature when they play their musical instruments, and the construction of the flute itself echoes it. The grand symbolic integration of Reason and Nature comes in the climax of the opera, act 2, scene 28. Nature is represented by the four elements named by the Men in Armor and shown in the theater scenery of fire and water, mountain (earth) and fog (air).[59] While the geometric form of the pyramid with the verses of the Men's song written on it represents Reason, the simple chorale they sing, reinforced with trombones and winds, against the complex and contrasting fugato in the strings seems again to hint at a synthesis of powers rather than the victory of one principle over another.[60] Pamina and Tamino walk through this landscape, embracing and speaking of courage and love. After the final defeat of the Queen and her retinue in the last scene, the Chorus sings of Wisdom, pairing it with beauty. These two concepts point to the integration of Reason and Nature, for not only is the Temple of Wisdom between that of Reason and that of Nature, but beauty is related to art in the eighteenth-century mind.

When we come to see Mozart's *Magic Flute* as a drama of education aimed at integrating the powers of Nature and Reason, the individual paths and progress of Papageno, Pamina, and Tamino command our attention and draw us into the opera, whereas the fairy tale triumph of sunlight over the forces of darkness is displaced to a more superficial level of meaning. The two very original and powerful musical passages which commentators have repeatedly stressed, the Three Temples scene in the first act and the Men in Armor scene in the second act, underline dramatically the progress in the opera from an open conflict between Reason and Nature to a synthesis of these forces. Love and art, the educative tools serving as a bridge, at the same time represent the dynamic union of Reason and Nature, which is symbolized on a more concrete level by the flute, the bells, and the Temple of Wisdom.

NOTES

1. Heinz Schuler, *Mozart und die Freimauerei* (Wilhelmshaven: Florian Noetzel, 1992), 43.

2. For an overview of the various sources for the opera, see Peter Branscombe, *W. A. Mozart: Die Zauberflöte* (Cambridge: Cambridge University Press, 1991), 4–34. The title of the opera and the queen who gives a magic flute to the man who is to rescue her daughter is taken from "Lulu oder die Zauberflöte," published in a fairy tale collection (1786) edited by Christoph Martin Wieland; see Alfons Rosenberg, *Die Zauberflöte: Geschichte und Deutung von Mozarts Oper* (Munich: Preste, 1964), 120–22. The play *Thamos, König von Ägypten*, for which Mozart had composed incidental music in 1773, is more closely related to the opera plot. Jean Massin and Brigitte Massin, *Wolfgang Amadeus Mozart* (Paris: Fayard, 1970), 1146, believe that Mozart suggested or imposed this plot on his librettist. The Papageno figure and a few other details are drawn from the popular stage. See E. M. Batley, *A Preface to The Magic Flute* (London: Dennis Dobson, 1969), 94–95, 108.

3. *Sethos, histoire ou vie tirée des monumens anecdotes de l'ancienne Egypte* was translated in 1777–78 by Matthias Claudius into German under the title: *Geschichte des ägyptischen Königs Sethos*. Mozart and Schikandeder knew the novel. See Paul Nettl, *Mozart und die königliche Kunst* (Berlin: Wunder, 1932), 103–18; and Edward Dent, *Mozart's Operas*, 2d ed. (London: Oxford, 1947), 224–28 (Dent's book hereafter cited parenthetically in the text).

4. Katharine Thomson, *The Masonic Thread in Mozart* (London: Lawrence and Wishard, 1977), 158.

5. Brigid Brophy, *Mozart the Dramatist*, 2d rev. ed. (London: Libris, 1988), 202.

6. Jessica Waldoff, "The Music of Recognition: Operatic Enlightenment in *The Magic Flute*," *Music and Letters* 75/2 (1994): 235.

7. Jacques Chailley, *The Magic Flute, Masonic Opera*, trans. Herbert Weinstock (New York: Da Capo, 1982), 95.

8. For example Batley, *Preface*, 117; Jean Massin and Brigitte Massin, *Mozart*, 1150. F. Robert Lehmeyer, who sees the focus of the opera in "the Artist-man divided into two characters," Papageno and Tamino (76), ignores the importance of Pamina in her own right and the reciprocal influence between the Prince and his side-kick. See Lehmeyer, "Artist and Man in *Die Zauberflöte:* An Attempt at Interpretation," in: *Literary and Musical Notes: A Festschrift for Wm. A. Little*, ed. Geoffrey Orth (Bern: Peter Lang, 1995).

9. Thomson, *Masonic Thread*, 158.

10. Rose Subotnik, "Whose Magic Flute? Intimations of Reality at the Gates of the Enlightenment," *Nineteenth-Century Music* 15 (1991): 150.

11. For a complete explanation of the concept of *Bildungsdrama*, see Margaret Scholl, "German 'Bildungsdrama': Schiller's *Don Carlos*, Goethe's *Torquato Tasso*, and Kleist's *Prinz Friedrich von Homburg*" (Ph.D. diss., Washington University,

1973). The *novel* is a more familiar venue in the eighteenth century for propounding Enlightenment ideas on the education of a prince (Fenelon's *Télémaque*; Wieland's *Agathon*; Terrasson's *Sethos*).

12. Schuler, *Mozart und Freimauerei*, 12–13.
13. Nettl, *Mozart und Kunst*, 123–24
14. Scholl, "German 'Bildungsdrama,'" 61.
15. Ibid., 47.
16. Oh eternal night, when will you vanish? When will my eyes find the light? (1.15). Quotations by act and scene number from the libretto are taken from the 1791 edition, reproduced in Judith Eckelmeyer, *The Cultural Context of Mozart's "Magic Flute,"* vol. 2 (Lewiston, N.Y.: Edwin Mellen, 1991).
17. Scholl, "German 'Bildungsdrama,'" iv.
18. Chailley, *Magic Flute, Masonic Opera*, 177–78. See also Alfred Einstein, *Mozart, His Character, His Work*, trans. Nathan Broder (1945; reprint, New York: Hesperides, 1962), 468.
19. Erich Smith, "The Music" (Branscombe, W. A. *Mozart*, 114–15), finds the harmonic pattern of sonata form for instance in Tamino's "Bildnis" aria and in Pamina's "Ach ich fühls" aria. Eckelmeyer, *Cultural Context*, 1.48, argues that "the macrostructure of the *Magic Flute's* harmonic process . . . takes on the characteristics of an enormous sonata consisting of the usual exposition, development and recapitulation."
20. Compare Jean Massin and Brigitte Massin, *Mozart*, 1152: "Pour la première fois, la musique s'assigne pour tâche d'exprimer le mûrissement progressif d'une conscience. . . ."
21. Chailley, *Magic Flute, Masonic Opera*, 216.
22. Ibid., 162–63. See also Waldoff, "Music of Recognition," who analyzes the music in this scene in great detail, 222–30.
23. Batley, *Preface*, 120; Christoph Wolff, "'O' ew'ge Nacht! wann wirst du schwinden?' Zum Verstandnis der Sprecherszene im ersten Finale von Mozarts Zauberflöte," in *Analysen: Beiträge zu einer Problemgeschichte des Komponierens*, ed. Werner Brieg et al. (Wiesbaden: Franz Steiner, 1984), 238.
24. Jean Massin and Brigitte Massin, *Mozart*, 1153; see also Wolff, "'O ew'ge Nacht,'" 240–41, 247.
25. Jean Massin and Brigitte Massin, *Mozart*, 1148, offer one of the few interpretations that discusses the symbolic import of the Temples; however, whereas they concentrate on the dichotomy Reason-Nature and claim Sarastro (Freemasonry) represents Reason, my claim is that Sarastro represents Wisdom, the synthesis of Reason and Nature.
26. Independently from me, Eckelmeyer, *Cultural Context*, 42–45, speaks of a dialectic and synthesis in this opera. However, she pictures act 1 through scene 14 as the thesis; scene 15 to the end of act 1 as the antithesis; and act 2 as the synthesis.
27. Chailley, *Magic Flute, Masonic Opera*, 210.
28. The Chorus that announces Sarastro's first entrance has the line "Stets mög er des Lebens als Weiser sich freun!" [ever may he enjoy life as a wise man, 1.18]. Later in that same scene he is referred to as "der göttliche Weise" [the divine wise

man]. The Speaker in 2.1 calls Sarastro's words "deine weisheitsvollen Reden" [your speeches full of wisdom].

29. May the teachings of wisdom be my victory (2.3).

30. Claudius's translation quoted according to Hans-Josef Irmen, *Mozart: Mitglied geheimer Gesellschaften*, 2nd rev. ed. (Zulpich: Prisca, 1991), 53: grant your spirit to the new servant; the *Flute* libretto reads: "grant the spirit of wisdom to the new pair!" (2.1).

31. Chailley, *Magic Flute, Masonic Opera*, claims that because the Temple of Reason is to the right of the Wisdom Temple that Reason "has supremacy over nature" (210). Subotnik, "Whose Magic Flute?" thinks that the opera reflects her general definition of Enlightenment, the "victory of reason over nature" (145).

32. Who am I? [*To himself*] What a stupid question! [*Aloud*] A man like you! (1.2).

33. Chailley, *Magic Flute, Masonic Opera*, 229.

34. See Irmen, *Mozart: Mitglied geheimer Gesellschaften*, 341.

35. Ibid.

36. Chailley, *Magic Flute, Masonic Opera*, shows many resemblances between what he calls the "initiation" of Tamina and Pamina, 127–57. He also makes many excellent points on how Papageno's "trials" mirror those of the royal couple (but the case he makes for Papagena's trials is not convincing). However his stress on ritual and initiation does not emphasize nearly enough the educational process, the personal growth. In fact, part of the education of the characters takes place in the Queen's territory, and most remains outside of the formal initiation rites.

37. This is the case in the interpretations of Nettl, *Mozart und Kunst*, and Rosenberg, *Zauberflöte Geschichte*.

38. Jean Massin and Brigitte Massin, *Mozart*, 1158.

39. Subotnik, "Whose *Magic Flute?*" 134.

40. See Brophy, *Mozart the Dramatist*, 223; Chailley, *Magic Flute, Masonic Opera*, 104.

41. Dent, *Mozart's Operas*, 260–61.

42. Thomson, *Masonic Thread*, 158.

43. I chattered—and that was bad—for that reason I now deserve what I'm getting (2.29).

44. Batley, *Preface*, 98; Herbert Zeman, "Altwiener Volkskomödie," *Zwischen Revolution und Restauration: Klassik, Romantik 1786–1813*, vol. 5 of *Deutsche Literatur: eine Sozialgeschichte*, ed. Albert Glaser (Hamburg: Rowohlt, 1980), 332.

45. Batley, *Preface*, 95.

46. Zeman, "Volkskomödie," 331, hints at the importance of such a synthesis in this opera when he notes that *The Magic Flute* "verweist auf einen neu erlangten . . . Ausgleich von Empfindung und Vernunft."

47. Most commentators assume that Sarastro's sentence of a bastinado of seventy-seven strokes for Monostatos is carried out, but Irmen, 340, demonstrates conclusively that it is not by quoting Monostatos in a subsequent scene: "Also bloß dem heutigen Tage hab' ichs zu verdanken, daß ich noch mit heiler Haut auf die Erde trete" [I have the present day to thank for the fact that I still walk on the ground with uninjured skin, 2.7].

48. Quoted in Schuler, *Mozart und Freimaurerei*, 206: "sanfte Belehrung gegen die Schwachheiten unsrer Brüder. . . ."

49. But if Sarastro had kept for you a girl that was just like you in clothes and color? (2.3).

50. Brophy, *Mozart the Dramatist*, 147, represents this view forcefully. It seems to me that Rosenberg, *Zauberflöte Geschichte*, 118–19, is closer to the truth in insisting that the flute partakes of both Sarastro's and the Queen's realms.

51. Rosenberg, *Zauberflöte Geschichte*, 122.

52. Compare Chailley, *Magic Flute, Masonic Opera*, 125.

53. In a magic hour, my father cut the magic flute deep out of the base of the thousand-year old oak, in the midst of thunder and lightening, storm and shower (2.28).

54. and amid the singing walk away as if marching (1.17). Most productions have Monostatos and the slaves do a dance while listening to the bells.

55. See Friedrich Schiller's "Letters on the Aesthetic Education of Man" (Briefe über die ästhetische Erziehung des Menschen, 1795), in which he advocates the arts as a way to educate the populace since they build on the sensual natural base, but have potential to educate the mind (or reason).

56. Be a man, then young man, you will triumph in a manly way (1.15).

57. A woman who is not afraid of night and death is worthy of being initiated (2.28).

58. The 1794 interpretation by the Freemason Ludwig von Batzko is quoted in Thomson, *Masonic Thread*, 157.

59. The long description of the stage set in the libretto includes two mountains, one with a waterfall and the other spouting fire. Near the water there is a "black fog" (2.28).

60. Compare Chailley, *Magic Flute, Masonic Opera*, 278–79; Rosenberg, *Zauberflöte Geschichte*, 101.

Gothic Gold: The Sadleir-Black Gothic Collection

FREDERICK S. FRANK

This narrative is the saga of the formation and content of the Sadleir-Black Gothic collection, monumental and compendious repository of rare Gothics and the premier collection of its type in the world. Maintained by the rare book department of the Alderman Library at the University of Virginia, the collection is a researcher's time capsule of a lost literary movement. It attracts dozens of working scholars annually as well as the merely curious and has continued to grow since Robert Kerr Black, antiquarian bookseller and sometime graduate student at the University of Virginia, donated it in perpetuity to the Alderman Library in 1942. Currently, Sadleir-Black holds 1,135 titles[1] representing every known mutation of the Gothic novel including many specimens of the shilling shockers or bluebooks, these short paperback Gothics once scorned by collectors to be the toxic literary waste and fin de siècle debris of the period. Twenty of the Gothic artifacts in the collection are vault items,[2] so scarce and so rare, that they are perhaps the final surviving copies of their single run printings. Mrs. Radcliffe's 1816 volume of poetry is but one rarity available to the working scholar who comes to the collection in quest of the real Gothic novel, that exciting body of literature that had been denounced by reviewers and devoured by readers during the last decade of the eighteenth century.

Readers who have made up their minds about what Gothic fiction is, who was reading it and why, who was writing it and why, or even what the physical appearance of the early Gothic novel was, will be enlightened by a research visit to Sadleir-Black, an experience which will alter many presuppositions about the Gothic, particularly for those scholars who approach the subject by way of feminist criticism or deconstructionist theory. For critics who dismiss the historical importance and literary worth of the Gothic, an investigation of Sadleir-Black might be conversionary. What lurks behind such intriguing titles as *The Cavern of Horrors; or, The Miseries of Miranda, The Ruins of Rigonda; or, The Homicidal Father, Düsseldorf; or, The Fratricide, Correlia; or, The Mystic Tomb, Louisa; or, The Black Tower, The Nuns of the Desert; or, The Woodland Witches, The Phantoms of the Cloister; or, The Mysterious Manuscript, The Recluse of the Woods; or, The Generous Warrior, A Gothic Romance, The Spectre of Landmere Abbey; or, The Mystery of the Blue and Silver Bag*, and two compelling titles which should not be omitted from any sequel to Isabella Thorpe's reading list of Gothic delicacies,[3] *The Idiot Heiress* and *Deeds of Darkness; or, The Unnatural Uncle*? A perusal of these and a myriad of other odd titles in Sadleir-Black will verify for the researcher a truth similar to what Mark Twain once said of Wagner's music—that it is not nearly as bad as it sounds.

Who was Michael Sadleir (1888–1957),[4] the motive force behind the collection? Most students of literature will associate his name with *Excursions in Victorian Bibliography*, especially the collecting and cataloguing of the Trollopes, the novelists Anthony and Frances. But between the years 1922 and 1937 when Sadleir sold his aggregation of terror novels to Robert K. Black, Sadleir was almost totally engaged in systematically collecting this unwanted kind of fiction. "The lust for Gothic romance," he wrote, "took complete possession of me."[5] But his was a controlled and rational lust always governed by the intellectual precision and persistence of this extraordinary bibliophile. His keen desire to own these books as physically pleasurable objects was balanced by a desire to possess them intellectually, an ideal combination of inquisitiveness and acquisitiveness. Sadleir had been drawn toward the accumulation of horror fiction as an undergraduate at Oxford. His literary affairs with Poe and such French decadents and symbolists as J. K. Huysmans and Mallarmé took him outside the Victorian mainstream of the novel and back to Charles Brockden Brown, America's first Gothic practitioner. By way of Brown, Sadleir began to gaze in wonder down the dark and forbidden corridor of Gothic fiction and to alternate his central collecting mania for the Trollopes with a diametrically opposite passion for things Gothic. By 1922, as he himself puts it in his account of the beginnings of Sadleir-Black, "With Poe, Brockden Brown, *Northanger Abbey*, the 'terror' elements in Dickens and a generalized passion for old novels as things to possess for their own sake, I was all set for an adventure in Gothicism."[6]

Sadleir's Gothic adventure was serendipitous to the limit of the laws of serendipity at its outset. Rummaging in the Oxford Street bookstore of Bumpus, he stared in disbelief as he held in his hands Karl Grosse's *Horrid Mysteries* and Regina Maria Roche's *The Children of the Abbey*, two extremely elusive Gothic titles. One of these books, *Horrid Mysteries* (1796), was not merely a lost or extinct Gothic; it was one of the seven titles in the "*Northanger* Septet,"[7] the gruesomely gratifying Gothics recommended to Catherine Morland by Isabella Thorpe in the pump room at Bath in Jane Austen's *Northanger Abbey*. The first time out—and the prospector had struck Gothic gold.

With the nonchalance of the neophyte, Sadleir had stumbled upon one of the missing *Northanger* novels whose very existence had been disparaged by the formidable critic, George Saintsbury. "I should indeed like some better authority than Miss Isabella Thorpe's to assure me of their existence,"[8] Saintsbury had erroneously pontificated. Sadleir was now demonically driven to locate and own the remaining six "*Northanger* Gothics": *The Mysterious Warning* and *The Castle of Wolfenbach* by Eliza Parsons; *Clermont* by Regina Maria Roche; *The Midnight Bell* by Francis Lathom; *The Necromancer; or, The Tale of the Black Forest* translated from the German by Lawrence Flammenberg and the Gothic which would challenge Sadleir's endurance as a collector, Eleanor's Sleath's *The Orphan of the Rhine*. As Sadleir pursued these ephemeral titles throughout the 1920s, the infrastructure of what was to become the collection began to assume a definite shape. The only hindrance to locating and purchasing first editions of major Gothics such as *The Mysteries of Udolpho*, *The Castle of Otranto*, and *The Monk* was their cost. The works of Walpole, Radcliffe, and Lewis were obtainable but prohibitively expensive as were the two teenage Gothics by Shelley, *Zastrozzi* and *St. Irvyne; or, The Rosicrucian*, which Sadleir craved and located but could not afford. But since nobody, neither antiquarian booksellers nor literary scholars, wanted the minor Gothics, Sadleir was able to spot and purchase such effluvia very cheaply because he and he alone could recognize the gold amidst the dross. At a Sothebys auction in 1923 which featured the dispersion of the Syston Park Library, Sadleir went early, stayed late, and at the jaded conclusion of the proceedings purchased several cases marked "contents unknown." Again, as with his beginner's luck at Bumpus's bookshop, he acquired an additional cache of forgotten fiction, much of it pure or high Gothic. Sadleir recalls: "When I got the books home and sorted them up, I found that my Gothic collection had ceased to be an aspiration and become a reality. No title of current market importance was in the bundles, but there were a large number of genuine minor Gothics of the kind most difficult to locate,"[9] including another *Northanger* title, Francis Lathom's *The Midnight Bell.*

During the mid-1920s, Sadleir also wrote some of the first serious criticism of the Gothic novel, thus opening the way for the questings of such figures as Montague Summers.[10] In November 1927 he published the important monograph, *The Northanger Novels: A Footnote to Jane Austen* for the English Association. By then this tenacious Gothophile had recovered six of the septet and was able to append a timely postscript when *The Orphan of the Rhine* fortuitously fell into his hands. Sadleir's view of Gothicism, its rise, its nationwide reign of terror, and its collapse and disappearance in the late 1820s became the critical basis for the renaissance in Gothic studies which began in the 1950s. Based partially on his familiarity with the form through zealous collecting, Sadleir theorized that the Gothic novel expressed "an eloquent disequilibrium of the spirit," "the triumph of chaos over order," "a fierce reaction against exhausted classicism which lay like a tired blight upon the civilization of western Europe." The Gothic's array of collapsing structures and magnificent devastation rendered it a singular example of subversive and negative Romanticism. "For qualities it had, and good historical and psychological justification also. The Gothic romance was not by any means a mere crazy extravagance. Like most artistic movements, it had its primitive incompetence and its over-ripe elaboration; but it sprang from a genuine spiritual impulse, and during its period of florescence produced work of real and permanent beauty."[11] In 1927, these opinions were the rankest heresy; in 1957, the year in which Devendra P. Varma's *Gothic Flame*[12] appeared, these same words had become doctrine. Thus, Sadleir became one of the first defenders and proponents of Gothic studies and the collection that was to bear his name is a confirmation that the Gothic could no longer be ignored or dismissed by cultural, intellectual, and literary historians.

If the vital core of the Sadleir-Black Gothic collection is the *Northanger* seven, its key years are 1923 and 1927. In 1927, Sadleir's *Northanger* monograph aroused new curiosity and even a modicum of respect in scholarly circles for Gothic fiction. By 1927, the last of the lost Gothics, *The Orphan of the Rhine*, had found a home and patron in Sadleir's collection. Previously, in 1923, Sadleir's Gothic quest for the *Northanger* titles and the enlargement of his Gothic collection gained impetus by way of a chance friendship with Arthur Hutchinson, clubman of the Omar Khayyam Club, conversationalist, raconteur, amateur collector and littérateur, editor of the *Windsor Magazine* and ceaseless scavenger of old books of any and every sort. Like Sadleir, Hutchinson was a bibliomaniac, but his bibliomania, unlike Sadleir's, took the peculiar form of undirected and undisciplined book accumulation.

Hutchinson foraged for books not caring what he found so long as they were old novels and so long as he possessed them in vast quantities. Driven by his gluttony for books as material items, Hutchinson had the acquisitive spirit of the true collector, but lacked literary inquisitiveness. It was the spines, wrappers, covers, and boards of his books which gratified Hutchinson more than their contents which he seldom examined. This Dickensian character who might have been a reincarnated resident of Mr. Brogley's cluttered pawnshop in *Dombey and Son*, this "queer" and "omnivorous" collector whose "lust for fiction was uncontrolled either by selective design or problems of space"[13] as Sadleir himself described his friend, bought up batches of novels on a daily basis, placing his random buys in packing crates stuffed with other miscellaneous items including railroad timetables and back numbers of periodicals on every subject imaginable. Hutchinson filled box after box until at the time of his death in 1927 this old novel maniac had amassed a bizarre literary estate of 140 packing cases, an enthusiast's primal hodgepodge. Somewhere in the depths of the Hutchinson "library"—to use the term very loosely—somewhere within these crates of unsorted books lay the disarranged corpus of what would become the Sadleir-Black Gothic collection. Here too was the Gothic gold mine, but its wealth would not yield itself easily. When Sadleir was named executor of the Hutchinson library upon Hutchinson's death in August 1927, he could only ponder "what a tremendous and in some ways macabre task had been laid upon me."[14] Sadleir describes his first viewing of the entire Hutchinson library in a scene suggestive of a Gothic victim's helpless awe during a spectral encounter or facing a premature burial.

> I shall never forget the first sight of that astonishing collection. After sending our credentials to the repository and fixing a time for a preliminary view, we asked for certain sample cases to be unpacked in readiness for the visit. Having arrived at the huge building, we were conducted to a sort of mezzanine floor—low ceilinged and in complete darkness. There were 140 packing cases of books, of which a random dozen or fifteen had been unpacked. We were given torches and left to investigate. The rays of light flickered across the vast floor on which—spines upward—were ranged row after row of books. It looked as though an over-floor of books had been laid down, with the narrowest passages here and there through which we crept, flashing our torches on title after title, and feeling every moment more appalled at the prospect of having to sort these thousands of volumes and prepare them for sale. For they were completely unclassified and desperately miscellaneous; quite half were still parcelled and would have to be undone and distributed before even a start could be made. Out in the daylight my colleague and I stared at one another in despair. What in the world were we to do?[15]

Somewhere in this disarray of books and unknown to Hutchinson himself was concealed the four-volume body of *The Orphan of the Rhine*—but where? As Sadleir faced the labor of sorting and organization he confronted the is-it-here?-and-if-so-where? problem repeatedly. The veins of Gothic gold would first have to be detected, then assiduously mined if any coherence at all were to be imposed upon the Hutchinson library. And to add to Sadleir's consternation, many three- and four-volume novel sets had been randomly separated by Hutchinson. If, for example, the first two volumes of *The Orphan of the Rhine* had filled a case to the top, then volumes three and four might have been consigned to another unnumbered box with no regard for sequence. Add to this the fact that there was no order or dating whatsoever among the boxes and therefore no way to determine whether Hutchinson had purchased all volumes of a multi-volumed novel or only fragments. Sadleir would just have to endure these dilemmas of identification as he began the process of classification and ranking that would occupy many months of eerie sequestration alone within the maze of the Hutchinson library. Because Sadleir could not anticipate what each box might contain, each moment of unpacking prolonged the tedium but offered the potential thrill of discovery. "Stultified with fatigue and dust, and feeling I never wanted to see a book again, I was listlessly unpacking perhaps the hundredth packing case when my jaded intelligence suddenly awoke to the fact that I was holding in my hand the four volumes of *The Orphan of the Rhine*. Hutchinson, though he did not know it, had had a copy afler all."[16] Similar moments would unearth some of the rare artifacts now the pride of the collection. Sadleir found most of the Gothics written by Francis Lathom including *The Midnight Bell*, several first editions of *The Monk*, the delicate volume of Mrs. Radcliffe's poems, Jane Porter's *Thaddeus of Warsaw* in first-rate condition with uncut boards, Lady Morgan's [Sidney Owenson's] *The Novice of St. Dominick* in opulent green morocco boards, ghoulish Gothics by the followers of Monk Lewis, lachrymose Gothics by the imitators of Mrs. Radcliffe, and an abundance of thirty-six and seventy-two page shilling shocker chapbooks, the Gothic novel in its most fragile and transient form.[17] There were bookplates bearing the *ex libri* of Richard Brinsley Sheridan and Samuel Whitbread, a prominent member of Charles James Fox's ministry. The large number of novels by Eliza Parsons, Regina Maria Roche, Elizabeth Helme, the Lee Sisters, Charlotte Smith, Charlotte Dacre [Rosa Matilda], Mary Charlton, and clusters of other forgotten favorites who had operated as Gothic novelist stringers for the Minerva Press reassured Sadleir of the uniqueness of his legacy. Once they had been reassembled, classified, and repaired by Sadleir, these books would come to constitute what may be the nucleus of the Sadleir-Black Gothic collection, its extensive holdings of minor and lost Gothics. In some boxes,

Sadleir found Germanic variations of the Gothic novel in the form of Ritter- and Räuberromane, Schauerromane, and French translations of the Gothic penned by the émigrés during the 1790s together with specimens of the roman noir or French Gothic novel by Ducray-Duminil, Baculard d'Arnaud, and Madame Genlis[18] Hutchinson's eclectic tastes in book covers was also evident in his ownership of Schiller's *Der Geisterseher*, Christiane Naubert's novel of the secret Fehmic tribunal or Vehmgericht, *Hermann von Unna*, and several splendidly lugubrious thrillers by Joseph Alois Gleich, in whose shrill craft the Schauerroman or German shudder novel attained its zenith. When the task of exhumation was completed and the waste discarded, Sadleir would have a residue consisting of more than a thousand titles embracing all forms of Gothic activity over a fifty-year span. All seven *Northanger* novels were now verified and descriptively catalogued. All that Sadleir's collection lacked were a permanent accommodation which would provide accessibility and an audience of general readers and scholarly specialists who would care enough about this fugitive genre to reread and revaluate it.

Robert Kerr Black, the third principal in the saga, would attend to these needs. Black had been introduced to Gothic literature at the University of Virginia by Professor Archibald Shepperson, whose witty account of the satiric face of the novel, *The Novel in Motley: A History of the Burlesque Novel in English* (1936), offered an amusing and informative history of the Gothic movement and its susceptibility to parody in the chapter "Gothic Nonsense."[19] Black's original interest in the Gothic was by way of Shepperson's admiration for such pastiches as Eaton Stannard Barrett's aggressive burlesque, *The Heroine; or, The Adventures of a Fair Romance Reader*, R. S.'s *The New Monk*, a sentence-by-sentence excoriation of Lewis's work, Thomas Love Peacock's *Nightmare Abbey*, Dennis Lawler's mock Gothic drama, *The Earls of Hammersmith; or, The Cellar Spectre* and, of course, *Northanger Abbey*. The parodies of the Gothic novel in Sadleir-Black are Black's most vital contributions to the collection. One of the most skillful lampoons in Sadleir-Black is *Love and Horror: An Imitation for the Present and a Model for All Future Romances*, bearing the cryptic pseudonym, "Ircastrensis."[20]

As a collector, Black's favorite quarry was Gothic satire in novelistic and dramatic form. In the late fall of 1937, he queried the bookseller, George Bates, a small dealer in the lower Haymarket, in an attempt to obtain Eaton Stannard Barrett's *Heroine* and anything else that might possibly be considered a Gothic pastiche. Bates and Black developed a bibliophile friendship centered around rare books, particularly Gothic books, a special interest that would eventually lead Black to Michael Sadleir and his archive of remarkable oddities. "'Have you ever heard of Michael Sadleir's fine collection of

Gothic novels?' Bates asked. 'I replied truthfully that I had—once,' Black responded. 'Did you know it was for sale?' I had not known and I showed my provincial Americanism by immediately and idly inquiring: 'How much?'"[21]

Bates arranged a meeting with Sadleir, a proposal was made, and Robert K. Black became sole owner of the collection for an undisclosed price. Why did Sadleir sell his so preciously refined Gothic gold? There were two reasons, neither involving monetary concerns. First, for all of his scrupulous searching and selecting, Sadleir's Gothic collecting habit was a recessive passion assuaged by his completion of the *Northanger* set and a renewal of his central bibliographical commitments to the Trollopes. By the mid-1930s, his bibliographical objectives in the Gothic field had been attained. In the 1940s and up until his death in 1957, he would write scholarly studies of Wassily Kandinsky, Herman Melville's prose, James T. Farrell's *Studs Lonigan* trilogy, Victorian railroad fiction, Bulwer-Lytton, and the political career of Richard Brinsley Sheridan, subject areas far removed from Gothicism. Second, Sadleir certainly sensed in Robert K. Black the ideal custodian and successor for the care and dispersion of such unusual and irreplaceable books. Black grasped both the material and intellectual worth of the Sadleir Gothics and their potential value to a future acceleration of Gothic studies. Black's academic connection with the University of Virginia was an additional assurance that Sadleir's Gothic collection would not be privately hidden away but have public scholarly accessibility.

Concentrating on gaps left by Hutchinson and Sadleir, Black purchased and added Beckford's *Vathek* and Shelley's juvenile Gothics which Sadleir had desired but could not afford, *St. Irvyne; or, The Rosicrucian* and *Zastrozzi*. Oddly, neither Hutchinson's crates nor Sadleir's lucky acquisitions contained the 1818 edition of *Frankenstein*, or *Northanger Abbey*, or any editions of any one of the Reverend Charles Robert Maturin's six novels. Among the approximately one hundred items appended by Black was a copy of *The Mysteries of Udolpho* bearing the bookplate of Elizabeth Shelley, the mother of the poet. Black's own Gothic explorations turned up the publisher's contract for five hundred pounds for *Udolpho* signed by Mrs. Radcliffe, this document found in the basement of a book dealer in Newark, New Jersey. He further enhanced the collection by installing several critical documents including Jakob Brauchli's first primary bibliography of the Gothic novel, *Der Englische Schauerroman um 1800*.[22]

By 1942, Black's role as informal curator and preserver of the Collection had run its course. Care and storage were immediate problems while the acid base composition of the paper meant that many of the Gothics, perhaps appropriate for a genre which indulged in so much desolation and decay, was almost visibly decomposing. Having been literally read to pieces two centuries earlier, the surviving relics were now confronted by another disintegration. Hence, Black's decision to give the collection to the University of Virginia was both an intellectually natural and a scientifically expedient gesture. Black decided to establish a viable, working collection of rare books, not wishing to see Sadleir's magnificent archive of forbidden titles gradually destroyed by lack of proper care.

From this account of its formation, the nature and scope of the Sadleir-Black collection as well as its incalculable usefulness to researchers can be discerned. Even the disposable titles which the collection retains have their value for what they can reveal about publishers' practices and the idiosyncracies of late-eighteenth-century readership. Perhaps it was for this reason that both Sadleir and Black did not eliminate all of the trash Gothic which the Hutchinson library contained, but reserved some aptly chosen representative samples in order to render as accurate a picture as possible of the huge and quirkish Gothic audience and its needs. Hence, not every single holding in the collection can be considered high Gothic, but the majority of the books do fall into this category either directly or marginally, which means that Sadleir-Black offers a purity of period and subject matter that surpasses more amorphous collections of its type. The holdings can be subdivided into discrete categories: first editions of the front rank Gothic writers who comprise the inner circle of Gothicism, Walpole, Clara Reeve, Beckford, Mrs. Radcliffe, Lewis, and Maturin; complete or nearly complete runs of the satellites of the great Gothics; second-level Gothic fiction by William Henry Ireland, Charlotte Dacre, T. J. Horsley Curties, Elizabeth Helme, Mary Meeke, George Moore, and Mary Robinson; tertiary and residual Gothics or shoddy imitations and straight plagiarisms; non-Gothic eighteenth-century fiction with strong Gothic overtones in style, plot, and characterization, such as the Jacobin and doctrinaire work of William Godwin, Robert Bage, and Thomas Holcroft; pastiches, parodies, and lampoons; French and German Schauerromane or "shudder novels"; miscellanies, annuals, keepsakes, and anthologies; and finally, the collection's extensive array of short Gothics in pamphlet format, the bluebooks, chapbooks, yellowbacks, shilling shockers, thirty-six and seventy-two page pulps and bloods, and serialized and periodical Gothics.

It is perhaps this chapbook element of the Sadleir-Black collection which draws the researcher rather than its ponderous triple-decker Gothics with their casual slaughters, serpentine plots, and complex turnings of the screw. The collection's chapbooks clearly indicate acute shifts in the tastes and expectations of the Gothic readership. As early as the 1790s as these primitive paperbacks began to seep into the system, the Gothic novel in long form as it was being mass produced by the Minerva Press was already becoming an endangered species. Gothic readers would still tolerate such performances as Agnes Maria Bennett's Gothic behemoth in six volumes, *Vicissitudes Abroad; or, The Ghost of My Father*[23] published in 1806; but by eliminating all moralism and by pushing the characters along a corridor of blood and bringing them either to the altar or the grave within the alloted thirty-six pages, the chapbookers would eventually drive out such lengthy Gothics and corner the market. Their phantasmic titles coupled with the garish vigor of their illustrations offered their devoted public instantaneous horror that the long Gothics could not match. It did not matter that almost every shilling shocker was a plagiarized reduction of *The Monk* or one of Mrs. Radcliffe's romances or a tawdry compression of Shakespeare's *Titus Andronicus, Macbeth, Hamlet, Measure for Measure,* or *Cymbeline.*

Statistically, the tally of chapbooks in Sadleir-Black validates that the national lust for the macabre in literature reached its apogee between 1810 and 1815 and extended well into the Romantic movement. Because only a small fraction of these little Gothics survive, we can only speculate about their grand totals in the period as the Gothic impulse accelerated toward critical mass in the 1810s. As he investigated Hutchinson's boxes, Sadleir must have been particularly alert to the chapbookers since the collection contains more than two hundred specimens of these abbreviated Gothic thrillers. Sadleir also realized that a typical bluebooker was often employed by several rapacious publishers simultaneously to fill their quotas of Gothics. One typical bluebooker, Isaac Crookenden, appears to have marketed the same plot to several rival publishers under variant titles, among these, *The Skeleton; or, The Mysterious Discovery, A Gothic Romance, The Spectre of the Turret; or, Guolto Castle,* and *Horrible Revenge; or, The Monster of Italy!!* Two anonymous chapbooks in the collection, *The Midnight Groan; or, The Spectre of the Chapel, Involving an Exposure of the Horrible Secrets of the Nocturnal Assembly, A Gothic Romance* and *The Bloody Hand; or, The Fatal Cup, A Tale of Horrors* are plagiarisms of prior plagiarisms in the chapbook trade. The drudge-and-sludge component of Sadleir-Black also reflects Sadleir's interest in Victorian proletarian horror fiction as represented in the collection's samples of the pulp publisher Edward Lloyd's chain novels putatively authored by Thomas Peckett Prest, creator of *Varney the Vampyre;* however, *Varney* itself is not to be found in Sadleir-Black.

Although the full-sized Gothics in Sadleir-Black are often elegantly bound and well-preserved, they are generally not, with a few exceptions from among the French and German translations, lavishly illustrated. The practice of Gothic illustration[24] is an area of lurid special effects restricted almost exclusively to the chapbooks and bluebooks. Fearsome engravings and woodcuts of variant artistic quality adorn numerous title pages and frontispieces and sometimes embellish the text at ten- or twelve-page intervals. It was the illustrator's task to select the most emetic, erotic, or sensationally supernatural episode in the chapbook, then pictorialize it to lure the Gothic consumer. If no such satisfactory horrific event could be located by the illustrator, the artist then fabricated his own. Thus, the connection between an illustration and a corresponding textual event is sometimes mysterious or nonexistent. In a few cases, the illustrations approach the nightmare brilliance of Fuseli, Goya, or Doré, but mainly they reflect a crassly promotional group style. The prototypical Gothic cover picture depicting the maiden in flight down a staircase or dark path as she glances hysterically over her left shoulder is a pictorial cliché of the Gothic illustrators.

NOTES

1. The primary documents relating to the formation and content of the Sadleir-Black Collection are: the pamphlet by Robert K. Black containing Michael Sadleir's account, "The Sadleir-Black Gothic Collection, An Address Before the Bibliographical Society of the University of Virginia" (Charlottesville, VA: The Alderman Library of the University of Virginia, 1949); the mimeographed Catalogue of the Sadleir-Black Gothic Collection prepared and distributed by the Rare Book Department of the Alderman Library; Sadleir's November, 1927 pamphlet for the English Association, *The Northanger Novels: A Footnote to Jane Austen*; David McKinney, *The Imprints of Gloomth: The Gothic Novel in England, 1765–1830, An Exhibition Featuring the Sadleir-Black Gothic Novel Collection* (Charlottesville, VA: Alderman Library of the University of Virginia, 1988). Other partial bibliographical descriptions of Gothic items in the Sadleir-Black Collection are: Dorothy Blakey, *The Minerva Press, 1790–1820* (London: Oxford Press for the Bibliographical Society, 1939); Montague Summers, *A Gothic Bibliography* (London: Fortune Press, 1941; New York: Russell and Russell, 1964); Ann B. Tracy, *The Gothic Novel, 1790–1830: Plot Summaries and Index to Motifs* (Lexington, KY; University Press of Kentucky, 1981); Frederick S. Frank, *The First Gothics: A Critical Guide to the English Gothic Novel* (New York: Garland, 1987).

2. The Sadleir-Black Collection Catalogue lists the following vault holdings:

Beckford, William. *Vathek: An Arabian Tale from an Unpublished Manuscript* (J. Johnson, 1786)

Goethe, Johann Wolfgang von. *The Sorrows of Werter: A German Story* (J. Dodsley, 1779)

Grosse, Karl. *Horrid Mysteries* (Minerva Press, 1796)

Hedgeland, Isabella [Kelly]. *Eva* (Minerva Press, 1799)

Kahlert, Karl Friedrich. *The Necromancer; or, The Tale of the Black Forest* (Minerva Press, 1794)

Lathom, Francis. *The Midnight Bell: A German Story* (H. D. Symonds, 1798)

Two editions of Lewis, Matthew Gregory. *The Monk: A Romance* (J. Bell, 1796)
Maturin, Charles Robert. *Bertram; or, The Castle of St. Aldobrand* (John Murray, 1816)
Ormsby, Mrs. Anne. *Memoirs of a Family in Swisserland* (Longman & Rees, 1802)
Parsons, Eliza [Phelp]. *Castle of Wolfenbach; A German Story* (Minerva Press, 1793)
Parsons, Eliza. *The Mysterious Warning, A German Tale* (Minerva Press, 1796)
Radcliffe, Ann [Ward]. *The Castles of Athlin and Dunbayne: A Highland Story* (T. Hookham, 1799)
Radcliffe, Ann [Ward]. *The Poems of Mrs. Ann Radcliffe* (J. Smith, 1816)
Reeve, Clara. *The Champion of Virtue. A Gothic Story* (W. Keymer, 1777)
Roche, Mrs. Regina Maria [Dalton]. *The Children of the Abbey. A Tale* (Minerva Press, 1796)
Roche, Mrs. Regina Maria [Dalton]. *Clermont. A Tale* (Minerva Press, 1798)
Shelley, Percy Bysshe. *St. Irvyne; or, The Rosicrucian: A Romance* (J. J. Stockdale, 1811)
Sleath, Mrs. Eleanor. *The Orphan of the Rhine* (Minerva Press, 1798)
Walpole, Horace. *The Castle of Otranto, A Gothic Story* (Thomas Lownds, 1765).

3. In chapter 6 of Jane Austen's *Northanger Abbey*, Isabella Thorpe provides the heroine, Catherine Morland, with a reading list of seven terrifying titles. These titles comprise the "*Northanger* Novels" or "*Northanger* Septet," the objectives of Sadleir's search and the core of the Sadleir-Black Collection. The seven titles with Sadleir-Black vault copy call numbers are: Eliza Parsons's *Castle of Wolfenbach* (PZ2.P377C) and *The Mysterious Warning* (PZ2.377mys), Mrs. Regina Maria Roche's *Clermont* (PZ2.R63C1), Karl Friedrich Kahlert's *The Necromancer of the Black Forest* (PZ2.K43N), Francis Lathom's *The Midnight Bell* (PZ2.L38Mi), Mrs. Eleanor Sleath's *The Orphan of the Rhine* (PZ2.S560), and Karl Grosse's *Horrid Mysteries* (PZ2.G77H).

4. The sole bio-bibliographical study of Sadleir's scholarly career is: Roy Stokes, *Michael Sadleir* (Metuchen, NJ, and London: Scarecrow Press, 1980). Sadleir specialized in collecting and writing about Victorian fiction and was an eminent bibliographer in the field. His *Excursions in Victorian Bibliography* (London: Caundy and Fox, 1922) and *Anthony Trollope, A Commentary* (Boston: Houghton Mifflin, 1927) remain standard references.

5. Sadleir, "The Sadleir-Black Gothic Collection," 5.

6. Ibid., 4.

7. The quest for the lost *Northanger* novels was initiated by Montague Summers. See: "'Northanger Abbey': 'Horrid Romances,'" *Notes & Queries* 2 (July 1, 1916): 9; "'Northanger Abbey': 'Horrid Romances,'" *Notes & Queries* 2 (July 29, 1916): 97–98; "'Northanger Abbey': 'Horrid Romances,'" *Times Literary Supplement*, 27 December 1917, p. 649. Summers refuted Saintsbury's denial of their existence. Another searcher, Alan D. McKillop, verified the authenticity and discussed the authorship of *The Necromancer; or, The Tale of the Black Forest* in "Jane Austen's Gothic Titles," *Notes & Queries* 9 (1921): 361–62. Sadleir's 1927 monograph (cited above) and a second version of this study, "'All Horrid?': Jane

Austen and the Gothic Romance," in *Things Past* (London: Constable, 1944), 167–200, summarize and analyze the *Northanger* Seven. For modern critical discussions of these Gothics, see: Bette B. Roberts, "The Horrid Novels, *The Mysteries of Udolpho* and *Northanger Abbey*," in *Gothic Fictions: Prohibition/Transgression*, ed. Kenneth W. Graham (New York: AMS Press, 1989), 89–111; Nelly Stéphane, "Une Parodie de Roman Noir: *Northanger Abbey*," *Europe: Revue Littéraire Mensuelle* 659 (1984): 19–28; Beth Lau, "Madeline at *Northanger Abbey*: Keats's Anti-Romances and Gothic Satire," *Journal of English and Germanic Philology*, 84 (1985): 30–50; Tara Ghoshal Wallace, "*Northanger Abbey* and the Limits of Parody," *Studies in the Novel* 20 (1988): 262–73; Mark Loveridge, "*Northanger Abbey*: Or, Nature and Probability," *Nineteenth-Century Fiction* 56 (1991): 1–29.

    8. George Saintsbury, *Tales of Mystery: Mrs. Radcliffe, Lewis, Maturin* (New York: Macmillan, 1891), 19.

    9. Sadleir, "The Sadleir-Black Gothic Collection," 6.

    10. Summers's history of the Gothic novel, *The Gothic Quest: A History of the Gothic Novel* (1938; reprint, New York: Russell and Russell, 1964), 398. Summers acknowledges the scholarship of Sadleir as helpful to his own Gothic questings. "Mr. Sadleir is rightly emphatic that the Gothic romance 'sprang from a genuine spiritual impulse.' I have chosen as the title of my book 'The Gothic Quest' to signify the spiritual as well as the literary and artistic seeking for beauty."

    11. Sadleir, *The Northanger Novels: A Footnote to Jane Austen*, 3–4.

    12. Devendra P. Varma, *The Gothic Flame: Being a History of the Gothic Novel in England; Its Origins, Efflorescence, Disintegration, and Residuary Influences* (London: A. Barker, 1957; New York: Russell and Russell, 1966; Metuchen, N.J.; and London: Scarecrow Press, 1990). The seven Northanger novels were made available to modern readers in editions by the Folio Press in 1968 with Varma's introductions. Additionally, thirty of the Sadleir-Black Collection's rarest Gothics were reprinted in three series by the Arno Press (1972, 1974, 1977) under Varma's general editorship.

    13. Sadleir, "The Sadleir-Black Gothic Collection," 6.

    14. Ibid., 7.

    15. Ibid.

    16. Ibid., 10.

    17. Except for William Whyte Watt's now-ancient fifty-four page monograph, *Shilling Shockers of the Gothic School: A Study of Chapbook Gothic Romances* (Cambridge, MA: Harvard University Press, 1932; New York: Russell and Russell, 1967), scholarly interest in these miniature Gothics has been minimal. Watt regarded the shilling shocker as the transitional link between the Gothic novel of the eighteenth century and the nineteenth-century short tale of terror as practiced by Poe, Maupassant, and Le Fanu. Recent reprintings of a few shilling shockers have been done by Peter Haining whose two anthologies, *Gothic Tales of Terror: Classic Horror Stories from Great Britain, Europe, and the United States, 1765–1840* (New York: Taplinger, 1972) and *The Shilling Shocker: Stories of Terror from the Gothic Bluebooks* (New York: St. Martin's Press, 1979) offer some examples. Chris Baldick's edition entitled *Oxford Book of Gothic Tales* (New York: Oxford Univer-

sity Press, 1992) contains Isaac Crookenden's *The Vindictive Monk; or, The Fatal Ring.*

18. "Bibliographie Chronologique du Roman 'Gothique' 1764–1824," a selective primary bibliography of Gothic fiction in Maurice Lévy's *Le Roman 'Gothique' Anglais, 1764–1824* (Toulouse: Association des Publications de la Faculté des Lettres et Sciences, 1968), 684–708, identifies numerous titles in Sadleir-Black and the New York Society Library's Hammond Collection. Maurice Lévy, "English Gothic and the French Imagination: A Calendar of Translations, 1767–1828," in *The Gothic Imagination: Essays in Dark Romanticism,* ed. G. R. Thompson (Pullman, WA: Washington State University Press, 1974), 150–176, concentrates on the work of émigré translators in Sadleir-Black, the New York Society Library, the British Museum, and the Bibliothèque Nationale. Lévy refers to the Gothics as "obsolete wonders," and mentions Sadleir-Black as "a unique collection . . . an invaluable help to such scholars as are reckless enough to investigate these futile but difficult matters."

19. Archibald Shepperson, "Gothic Nonsense," in *The Novel in Motley: A History of the Burlesque Novel in English* (Cambridge, MA: Harvard University Press, 1936), 154–81. The incontinence of the Gothic novel gave rise to parodies and burlesques, with "the same burlesque usually ridiculing both excessive sensibility and excessive Gothicism."

20. This puzzling pseudonym is attached to one of the most acerbic parodies of the Gothic in the Sadleir-Black Collection. *Love and Horror: An Imitation for the Present and a Model for All Future Romances* (PZ2.I65L; London: J.J. Stockdale, 1815) delivers a coup de grâce to all "Gothic nonsense" as well as to the stilted young hero and menaced maiden of the typical Gothic romance. Discontented with dull normality, Ircastrensis's hero, the plain and pedestrian Thomas Baily, sets out to reshape his life as a Gothic ordeal. He falls in love with a woman who has been deceased for two hundred years and determines to reincarnate the posthumous beloved of his dreams as the ravishing Ethelinda Tit by persuading Ethelinda's last surviving relative, Annabella Tit, to impersonate her in a series of contrived Gothic emergencies which allow Baily to excel in the role of Gothic hero. The irate brilliance of the satire may be a clue to the pseudonym, a compound of the Latin "ira" or anger and "castrametari," or "castrametation," the term for the construction of a defensive military encampment of the legion on campaign. The pseudonym then explains itself as "angry defensive position against" all forms of Gothic flummery.

21. Black, "The Sadleir-Black Gothic Collection," 11.

22. Jakob Brauchli, *Der Englische Schauerroman um 1800: Unter Berücksichtigung der Unbekannten Bücher. Ein Beitrag zur Ceschichte der Volksliteratur* (Weida, Germany: Thomas und Hubert,1928). Brauchli's bibliographical pamphlet, the first systematic bibliography of Gothicism, is itself a rare book. Entries are not annotated, print is miniscule, and publication data is often omitted or erroneous. Nevertheless, Brauchli's listings of the first Gothics are indispensable to Gothic bibliography and can survive Montague Summers's complaint that they "are not merely incomplete but muddled in their arrangement."

23. Agnes Maria Bennett, *Vicissitudes Abroad; or, The Ghost of My Father* (London: Minerva Press, 1806) is exemplary of the fashion in giant Gothics and is perhaps the lengthiest novel in Sadleir-Black. The page counts of the six volumes are: volume 1, 384 pages; volume 2, 340 pages; volume 3, 323 pages; volume 4, 355 pages; volume 5, 316 pages; volume 6, 308 pages, yielding a grand total of 2,026 pages.

24. Gothic illustration is yet another nearly uncharted area of Gothic study. The Gothic bibliographers, Summers and Lévy, have included an assortment of plates from the translations, longer Gothic fiction, and chapbooks in their writings, but no full-length study exists. See: Montague Summers, "The Illustrations of the Gothick Novels," *Connoisseur* 98 (1936): 266–71; Maurice Lévy, Images du Roman Noir (Paris: Eric Losfeld, 1973); Maurice Lévy, "Images du Roman Noir," *Die Buchillustration im 18. Jahrhundert: Colloquium der Arbeitsstelle 18. Jahrhundert Gesamthochschule Wuppertal Universität Münster / Düsseldorf vom 3. bis 5. Oktober 1978* (Heidelberg: Heidelberg University Press, 1980), 156–65; Maurice Lévy, "Les llustrations du Roman 'Noir' en France à la Fin du XVIIIe Siècle," in *L'Illustration du Livre et la Littérature an XVIIIe Siècle en France et en Pologne*, ed. Zdislaw Libera (Warsaw: University of Varsovie, 1982), 123–34.

25. Tracy, *The Gothic Novel, 1790–1830: Plot Summaries*, 15. The Gothics in the Sadleir-Black Collection furnish a partial database for the titles described in the Tracy bibliography. In compiling the bibliography, Tracy notes that "the University of Virginia's Sadleir-Black Collection of Gothic novels is much the most extensive on this side of the Atlantic, and the staff is especially courteous and reasonable."

26. Devendra P. Varma, "The Starhemberg Collection," *Illustrated London News*, Christmas Number, 1983: 67–68. Varma rates this collection as on a par with the Sadleir-Black Collection and superior to Sadleir-Black in certain areas.

Appendix

Commentaries on the Engravings and Woodcuts

The nine specimens of Gothic chapbook illustrating which follow are selective reproductions of covers and frontispieces facing the title pages of nine short Gothics in the Sadleir-Black collection and are arranged chronologically by author with unsigned Gothics following the signatured titles. The illustrations demonstrate publishers' preferences for certain type scenes and horrid situations. Approximately one-third of the titles in Sadleir-Black are chapbooks, shilling shockers, and penny dreadfuls. The nine samples have been selected to give an overview of the typical chapbook cover and frontispiece of this primitive paperback industry. A statistical survey of the Sadleir-Black collection's illustrated Gothics remains to be accomplished. Such a survey would also identify the number of titles in the collection that are unique or sole surviving copies, a category which embraces most of the chapbooks. Sadleir himself never attempted to determine what percentage of the novels in the collection were pure or high Gothics and which books were other shades of terror fiction. Except for the chapbooks which are all dependably horrid, the titles of the novels are not always an accurate guide to their Gothicity. In her bibliographical inventory of Sadleir-Black titles, Ann B. Tracy has noted that "Some quite promising titles led to disappointingly bland novels, while some rather neutral titles [e.g., *Mary Jane* by Richard Sickelmore] proved satisfyingly horrid."[25]

There are other collections of Gothic fiction elsewhere in the world, but none can rival the riches and wonders of Sadleir-Black. The Harvard, Yale, Illinois, and University of Toronto libraries have Gothic holdings. The Hammond collection of the New York Society Library, the Larpent collection of eighteenth-century plays in the Huntington Library, and a dispersion of American Gothic titles in the stacks of the American Antiquarian Society in Worcester, Massachusetts present opportunities and resources for the Gothic researcher. The Prince Ludwig Starhemberg library of Gothics recently discovered by Devendra P. Varma at Schloss Eferding in Austria has profuse deposits of Gothic gold. But the supremacy of Sadleir-Black in this field will continue so long as these rare books are sought after and read. Writing of the Starhemberg discovery, Devendra P. Varma has commented that "the pages of Gothic fiction turn with a ghostly flutter."[26] That same ghostly flutter remains eternally audible throughout the fascinating labyrinth of Sadleir-Black.

ROUND TOWER.

C. F. Barrett, *The Round Tower; or, The Mysterious Witness, an Irish Legendary Tale of the Sixth Century* (London: Tegg and Castleman, 1803), 36 pages.

The chapbook frontispiece shows a tripartite figure arrangement depicting a Duncanesque *deus ex machina*, "his silver skin lac'd with his golden blood," pronouncing last judgement on the two Macbethian usurpers, Sitric and Cobthatch. As the murderers extend their left arms, the regal deity raises a righteous right arm in retribution. This is a Macbethian Gothic, a subtype of the shilling shocker designed to thrill the reader with gory supernatural spectacle.

Isaac Crookenden, *The Skeleton; or, The Mysterious Discovery, A Gothic Romance* (London: A. Neill, 1805), 38 pages.

    A typical chapbook by the master counterfeiter of long Gothics, Isaac Crookenden. The illustration shows that mandatory moment of supernatural startle when the castle explorer comes face-to-face with the deceased or missing owner. Crookenden plundered the plot from *The Animated Skeleton*, a 1798 Minerva Press Gothic, and melted down its four hundred pages to the requisite thirty-eight page quota. If the baron's bones are not quite animated here, neither are they immobilized as the illustrator has succeeded in giving an air of aliveness to the ossuarial figure which seems about to descend from its niche.

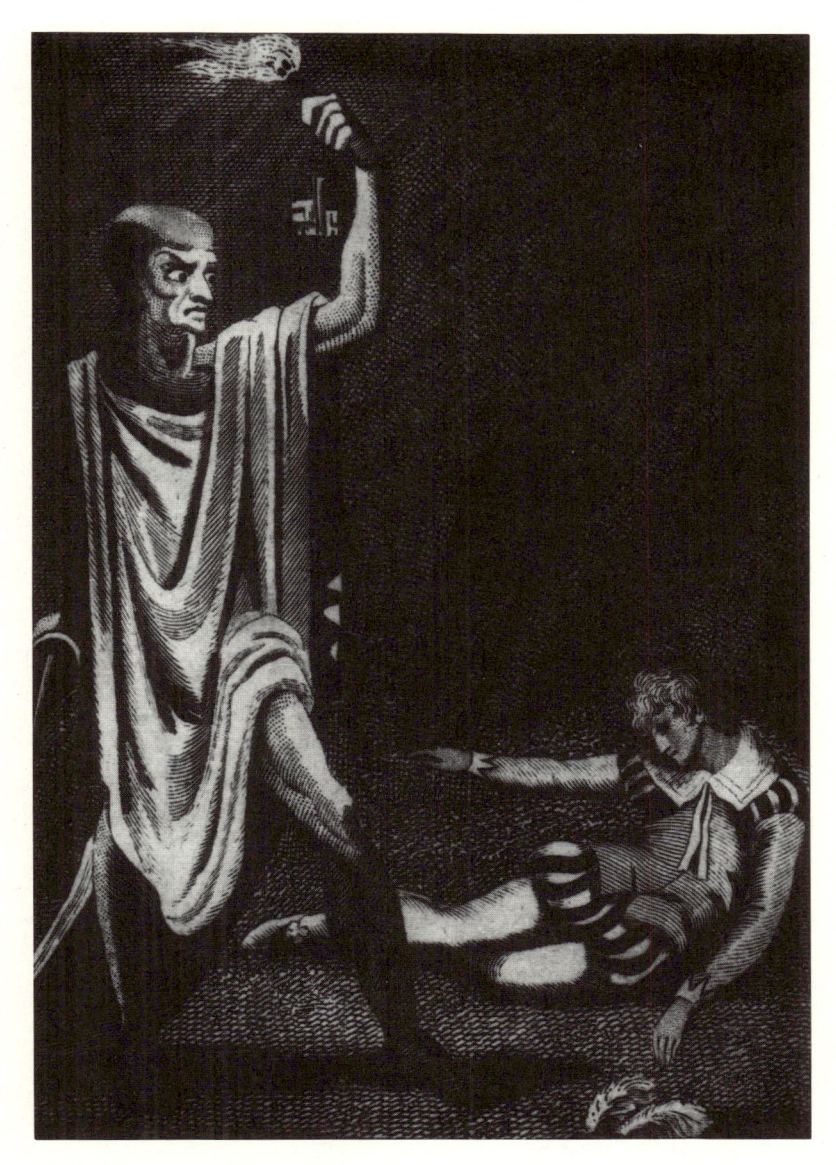

Lucy Watkins, *Romano Castle; or, The Horrors of The Forest* (London: Dean and Munday, n.d.), 35 pages.

    The signature of Lucy Watkins is to be found frequently among the chapbook authors. The chapbook also uses the device of the page direction which sends the reader without delay to the ghastly scene shown on the title page. Page 5 of *Romano Castle* reads: "As Alfonso advanced, he saw that the light was held by a gigantic being, a skeletal form with two flaming red eyes." Brandishing the torch, keys, and cutlass, the skeletal apparition confronts and converts the rationalist who is seen in a stylized swoon as the figure nears.

Sarah Wilkinson, *The Castle of Montabino; or, The Orphan Sisters* (London: Dean and Munday, 1810), 38 pages.

   A chapbook from the prolific pen of a leading lady chapbooker, Sarah Wilkinson, who haunted the chapbook marketplace for more than two decades and whose palette oozed every shade of blood. The single source of light in the engraving radiates from the phantom silhouetted in the Gothic archway. The moment is another stock Gothic scene, the spectral encounter when the thing from the other world confronts the maiden causing here a triple swoon of awestruck belief. Although the moral nature of the specter in the portal is indeterminate, the well-versed Gothic maiden, like *The Mysteries of Udolpho's* Emily St. Aubert, when the black veil drops away from the portrait, will faint on cue during every liaison with the supernatural.

ZITTAW THE CRUEL.

Zittaw gaining the Affections of Amelia Perowitz.

Sarah Wilkinson, *Zittaw the Cruel; or, The Woodsman's Daughter, A Polish Romance* (London: B. Mace, n.d.), 36 pages.

Another curious corner of the Sadleir-Black Collection features Slavonic or Polish Gothic romances which seem to have enjoyed a steady vogue. Lengthy Slavonic Gothics such as Mary Charlton's four-volume romance *Phedora; or, The Forest of Minski* (1798) and Thomas Pike Lathy's *The Invisible Enemy; or, The Mines of Wielitska, A Polish Legendary Romance* (1806) published by Lane and Newman's Minerva Press were widely read and went through successive editions. In chapbook form, Slavonic Gothics such as *Zittaw the Cruel* appealed strongly to the chapbook audience. The woodcut shows Zittaw in the uniform of a Russian hussar engaged in the arboreal seduction of the heroine, Amelia Perowitz.

Ildefonzo and Alberoni; or, Tales of Horror (London: Tegg and Castleman, 1803).
    Argosies and anthologies such as *Ildefonzo and Alberoni* offered the Gothic reader sundry horrors based on medieval ballads and legends of the demon huntsman and ghostly rider. Shown here amidst "darkness visible" is the Gothic sampler's frontispiece with the beckoning cadaverous figure inviting the human figures to take death's last ride with him. The allegory of death's victory over life has been captured by the illustrator's rendition of death's black stallion or the devil's stud looking on appreciatively as the two mortals prepare to accompany their fiendish guide.

Maximilian and Selina; or, The Mysterious Abbot, A Flemish Tale (London: Tegg and Castleman, 1804), 36 pages.

Sadleir-Black contains many short unsigned Gothics manufactured and marketed by Tegg and Castleman. Fatal peril or deadly predicament atop a tower is a common dilemma for the Gothic victim. The perilous or infernal tower also figures prominently as a place of nefarious aspiration in Beckford's *Vathek*. About to be hurled from the turret by his malicious brother, Adolphus de Monvel, Maximilian's doom seems sealed as a pathetic mother figure murmurs an ineffectual prayer unheard in the fallen and godless universe. The scene is the chapbook's initial spectacular incident in a series of unremitting crises.

The Midnight Assassin; or The Confessions of the Monk Rinaldi, containing a complete history of his diabolical machinations and unparalleled ferocity. Together with a circumstantial account of that scourge of mankind, the inquisition, with the manner of bringing to trial those unfortunate beings who are at its disposal. Marvellous Magazine and Compendium of Prodigies, May 1802. (facing page)

Serialized Gothics appearing singly or in installments in periodicals such as *The Marvellous Magazine and Compendium of Prodigies* are yet another mutation of the Gothic novel. *The Midnight Assassin* is Mrs. Radcliffe's *The Italian* reduced from three volumes to 30,000 words and heavily eroticized. The incubus poised at the maiden's bedside is a creature of sexual nightmare complete with phallic dagger. The guardian locket on the maiden's breast causes the Monk Rinaldi to hesitate just as Father Schedoni had wavered over the sleeping figure of his niece, Ellena de Rosalba, in *The Italian*'s climatic horror-and-recognition scene.

The Secret Tribunal; or, The Court of Wincelaus (London: Tegg and Castleman, 1803). Overleaf.

A considerable number of novels in Sadleir-Black deal with the plots and counterplots of the Vehmgericht or secret Fehmic court, the Illuminati, Masonic societies, and other secret societies dedicated to international conspiracy and ritual sacrifice. The anonymous *Secret Tribunal; or, The Court of Wincelaus* (1803) is an utterly ordinary chapbook example of this *Horrid Mysteries* strain of Gothicism. The title page illustration, however, is an extraordinary projection of Gothic sublimity whose power overshadows the chapbook's vapid text. All of the distorted religious iconography of the Gothic romance converges in this remarkable engraving. The melodramatic flight of the maiden through an eternal night and from some pursuing unseen force resonates with paradises lost forever. The castle or cathedral, once a refuge or sanctuary, now glowers on the horizon like Milton's Pandemonium. The stark granite cross which the fleeing maiden embraces so desperately has ceased entirely to be a sacramental object and has become its very opposite, an emblem of ultimate terror. It is black, monstrous, and malignantly animated, its traditional salvational properties replaced by the graveyard gloom. Her hopeless flight has brought the maiden from one place of darkness and damnation to another equally dark and foreboding. Yet, she is determined to cling heroically to those decadent symbols of a religious and social order now morally transformed. The maiden in this illustration symbolizes the essence of the Gothic experience, that same "eloquent disequilibrium of the spirit" of which Sadleir had spoken in characterizing the Zeitgeist of Gothic romance.

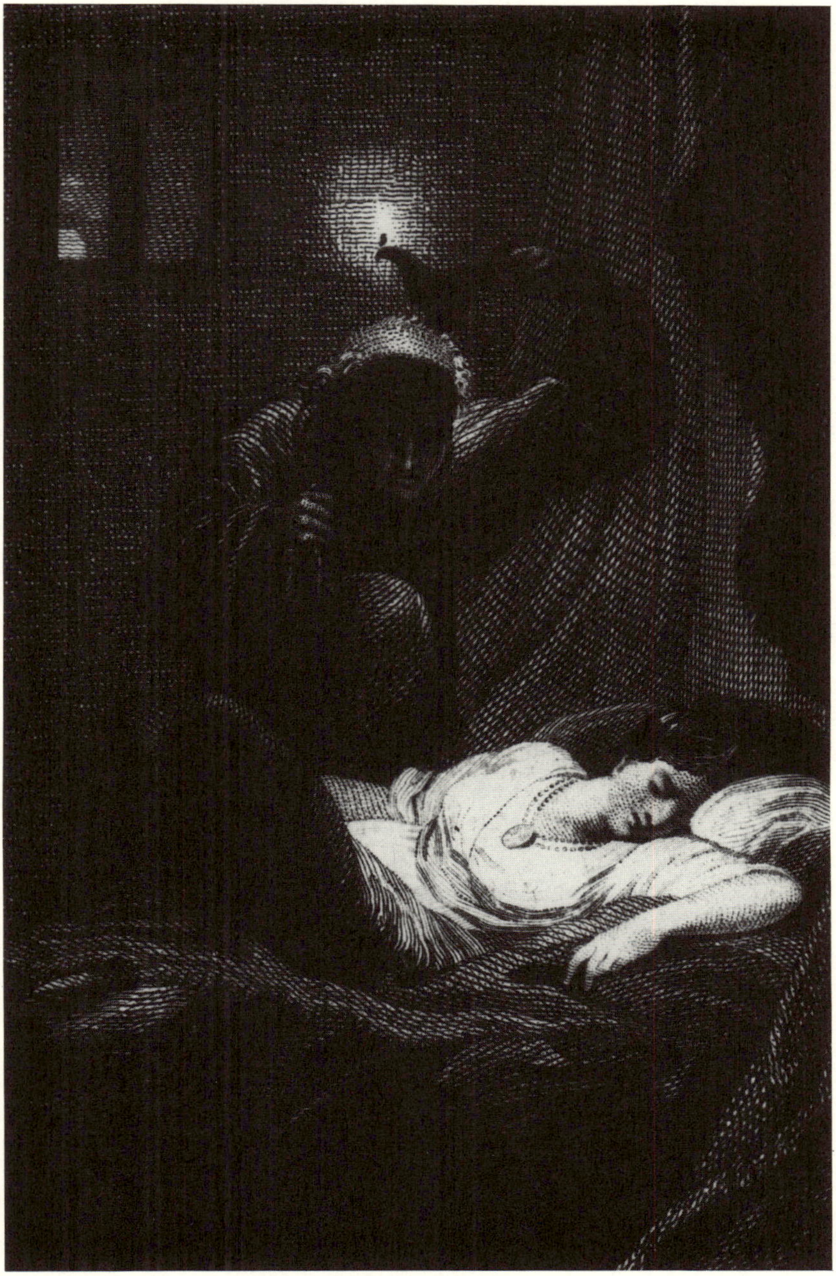

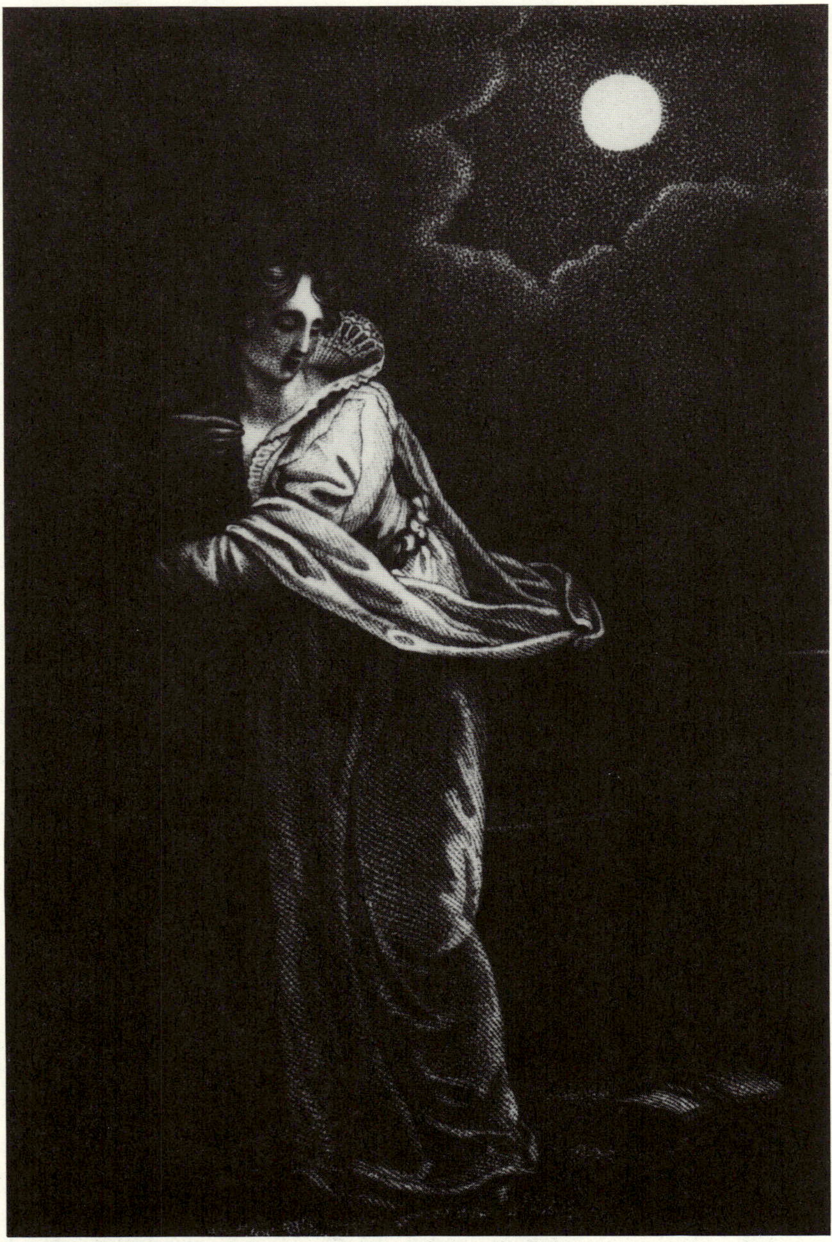

Contributors to Volume 26

Franz A. Birgel is an Assistant Professor of German at Muhlenberg College in Allentown, Pennsylvania. In addition to Wieland and Wezel, his research interests also include German cinema, and he has published articles on the films of Werner Herzog, Edgar Reitz, Luis Trenker, and Veit Harlan.

Huguette Cohen is a Research Associate in French at the University of Illinois, Urbana-Champaign. She is the author of *La Figure dialogique dans Jacques le fataliste* and of numerous articles on Diderot. She is at present engaged in a lengthy study of his *Paradoxe sur le comédien*.

Glen Colburn, an Assistant Professor of English at Morehead State University in Morehead, Kentucky, has done several conference papers on Fielding, the novel, and hysteria. He is currently working on a book-length study of hysteria and hypochondria as a cluster of traits that characterize eighteenth-century Britain's self-perception and novelistic narratives.

Sharon Long Damoff teaches English at Rollins College Brevard and is a doctoral candidate at the University of Florida, where she is currently completing a study of the novels of Frances Burney.

A. P. Dierick, whose most recent book is *Gottfried Benn and His Critics: The Major Interpretations*, serves as Associate Professor and Chair of the Department of Germanic Languages and Literatures at the University of Toronto. He has published numerous articles on German and Dutch literature and is currently researching eighteenth-century German aesthetics and political polarization in the writings of the Weimar Republic.

Frederick S. Frank, Professor Emeritus of English at Allegheny College, Meadville, Pennsylvania, and former NEH Research chairholder at Allegheny, has published widely on early British and American Gothic fiction. Among his newest publications are *Montague Summers: A Bibliographical Portrait* and *Guide to the Gothic II: An Annotated Bibliography of Criticism, 1983-1993*. He is currently writing *The Poe Encyclopedia,* to be published by Greenwood Press.

Thomas Kaminski teaches in the English Department at Loyola University in Chicago. He is the author of *The Early Career of Samuel Johnson*.

Barbara Knauff is Assistant Professor of French at St. Mary's College of Maryland. She is currently working on seventeenth- and eighteenth-century imaginary voyages and their portrayal of the linguistic encounter with the Other.

Jacqueline Letzter, Assistant Professor of French at the University of Utah in Salt Lake City, has recently completed her Ph.D. dissertation entitled "To Read or Not to Read: Questions of Education in the Works of Isabelle de Charrière." She is currently studying the debate over the legacy of Rousseau among women intellectuals during the French Revolution.

Michael McKeon, Director of English Graduate Studies at Rutgers University, is the author of *Politics and Poetry in Restoration England* and *The Origins of the English Novel*, which won the Modern Language Association's James Russell Lowell Prize for the year 1987. He is currently investigating the way the early modern division of knowledge gave to modernity its familiar separations and oppositions. The essay in this volume was the eleventh Clifford Lecture given at the ASECS meeting in Tucson in April of 1995.

Julie D. Prandi is Professor of German at Illinois Wesleyan University. She has published articles on German dramas of Goethe, Kleist, and Büchner; and her most recent book is *"Dare To Be Happy!" A Study of Goethe's Ethics*. Her work on Anna Louisa Karsch, an eighteenth-century German poet, has been included in two recent anthologies of German women writers.

Ronald C. Rosbottom was Executive Secretary of ASECS 1978–82, chairman of Romance Languages at Ohio State 1982–88, and then Dean of the Faculty at Amherst College 1989–95. In 1995, he returned to the classroom as a Professor of French and European Studies, and teaches courses in eighteenth-century art, the history of Paris, and autobiography.

John Sainsbury is Associate Professor of British History at Brock University, St. Catharines, Ontario. His publications include *Disaffected Patriots: London Supporters of Revolutionary America, 1769–1782*. At present he is working on various aspects of the career of John Wilkes.

Mary Sheriff is Professor of Art and Adjunct Professor of Women's Studies at the University of North Carolina at Chapel Hill. She has recently published *The Exceptional Woman: Elizabeth Vigée-Lebrun and the Cultural Politics of Art* and is co-editor of *Eighteenth-Century Studies*.

Frank Shuffelton teaches American Literature at the University of Rochester. He has published a biography of Thomas Hooker, two bibliographic volumes that record and comment on the writings about Thomas Jefferson from 1826 to the present, and has edited volumes of essays on ethnicity in early America and on the American Enlightenment.

Miriam L. Wallace is Assistant Professor of British and American Literature at New College of the University of South Florida. She has published on Virginia Woolf and Walter Scott, and is currently completing an essay on historical constructions of gender and genre in Elizabeth Inchbald's *A Simple Story*, as well as writing a book on changing constructions of gendered subjectivity in eighteenth-century British literature.

Executive Board 1995–1996

President: **Barbara Stafford**, William B. Ogden Distinguished Service Professor, University of Chicago
First-Vice President: **J. Paul Hunter**, Chester D. Tripp Professor of Humanities, University of Chicago
Second-Vice President: **Marie Hélène Huet**, Frederick Huetwell Professor of French, University of Michigan
Past President: **Ronald C. Rosbottom**, Professor of French, Amherst College
Treasurer: **Catherine Lafarge**, Graduate School of Arts & Sciences, Bryn Mawr College
Executive Secretary: **Jeffrey Smitten**, Professor of English, Utah State University

Members-at-Large
John Bender, Professor of Comparative Literature, Stanford University
Carol Blum, Professor of French, State University of New York-Stony Brook
Dena Goodman, Professor of History, Louisiana State University
Anita Guerrini, Professor of History, University of California-Santa Barbara
Jeffrey Merrick, Professor of History, University of Wisconsin-Milwaukee
Gordon Schochet, Professor of Political Science, Rutgers University

Administrative Office
Accounts Manager: **Hailey Brady**, Utah State University
Office Manager: **Deborah Gessaman**, Utah State University

**For information about the
American Society for Eighteenth-Century Studies, please contact:**
ASECS
P.O. Box 7867
Wake Forest University
Winston-Salem, NC 27109
Telephone: (336) 727-4694
Fax: (336) 727-4697
E-mail: asecs@wfu.edu
Web Site: http://direct.press.jhu.edu/associations/asecs

American Society for Eighteenth-Century Studies

Patron Members 1995–1996

Paul Alkon
Mark S. Auburn
James G. Basker
Barbara Becker-Cantarino
R. Bernasconi
Theodore E. D. Braun
Peter M. Briggs
Morris Brownell
Patricia Brückman
Joseph A. Byrnes
Marilyn Carbonell
Louis Cornell
Robert Adams Day
Roland Desne
Frank H. Ellis
Roger J. Fechner
Jan Fergus
Dustin H. Griffin
Phyllis Guskin
Basil Guy
Roger Hahn
Robert H. Hopkins

Lynn A. Hunt
Margaret C. Jacob
Annibel Jenkins
Gary Kates
David H. Koss
J. Patrick Lee
Geoffrey Marshall
H. W. Matalene
Helen Louise McGuffie
Donald C. Mell, Jr.
John H. Middendorf
Earl Miner
Dennis Moore
Frank Palmeri
Virginia J. Peacock
Jane Perry-Camp
R. G. Peterson
John Valdimir Price
Ralph W. Rader
John Radner
Ronald C. Rosbottom
Treadwell Ruml II

Harold Schiffman
Richard Sher
English Showalter
John Sitter
Patricia Meyer Spacks
Susan Staves
Mary M. Stewart
Ann T. Straulman
Masashi Suzuki
Diana M. Thomas
Connie C. Thorson
James L. Thorson
David F. Venturo
Howard D. Weinbrot
David H. Weinglass
James A. Winn
Calhoun Winton
James Woolley
William J. Zachs
Lisa M. Zeitz

Sponsoring Members 1995–1996

David R. Anderson
Jack Armistead
Paula Backscheider
Jerry C. Beasley
David Blewett
Carol Blum
Thomas F. Bonnell
Martha F. Bowden
Leo Braudy
Leslie Ellen Brown
Martine W. Brownley
Martha L. Brunson
Thomas M. Columbus
Michael J. Conlon
Edward Copeland
Brian Corman
Howard Coughlin, Jr.
Patricia B. Craddock

William Cunningham, Jr.
Alix S. Deguise
Pierre Deguise
Margaret Anne Doody
William F. Edmiston
JoLynn Edwards
A. C. Elias, Jr.
Antoinette Emch-Deriaz
Clarissa C. Erwin
Timothy Erwin
David Fairer
Charles N. Fifer
Bernadette Fort
James D. Garrison
Josephine Grieder
Joyce Grossman
Diana Guiragossian-Carr
Elizabeth Harries

Karsten Harries
Phillip Harth
Donald M. Hassler
Carla H. Hay
Robert P. Hay
Daniel Heartz
Charles H. Hinnant
J. Paul Hunter
Kathryn Montgomery Hunter
Adrienne D. Hytier
Malcolm Jack
Regina Mary Janes
Thomas Jemielity
Loftus Townshend Jestin
Claudia L. Johnson
Robert P. Kalmey
Frederick M. Keener
Shirley Strum Kenny

320 / *Sponsoring Members*

Charles A. Knight
Philip Koch
Gwin J. Kolb
Colby H. Kullman
Catherine Lafarge
Darline Gay Levy
Joanna Lipking
Lawrence Lipking
Florence Mack
Maynard Mack
David D. Mann
John A. McCarthy
Alan T. McKenzie
David McNeil
Shirley McNerney Rendell
Linda E. Merians
Dewey F. Mosby
Maureen E. Mulvihill
Felicity Nussbaum
Mary Ann O'Donnell
Hal N. Opperman

Douglas Lane Patey
Stuart Peterfreund
J.G.A. Pocock
James Pollak
Irwin Primer
Tom Prins
Richard E. Quaintance, Jr.
Ruben D. Quintero
Thomas J. Regan
W. E. Rex
John Richetti
Albert J. Rivero
Betty Rizzo
Raymond Rizzo
Lawrence A. Ruff
Peter Sabor
Mona Scheuermann
Barbara Brandon Schnorrenberg
Gordon J. Schochet
Robert G. Schwartz
Donald T. Siebert

Jeffrey Smitten
Robert Spector
G. A. Starr
Joan Koster Stemmler
Damie Stillman
Zenzo Suzuki
A. G. Tannenbaum
Janice Thaddeus
Dennis Todd
Betty Perry Townsend
Daniel Townsend
Linda Veronika Troost
Randolph Trumbach
Jack Undank
Charles Vallely
Peter Van Roijen
Peter Wagner
Renee Waldinger
Tara Ghoshal Wallace
Jan Widmayer
Charles G. S. Williams

Institutional Members 1995-1996

American Antiquarian Society
Arizona State University Library
Brown University–John Carter Brown Library
University of California Library
Carlyle House Historic Park
Case Western Reserve University–Freiberger Library
Claremont College–Honnold Mudd Library
Colonial Williamsburg Foundation
University of Connecticut–Homer Babbidge Library
Dalhousie University Library
Darnall's Chance
Early American History & Culture Institute
Emory University–Robert W. Woodruff Library
University of Evansville Library
Florida State University
Folger Institute
Fordham University Library
Harvard College Library
Herzob August Bibliothek
Indiana University at Kokomo Library
Johns Hopkins University–Milton S. Eisenhower Library
Mount Saint Vincent University Library
University of North Carolina–Davis Library
Northern Illinois University Libraries
University of Notre Dame–Hesburgh Library
Ohio State University Libraries
University of Pennsylvania Library
University of Rochester Library
Rutgers University–Alexander Library
SUNY at Binghamton Library
Smithsonian Institution
University of Southern California
University of Southern Mississippi
Stanford University–Green Library
Swarthmore College Library
University of Tennessee Library
University of Texas at Austin
Towson State University
Tulane University Library
University of Tulsa–McFarlin Library
University Press of Kentucky
Utah State University–Merrill Library
Utrecht Universiteit Letterenbibliotheek
University of Victoria–McPherson Library
Wm. Andrews Clark Memorial Library
Washington University–Olin Library
Westfalische Wilhelms University
Yale Center for British Art Reference Library
Yale University–Sterling Memorial Library
York University–Scott Library

Index

Every effort has been made to include in this index all identifiable persons named in essays who lived during the long eighteenth-century or before. Readers seeking twentieth-century critics' names should check the endnotes of individual essays. Note numbers are cited in cases when persons are mentioned only in endnotes, but not in the body, of a particular essay.

Addison, Joseph, 20, 60, 74, 251, 258
Aesthetics: in early American literature, 74–75; origin of, 74
African influence, 82–83
Age of Reason, 147
Alderman Library, University of Virginia, 287
Alembert, Jean le Rond d', 249
Alexander, 52: and Apelles, 52
Almon, John, 159
Alphabet, 34–35, 37–38, 48
Alter, Robert, 87
Althusser, Louis, 179
Ambivalence, 226–27
Anglican Church, 152, 156–58, 161
Anglicanism, 232, 237–38, 240–41
Anne, Queen of England, 69
Ariosto, Ludovico, 32
Aristotle, 74, 187, 254
Armstrong, John, 159
Augustanism: opposition, 57, 61, 64–65, 68
Augustus (Roman Emperor), 57–62, 66, 68
Austen, Jane, 289–90
Arnaud, François Thomas Marie de Baculard d', 293

Bage, Robert, 295
Barrett, C. F., 303
Barrett, Eaton Stannard, 293–294
Batteux, Charles, Abbé, 74
Baumgarten, Alexander, 74
Baxter, Andrew, 155

Beckford, William, 294–95, 309
Belles-lettres, 76–77
Bennett, Agnes Maria, 296
Bible, the, 236–40
Blake, William, 26
Bodmer, Johann Jakob, 251, 256–59, 261
Body, the, 175–93
Boileau-Despréaux, Nicolas, 141, 253–54
Bolingbroke, Henry St. John, Viscount, 155, 162
Boswell, James, 11, 23, 151, 153, 155–56
Boucher, François: *La Toilette*, 43
Bowdoin, James, 78
Bradley, James, 166
Brecht, Bertolt, 147
Breitinger, Johann Jakob, 251, 256–61
Brown, Charles Brockden, 288–89
Büchner, Georg, 147
Burgh, James, 167
Burke, Edmund, 200, 204–5, 252–53
Burney, Frances, 231–46
Bute, John Stuart, third Earl of, 161–62, 165
Butler, Joseph, 240–41, 243

Cabanis, Pierre-Jean-George: *On the Relations Between the Physical and Moral Aspects of Man*, 45
Cassatt, Mary, 48
Challe, Charles-Michel-Ange, 198

Chardin, Jean-Baptiste-Siméon, 196, 200
Charity, 231–46
Charles II, 60–61, 65
Charlton, Mary, 292, 307
Charrière, Isabelle de, 209–30
Chateaubriand, François René, 250
Chatterton, Thomas, 11
Cheyne, George, 89–91, 95–96, 103–5, 108, 111–12
Christianity, 231–32, 237–41
Churchill, Charles, 157, 160
Cibber, Colley, 62
Cicero, 74
Claudius, Matthias (as translator), 276
Cochin, Claude-Nicholas, 40
Coleridge, Samuel Taylor, 26, 250, 253
Collier, Mary, 23
Collins, William, 11–12
Colonialism: and pastoral, 8–9, 11–14, 26
Condillac, Étienne Bonnot de, 247
Constant, Benjamin, 222
Corday, Charlotte, 32, 50–52
Corneille, Pierre, 67
Corradini, Gertrude, 158
Craftsman, The, 61
Crookenden, Isaac, 296, 304
Crousaz, Jean-Pierre de, 254
Cultural comparison, 125–28, 130, 134
Curties, T. J. Horsley, 295

Dacre, Charlotte ("Rosa Matilda"), 292, 295
Dance, Nathaniel, 45
Dashwood, Sir Francis, 165
David, Jacques-Louis: and Napoleon, 52; *Marat Assassinated*, 32, 48–52
Defamiliarization: figures of, 125–36

Deshays, Jean-Baptiste, 196–97, 200
Deism, 154–57, 161
Delarivier Manley, 23–24
Delaunay, Nicholas: *Chiffre d'Amour, Le*, 32–34
Dent, Edward (musicologist), 274–75
Dibutadis, 37–38, 40–41, 46
Dickens, Charles, 289, 291
Diderot, Denis, 154, 195–207, 247, 251, 254, 263–64
Dilettanti, Society of, 158
Doyen, Gabriel-François, 197; 199
Dryden, John, 14, 60–61, 65, 67, 70–71
DuBos, Jean-Baptiste, 74, 197, 257, 259, 262
Duck, Stephen, 21–23
Ducray-Duminil, François Guillaume, 293

Education: art as, 280; corporal punishment as, 278–79; drama of [*Bildungsdrama*], 274–75; towards Enlightenment, 281; love as, 279; women's, 209, 211, 221, 226–27
Ekphrasis, 206nn6, 12
Elegiac poetry, 81, 83
Empire, British, 77–79
Enargeia, 197, 206nn6, 15
Enlightenment, 152, 154, 159, 161–62, 281; aesthetics, 280; German, 139, 147; ideals, 273
Essay on Woman, 152, 160–64
Eusden, Laurence, 62
Eve, 35–36, 38, 47–48

Farrell, James T., 294
Female virtues: charity, 235–38, 241, 243–44; modesty, 235–38, 241–44
Femininity, 178–80, 188, 190

Feminism / feminist, 175–76, 180, 190
Ferry, Luc, 75
Fichte, Johann Gottlieb, 270n.42
Fielding, Henry, 144, 146; *Amelia*, 87–91, 93–94, 96, 98–100, 102–3, 105, 107–11, 115–16, 118, 120
Finch, Anne, Countess of Winchilsea, 14–16
Flammenberg, Lawrence, 289
Foucault, Michel, 116n14, 118n38, 119n51, 175, 179
Fox, Charles James, 292
Fragonard, Jean-Honoré: *If he were only as faithful!*, 32; Fantasy portrait of an old man, 38; *Love Letters*, 32; *Souvenir, The*, 30–32, 35–38, 43, 45–49, 199
Franklin, Benjamin, 74
Freemasons, 273–74, 281; Masonic ideas and traditions, 273; Masonic eulogy, 278
Freethinking, 153–55, 167
Freud, Sigmund, 45

Gallitzin (Princess), 247–48, 262, 265
Gallitzin, Dimitri (Prince), 247
Gay, John, 10
Gefühlskultur, 250, 259
Gélieu, Isabelle de, 222–23
Gellert, Christian Fürchtegott, 141
Gender, 175–83, 186–90; and genre, 136; and pastoral, 9, 14–17, 19–25; and stylistic devices, 136; and medicine and the novel, 103–5, 110–12, 108–11, 116, 122–24
Genius, 256–58, 260
Genlis, Félicité de Saint-Aubin, 293
George I, 62–63
George II, 57, 61–62, 64–66, 68–69
George III, 162
German Enlightenment, 139, 147

Gessner, Salomon, 197, 250
Giseke, Nicolaus Dietrich, 141
Gleich, Joseph Alois, 293
Godwin, William, 295
Goethe, Johann Wolfgang von, 142, 144, 248–50, 252, 262; 310
Goldoni, Carlo, 138n18
Goldsmith, Oliver, 10, 18–19
Gordon, Thomas, 155–57
Gothic bibliographers: Robert Kerr Black, 287–88, 293–95, 297, 313; Dorothy Blakey, 297; Jakob Brauchli, 294, 300; Frederick S. Frank, 287–313; Maurice Lévy, 300–1; David McKinney, 297; Michael Sadleir, 287–302; Montague Summers, 290, 298–301; Ann B. Tracy, 297, 301–2; Devendra P. Varma, 290, 299, 301–2; William Whyte Watt, 299
Gothic fiction collections, 287–313
Gothic illustrations, 302–13
Gottsched, Johann Christoph, 253, 256–259
Gouges, Olympe de, 209
Graffigny, Françoise de: *Lettres d'une Péruvienne*, 125–38
Gray, Henry, 191n3
Gray, Thomas, 18, 250
Greuze, Jean-Baptiste, 196–97
Grimm, Friedrich, 195–96, 201
Grosse, Karl, 289, 297
Guez de Balzac, 60, 70n13

Habermas, Jürgen, 77–78
Hallé, Noël, 198
Haller, Albrecht von, 250
Hamann, Johann Georg, 252
Hedgeland, Isabella (Kelly), 297
Helme, Elizabeth, 292, 295
Hemsterhuis, François (Frans), 247–71
Hemsterhuis, Tiberius, 248

Herder, Johann Gottfried, 48, 247–48, 252, 257, 260, 263, 266
Herring, Thomas, 156
Hervey, James, 250
Hogarth, William, 36, 38, 45, 54–55, 254
Holbach, Paul-Henri, Baron de, 154
Holcroft, Thomas, 295
Home, John, 12
Homer, 76
Horace, 13, 18, 57–59, 62, 64–69, 72, 76, 140–41, 197
Huber, Ludwig Ferdinand, 223
Hume, David, 74, 155–56, 251, 257
Hutcheson, Francis, 251–53, 263
Hutchinson, Arthur, 290–96.
Huysmans, J. K., 288
Hysteria, 88–91, 94–96, 98–100, 101–4, 106, 108–17, 119–23; cultural hysteria, 89, 91; discursive hysteria and its symptoms: —incoherence, 88–92, 97–98, 123; —digressions, 103–8

Idealism, 139, 145
Imaginary, the: 177–79, 182–83, 185, 188–89
Imaginary voyage, 126, 135–36
Interdisciplinarity: and disciplinarity, 1–5
Ircastrensis, 293
Ireland, William Henry, 295
Irigaray, Luce, 176–80, 182–83, 188–90
Irrationalism, 252, 262

Jacobi, Friedrich Heinrich, 248, 252, 263
Jacobi, Johann Georg, 144
James II, 60
Johnson, Samuel, 12–13, 151, 164, 167

Jonson, Ben 72
Juvenal, 12, 57, 59, 62, 64, 68–70, 140–41

Kahlert, Karl Friedrich, 297
Kandinsky, Wassily, 294
Kant, Immanuel, 48, 74–75, 260
Kauffman, Angelica, 45
Kidgell, John, 163, 165

Laclos, Pierre Choderlos de, 154
Lagrenée, Jean-Louis-François the Elder, 196, 198
La Mettrie, Julien Offray de, 139
Laqueur, Thomas, 115, 120–21, 123, 175–77, 180, 181
La Roche, Sophie, 147
Lathom, Francis, 289–90, 292, 297–98
Lathy, Thomas Pike, 307
Latitudinarianism, 157
Lavater, Johann Caspar, 257
Lawler, Dennis, 293
Leapor, Mary, 15–19
Leibniz, Gottfried Wilhelm, 254, 257
Le Fanu, Joseph Sheridan, 299
Lee, Harriet, 292
Lee, Sophia, 292
Leonardo da Vinci, 257
Leprince, Jean-Baptiste, 199, 201
Lessing, Gotthold Ephraim: *Laokoon*, 74, 268
Letter, 29, 32, 34–38, 41, 48, 51
Lewis, Matthew Gregory, 289, 292–93, 295, 298–99
Libera, Zdislaw, 301
Libertinism, 151–68
Limits, transgression of, 195, 198–99, 202, 204–5
Locke, John, 139, 185
Lomazzo, Giovanni, 45

Longinus, 200
Louis XIV, 52, 60; and Charles Le Brun, 52
Loutherbourg, Jacques-Philippe, 199, 201
Lowth, Robert, 156
Lucian, 32, 141
Lytton, Edward Bulwer, first Baron, 294

Maecenas, 58–59, 66, 70, 76–77
Malherbe, François de, 60
Mallarmé, Stéphane, 288
Mandelbaum, Maurice, 92
Mandeville, Bernard, 91–92, 94–96, 98–101, 105, 108
Mannerists, the, 45
Manningham, Sir Richard, 93, 95, 103
Marie–Antoinette, 38, 41
Martial, 57–59, 62, 64, 68, 70
Marvell, Andrew, 17
Masculinity, 176, 178, 180, 181–84, 186, 188–90
Maturin, Charles Robert, 294–95, 298–99
Maupassant, Guy de, 299
Medical theory of the eighteenth century, 92–96
Medicine: and the new mechanical philosophy, 96–99, 102–5; gender, and the novel, 103–5, 110–12
Medmenham monks, 159, 165
Meeke, Mary, 295
Melville, Herman, 294
Merck, Johann Heinrich, 142–44
Michelangelo, 45
Milton, John, 36, 66, 81, 258–59
Miramond, M. de, 54n16
Molière, Jean-Baptiste, 226
Moment, 197–99, 201

Montaigne, Michel de, 254
Montesquieu, Charles de Secondat, Baron de la Brède et de, 254
Moore, George, 295
Montagu, Edward Wortley, 24
Montagu, Lady Mary Wortley, 24
Montesquieu, Charles, Baron de: *Lettres persanes*, 125–27, 136
Mozart, Wolfgang Amadeus: as Freemason, 274; *The Magic Flute* music, 275, 280–81; *Magic Flute* libretto, 282n2; incidental music for *Thamos*, 282n2

Napoleon, 52; and Jacques-Louis David, 52
Natural: the concept of, 93, 96–97, 101–3, 107–9, 112–13; man, 276; philosophy, 89–90, 97
Nature: and Reason, —integration of, 276–78, 281; —synthesis of, 277, 280; as emotion, feeling, sensibility, 276, 280; as sensuality, Eros, sexuality, 276–77, 279–80; religion of, 154, 159; represented by the four elements, 280–81
Naubert, Christiane Benediktine, 293
Northanger Novels, the, 289–90
Novalis [Friedrich von Hardenberg], 252, 255, 263
Novel: gender, medicine, and the, 103–5, 110–12
Novels: reading, 217–20

Opposition (to Sir Robert Walpole), 57, 61, 64–66, 68
Oppositional reading, 29–30, 32, 38, 50, 52
Organ morale, 263–64
Ormsby, Ann, 298
Otway, Thomas, 67

Ovid, 32, 59, 70
Owenson, Sidney (Lady Morgan), 292

Panegyric, 62, 64
Parsons, Eliza, 289, 292, 298
Pastoral, 7–26, 32, 34–35, 38; and colonialism, 8–9, 11–14, 26; and culture, 7–26; and environmentalism, 26; and gender, 9, 14–17, 19–25; and the Golden Age, 9, 16; and nature, 7–26; and Romanticism, 26; and social status, 10, 14, 19–25; conception, 199
Patronage, 58–59, 61, 68
Peacock, Thomas Love, 293
Perception: Hemsterhuis's theory of, 264–66
Perfectibility, 147
Periphrasis, 125–36
Phallicism, 158–60
Philosophy: natural, 89–90, 97; new mechanical and medicine, 96–99, 102–5
Pierre, Jean-Baptiste-Marie, 198–99
Pitt, William, the Elder, 161, 164
Plato, 74
Pliny the Elder, 37, 40
Poe, Edgar Allan, 288, 299
Polite letters, 60–61, 66, 68–69
Pope, Alexander, 10, 57, 69, 81, 141, 161; *Epistle to Augustus*, 57, 61–69
Porter, Jane, 292
Potter, Thomas, 160–61
Prest, Thomas Peckett, 296
Prévost, Antoine-François, 40
Price, Richard, 167–68
Priestley, Joseph, 155, 167
Public sphere, 78–81
Purcell, John, 92, 94, 104–5, 110

Quipos, 129, 132–33

Racine, Jean, 67
Radcliffe, Ann, 287, 289, 292, 294–96, 298, 310–11
Radicalism, 152, 164–68
Realism, 139, 144
Reeve, Clara, 295, 298
Richardson, Samuel, 254
Robert, Hubert, 199
Robinson, Mary, 295
Roche, Regina Maria, 289, 292, 298
Romanticism, 249, 251–52, 257, 264; and pastoral, 26; and pre-Romanticism, 249–51, 257–59, 264, 266
Rousseau, Jean-Jacques, 34, 45, 47, 50, 139, 146, 149, 210–11, 214, 250–51, 262–63, 274
Rushton, Edward, 11

Sackville, Lord George, 161
Saint-Aubin, Gabriel de: *The Private Academy*, 30, 43–46
Sainte-Beuve, Charles Augustin, 127
Saint-Evremond, Charles, 70
Sandwich, John Montagu, fourth Earl of, 159, 165
Sannazaro, Jacopo, 10, 32
Satire, 139–50
Savage, Richard, 62–63
Schelling, Friedrich Wilhelm von, 270
Schickaneder, Emanuel (as librettist), 274, 282
Schiller, Friedrich, 261, 293; *Don Carlos*, 274; theory of aesthetics, 280
Schlegel, Friedrich, 252, 263
Schmidt, Christian Heinrich, 142
Sensibility, 153, 159–60

Serpentine line, 36, 38, 43, 45, 47
Sex / sexuality / heterosexuality / homosexuality, 175–84, 186, 188–90
Shaftesbury, Anthony Ashley Cooper, third Earl of, 74, 76, 155, 196, 251–52, 254, 257–59, 262–63
Shakespeare, William, 65–66, 296
Shebbeare, John, 164
Shelley, Elizabeth, 294
Shelley, Percy Bysshe, 289, 294, 298
Sheridan, Richard Brinsley, 292, 294
Sickelmore, Richard, 302
Sidney, Sir Philip, 66, 72
Signature, 37–38, 45–46, 48, 51–52
Sister arts, 196
Sleath, Eleanor, 289, 298
Smeth, Théodore de, 248
Smith, Charlotte, 292
Smollett, Tobias, 11–12, 233
Sodomy, 152, 159–60
Southey, Robert, 11
Spenser, Edmund, 66
Spinoza, Baruch de, 248
Stanton, Domna, 59
Steele, Sir Richard, 10, 19–20
Sterne, Laurence, 143, 176, 180–81, 189–90
Stone, George, 161
Storm and Stress [*Sturm und Drang*], 140, 144, 247, 249, 251, 266
Strother, Edward, 90–91, 94
Sublime, the, 199, 204–7
Swift, Jonathan, 10–11, 140, 146–47, 149
Subjectivity, 179–80, 184–85, 188, 190
Sydenham, Thomas, 92, 94–95, 102, 108, 112
Symbolic, the: 177–80, 182–83, 185–86

Tableau, 197
Tacitus, 57–58, 69
Tacking, 212, 221, 227–30
Tasso, Torquato: *Jerusalem Liberata*, 32, 46
Temple, Richard Grenville, second Earl of, 160; neoclassical palace of named Stowe, 160
Terrasson, Jean: his novel *Sethos*, 273, 276–78, 280
Teutsche Merkur, Der, 141–50
Thompson, Edward, 166
Thomson, James, 17, 250
Tickell, Thomas, 10, 14
Tieck, Ludwig, 147
Tillotson, John, 163, 238
Trollope, Anthony, 298

Urfé, Honoré d', 32

Varius, 66
Vernet, Claude-Joseph, 195–96, 199, 201–7
Vien, Joseph-Marie, 196–97
Vigée-Lebrun, Elisabeth: *Self-Portrait*, 29–30, 36, 38–42; *Souvenirs*, 42; *Venus Tying the Wings of Cupid*, 36
Virgil, 9, 11, 15, 58–59, 66, 76
Voltaire, François Marie Arouet, 125–28, 146, 149–50, 154, 247; *Alzire*, 125; *Contes philosophiques*, 126; *L'Ingénu*, 126; *Lettres philosophiques*, 126

Wainewright, Jeremiah, 119
Waller, Edmund, 67, 71
Walpole, Horace, 151, 289, 295, 298
Walpole, Sir Robert, 57, 61–62, 64, 68
Warburton, William, 161–62, 165
Watkins, Lucy, 305
Wezel, Johann Karl, 139–48

Wheatley, Phillis, 75–83
Whiggism, 151, 153, 155, 157–58, 162, 164–66
Whitbread, Samuel, 292
Whytt, Robert, 101–2
Wieland, Christoph Martin, 139–48, 250, 282–83
Wilkes, John, 151–68
Wilkes, Sarah, 153, 168
Wilkinson, Sarah, 306–7
William III, 61, 70
Winckelmann, Johann Joachim, 154, 248, 253–54
Wirkungsaesthetik, 251, 256, 260

Wisdom, Temple of, 275–76, 281
Wit, 256–57
Wolfe, General James, 79
Wolff, Christian, 256
Woman: question, the, 210–11; writers, 135–36
Word-*tableau*, 197, 199, 201, 204
Wordsworth, William, 26, 250
Writing systems, 129, 131–32

Xenophon, 254

Young, Edward, 74, 81, 250, 252, 257